Salonnières, Furies, and Fairies

Salonnières, Furies, and Fairies

The Politics of Gender and Cultural Change in Absolutist France

Anne E. Duggan

DELAWARE

Newark: University of Delaware Press

Associated University Presses
2010 Eastpark Boulevard
Cranbury, NJ 08512

Library of Congress Cataloging-in-Publication Data

Duggan, Anne E., 1967–
    Salonnières, furies, and fairies : the politics of gender and cultural change in absolutist France / Anne E. Duggan.
        p.   cm.
    Includes bibliographical references and index.
    ISBN 0-87413-897-3 (alk. paper)
    1. French literature—17th century—History and criticism.   2. France—Intellectual life—17th century.   3. Women and literature—France—History—17th century.   4. Women in literature.   5. Social change in literature.   6. French literature—Women authors—History and criticism. I. Title.
PQ245.D84   2005
840.6'9287'09032—dc22   2004065907

In loving memory of my fairy godmother,
Aunt Frieda.

Contents

Illustrations

Preface

We believed romanticism was the historical genre . . . that only recently led our novelists to name their characters Charlemagne, François I, or Henri IV, instead of Amadis, Oronte, or Saint-Albin. Mlle de Scudéry is, I believe, the first example of this trend in France, and many people say bad things about her works without ever having read them. . . . But they seem as realistic, better written, and hardly more ridiculous than certain novels of our times that will not be remembered as long.

Alfred de Musset, Lettres de Dupuis et Cotonet (1836)

Presently I'm reading the children's tales of Mme d'Aulnoy in an old edition whose pages I colored when I was six or seven. The dragons are pink and the trees blue; there's one page where everything is colored red, even the sea. They really amuse me, these tales.[1]

Gustave Flaubert, Correspondance (1853)

THE SEVENTEENTH CENTURY WAS TRULY A PERIOD OF TRANSITION and cultural change for French subjects in general and aristocratic women in particular. With the end of the Religious Wars, absolutism increasingly became a political reality, especially under Richelieu, and, of course, Louis XIV. Notions of nobility, already destabilized in the sixteenth century, became only more problematic, evident in the seventeenth-century preoccupation with the distinction between appearance and reality. Uprooted from a crumbling feudal system and freely circulating, traditional signs of prestige could be appropriated by bourgeois social climbers to redefine themselves. At the same time that the upper echelons of the traditional merchant class engaged in a process of self-legitimation, aristocratic women also sought to develop more favorable and dignified definitions of womanhood. With the emergence of the salon at the beginning of the century, elite women now had a place in which to cultivate themselves as critics, writers, and more generally, as beings endowed with reason. By midcentury, and especially after the Revocation of the Edict of Nantes in 1685, which gave new impetus to the Counter-Reformation, salon culture and the genres associated with it were criticized for their "bad influence" on society and particularly on women. By the century's end, *mondain* women, or the aristocratic women who participated in salon culture, came under harsh attack.

The present study situates two of the most prolific seventeenth-century women writers, Madeleine de Scudéry (1607–1701) and Marie-Catherine d'Aulnoy (1650/1–1705), within the context of these episodes of French cultural history. I highlight the ways in which both writers responded to and participated in the cultural changes of their society, albeit from different generational and ideological positions, as salon women and as writers who contributed significantly to the evolution of genres like the novel and the fairy tale. I also take into account the response of two male writers and academicians, Nicolas Boileau (1636–1711) and Charles Perrault (1628–1703), to the active presence and participation of *mondain* women within the public sphere. Although scholars traditionally have focused on their differences, particularly within the context of the *Querelle des Anciens et des Modernes* [Quarrel of the Ancients and the Moderns], I will draw from Counter-Reformation discourse to demonstrate that, despite their differing positions on aesthetics and class, Boileau and Perrault both depict *mondain* women as threats to social and political order.

To emphasize what I consider to be at stake in the study of these writers, I would like to situate this study within the larger field of early modern studies and particularly early modern women's studies. On the one hand, it is important to examine the historical reasons, particularly regarding canon formation, that explain the exclusion of Scudéry and d'Aulnoy from the traditional French literary canon, despite the vast popularity of their works in both France and England. This exclusion resulted in the lack of scholarship on their works, which only began to receive serious critical attention in the late 1980s, not inconsequentially a period when scholars began to put into question the traditional canon.[2] On the other hand, and precisely because of the historical marginalization of women writers within literary history, I would like to address some of the paradigms presently being used in the study of early modern women writers that risk marginalizing them yet again by limiting the scope of our approaches to their texts. As we "excavate" texts by early modern women writers and validate their study, we need to work on incorporating texts by women writers into the larger field of early modern studies and highlight how women writers contributed to general literary history, influencing generations of both male and female writers.

LITERARY LEGACIES

That Scudéry and d'Aulnoy had an impact within the history of French literature is evident in the seventeenth century in the various reactions to their works, which we will explore in relation to Scudéry in chapter 4, as well as in the extent to which their works were published and read over the century.[3] Scudéry was perhaps the most influential novelist of the middle of the seventeenth century, and every novelist of the period—male or female—wrote in her wake. Although her novels appear archaic and inaccessible to a contemporary readership, they were the talk of *la cour et la ville* in seventeenth-century Paris, and paved the way for other novelists, from Marie-Madeleine Pioche de La Vergne, comtesse de Lafayette, to Jean-Jacques Rousseau. Even the criticism of her works by writers like Molière and Boileau attest to the impact her works made at the time. In the case of the fairy tale, a 1677 letter by Marie de Rabutin-Chantal, marquise de Sévigné, indicates that tales were already being told at court as a *jeu d'esprit*. Although few literary critics of the period made references to the 1690 fairy-tale vogue, Lewis Seifert attributes this to critics like Boileau who did not wish to elevate the genre "by openly denouncing it" (64). Nevertheless, the testimony of the Abbé de Villiers, who wrote an entire treatise against the genre, does suggest that fairy tales indeed had attained the popularity of the novel: "women who used to be enchanted by the *Princesse de Clèves* are today stubbornly attached to *Griselidis* and *la Belle aux cheveux d'or*" (quoted in Seifert, 79).

In the seventeenth and eighteenth centuries, Scudéry's and d'Aulnoy's works regularly were included in what Joan DeJean has referred to as "worldly anthologies," essentially unofficial canons targeted at a readership of salon-goers ("Classical Reeducation," 23–27). For the upper-class Parisian literati, works and portraits of Scudéry and d'Aulnoy regularly appeared in their readings, from Fontenelle's *Recueil des plus belles pièces françois* (1692) and Vertron's *La Nouvelle Pandore ou les Femmes illustres* in the seventeenth century, to Charles-Joseph Mayer's *Cabinet des fées* (1785–1789) and Louise Keralio Robert's *Collections des meilleurs ouvrages françois composés par des*

femmes (1786–1789) in the eighteenth century.[4] The literary legacy of Scudéry and d'Aulnoy survived the Revolution. Charles
Augustin Sainte-Beuve, the renowned literary critic, dubbed
Scudéry the *institutrice* or teacher of French society, and the
philosopher Victor Cousin praised Scudéry's depictions of seventeenth-century France. In his novel *Sous les Tilleuls* (1832), Alphonse Karr has one of his characters discuss Scudéry's "carte
du pays de tendre." Victor Hugo drew from d'Aulnoy's works on
Spain for his *Ruy Blas* (1838), Maurice Maeterlinck's *L'Oiseau
bleu* (1908) was inspired by d'Aulnoy's tale of the same name, and
Georges Sand recalls in *Histoire de Ma Vie* (1855) the years she
spent in her youth reading d'Aulnoy's tales.

    Both writers, and especially d'Aulnoy, had a significant impact
on English literature as well. Scudéry's *Artamène, ou le Grand
Cyrus* (1649–1653) was translated into English by 1653, and the
first volume of *Clélie, Histoire Romaine* (1654–1660) was translated as early as 1655 as *Clelia, an Excellent New Romance*.
From roughly 1652 to 1744, Scudéry's works regularly were
translated and republished in England. According to James S.
Munro, French seventeenth-century romances constituted the
tradition of prose fiction from which eighteenth-century English
novelists drew, and Scudéry's works were among the most influential: "[a]uthors of these romances, in particular La Calprenède and Mlle de Scudéry, enjoyed enormous vogue well into the
eighteenth century and gave rise to numerous imitations" (752–
53). John Dryden's *Secret-Love, or, The Maiden-Queen* (1668),
for instance, was inspired by Scudéry's *Grand Cyrus*, and for his
Lucius Junius Brutus (1681), Nathaniel Lee drew from Scudéry's story of Brutus as depicted in *Clélie, Histoire Romaine*.

    D'Aulnoy's works also were widely popular in England.[5] While
translations and imitations of her fairy tales initiated the vogue
for French fairy tales in England, her novel *Histoire d'Hypolite,
Comte de Duglas* (1690), translated into English as *Hypolitus
Earl of Douglas* (1708), enjoyed great popularity from the 1740s
through the 1770s, "a period significant for a revival of romance
and the development of Gothic fiction in England" (Palmer, "Madame," 245; see also Palmer and Palmer, "English Editions,"
227). In fact, d'Aulnoy's novels influenced the gothic fiction of Ann
Radcliffe, whose *Sicilian Romance* (1790) borrows elements
from d'Aulnoy's *Hypolite*. D'Aulnoy's writing had a particular appeal for English women writers like Radcliffe, Maria Edgeworth,
and Anne Thackeray Ritchie. Indeed, accounting for Scudéry or
d'Aulnoy's literary and cultural legacy would make for an inter-

esting study. For my present purposes, that this legacy exists is in itself sufficiently noteworthy.

Despite their vast popularity and impact, works by Scudéry and d'Aulnoy were excluded from the "pedagogical canons" that emerged in the eighteenth century and that became the foundation for the twentieth-century classical canon. Whereas the worldly canons in which their works regularly were included served the socializing function of educating adult men and women in the ways of salon culture, the pedagogical canon was aimed at quite a different audience: male students of the *collèges*. Both canons claimed to provide a pool of models for writing and behavior, but Enlightenment philosophers like Voltaire and Diderot, who laid the conceptual basis for the pedagogical canon, apparently did not deem works by writers like Scudéry and d'Aulnoy appropriate models for young men. Like the pedagogical canon, the earlier worldly canon purported to include texts or portraits of universal value.[6] Nevertheless, Enlightenment thinkers like Voltaire were "obliged to attribute to the prominent dramatists of Louis XIV an impact that transcended their own present, and to set in contrast with it 'the spirit of the time' as a bias against all noncanonized authors of the seventeenth century" (Gumbrecht, 146). Of course, as DeJean has argued, the exclusion of worldly texts was ideologically motivated and based on prejudices against women writers in the spirit of and perhaps influenced by, I would contend, writers like Boileau and Perrault.

Taking into account the importance of works by Scudéry and d'Aulnoy in literary history, on the one hand, and the ideological factors leading to their exclusion from the canon, on the other, suggests that the classical canon does not adequately represent the literary field of the seventeenth century. Indeed, such considerations put into question the marginality of their texts by revealing the institutional strategies of marginalization that have shaped our perceptions of the seventeenth-century literary field and their place within it. By canonizing (reading) Boileau and marginalizing (not reading) Scudéry, for instance, French literary history has turned a debate or dialogue about emerging models of subjectivity and the influence of salon culture into a monologue about the frivolity of women. Such a move does not do justice to Scudéry's sociocultural project or to Boileau's critique of Scudéry. It is for this reason that Gumbrecht calls for an *"archeology of literary communication"* (160) as a legitimate basis to open up literary studies.

In line with Gumbrecht's archeology, I would argue that the

function of the canon should be twofold. First, the canon should include works representative of the multiple trends constitutive of the literary and sociocultural field of a period, including debates and tensions between literary styles and ideological positions. This would mean, for instance, that Boileau's critique of Scudéry and salon women would not be taken at face value, but rather it would be read in terms of the debates about literary styles and women's role in the public sphere that were actually taking place. Second, in revising the canon we should also take into account texts from earlier periods that had an impact on later writers. In other words, the canon's function can be defined in terms of synchrony, as a collection of texts from a single period constitutive of that period's literary field; and in terms of diachrony, or the inscription of a text within literary history, taking into account its literary legacy. Finally, we should think of "the canon" as a flexible collection of texts that need not be fixed once and for all, but that nevertheless adheres to our idea of its overall function in delineating the literary field of a specific period or in navigating literary history. Such a definition avoids the arbitrary and often ideological charged notion of "great works" that has served to exclude women writers and genres like the fairy tale from the canon, and consequently, from serious critical consideration. Opening up the canon can only enrich our understanding of the seventeenth century, whose literary field cannot be fully understood without taking into account Scudéry's monumental role as a novelist and a *salonnière* (salon woman), or the 1690s fairy-tale vogue largely dominated by d'Aulnoy.

A ROOM OF THEIR OWN

Theorists of the classical canon believed works by writers like Scudéry and d'Aulnoy expressed the "spirit of the time" and thus belonged to the realm of the particular. As such they denied their texts the universality attributed to, for instance, classical theater or Boileau's *Satires*. It is precisely because women writer's works have been put in the category of the "particular" that as feminist scholars we must be careful not to lock them into this position. As such, we need to carefully examine the paradigms presently used to legitimate the study of early modern women writers.

Joan DeJean and Nancy K. Miller have truly defined the parameters of scholarship in this area. For most young scholars, it was their work that facilitated access to an area of study previously inaccessible and ignored. Miller's theoretical work problematizing, for instance, woman-as-particular and man-as-universal in relation to authorship, and DeJean's historical work on the institutional practices that excluded women writers from what has become the French canon, have been indispensable to all scholars of the period. Their approach to early modern women writers, however, is not unproblematic. In particular, I would like to address Miller's influential definition of "feminist writing," as well as Miller's and DeJean's notions of dissent in works by early modern women writers.

In her definition of "feminist writing," Miller lays out three key principles. First, feminist writing "articulates as and in a discourse a self-consciousness about woman's identity. . . . Second, feminist writing makes a claim for the heroine's singularity by staging the difficulty of her relation as a woman in fiction to Woman. Third, it contests the available plots of female development of *Bildung* and embodies dissent from the dominant tradition in a certain number of recurrent narrative gestures, especially in the modalities of closure" (Miller, 8). Perhaps the first question that needs to be addressed pertains to the idea of "feminist writing" itself. If "feminist writing" is one aspect of a woman author's writing, the concept is not problematic. However, if we limit a woman writer's project to "feminist writing," some difficulties arise. For example, if the notion of a "woman's identity" concerns only gender—however important that might be—are we ignoring the sociopolitical identity of a woman writer, her identity as a member of a particular class, region, country, political party, or social group?

The analysis of other aspects of a woman writer's affiliations does not take away from her identity as a woman, but it highlights how she positions herself within the broad spectrum of historical processes. DeJean's affirmation that women writers, in the wake of Scudéry, "strove to create an *écriture* that was beyond person and beyond class, but not beyond gender" fixes women writers in their identity as women and at the same time takes them out of the overall sociopolitical arena (*Tender*, 92). I hope to show in the chapters to come how writers like Scudéry and d'Aulnoy took part in formulating concepts and discourses that would define the social, political, and gender identity of both male and female members of their class or *condition*. Far from being concerned solely with the question of gender, Scudéry and d'Aulnoy found ways to conceptualize gender relations that conformed more generally to their sociocultural and political ideals.

Miller's second key principle concerns how women writers often problematize through their heroines their relation to normative constructs of women and gender relations characteristic of their society. While this might be a significant element in works by many women writers, it is important not to limit our analyses of their works to problematizing this relation. To open up the question, it would be important to look at how women writers problematize more generally their relation to their society. Lafayette's Princesse de Clèves and Françoise de Graffigny's Zilia reject their society not only as women, but also as people who contest a certain model of social (including gender) relations. Through her heroines, Scudéry not only wishes to construct new models of gender relations, but also and quite consequently new models of social and political relations. Similarly, d'Aulnoy's heroines contest their society with respect, again, to gender, social, and political relations. Each writer gives the question of gender more or less centrality in her works, which must be taken into account accordingly. We might furthermore ask ourselves to what extent we can separate gender from social, political, and cultural questions. From the examples cited above, early modern women writers would say, it seems to me, that we cannot.

With respect to Miller's third key point regarding women writers' contestation of available plots of female development and dissent from the "dominant tradition," we must ask ourselves exactly what constitutes this "dominant tradition." In France, seventeenth-century women writers clearly responded in their works to patriarchal models of female development propagated by humanist and religious discourses and texts. However, we must qualify the concept of "tradition" (which tradition?) in light of DeJean's thesis in *Tender Geographies* (1991), which affirms that the French novelistic tradition was formed largely by women writers. That is, women played highly influential roles as *salonnières*, novelists, and poets in the constitution of the seventeenth-century French literary field, and especially in the development of the novel. Despite the fact that most of these women writers' works have been excluded from the classical canon, they nevertheless constituted an important part of the period's literary field. Works by women authors circulated and influenced male and female writers alike. Moreover, women writers like d'Aulnoy contested the available plots of female development proposed by writers like Scudéry and especially Catherine Bernard (see chapter 5), which suggests that the "dominant tradition" is not always a patriarchal one, or at least one defined predominantly by men.

Even though women writers often problematize certain narrative models and reflect upon their relation to authority, dissent in their writings should not be restricted to resisting the "patriarchal plot" or deconstructing the male gaze—unless the writer herself clearly does so. At times Miller and DeJean seem to conceive of women's political dissent exclusively with respect to patriarchal practices and as women, which is exemplified in DeJean's discussion of the Fronde. This complex, multifaceted civil war saw women like Anne Marie Louise d'Orléans, duchesse de Montpensier, and Anne Geneviève de Bourbon-Condé, duchesse de Longueville, fighting next to their kinsmen and leading troops. Admitting she simplifies the story, DeJean describes those events as "a woman's war" and later states: "Had the *frondeuses* who directed their revolution recreated the legendary state of the amazons, the most absolute of French monarchies, that of Louis XIV, might have been avoided" (*Tender*, 42).

Clearly DeJean is engaged in a historical debate concerning the significance of the *frondeuses*, foregrounding the role they played in the war. However, scholars like Marlies Mueller, Joan Kelly, and James Collins put into question such overgeneralizations. They argue instead that, until the consolidation of European states, noble women defended when necessary their territories, fighting not as women, but as members of a particular lineage.[7] This would suggest that the women warriors of the Fronde bear traces of their feudal ancestors, and their unsuccessful last stand against absolutism marks the decline not only of feudalism, but also of noble women's political and military power, with the foundation of the centralized, monarchical state. We must ask ourselves to what extent the *frondeuses* were in fact fighting as women, and to what extent they were fighting as members of, for instance, the Condé family. Similarly, we must also ask ourselves to what extent a particular woman author writes as a woman, and perhaps this demands that we begin to think of women not in terms of radical otherness, but rather as existing within a tension between the same and other, as each woman author negotiates her relationship to her gender as well as to her literary tradition, social class, and national identity.

Although Miller and DeJean have sought to rectify the situation of the woman writer with respect to the canon and within the corpus of scholarship on the early modern period, their discursive practices inadvertently fix women writers in the position of the particular, mainly by limiting their analyses to women writers' experience *as women*. Certainly it is important, as Miller and DeJean have eloquently demonstrated in their various works, to highlight women writers' oftentimes problematic relationship to their identity as authors and as women. The question here concerns the scope not the validity of their theories.

I am arguing that we not limit the scope of women writers works to their situation in the world as a woman. Such limitations confine them to the particular, to a room of their own, thus legitimating their marginal status within French literary history. We must recognize the multiple positions women took with respect to their culture, acknowledging their contributions not only to all things feminist, but also to the creation of the modern French language, a modern French identity, salon culture, republicanism, and romanticism. Without neglecting the position a women writer takes as a woman, it is imperative to examine her position with respect to politics (a royalist, a feudalist, a republican), cultural change (reactionary or progressive), and social mores (conformist or critical). At times we may discover tensions, contradictions as well as continuities between the various positions a particular (woman) writer takes. This approach supposes that works by any writer, male or female, constantly move between the particular (her or his personal history and identity) and the universal (her or his contributions to overriding cultural trends). As it regards specifically women writers, we need to resituate them within literary history first and foremost as human beings, who happen to be women. Focusing solely on how women writers have contributed to a female (read: marginal) literary history can become a trap. It can be used to legitimate their exclusion from the "universal" canon to which they indeed have contributed. These, then, are the issues at stake in this study of works of Scudéry and d'Aulnoy.

Part of what I am trying to do through *Salonnières, Furies, and Fairies* is to tell a story, one that begins with Scudéry, whose works mark the apogee of French salon culture and the public influence of upper-class women in seventeenth-century France. The second part of the story concerns the post-1660 patriarchal reaction of writers like Nicolas Boileau and Charles Perrault to the influence and presence of women in the public sphere—a reaction that coincides with the *prise de pouvoir* of Louis XIV, the proliferation of all-male academies, and the new impetus given to the Counter-Reformation around the time of the Revocation of the Edict of Nantes. Finally, the concluding section of the story looks at d'Aulnoy's response, written from a position much less powerful than that of Scudéry, to the decline of the salon, to the demise of feudalism, and last but not least, to concepts limiting the scope of women's actions. Although the main narrative of this story places Scudéry and d'Aulnoy in a relation of continuity, the details will bring forth many discontinuities, not only with respect to their concepts of gender, but also concerning their positions toward cultural change. Whereas Scudéry picks up the pieces of a shattered feudal order, reconfiguring them to create a new brand of aristocracy, d'Aulnoy remains nostalgic for an idealized feudal past, taking a much more critical position than Scudéry—for both historical and political reasons—to the changes that have occurred over the course of the century.

Acknowledgments

I would like to convey my deepest gratitude to Jack Zipes for introducing me to the world of fairies and French salons, and for his generous support and encouragement in my professional development from graduate student to Assistant Professor. In the same vein I wish to express my appreciation to Susan Noakes, who always had confidence in my work and to whom I am indebted for her constant support and advice, all of which was a great inspiration for me. I would also like to thank: Tom Conley, whose approach to the early modern period is nothing less than electrifying, not to mention inspirational; Mária Brewer, for her generous ongoing encouragement in "my early years" and for her theoretical finesse; Ellen Messer-Davidow, whom I still wish to thank for making me write that MA essay on Descartes over and over again; Joseph Waldauer (may he rest in peace), for his wonderful stories and sense of humor; and last but not least, Maria Paganini, from whom I feel I learned how to read literature.

At Wayne State University, I am fortunate to have terrific colleagues whose support carried me through the day. Charles Stivale closely read the opening chapters of the manuscript and has given me so much feedback, advice, and assistance that I wouldn't know where to begin in showing my appreciation. Michael Giordano also read parts of the manuscript and has been a most enthusiastic colleague. When I first came to WSU, Donald

Haase kindly welcomed me into the Wayne fairy world, and it truly has been a great pleasure working with him on *Marvels & Tales* and discovering new fairy dimensions in our Humanities Center Working Groups. I would also like to thank Walter Edwards, Director of the WSU Humanities Center, and Lisabeth Hock, both of whom offered me a "room of my own" just when I needed it most, without which the completion of this project would have been impossible. Finally, I am much obliged for the generous support provided by the WSU Humanities Center Faculty Fellowship Competition, the WSU Research and Inquiry Grant Program, the WSU University Research Grant Program, and the WSU Minority/Women Summer Grant Program.

An abbreviated version of chapter 2 appeared in *Le savoir en France au XVIIe siècle, Actes du colloque organisé par la North American Society for Seventeenth-Century French Literature* (Tübingen: Gunter Narr Verlag, 2003); and a section of chapter 6, "Women and Absolutism in French Opera and Fairy Tale," appears in *The French Review* (December 2004). I am grateful for permission to reprint these pieces here.

Salonnières, Furies, and Fairies

1

Politics, Gender, and Cultural Change

CULTURAL CHANGE IS A CONTINUAL PROCESS IN EVERY SOCIETY, FOR culture is not simply a collection of permanent monuments, nor are the discourses, stories, techniques of power, or rituals constitutive of a particular culture set in stone. Current events, modifications in the economic or political structure, the creation of new concepts, discourses, and technologies, and new controversies constantly emerge that affect, and are affected by, our ways of understanding and living in the world. Generally the overall framework of a culture, which slowly evolves over time, can accommodate such change. At certain historical moments, however, the accumulation of minor structural modifications, or the conjunction of several major ones, comes to a head in radical cultural change. Basically, radical cultural change takes place when the very framework defining a particular culture has crumbled for, reaching a point of saturation, this framework can no longer accommodate change and must itself be transformed.

Over the course of the sixteenth and seventeenth centuries in France (and more generally in western Europe), such radical cultural change did indeed occur. A conjunction of political, social, and economic transformations clearly point to a significant epistemological shift in French culture and society. In the following discussion, I would like to lay out what I regard as the important changes Madeleine de Scudéry, Nicolas Boileau, Charles Perrault, and Marie-Catherine d'Aulnoy address in their works. Shifts in notions of social identity, art, culture, and gender inform directly and indirectly my reading of these writers and their sociopolitical objectives. In general and most simplified terms, the overriding cultural change concerns the decline of "feudal" culture and the rise of "modern" culture.

FROM FEUDAL TO EARLY MODERN

Part of the legacy of "modernist" writers to our own culture is a prejudiced idea of "feudalism," a term that, along with "medieval," has come to connote a backward or unenlightened society steeped in superstition, intolerance, and misogyny. In order to fully grasp the sense of the radical changes of this period and to do justice to the various responses to them, we must modify our inherited notions of "feudalism," in part by recognizing the historical specificity of feudalism as a sociopolitical structure and as a culture. That is, we must be prepared to put into question our inherited notions concerning the superiority of modernity over everything feudal. Rather than compare societies in relation to a limited, often technological notion of progress, and consequently in terms of inferiority and superiority, it would be more fruitful to study each society on its own terms, as a system with both strengths and weaknesses.[1]

I have suggested that at moments of radical cultural change, the overall framework of a society in effect collapses and needs to be transformed. The framework that collapsed by the seventeenth century emerged around the twelfth and thirteenth centuries, when a bellicose form of feudalism was replaced by a more courtly and politically stable one. As a preliminary definition of the overall sociopolitical framework of the High Middle Ages, let us take P. Michaud-Quantin's broad characterization: "according to the image of nature, society depends on the inequality of elements that compose it, and from one element to another there is not a rift or rupture, but a continuous transition from the greatest element to the smallest" (81). The idea that the elements making up society are unequal yet maintain a relation of continuity is an important one, and is relevant to many aspects of feudal culture.

As it pertains to the sociopolitical hierarchy, the inequality of elements was determined by one's position—or more precisely, one's function—within society. For instance, inequality in the hierarchical ordering of the nobility (king, duke, count, and baron) or in the ordering of society (clergy, nobility, peasants) was determined by the perceived importance and scope of each function in relation to the others, each one being necessary to the performance of the whole. Although the value of each function was unequal (i.e., a baron had less value than a king, a peasant less than a baron), every function within society nevertheless carried a certain value. The sociopolitical value and identity of the individual was constructed in terms of exteriority. Because it was one's function that conferred value and was the basis for one's social identity (as a peasant, bourgeois, or noble), human value and identity were not perceived to be presocial, located in the "soul" or "mind" (the interior) of a person. Despite the fact that the notion of bloodlines existed since the twelfth century—locating identity in the body—the instability of family lineages and the constant replenishment of the nobility with members of the lower orders suggests that, in the final analysis, function superseded bloodlines.[2] I do not mean to suggest that social or political injustices did not play a role in the hierarchical system of the feudal period. I do wish to suggest, however, that the value of an individual within the framework of feudalism, integrally related to one's function, was quite different from how the value of individuals would be constructed in the early modern period.

One important feudal institution that maintained a sense of continuity between the orders, not to mention the sexes, was Catholicism. On the one hand, Catholicism allowed for the redemption and valuation of all (Christian) members of society. Peasant or noble, man or woman could be damned or saved and potentially accede to sainthood. Although official Catholic discourse was imbedded with misogynous concepts, nevertheless there was clearly a place for women within Catholicism on the whole, whether in its hagiographic representations of women saints, or in church institutions like the abbey, or simply as worshippers. It is important to note here that the misogyny of the Catholic Church was amplified during the Counter-Reformation of the sixteenth and seventeenth centuries.[3] On the other hand, Catholicism provided a general cultural framework shared by all orders. Diffused through oral stories and all forms of art (tapestries, paintings, sculptures), the lives of the saints were accessible to the literate and illiterate alike. It would be naive to think that the diffusion of hagiography was ideologically neutral, that representations of the saints were not caught up in techniques of power. However, for my present purposes, I simply wish to emphasize the general accessibility of such representations, constitutive of a pool of shared cultural references, to all orders of society.

Similarly, folklore (including hagiography) was another common denominator connecting the orders. Nobles, bourgeois, and peasants all told stories with either legendary personages (Saint-Etienne, Geneviève de Brabant) or archetypal characters usually referred to by their function: the priest, the princess, the good bourgeois, and the old peasant woman. Fairies appeared everywhere, from literary works like Jean d'Arras's *Mélusine* (1392–1393), to the women's workplace in sixteenth-century Lyon, remaining a part of French peasant lore until the beginning of the twentieth century.[4] Though we do not have access to the

tales that were told by the illiterate (the majority of the population), those related by writers of the period interestingly depict
the lives of all members of society and the relations between
them.[5] The point I would like to make here is that, for all intents
and purposes, there was no clear delineation in the High Middle
Ages between "high art" and "low art," nor for that matter between written and oral traditions, again suggesting that all orders of society shared common cultural (folkloric, literary)
references.[6] This delineation did not become characteristic of
French and more generally western cultures until the period of
the Renaissance.

Politically, France was a decentralized kingdom: each village,
city, and region enjoying various degrees of autonomy with respect to feudal lords and the king. Beginning in 1150, many feudal
lords, especially in the regions of Catalonia, Béarn, Champagne,
Burgundy, and Lorraine, legislated *chartes de franchises*, char-
ters establishing the rights and privileges conceded to a community by its lord. A system originally imposed by force sought to
legitimate itself by normalizing and regulating relations between
lords and peasants both legally and fiscally, taxes being the price
of the latter's freedom. In the twelfth and thirteenth centuries,
during the "communal movement," some cities in the kingdom of
France attained the semiautonomous status of "commune." This
status was the result of negotiations between the bourgeoisie of
a particular city and the city's lord, ratified by a *charte de commune* fixing the distribution of juridical and political power between the two parties.[7] Within such a decentralized structure,
the king's function was that of protector of the kingdom, understood as an association of *corps* or corporations consisting of orders, provinces, cities, communities, and trades. Strictly
speaking, the king was a suzerain, lord of lords at the top of the
feudal pyramid constituting the body politic over which he did not
exercise direct control.

Of course, change did not happen suddenly. As Erich Köhler
has shown in his acclaimed study of Chrétien de Troyes, tensions
between the various orders and conflict over the definition of
their respective functions existed already in the twelfth century.
Lower-level members of the nobility felt disenfranchised by the
concentration of wealth in the hands of a few powerful princes,
and writers like Chrétien de Troyes tried to reiterate the obligations of the latter to the former. Moreover, various writers expressed the potential danger to feudalism in the king's practice
of promoting members of the bourgeoisie to the level of royal ad-

ministrators, whose consequent social value and identity would depend entirely on the king rather than on traditional feudal alliances. Throughout the High Middle Ages, the balance of power was relatively unstable, favoring at times the social and political promotion of the bourgeoisie, the centralizing tendencies of the king, or the authority of feudal lords. During the Hundred Years War, conflict particularly between the high nobility and the king intensified, finally resulting in the strengthening of the monarchy.

One factor in the monarchy's increased power after the war had to do with taxation. Extraordinary taxes levied during the war became permanent afterwards, marking the beginning of the monarchy's infringement on the customary rights of France's diverse communities, an infringement more generally taking shape in the centralization of France's financial and juridical institutions.[8] With the monarchy's solid tax base and an increasingly centralized administration, the traditional rights of the nobility could also be contravened, perhaps most importantly in the area of military affairs. The monarch could now maintain an army of mercenary troops armed with firearms, releasing him from dependency on the nobility for military support (see Elias, 154–55). Over the course of the sixteenth and early seventeenth centuries, the nobility lost their private armies, maintaining only privileges in the king's army by 1650, meaning that very raison d'être of the feudal nobility (referred to by the seventeenth century as the nobility of the sword in contrast to the newly created nobility of the robe) had been thwarted by the historical and political developments favoring absolutism (see Billacois, 270). The monarchy's monopolization of political and military power impacted the role of noble women as well, who had exercised "governing and military power in times of need" during the High Middle Ages, and who would be excluded from all such functions (with the exception of the queen regents) within the absolutist state.[9]

Generally speaking, the absolutist movement was transforming the nature of relations within the body politic. Alliances based on orders, kinship, and local communities mediated the relation of French subjects to the king. Gradually this structure gave way to a new configuration in which subjects were directly attached to the body of the king with the centralization of French administration. Another way of imagining these changes is in terms of a decentralized political patchwork (feudalism) made up of networks of households, which was giving way to a centralized and homogenous state (absolutism), conceived of as the king's household. In the words of Norbert Elias, "[t]he king's rule over the country was nothing other than an extension of and addition to the prince's rule over his household. What Louis XIV, who marked both the culmination and the turning point of this development, attempted, was to organize his country as his personal property, as an enlargement of the household" (42). Thus at the same time that absolutism sought "a monopoly on public space" (Clark, 418), public space quite ironically was becoming the "private property" of the king. Indeed, during the French Revolution Republicans would contest the concept of the nation-as-seigneurie. Nevertheless, absolutism, in its move to consolidate France's political and economic structures, prepared the way for the modern nation-state.

For its part, the feudal nobility not only had difficulty retaining its traditional political power with respect to the monarchy, but also was losing out financially to the nobility of the robe and to the higher ranks of the bourgeoisie. With the general inflation of the sixteenth century, the nobility's earnings from their land was devalued, undermining their economic base (see Elias, 151–52; Billacois, 267). As the idea of "living nobly" (living off revenues from the land or seigneuries) increasingly became defined in terms of conspicuous consumption, many nobles ruined themselves keeping up appearances, consequently relying more and more on the monarchy for pensions—not to mention a sense of identity. During the seventeenth century, and particularly under Louis XIV, the feudal nobility was transformed into a court nobility, a phenomenon that reaffirmed a noble's sense of status, yet marked his or her total dependence on the king.[10]

According to Georges Huppert, the rising bourgeoisie also played a role in the economic decline of the feudal nobility. In the sixteenth century, members of the upper echelons of the bourgeoisie sought to distance themselves from their condition, and one way to do this was to acquire a fief. The *bourgeois conquérant* would grant nobles as well as *laboureurs* loans, "with the particularity that the borrower, instead of paying off the principal plus interest, keeps paying the interest indefinitely without ever reducing the principal" (Huppert, 35). Eventually the landowner would be forced to sell, and the bourgeois lender could then buy up the property. Acquiring land did not immediately confer noble status onto the *bourgeois conquérant*. After one or two generations, however, land could be used to back up the claim that he had lived nobly.

ENNOBLING EDUCATION

As the political and economic configuration of French society was being transformed in the sixteenth and seventeenth centuries, new concepts of nobility were emerging. With the decadence of medieval cathedral schools in the sixteenth century, members of the local gentry and city councils started what Huppert refers to as the "feverish foundation of *collèges*" (63) or humanist schools, which was taking place all over the country, from Rouen to Bordeaux and Lyon, to even smaller provincial cities like Albi, Aurillac, and Auxerre. Although the Jesuits took over the administration of *collèges* in the seventeenth century, they maintained the humanist curriculum established by the schools' founders. Huppert emphasizes the revolutionary nature of the creation of the *collège*: "The celebration of letters must be understood not merely as an intellectual fashion but also as a profound cultural revolution. The King, as 'Protector of Letters,' was also protector of the status of the high bourgeoisie. The Renaissance in France was the creation of this class and its passport to honors" (60).[11] In other words, the high bourgeoisie sought nobility not only through the acquisition of land, but also through a humanist education. Education as a sign of nobility was a new concept that had not indicated nobility in previous periods. By the middle of the seventeenth century, however, the cultivation of letters would become a general indicator of nobility shared by noble and bourgeois alike, suggesting that the aristocracy forming in the early modern period was based on a fusion between noble and bourgeois values. As Carolyn Lougée has aptly demonstrated, this fusion manifested itself as well on a sociopolitical level in the intermarriages between the nobility and the high bourgeoisie that often took place within the salon, which combined noble status with money (*Paradis*, 151–70).

The "takeover" of cathedral schools by humanist ones is representative of a more general shift occurring in French society. Within the upper classes, secular humanism slowly was replacing Catholicism as a source for cultural references.[12] This shift had repercussions for class as well as gender relations. With respect to class, Delumeau argues that the increasing gap between rich and poor in the sixteenth and seventeenth centuries played out both geographically, in the location and architecture of noble lodgings, as well as culturally:

[T]he custom of organizing royal and aristocratic residences around an interior court and the fashion of pleasure palaces and villas con-

tributed to physically and materially separating the rich from the
poor. Occasions where the people and the aristocracy or the people
and sovereigns could meet were increasingly rare. Certainly, the
"joyous and triumphant entrances" of princes in Italy, Flanders, and
France, carnivals and the marriages of the great dukes of Tuscany
and those of the Valois were occasions for public festivities, with dec-
orated streets, parades, and the construction of floats. But the
themes used by the decorators and artists in charge were increasingly mythological, thus often esoteric and unfamiliar to the mental-
ity of the people. (129)

Taken from Greco-Roman literature (the emerging humanist
source of cultural references), the mythological themes for royal
festivals were accessible primarily to the literate upper classes.
Increasingly, the economic and geographical disparity between
rich and poor was reflected in the development of what we now
call "high culture" as opposed to "low culture." Humanism would
be the springboard for the seventeenth-century creation of a
classical French literary tradition that would maintain the cleav-
age between the cultural references of the classes, exemplified
in the virtual absence of any lower-class characters in Ancien
Régime poetry, theater, or novel. Inseparable from the cultivation of a French literary tradition was that of the French
language, fostered in the salons and academies, creating furthermore a linguistic gap between upper and lower classes.

With its focus on illustrious men of antiquity, humanist tradition similarly reserved little room for positive representations of
women. Already in the fifteenth century, the humanist-educated
Christine de Pizan laments this state of affairs, which she attempts to rectify in her *Cité des dames* [The City of Ladies]
(1405) by inserting the examples of women of antiquity, as well
as women from Biblical and French history and popular culture,
into the narrative of world history. In the same vein Scudéry published *Les Femmes Illustres ou les Harangues héroïques* (1642),
literally "giving a voice" to fifteen famous women of Antiquity.
Not only were representations of women lacking in the pool of
humanist cultural references, but the concept of "reason" (*raison, esprit, bon sens*) did not automatically apply to women—or
the lower classes for that matter. As Joan Kelly has argued, "humanism was far more narrow in its views of women than traditional Christian culture. The religious conception of women,
although misogynist in its own way, did regard women as equally
capable of the highest states 'man' could attain: salvation and
sainthood" (8).

From Pizan's first feminist critique of humanism to Scudéry and Poulain de la Barre in the seventeenth century, feminist writers were forced to argue that women indeed were endowed with the same reason as men. In chapter 4 on Boileau and Perrault, I will examine in more detail the importance of reason as it relates to women, but I would like to note briefly here that such writers tried to discredit women, whether in reference to their political or literary aspirations, in terms of their lack of reason, creating an implicit dichotomy opposing male reason to female folly. Such a dichotomy legitimated women's exclusion from a public sphere, defined in terms of an implicitly male civic virtue that Scudéry challenges in works like *Les Femmes Illustres* and *Clélie, Histoire Romaine*, which we will examine in chapter 2. In the same way that the monarchy was attempting to dominate the administration of the body politic, many men in positions of power sought exclusive rights to public space.

It is notable that the high season for witch trials in France (1580–1630) was initiated by the humanist Jean Bodin with the publication of his *De la démonomanie des sorciers* [On the Demon-Mania of Witches] (1580), and was carried out not by the church, but by the Parlement de Paris and other secular courts. Although between 1540 and 1670 only a small percentage of those tried by the Parlement de Paris (roughly 9 percent) were actually convicted and burned at the stake, the trials nevertheless had a significant impact in France. Witch trials served as a legal mechanism to repress and stigmatize cultural practices deemed passé, barbaric, unenlightened, or simply inferior. In the Middle Ages peasants and elites alike practiced forms of magic that would later be denounced by the courts. With the rise of humanism and the centralizing efforts of the Catholic Church of the Counter-Reformation, "superstitious" and marginal practices generally came under attack, the trials reinforcing the divide between lower and upper classes through institutionalized terror. According to Robert Muchembled, the principal result of this repression was to clearly separate the universe of peasant superstitions from those of established religion and learned knowledge (236–74; also see his entry in *Dictionnaire* II: 1489–91). In other words, witch hunts reinforced the emerging divide between high and low culture, not to mention dichotomous conceptions of men and women.

Overall in Europe, women were tried at a rate of four to one, resulting in the execution of over 100,000 women in the sixteenth and seventeenth centuries, suggesting that superstition was not the only target of the trials. As a matter of fact, some historians have argued that Bodin's opposition to witchcraft was intricately connected to his opposition to birth control, ultimately for economic reasons (see Heinsohn and Steiger). It was necessary for the state to control women's bodies in order to prevent them from limiting the size of their families and consequently the country's population, which was believed to be a significant source of national wealth. As such, Bodin's position anticipated that of many eighteenth-century "enlightened" theorists who also associated population with national wealth.[13]

WOMEN, CLASS, AND CONSOLIDATION OF THE PUBLIC SPHERE

Evident in the history of the witch trials, the early modern backlash against women had much to do with the reconfiguration of the state. Feminist historians from Joan Kelly and Natalie Zemon Davis to Sarah Hanley all agree that the burgeoning French nation increasingly placed restrictions on women's legal rights, putting the fate of women of all classes in the hands of men. This was done through a series of institutional restrictions and edicts, issued from the middle of the sixteenth century onwards, prohibiting women from voting in mixed gender guilds, requiring parental consent for a valid marriage (1556), limiting women's rights to dispose of property, controlling reproductive customs, and regulating conditions of marital separation.[14] In her monumental essay, "Engendering the State: Family Formation and State Building in Early Modern France," Sarah Hanley argues that, at least with respect to the upper classes, such legal restrictions on women were part of the Family–State compact, the purpose of which was to consolidate the professional administrative elite, consisting of the high bourgeoisie and nobility of the robe, or former *bourgeois conquérants*: "These professional legists purchased judicial offices with family funds, inherited offices from family predecessors, and received offices (in usufruct) from spouses through female dowries of allied families. From the outset the officeholders (male) and office owners (male and female) strategically retained these prestigious charges within family networks, because offices (hereditary property by 1604) made good investments in the proto-capitalistic economy, opened other patronage doors, and conferred noble status over several generations" (7). Even if socially the notion of bloodlines never quite disappears, in practice feudal lineages based on bloodlines were being replaced by *officier* ones. Marriage as sacrament was superseded by a contractual notion of marriage that maintained the *officier* lines.[15]

Marriage had become virtually indissoluble and, according to Hanley, "husbands who suspected wives of contemplating separation suits stalled such moves by initiating charges of adultery, fabricated or not" (24). Such charges led to wives being confined to a convent for an extended period of time (up to two years), during which the husband had the option of taking her back into the household. If there was no reconciliation, the wife "was obliged to spend the rest of her life in the cloister" (Gibson, 64; see also Portemer, 458). Convents in the later seventeenth century had to be reoriented for at least two reasons: "first, the need of families to mobilize convents as alternative prisons; and second, the need of some convents to increase income with boarding fees, gifts, and bribes" (Hanley, 25). Whereas women writers of the first half of the century like Scudéry were quite critical of parental control over marriage and of the limitations marriage imposed on women, it was not until the second half of the century that writers like d'Aulnoy treated the question of the cloistered woman, suggesting that the full impact of the Family–State compact hit women later in the century.

The increased cloistering of women is exemplary of the various efforts made on the part of different institutions to exclude women from the "public sphere." Many factors in the early modern period contributed to the creation of a public sphere, a place in which women would have to fight for over the next centuries. In the High Middle Ages, the distinction between "private" and "public" interests did not exist as such. Within the decentralized structure of the body politic, noble men and women exercised political power in the interests of the household. With the emergence of absolutism, an abstract political entity (the nation) understood primarily as a public entity (*res publica*) was slowly replacing the household as the locus of political interests. Economically, a similar phenomenon was happening, whereby the economic unit of the household slowly was being supplanted, particularly in urban areas, by manufactures. In the sixteenth century, industry was based primarily on workshops run by master craftsmen and their families; master craftsmen owned their own shops and sold their own goods within local markets. By the mid-seventeenth century protoindustrial manufactures, headed by entrepreneurs, were on the rise, selling generally luxury goods in national and international markets.[16]

Far from being uninterested in the development of French manufactures and commercial trade, the monarchy was directly involved in their protection. Escalating production and trade was a significant factor in the augmentation of state revenues, which increased sevenfold between 1610 and 1643.[17] Under the reigns of Henri IV and Louis XIII, some sixty manufacturers received the title of "manufacture privilégiée," conferring for twenty years a monopoly on the production and distribution of a particular good within a determined geographical market, with the purpose of supporting a national industry of luxury products.[18] It was not until this period that "economy," originally used with respect to the acquisition and management of goods within the domain of the household, came to be associated with the well-being of the state (Clark, 420, 429). This overall shift from local to national economic and political structures split the politico-economic realm of life from the household unit, resulting in the conceptual division between and consequent gendering of "public" and "private" spheres. In the words of Merry Wiesner, the "advent of national governments and the end of the household form of production may have made the public/private, work/home, male/female divisions which did develop inevitable" (6). I would like to emphasize the conceptual nature of this division for, as the Family–State compact exemplifies, "public" policy regarding marriage and reproduction clearly had an impact on the domain of the "private" or domestic.

Such changes furthermore mark the beginnings of a "modern" class-type structure of society, whereby relations based on continuity (master, journeyman, apprentice) gave way to relations based on rupture (entrepreneur, worker). This rupture developed over the course of the seventeenth century with the establishment of various types of Academies, institutionalizing a division of labor privileging intellectual work (i.e., the artist, architect, engineer) over manual labor (i.e., the artisan, mason, and so forth). As Jean-Marie Apostolidès suggests, this division of labor furthermore legitimates the exclusion of lower classes from the public sphere by sanctioning the separation between the people and the nation (*Roi-Machine*, 38). Humanist and seventeenth-century classical discourse reinforced the division of labor in the same way that it reinforced gender distinctions, affirming that members of the lower classes, much like women, lacked reason. It is notable that women writers like Scudéry (and many after her) who supported women's claim to reason often, in compliance with their own class prejudices, maintained the intellectual inferiority of the lower classes.

SIGNIFYING DISTINCTION

Despite the fact that the early modern period marks the emergence of a modern commercial society and class structure, it would be incorrect to characterize seventeenth-century French society in terms of "bourgeois" culture or modern capitalism. In the early modern period, the bourgeoisie did not have an identity as such, for some members of the bourgeoisie aspired to noble status, whereas others continued to base their identity on traditional trade affiliations. There was no clearly bourgeois discourse, although writers like Charles Perrault began to formulate one. Rather, seventeenth-century France witnessed the birth of an aristocracy that was seriously challenged during the French Revolution and saw its final decline in the late nineteenth and early twentieth century—an aristocracy whose identity was made up of certain indicators formerly associated with the feudal nobility, and newly emerging signs of nobility coming out of humanist discourse and more generally from the culture of the Haute-Bourgeoisie and Robe.

As the overall feudal framework crumbled, signs previously attached to a nobility based on function were freed up, so to say, and circulated in society in such a way that they could be appropriated and recombined with new signs of nobility to legitimate a new aristocracy. One example of this is the manner in which land, a traditional indicator of nobility as well as the nobility's main source of income, was appropriated by wealthy bourgeois as a purely symbolic indicator of nobility. The use-value or concrete function of land within the feudal framework was superseded in the early modern period by its primarily abstract value as a sign of social prestige.

The "self-made man" was rising out of the debris of a feudal order, traces of which still composed the necessary elements of his social legitimization. In the early seventeenth century Turquet de Mayerne argued that true nobility "represente un ordre singulier d'hommes façonnez et qui se façonnent, par continuelle instruction . . . aux grandes charges et plus honorables devoirs de la Republique" [represents a singular order of cultivated men who cultivate themselves through continual instruction . . . for important positions and the most honorable duties of the Republic] (quoted in Huppert, 203). Whereas the singularity of the feudal nobility resided on a symbolic level in their "blue blood," the singularity of the *officier*-commercial nobility which made them a distinguished order rested in their *reason*, the foundation of the early modern (noble) self expressed so clearly in the works of Descartes. An innate, presocial quality in the *Discours de la Méthode*, reason is the raw material constitutive of the self-made man, which must be formed—*façonnez* in Turquet de Mayerne, *réformer* in Descartes—by means of some sort of education or *méthode*: "Jamais mon dessein ne s'est étendu plus avant que de tâcher à réformer mes propres pensées, et de bâtir dans un fonds qui est tout à moi" [Never has my intention gone beyond trying to reform my own thoughts, building upon a foundation all my own] (Descartes, 44).

I have emphasized the idea of *man* in the concept of the self-made man. The question of women fashioning themselves was problematic in the early modern period. In her discussion of the sixteenth-century poets Madeleine and Catherine des Roches, Tilde Sankovitch remarks: "She [Madeleine] and her daughter yearn for what is man's birthright: the possibility of fashioning themselves. The wish to give form and shape to themselves by writing, and to gain *honneur*, that is, poetic immortality, in the process" (232). We have already noted that reason was not automatically attributed to women, and as reason was the basis of the self-made man, the concept of the self-made woman was not an obvious one. Furthermore, the traditional association between woman and the flesh in Christian discourse, along with the rise of neo-Platonism in the Renaissance based on the opposition between the "formless body" and the "forming mind," could only have reinforced the dichotomy of woman-as-*matter* and man-as-form, particularly at a time when members of the upper echelons of society increasingly defined themselves not in the material terms of their sociopolitical or economic *function*, but in the idealist terms of educational *formation*. How could matter, the body, woman, form itself?

It comes as no surprise that the postulation of a presocial rational subject emerged at the same time that feudalism's functional model of subjectivity was becoming obsolete. The detachment of signs from functions, in other words, the detachment of signifiers from their traditional signifieds, led to the ongoing debate in seventeenth-century France concerning the relation between appearance and reality—not only as it pertained to social rank, but also in reference to other social signs.

Molière's plays are particularly insightful in the way they draw attention to the ridiculous side of appropriating signifiers to create a singular identity. In *Le Bourgeois Gentilhomme* (1670), for instance, Molière highlights the financial side of appropriating noble signifiers and negotiating a noble identity:

> C'est un homme [Monsieur Jourdain] à la vérité, dont les lumières sont petites, qui parle à tort et à travers de toutes choses et n'applaudit qu'à contre-sens; mais son argent redresse les jugements de son esprit. Il a du discernement dans sa bourse. Ses louanges sont monnayées; et ce bourgeois ignorant nous vaut mieux, comme vous voyez, que le grand seigneur éclairé qui nous a introduits ici. (2:502)

> [In truth [Monsieur Jourdain] is a man whose wits are dim, who speaks erroneously about everything and who applauds at the wrong moment; but his money rectifies the judgments of his mind. He shows discernment in his pocketbook. His praises are minted; and this ignorant bourgeois is worth more to us, as you see, than the great and enlightened lord who introduced us to him.]

Signs such as "judgement" and "discernement" were relatively new indicators of nobility, suggesting that the values of the sixteenth-century high bourgeoisie (spiritual and not physical prowesses) indeed had become the noble values of the seventeenth century. Just as noble indicators could be co-opted by a bourgeois to reinvent himself, so other types of signs could be appropriated to give one sort of appearance or another. In *Les Précieuses Ridicules* (1659), Cathos and Magdelon adorn themselves with signs of *préciosité*; in *Le Tartuffe* (1664), it is a question of religious signs being manipulated.[19]

What Gilles Deleuze has proposed about the nature of signs in Marcel Proust's depiction of nineteenth-century French aristocratic society would also be valid to some extent in seventeenth-century France. Deleuze argues that such signs had no transcendental value but replaced, stood in for, both thought and action: "judged from the perspective of actions, *mondanité* appears deceiving and cruel; and from the perspective of thought, seems stupid. One does not think nor act, but one signals [*faire signe*]" (13). The value of these empty signs resides purely in their ritualistic aspect: "They are empty, but this vacuousness grants them a ritualistic perfection" (Deleuze, 13).[20] One makes a sign, *faire signe*, of belonging to a particular group or social category, but this sign has no inherent value, no "end in itself." Monsieur Jourdain, for example, cares little for music or philosophy in itself; the value of art for him lies in the social prestige he can potentially attain by signaling his good taste.

It is important to recall here that in early modern France commerce was socially looked down upon, despite the fact that it constituted the economic base of the new aristocracy. Whereas the feudal nobility was ennobled by their political and economic functions, the rising aristocracy, for reasons of social prestige, had to distance themselves from their actual function in society and build their identity from signs that were detached from it. Signs of social prestige existed in a relation of discontinuity with the actual economic and political functions of the persons who appropriated these signs: thus the need to signal belonging to a particular *social* group—defined in terms of artistic taste or philosophical tendencies—rather than to a particular *condition* or "class."

One broad characteristic of cultural change in the early modern period is clearly *rupture*: geographical, cultural, and linguistic rupture between upper and lower orders or classes of society, marking the beginnings of the distinction between "high" and "low" culture; a rupture in the traditional working relationship between master, journeyman, and apprentice, as slowly a more "class-oriented" relationship develops, based on the distinction between manual and intellectual labor, worker and entrepreneur; the breakdown of the household unit resulting in a rupture between the public (politico-economic, masculine) sphere and the private (domestic, feminine) sphere, a divide reinforced by emerging concepts of reason and noble identity; a rupture between one's social identity and one's politico-economic function in society; and finally, a rupture between social signifiers from their traditional signifieds, accounting for the seventeenth-century preoccupation with the relation between appearance and reality. Overall a gap was forming that separated the "haves" (those who possess financial and cultural capital) from the "have-nots." Upper-class women found themselves on both sides of the gap. Financially separated from women and men from other "classes," they nevertheless found themselves at times on the other side of the tracks when it came to cultural capital, not to mention legal rights.

WOMEN AND CULTURAL CHANGE IN SEVENTEENTH-CENTURY FRANCE

I have focused extensively on how cultural change in the early modern period negatively affected women. However, women

were not simply passive bystanders to their own fate, and patriarchal practices were far from being monolithic. Despite the proliferation of laws and practices prejudicial to women, women did
engage in the cultural and material production of French society.
Regarding the proliferation of laws regulating marriage and limiting women's legal rights, Hanley remarks that it "widened the
gap in social entitlement by empowering male heads and placing
females at risk. At the same time, the women in these particular
cases fashioned a counterfeit culture both to suit themselves and
to minimize the risks" (21). And according to James Collins, "despite increasing institutional (especially legal) restrictions
against women, the statistical evidence implies that the number
of businesswomen was growing in the seventeenth century"
(464). In spite of institutional restrictions and discourses purport-
ing women's lack of reason and self-control, women did indeed
"fashion themselves," evidenced in the very existence of the
play, *Les Précieuses Ridicules*. It would seem that women had
greater real than theoretical power in early modern France, as
they found ways around legal and institutional practices that
sought to limit their economic and sociocultural activity.

For upper-class women, the emergence of the salon provided
an antidote to barriers impeding women from actively and officially engaging in the public (politico-economic) sphere. Along
with informal and institutionalized academies, salons formed
part of what could be called the "public *sociocultural* sphere."
After Reinhart Koselleck, Dena Goodman advances the idea that
in the eighteenth century there existed two public spheres: the
"inauthentic" public sphere of state authority (which I will refer
to as the politico-economic sphere), and the "authentic" (or sociocultural) public sphere where people came together through
the public use of their reason (5).[21] Daniel Gordon already sees
a split occurring between what he calls the "political" and the
"apolitical" public sphere in the seventeenth century.[22] Of
course, the distinction between these two spheres—like the distinction between public and private—is a conceptual one, for
within salons and academies relationships were cultivated that
had implications in the politico-economic sphere.

As theorists from Habermas to Goodman and Gordon have
suggested, the "authentic" or sociocultural public sphere developed at the same time that the monarchy was consolidating its
power within the *res publica*, or the politico-economic public
sphere. In the first half of the seventeenth century, particularly
after the death of Richelieu (1642), informal academies and sa-

Table 1

Salons	Informal Academies (cercles, cabinets)
Marguerite de Valois (1605–1615)	François Malherbe (1607–1633)
Catherine de Vivonne, marquise de Rambouillet (1610–1645)	cercle des amis de Régnier (1615–1630)
Marie le Jars de Gournay (1620–1640)	cercle d'A. Brun (1620s)
	Guillaume Colletet (1620s)
Charlotte des Ursins, vicomtesse d'Auchy (1630s–1640s)	les frères Du Puy (1620–1650)
Madeleine de Scudéry (1650s)	abbé Marin Mersenne (1630s)
Henriette de Coligny, comtesse de La Suze (1650s; model for the abbé de Pure's Eulalie)	Nicolas Bourbon (1637–1644)
	Le Pailleur (académie Parisienne des sciences; 1642–1654)
Madeleine de Souvré, marquise de Sablé (1650s–1660s)	Marolles (1650s)
Ninon de Lenclos (1660s)	Gilles Ménage (1650s)
	Olivier Patru (1650s)
Marie-Madeleine Pioche de la Vergne, comtesse de La Fayette (1660s)	Guillaume de Lamoignon (1650s–1660s)
Marguerite Hessein, Madame de La Sablière (1660s–1670s)	François Hédelin, abbé d'Aubignac (1650s–1660s)
Anne Thérèse de Marguenat de Courcelles, marquise de Lambert (launched in 1690s and frequented by fairy-tale writers)	

lons quickly sprung up. In the above list I have included some of the important salons and informal (that is, noninstitutional) academies, along with their approximate dates.[23] The distinction I am making here between salon and academy—which was not a clear one in the seventeenth century—is based on gender: the salon is a mixed social group, and the academy an exclusively male one (see Table 1). Each salon and informal academy was of a different social and literary tendency. The salon of Catherine de Vivonne-Savelli, marquise de Rambouillet, was more aristocratic than that of Scudéry, and less erudite than that of Charlotte des Ursins, vicomtesse d'Auchy, whose salon was "surrounded by astrolabes and mathematical instruments" (Maclean, 142). Whereas Ninon de Lenclos's salon, frequented by Molière and Scarron, was dominated by libertine tendencies, that of Madeleine de Souvré, marquise de Sablé, consisting of disillusioned *frondeurs* like La Rochefoucauld, was distinctly Jansenist in character. Cartesian philosophy was disseminated through salons like that of Madame de Bonnevaut. With respect to informal academies, we generally find the same kind of diversity: the *cercle des amis* de Régnier and that of the brothers Du Puy were of a libertine tone; the Le Pailleur circle primarily dealt with scientific questions; and the entourage of Nicolas Bourbon adhered to erudite humanism.

The diversity of the sociocultural public sphere presents a stark contrast to the increasingly homogeneous politico-economic public sphere. Through the creation and proliferation of salons, elite women carved out a place for themselves in this "second" public sphere. However, women's new public role would not go uncontested. In Harth's words, "[t]he salon and the academy entered into a gendered competition with each other for intellectual space" (*Cartesian,* 17). By situating this gendered competition within the sociocultural sphere, we can better understand seventeenth-century debates about women and their public role, not to mention the ways in which women shaped early modern French culture and society.

In essence, the salon was an unofficial institution created and run by women. Initiating the salon movement around 1610, Rambouillet not only defined the general character of salon culture, but also designed herself the *Chambre bleue,* an architectural plan that would be imitated in the construction of other Parisian *hôtels.* Within French society, the salon fulfilled multiple functions. First, at a time when women were being excluded from the politico-economic public sphere, the salon, as noted above, allowed elite women to play a role in the sociocultural public sphere. Second, the salon provided a literary and philosophical forum in which women could legitimate themselves as beings endowed with reason, often adopting feminist versions of Cartesian philosophy to argue that "the mind has no sex." Third, through the salon women could actively take part in the production and dissemination of literature, science, philosophy, and new sociocultural concepts. The interconnections between literary production and salon culture are emphasized by Ian Maclean, who states that seventeenth-century literature "owed as much to the *salons* as the *salons* owed to literature" (149).[24] Fourth, salon women took the authority to reform the French language. Fi-

nally, the institution of the salon was caught up in a larger social
project of developing the precepts for and forming a new aristocracy. In chapters 2 and 3 concerning Scudéry and her works, we
will examine some of these functions in great detail; for the time
being, I would like to comment briefly on salon women's linguistic and social role in seventeenth-century France.

Salon women's contribution to the formation of the modern
French language cannot be underestimated: they sought to eliminate Greek and Latin derivations; they developed, cultivated,
and diffused the use of adverbs, metaphors, and expressions still
used today; and they reformed orthography. Their linguistic influence, the authority of which was acknowledged by Vaugelas in
his *Remarques sur la langue françoise* [Remarks on the French
Language] (1647), sparked retaliation by grammarians like Scipion Dupleix, who wished to exclude women from participation in
the development of the language by setting educational standards inaccessible to them.[25] Indeed, Dupleix's reaction attests
to the extraordinary influence women did have in linguistic matters of the period. Acknowledging women's active role in the development of modern French is important to recall today.
Psychoanalytic theorists who insist on the inherently patriarchal
nature of language take away women's voices by rendering them
"inauthentic." Such theories rest upon the assumption that
women have not actively played a role in the production of languages.

The "reformation" of the French language was connected to
the formation of a new aristocracy: the new nobility distinguished itself from other "classes" in part through its speech.
Cultivated in the salons, proper conversation, as we will see in
the discussion of Scudéry's salon chronicles, required the exclusion of certain topics, words, and concepts associated with the
domestic sphere, the politico-economic public sphere, and lower
classes. Provincialisms were frowned upon. Unlike the feudal nobility, whose identity was connected to a fief in the *countryside*,
the new nobility was of a distinctly civil or civic (related to the
city) and especially *Parisian* character. Proper language and
consequently nobility now had a geographical locus: Paris.

We have already noted that the rising aristocracy sought to
build their identity from signs that were detached from their actual function in society (in other words, detached from their function in the politico-economic public sphere). The salon was, so to
say, the construction site of one's social identity, a place where
elite men and women could refashion themselves. Like the High

Bourgeoisie and the Robe, women had an interest in reshaping themselves in a way that was discontinuous from their function in society. Within the sociocultural public sphere of the salon, women were no longer wives or mothers, but reasonable beings engaged in literary production, as well as in the production of a new social elite, accomplished through conversations, debates, and literary works treating proper behavior. Proper behavior was defined in terms of both gender and social relations, and the two were often inseparable, as we will see in both Scudéry's and d'Aulnoy's models of subjectivity. Through social practice and the continual production of books over the course of the century Scudéry, perhaps more than any other salon woman, contributed to developing new definitions of nobility. Her overwhelming influence in seventeenth-century France accounts for the fact that Nicolas Boileau aimed his attack of the novel and new models of subjectivity at her in particular, Scudéry being the embodiment of the new cultural trends he opposed.

In some respects the proliferation of salons and informal academies in the beginning of the seventeenth century reproduced at a sociocultural level the political decentralization of earlier periods. In the same way that the monarchy infringed upon communal rights within the politico-economic public sphere, so it attempted to monopolize sociocultural public space in the second half of the seventeenth century with the construction of Versailles, the monopolization of patronage, and the institutionalization of academies. With the construction of Versailles, Louis XIV widened the scope of court culture and increased the high nobility's submission to him by imposing a model of etiquette glorifying the king above all other nobles, and by granting and refusing favors in such a way as to increase the nobility's social, political, and economic dependence on the monarchy. Louis XIV was going to avoid at all costs another Fronde, and Versailles was his vehicle of repression and surveillance.[26]

In the beginning of the century, it was quite common for writers, who also functioned as their administrators, to be pensioned by members of the high nobility (i.e., members of the Longueville or Condé family). Again, the sociocultural public sphere reproduced the type of decentralization characteristic of the medieval body politic. In fact, the patron–client relations of the early modern period came to replace traditional bonds of vassalage with the transformation of social and political structures, a phenomenon referred to as "bastard feudalism" (Kettering, 207). The degree to which clients and patrons of the period construed their relation in feudal terms will be examined in chapter 3.

After the fall of Nicolas Fouquet, the last great independent patron of the arts, Louis XIV erected himself as the country's sole Maecenas. Although patronage does not disappear, particularly with regards to managing noble estates, Louis XIV clearly attempted to eliminate competition within the sociocultural field. It was due to the institutionalization of academies that the king could put himself forth as sole national patron, at the same time that officializing academies allowed the king to co-opt artistic and scientific energies for his own purposes, monopolizing (or attempting to monopolize) sociocultural public space—in the provinces as well as in the capital. Several provincial academies, with official *Lettres Patentes*, were established from 1658 to 1706. Members not only modeled their academies on Parisian "originals," particularly the Académie Française and the Académie Royale des Sciences, but they also had direct connections to the capital through Parisian *académicien* patrons who helped them attain their *Lettres Patentes* (see Table 2).[27]

With the institutionalization of academies, which took off in the 1660s, the configuration of the sociocultural public sphere was modified. One effect appears to be the diminution of the extent of the salon's influence in French society, at least until the death of Louis XIV. As DeJean has remarked, "the salons were displaced by the academies" as locuses for writing in the latter part of the century (*Tender*, 129). Because a full-scale history of the seventeenth-century salon has yet to be written, it is not clear, moreover, whether there were fewer salons established during Louis XIV's personal reign, or if salons simply did not carry the same weight within the sociocultural public sphere—at least as reflected in literary history—as salons of the earlier part of the century (i.e., those of Rambouillet, Sablé, and Scudéry). In any case, the establishment of official academies encroached upon the scope of the salon's sociocultural function.

Conferring *Lettres Patentes* to academies and making their status official further reinforced gendered conceptions of sociocultural space, and quite consequently, gendered notions of knowledge. Whereas the more learned salons of Gournay and d'Auchy were often referred to as "academies," later salons would no longer be confused with what increasingly was thought of as purely masculine institutions. Londa Schiebinger emphasizes the consequences of "masculinizing" the academy as it pertains to scientific knowledge: "With the founding of the academy

Table 2

Parisian Academies	Lettres Patentes
Académie Française	1635
Académie Royale de Peinture et de Sculpture	1648
Académie Royale de Danse	1661
Académie Royale des Inscriptions et Belles-lettres (la Petite Académie)	1663
Académie Royale de France à Rome	1666
Académie des Sciences	1666
Académie Royale de Musique	1669 (A. Viala gives 1672)
Académie Royale d'Architecture	1671

Provincial Academies	Lettres Patentes	Affiliation	Parisian Patrons
Avignon	1658	Académie Française	Paul Pellisson (AF)
Castres	active 1648–1670	Académie Française	Daniel Huet (AF)
Caen	active 1652–1705	independent	Saint-Aignan (AF); le cardinal de Vendôme
Arles	1669	Académie Française	Olivier Patru (AF); Pellisson; le cardinal d'Estrée (AF)
Soissons	1674	Académie Française	
Nîmes	1682	Académie Française	chancelier Le Tellier; Esprit Fléchier (AF)
Angers	1685	Académie Française	Gilles Ménage
Villefranche	1695	Académie Française	
Toulouse	1695	Académie Française	
Lyon	1700	independent	Villeroy
Montpellier	1706	Académie royale des sciences	Bishop Colbert de Croissy
Bordeaux	1706	Académie royale des sciences	duc de La Force

AF = member of the Académie Française.

system in Europe, a general pattern for women's place in science begins to emerge: as the prestige of an activity increases, the participation of women in that activity decreases" (20). Only one academy, the Académie Royale de la Peinture et de la Sculpture, admitted women (seven from 1663 to 1682), but closed its doors to them by 1706 (Schiebinger, 27). Science, architecture, and philosophy were perceived to be male disciplines, whereas the novel and conversation were associated with women—a gendered conception of knowledge still part of our own cultural heritage in twenty-first-century America.

The exclusion of women from the official academies must also be looked at within the broader context of Louis XIV's overall political project. Jean-Marie Apostolidès attributes the acceleration of the establishment of official academies to the monarch's will to possess and control the nation's intellectual activity.[28] Along with male intellectuals, like the ill-fated Claude Petit who failed to yield to monarchic authority, women also were marginalized, as if by their very nature women would be incapable of submitting to the monarch's patriarchal authority. (We might recall here that in Ancien Régime absolutism, the monarch was conceived of as the head of the nation-household.) Under Louis XIV, the institutionalization of academies resulted in both the subordination of academies to the monarchy's own purposes, and the marginalization of salon culture and consequently of women within the sociocultural public sphere. However, as Joan DeJean has pointed out, it is under Louis XIV that women writers were the most prolific (*Tender*, 127–28). Absolutism in all its repression failed to put a stop to women's participation in the cultural production of French society.

As a period of transition, seventeenth-century France was ridden with tensions. Class tensions revolved around definitions of nobility: some people were nostalgic for what they took to be a more "stable" feudal order of signification, whereas others saw the freeing-up of signs of prestige as an opportunity to redefine themselves in more dignified terms. Tensions existed between the rights of particular communities and those of the monarchy, which manifested themselves most explicitly in the Fronde. Tensions concerning gender played out in terms of legally limiting women's rights at the same time that elite women were exercising their reason and right to self-fashioning within the salons, which in turn posed a threat to male authority within the sociocultural public sphere. Considered together the chapters that follow push and pull between these various points of tension, constantly moving from politics to class to gender as the four writers studied here position themselves differently from one another, just as they are all connected, defining themselves with and/or against the others in implicit and explicit ways.

2

Love Orders Chaos: Madeleine de Scudéry's
Clélie, Histoire Romaine

WRITING HISTORY HAS OFTEN MEANT WRITING THE NATION. CONSIDER the sixteenth-century historian Etienne Pasquier's *Des recherches de la France* [Research on France], (1560), in which Pasquier affirms France's Gallic and not Trojan origins in order to postulate the nation's nonmonarchical origins; or the nineteenth-century historian Victor Cousin's *La Société française au XVIIe siècle d'après Le Grand Cyrus de Mlle de Scudéry* [French Society in the 17th Century according to the Great Cyrus by Mlle de Scudéry] (1858), in which Cousin opposes the glory of France's monarchical and civil past to the social and political upheaval of the 1850s. In these two examples, the historian's claims to accurately represent the nation's past are ideologically motivated, and have implications in the historian's own present. Writing history has also often meant telling the story of national heroes, who provide models of subjectivity believed to be at the foundation of the nation. A historian who focuses on the role of great men in the history of the nation obviously infers quite a different national reality and relations between the nation's citizens than the historian who focuses on the contributions of women, lower classes, and minorities to that nation's evolution.

In writing *Clélie, Histoire Romaine*, Madeleine de Scudéry borrows techniques from early modern historiography to allegorically write the history (or history to be) of the French nation, and of the heroes and heroines at its foundation. Although Scudéry sought to include heroines in the narrative of universal history, her ultimate goals go beyond feminist revisionism. Taking into account both the structure of the novel and the concepts she deploys, it becomes clear that through *Clélie* Scudéry was putting forth a republican model of state and individual that would free women from oppressive social practices, and more generally reconcile the private interests of the individual with the public interests of the state. Through her appropriation of early modern historiographical practices, Scudéry engages in ideologically charged debates about glory and heroism, concepts that were to define the emerging French nation.

Scudéry's fictional histories are in part feminist revisions of those classical texts constitutive of early modern French historiography revived by sixteenth-century humanists. *Les Femmes Illustres ou les Harangues héroïques* [Les Femmes Illustres, or Twenty Heroic Harangues of the Most Illustrious Women of Antiquity] (1642) is a feminocentric version of Plutarch's *Lives* and recalls the earlier work of Boccaccio and Christine de Pizan. In *Artamène, ou Le Grand Cyrus*, Scudéry draws from Herodotus's *The Persian Wars* to allegorize the Fronde and its women warriors; and in *Clélie, Histoire Romaine* she highlights the role played by women in Livy's *History of Rome*. In some respects, Scudéry's way of appropriating traditional historical models and rewriting a history inclusive of women resembles contemporary revisionist efforts on the part of scholars of Women's Studies, African-American Studies, Native-American Studies, and Hispanic Studies. As we can acknowledge in twenty-first-century America, such revisionism modifies our notions of heroism, subjectivity, and the nation, and thus transforms contemporary culture and society. Writing at a time of sociopolitical instability, Scudéry's revisionism contributed to the processes of cultural change in her society by redefining concepts such as heroism, glory, and virtue through a form of fiction largely influenced by early modern historiography. Redefining such concepts, as we shall see, not only had implications for female and male subjectivity, but also marks Scudéry's engagement in the struggle to defend a particular image of the newly emerging French nation.

THE ORDER OF HISTORY

Based on her personal relationships, it is likely that Scudéry was well versed in contemporary theories of historical writing. Jean Chapelain and Paul Pellisson, both of whom receive their own chapter in Orest Ranum's *Artisans of Glory* (1980), were among Scudéry's closest friends. Chapelain spent years writing his only historical narrative, *La Pucelle* [The Maiden of Orléans] (1656), and was more of a critic and administrator of other writers' historical works than a historian in his own right. Pellisson did succeed in writing his *Relation contenant l'histoire de l'Aca-*

démie Française [The History of the French Academy] (1652),
which earned him election to the Academy, but for the most part
he was a failed historian. His *Lettres historiques*, consisting of
his correspondence with Scudéry, and his *Histoire de Louis XIV,
depuis la mort du Cardinal Mazarin en 1661 jusqu'à la paix en
1678* [The History of Louis XIV, from the Death of the Cardinal
Mazarin to the Peace of 1678], based on his notes as historiographer to the king, were published posthumously, in 1729 and 1749
respectively. Given the extent of Scudéry's interest in questions
of history—reflected in her decision to fictionalize the histories
of Plutarch, Herodotus, and Livy—and the intimate nature of her
relationships with Chapelain and Pellisson, we can fairly conclude that Scudéry would have influenced their concept of history at least as much as they had influenced hers.

Early modern notions of history were closely tied to the genre
of the exemplum, in that the primary purpose of historical writing was to put forth models of human perfection. For Chapelain
the role of history was to prescribe norms of civic virtue: "Je
tiens pour moy, que l'histoire est instituée seulement pour l'uti-
lité de la vie civile, et qu'on y doit regarder le vice moral, pour le
rendre odieux, et la Vertu, sa contraire pour en persuader l'a-
mour aux peuples" ["For me history is instituted only for the
usefulness of civil life, and one must observe in history moral
vice, in order to render it odious, and Virtue, its contrary, in
order to instill in peoples the love of virtue"] (quoted in Ranum,
Artisans, 183). Communicating hatred of vice and love of virtue,
history's function resides for Chapelain in its prescriptive rather
than descriptive qualities, a view generally shared by early modern historiographers. Drawing lessons from the past, "lessons
that strictly speaking had little or no relation to actual events,"
was a perfectly legitimate historical approach (Ranum, *Artisans*,
249). Moreover, in a country ridden with religious conflict, Catholicism was no longer a feasible foundation for national morality. Rather than draw from the lives of the saints as exemplary
models of human perfection, early modern writers—particularly
those humanist-educated writers of the Robe and Upper Bourgeoisie—took their models from Greco-Roman history, especially Plutarch and Livy, whose use of character depictions or
portraits "satisfied a need for edification" (Ranum, *Artisans*,
257). Pellisson comments on the necessity for such devices in
historical writing: "C'est un des grands secrets pour rendre l'histoire animée, et pour empecher qu'elle languisse" ["This is one

of the great secrets for invigorating history, and preventing it from languishing"] (quoted in Ranum, *Artisans*, 262]).

Of course, the notion of perfection to be foregrounded in historical writing was an early modern one, itself under debate by those defending the monarchy, the traditional nobility of the sword, or the nobility of the Robe and Upper Bourgeoisie. As such, early modern historiographical models were subject to the rules of verisimilitude or *vraisemblance*. Reflecting on seventeenth-century notions of *vraisemblance*, Gérard Genette remarks: "The verisimilar narration is thus a narration whose actions correspond, like so many applications or particular cases, to a corpus of maxims accepted as true by the public it addresses" (76). To say that historical narration is verisimilar, then, means that the actions constitutive of it are used to illustrate maxims that convey norms of behavior or human nature to which a particular group or society adheres. Consequently, the truth-value of history resides less in its depiction of "the facts" than in the morality it communicates; it is less *vraie* [true] than *vraisemblable* [verisimilar]. It is perhaps for this reason that "literature of praise, contemporary history, and fictionalized memoirs and histories seemed to resemble each other more and more during the 1660s and 1670s" (Ranum, *Artisans*, 235). Indeed, the demarcation between history and fiction was as ambiguous as the term *histoire*, which signifies both *story* and *history*.

Whereas historical characters were put forth as models of human perfection, historical narrative itself was structured, according to Karlheinz Stierle, like a *macro-example*: "History is recounted, on the one hand, within the syntagmatic framework of universal history, and on the other, within the paradigmatic framework of a collection of exempla illustrating what always remains identical in human baseness [or glory]" (184–85). Stierle's analysis suggests that early modern historiography was not simply a collection of exempla arbitrarily strung together. Instead, these portraits were integrated into the larger framework of universal history, structured according to two underlying and analogous types of metanarratives: the classical medical narrative, on the one hand; and the Platonic one, on the other.

In the first case, the syntagmatic framework moves "from some zero-degree of vulnerable healthiness, that then builds up, through a series of significant symptoms to a predictable dramatic climax at a moment of required 'crisis' . . . after which the disease completes its predetermined and internally directed course, when the patient either dies or returns to health" (Fineman, 55). In the second case, the narrative proceeds from an initial situation of vulnerable stability to ontological degradation, to finally a return to stability: "the history of the world follows the vertical movement of degradation and ascension . . . a dynamic founded on the return to initial Unity, and [following] the cycle of a degradation then a reconstitution of Being" (Dubois, 18–19). In both cases, history is constructed according to some sort of Fall (physical or ontological disintegration) and the subsequent *rétablissement* (recovery, reestablishment) of unity or oneness, a movement or process we might characterize in terms of *chaos and a return to order.*

The paradigmatic and syntagmatic frameworks function together in such a way that the syntagmatic guides the general narrative from chaos towards order, while the paradigmatic accumulation of exempla puts forth ideal models of subjectivity (or models of human perfection) at the foundation of this order. That exempla or the examples of usually illustrious men are the means by which a return to order is effectuated has to do with the common early modern topoi of a correspondence between the microcosm and the macrocosm, between the individual and the state. Accordingly, it is by ordering the individual that order in the body politic can be restored. Competing narratives foregrounding the exemplarity of the feudal nobility or that of the monarchy had repercussions, then, regarding the model of the nation the historian was attempting to defend. Ranum notes, for instance, that Colbert "found in Priolo what Richelieu had found in François de Fancan, Jean Sirmond, and Mézerai: the young writer who would write history to undermine the aristocratic, *parlementaire*, and ecclesiastical ideals and to support the Crown" (*Artisans*, 168). The type of heroes chosen by a particular writer was inextricably tied to the model of the nation he or she proposed as ideal.

In writing *Clélie, Histoire Romaine*, Scudéry appropriates and develops certain historiographic techniques to construct a genre she earlier dubbed the *fable*, referred to today as the historical novel.[1] Like conventional history, Scudéry's fable is structured according to 1) a paradigmatic collection of exempla or portraits based on historical personages, for which she creates correspondences with members of the Parisian salon elite, establishing keys between ancient and modern heroes and heroines;[2] 2) a syntagmatic framework moving from chaos towards order; and 3) the principle of *vraisemblance*. Unlike conventional history, the paradigmatic is privileged over the syntagmatic almost to the point of bringing the forward movement of the narrative to a halt. Joan DeJean sums up this strategy by noting that "Scudéry broadens her rejection of action-oriented fiction, turning increasingly to an oblique presentation of events and continuing to slow down the pace of the narrative" (*Tender*, 55). *Clélie* is based on sections of books 1 and 2 of Livy's *History of Rome* concerning the usurpation of the Roman throne by Tarquin, the events leading to Tarquin's demise, and the establishment of the Roman Republic, all of which is recounted in less than one hundred pages. Scudéry's novel relates essentially the same story in over seven thousand. Her emphasis on the paradigmatic makes the fable distinct from history and, as we will see, has implications for both female and male subjectivity.

In *Clélie*, the paradigmatic consists not only of portraits or *histoires* (the term used by Scudéry within the novel to refer to portraits) of the various characters, but also of conversations. Interspersed within and between portraits/stories, conversations provide a space for commentary and abstract discussion for the *compagnie* (a term generally used to refer to a group of *salonniers* or salon participants) of listeners. Socratic-like debates, conversations revolve around the positive and negative qualities conveyed in the story through the behavior or example of the story's characters. Derived directly or indirectly from the concepts inscribed in the Carte de Tendre, Scudéry's celebrated map of interpersonal relations first published in *Clélie*, these qualities are expressed as maxims within the context of the conversations, maxims by means of which the reader is to understand the various characters' behavior.[3] As such, the novel does not rely on the reader's own pool of maxims but generates its own, thereby regulating what constitutes *vraisemblance* within the text. Evident in the responses of her contemporaries, particularly that of Nicolas Boileau, which we will examine in detail in chapter 4, Scudéry's notion of *vraisemblance* propagated in *Clélie* did not go uncontested.

REDEFINING GLORY

The way in which Scudéry privileges the paradigmatic over the syntagmatic gives much more importance to conversation and social behavior than to heroic action. In effect, this structural modification of conventional historical discourse has repercussions for her notion of heroism, aggressively attacked by Boileau in his *Dialogue des héros de roman*. Throughout the novel, Scudéry displaces the notion of heroic virtue or *gloire* from the domain of external military action to that of conversation and behavior in society or in the love relation. *Gloire*, then, comes to express a character's interior virtue. In fact, the novel pushes the reader to consider the exterior—in other words, the public virtue of a particular character—as an extension of his or her interior or private virtue. In so doing, Scudéry makes heroism or glory accessible to women, exemplified at the end of the novel in the erection of two statues: one dedicated to the military glory of Horace, the other commemorating Clélie's virtue, specifically her active defense of her chastity. It is the emphasis on conversation and behavior, and the displacement of heroism from military to social affairs, that allows Scudéry to include women in universal history.

Scudéry's displacement of the concept of glory also opens up heroism to all non-military people by redefining the virtues of the heroes of Antiquity. For instance, in the opening of Brutus's story, Herminius (alias Paul Pellisson) states that this will not be one filled with great events, but claims that his listeners will nevertheless admire Brutus: "Ne vous preparez donc pas à luy voir gagner des batailles, assieger des Villes, et faire de ces actions esclatantes, dont ordinairement la vie d'un Heros est remplie: Mais ne laissez pas de vous preparer à luy donner toute vostre estime, et toutes vos loüanges" ["Do not expect to see him winning battles, laying siege to Cities, or performing dazzling actions, which normally fill the life of a Hero: But do not prevent yourself from preparing to give him all your esteem, and all your admiration"] (3: 168). In *Clélie*, the Roman hero Brutus will be defined first and foremost in terms of his social virtues as well as his capacity to love, and only later in the novel will his political and military virtues, arguably extensions of his virtues in love and friendship, be highlighted.

Inserted within Brutus's story is, significantly, a conversation on glory that serves to reflect upon the particular story of Brutus at the same time that it allows the characters to examine the concept in more general terms. In the end, the debate works to redefine the concept by negating the importance of its military and public meaning, and by valorizing a more private and inclusive definition. This negation is expressed in the *compagnie*'s mocking Mutius, who defends the traditional military definition of glory. Whereas Mutius argues that glory is reserved for military actions and must be brought to public attention, Hermilie contends that Mutius's definition excludes women. To the approval of the *compagnie*, Herminius proposes a more inclusive definition of glory: "la gloire despend plus de la vertu, que de la Renommée . . . il y a de la gloire à estre savant, il y en a à estre genereux, equitable, et bon; il y en a à posseder toutes les vertus en general, et chaque vertu en particulier: il y en a à tous les Arts liberaux; il y en a mesme à sçavoir bien tous les Arts mecaniques . . . [et] à sçavoir aimer constamment ses Amis" ["glory depends more on virtue than on Renown . . . there is glory in being knowledgeable, generous, impartial, and good; there is glory in possessing all the virtues in general, and each virtue in particular: there is glory in the liberal Arts; there is even glory in knowing well all the mechanical Arts . . . [and] knowing how to faithfully love one's Friends"] (3:482–83). Opening up the definition of glory, Herminius makes it a general virtue that can describe many different types of activities and behaviors. It is both a private and a public virtue, applicable to women and men, bourgeois and noble.

By realigning glory with virtue in general, and with the liberal (versus martial) arts and love in particular, Scudéry puts forth in *Clélie* a feminized model of heroism, already suggested by the novel's title—a type of heroism accessible to women and members of the bourgeoisie alike. As Marlies Mueller has pointed out, the domesticating efforts of salon women like Scudéry were perceived by many as an "emasculating education" taking place "at court, in the salons, and at the academies" ("Taming," 220). Scudéry's redefinition of glory or "vertu heroïque" recalls that of her friend Guez de Balzac, who argued: "Il est certain que toutes les actions hardies ne se font pas à la guerre: il faut aussi de la resolution et du courage pour estre chaste" ["Certainly not all bold actions take place in war: resolution and courage are also necessary in order to be chaste"]. He was well aware of the critiques of this "emasculating" model of heroism: "Je scay bien qu'en cet endroit j'estime une qualité méprisée du monde, et que la pluspart de ceux qui font profession de la galanterie, me reprocheront que je loüe les hommes des vertus des femmes" ["I recognize that I value a quality scorned by high society, and that most of those who claim to be gallant, will reproach me for praising in men the virtues of women"] (Balzac 121–22). We must keep in mind that at the time Scudéry was writing *Clélie* many members of French high society still valued military prowess as a noble quality. Neither Scudéry's nor Balzac's valorization of moral virtue and social prowesses was universally accepted;

however, it was increasingly becoming the norm in French society.

Indeed, the very concept of *gloire* was under debate in French society. Whereas pro-Richelieu writers were critical of the high nobility's *faim de gloire* (thirst for glory) exemplified in the Fronde, other writers with a more critical view towards the ministerial regime put into question Richelieu's *politique de gloire* [politics of glory] for the French nation. In his study of Pierre Corneille, David Clarke lays out the position of various writers of the period vis-à-vis the minister's *politique de gloire*, often discussed in conjunction with the history of Rome. Writers indirectly criticized the minister's policy of national glory—perceived to be executed at the expense of the French people—by discussing Rome's unethical pursuit of glory. The *"monarchie seigneuriale* of pagan antiquity, totally unrestrained in the possession and use of its subjects' lives and wealth," was contrasted with "the sanctity and excellence of the 'most Christian' French monarchy," a sanctity perceived to have been violated by the "coup d'état" of Richelieu (and later, by the "usurper" Mazarin), whom many believed to be reigning in the king's stead (Clarke, 24, 29). Specifically as it relates to Corneille's *Horace*, Clarke argues that the title character, who sets aside nature and natural law for the glory of the Roman monarchy, embodies the moral ambiguity of Richelieu's *politique de gloire*, in which morality and ethics were superseded by *la raison d'état*.[4]

Through the writing of *Clélie*, Scudéry engages in this debate in an interesting way. At the same time that Scudéry redefines glory or national virtue to include women, she also reconceptualizes heroic virtue and national glory in such a way as to reconcile the public interests of the Roman Republic with the private interests of its citizens, as will become clear in the pages to come. She thus undoes the dichotomy present within the political discourses of her time between public and private interests. As opposed to other writers who used the Roman seigniorial *monarchy* as a springboard for criticism of Richelieu, Scudéry has her virtuous heroes (and to some degree heroines) overthrow the Roman monarchy ruled by the usurper Tarquin to establish a *Republic*. (It is important to note here that both Richelieu and Mazarin were considered by their critics as "usurpers.")[5] Although DeJean is correct in stating that *Clélie* is "a chronicle of salon life" (*Tender*, 55), we should not limit our reading of the novel to the confines of salon discourse. We must also pay attention to the ways in which Scudéry engages in and works through the political discourses and concepts of her time. Scudéry's reconceptualization of the notion of *gloire* in the novel is exemplary of how she creates a dialectics between private and public interests, between love and politics, to build her ideal society.

FABLE VERSUS HISTORY

What distinguishes the genre of the fable from that of history is love or *tendresse*. Love is a concept that governs both the syntagmatic movement of the fable's narrative as well as its paradigmatic string of exempla, and not inconsequentially is a principal that applies to the personal as well as the political. With respect to the overall syntagmatic movement of the novel, love functions as the overarching cause of events, creating a logical connection between the accidental, disordered, and sometimes illogical elements constitutive of "true" or descriptive history. This is highlighted in the conversation following Amilcar's account of the *histoire* of Hesiode and Clymene. Anacreon remarks that Amilcar's version not only is "plus belle que la verité, mais encore plus vraysemblable" ["more beautiful than the truth, but also more verisimilar"] (8: 1120), for history only mentions the banal and unordered facts of Hesiode's life such as his place of birth, the inspiration of the Muses, his travels, his reception of the Tripod, his victory over Homer, and his death at the hands of Clymene's brothers for being the confidant of her lover. Anacreon characterizes "true history" as a rather boring string of events rather loosely tied together, lacking both beauty and *vraisemblance*. Beauty must be understood here in its association with the notion of order, in the neo-Platonic tradition of Ficino or Pierre Nicole. In the early modern period, what was ordered was beautiful, what was beautiful was ordered.

In his version of the story, however, Amilcar invents the love affair between Hesiode and Clymene, and as such corrects history by making it more believable or *vraisemblable*:

Lors qu'on veut faire arriver des evenemens extraordinaires, il est sans doute bien plus beau d'y introduire l'amour, que nulle autre cause ... car en suposant l'amour du Prince de Locres, celle de Lysicrate, et celle d'Hesiode, pour Clymene, il vous a fait connoistre toutes ces diverses personnes, et vous a obligé d'aimer celles qui de-

voient estre les plus malheureuses. En suite il a donné de la vray-
semblance à ce qui n'en avoit guere; car il y a bien plus d'aparence
que deux freres ambitieux et méchans, se portent à tuer un homme
qu'ils croyoient faire obstacle à leur fortune, en empeschant leur
soeur d'estre favorable à un Prince dont ils attendent leur establisse-
ment, que non pas de le tuer comme confident d'un Amant de leur
soeur; car crime pour crime, il valoit mieux tuer l'Amant que le Confident"

[When one wishes to have extraordinary events occur, it is undoubtedly more beautiful to introduce love than any other cause . . .
for supposing the love of the Prince de Locres, Lysicrate, and Hesiod
for Clymene, love caused you to get to know these various people,
and compelled you to love those who were the most unfortunate.
Then love gave verisimilitude to that which had little; for it makes
more sense that two ambitious and mean brothers are led to kill a
man who they believed presented an obstacle to their fortune, by preventing their sister from favoring a Prince from whom they expected
their establishment, than to kill him as the confidant of their sister's
lover; crime for crime, it is better to kill the Lover than the Confidant.
(8:1122–23)

Love as the overarching cause of events serves several purposes, first and foremost, that of creating a logical connection between the accidental, disordered, and illogical elements of "true"
(or descriptive) history. Inventing the love affair between Hesiode and Clymene corrects history by making it more believable
or *vraisemblable*; it provides a logic or order to the story that
history itself could not provide.

Although not discussed by the characters here, the story of
Brutus and Lucrece offers a similar example of love operating
as the organizing principle for their story. As opposed to other
historical versions of the rape of Lucretia, Scudéry's version
strengthens the connection between Brutus and Lucrece by
making them lovers forced to forego their relationship when Lucrece must marry Collatin, thus rendering more *vraisemblable*
Brutus's thirst for vengeance against Sextus and the Tarquins.
In the neo-Platonic tradition, love for Scudéry serves as the ultimate force behind the narrative's order and beauty. Love furthermore serves as the pretext for character development,
allowing the reader to get to know the characters, making history, in Pellisson's words, more "animated." Getting to know the
characters also means knowing "le fond du coeur de tous les
hommes" ["the bottom of all men's hearts"] (8: 1126). Love fur-

nishes a way to get inside the characters through their words (conversations, love letters) in a way that external action cannot, at the same time that it functions as the internal motivation or cause of the story's syntagmatic movement.

Anacreon goes so far as to argue for the superiority of the fable over history. A fable gives the reader more pleasure and is more useful than history, for it can more effectively teach virtue through lessons of universal appeal. Most of the conversation on the fable revolves around its pedagogical function, in a defense against its detractors, who argue that the prevalence of love in the genre corrupts young people. To the contrary, Herminius contends that reading fables/novels would prevent women from responding naively to male advances, for the discrepancy between the behavior of fictional heroes and that of actual men would teach them to distinguish between men's apparent and actual intentions. Not only are characters to use the fable to help them interpret the behavior of other people, but also they are to observe and correct their own. In the conversation on *le mensonge* [lying], for instance, Plotine is so convinced by Herminius's condemnation of lying that she is determined never to do it again (9: 114). *Clélie* is constructed according to a textually inscribed addressee or *destinataire* of pedagogical lessons, or the characters listening to the story and internalizing its lessons; and an extratextual *destinataire*, or the reader, whose response to the text is guided by that of the inscribed addressees. It is the fable's basic structure that teaches both female and male readers not only the distinction between virtue and vice, but also how to apply these lessons to their own lives based on the textual *destinataire*'s responses.

Specifically as it relates to women, the fable can show them how to choose an appropriate partner by teaching them to distinguish, by means of exempla and conversations, between a virtuous, reasonable lover or husband and an immoral or mediocre one. The African Amilcar argues that Roman women, cloistered by their families like so many *captives*, do not know how to choose a husband because they cannot engage in conversation with men: "je suis persuadé qu'elles le [l'amour] donne de mauvaise grace, et mal à propos, car la conversation n'estant pas aussi libre icy qu'elle est en Afrique, il faut qu'elles le donnent sans sçavoir à qui; et qu'elles prennent les Gens sur leur bonne mine seulement, ce qui est la chose du monde la plus trompeuse" ["I am persuaded that they give love ungraciously and inappropriately, and because conversation is not as free here as in

Africa, women are forced to give their love without knowing to whom; they take people at face value, which is most misleading"] (3: 112). Conversation allows women to know to whom they give their love by teaching them how to penetrate appearances, revealing a man's (and more generally, peoples') true intentions or merit. Within the context of the novel, it is the precepts of the Carte de Tendre that serve as a guide for the textual and extratextual *destinataire*'s interpretation of a character's words and behavior, helping them distinguish between the appearance and reality of virtue in a particular character. For the female reader and female characters, determining the virtues of a suitor has repercussions for themselves: women must learn to resist certain forms of love that can enslave them or prove detrimental to their own virtue, and to accept others that are compatible with their freedom and reputation.

In *Clélie, Histoire Romaine*, freedom and slavery, virtue and vice, are terms relevant to the situation of the individual, the Roman people, and even Rome itself. In the novel, these concepts are organized overall in terms of good or reasonable love, and bad or mad love which leads to chaos in the individual and consequently in the state. The Carte de Tendre provides the key to the distinction between the two, and exemplifies the correspondence between the individual (or microcosm) and the state (or macrocosm) in its very form, representing both the way to a woman's heart and the road to the *Empire de Tendre*. Good love, or in Scudéry's words, *tendresse*, is the conceptual foundation for the novel's exempla and thus the overriding corrective principle for the characters' and reader's behavior. Love is the ordering principle for both the individual and the nation, precisely because order in the individual microcosm eventually leads to order in the nation or macrocosm, much in the tradition of Plato's *Republic*.[6]

THE CARTE DE TENDRE, OR ORDERING THE INDIVIDUAL

Clélie, Histoire Romaine is best known for its Carte de Tendre [Map of Tenderness], too often to the neglect of the novel's other dimensions and stories. However, the centrality of the Carte to discussions of the novel is not without merit. In fact, it is arguably the key of keys to this *roman à clés*. With its inscribed precepts or *opérations*, the Carte generates the pool of maxims that constitute the rules of *bienséance* or decorum underlying the exem-

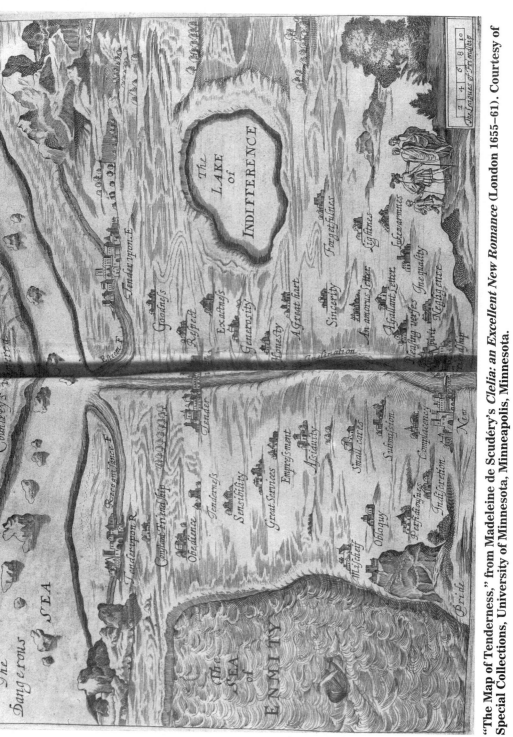

"The Map of Tenderness," from Madeleine de Scudéry's *Clelia: an Excellent New Romance* (London 1655–61). Courtesy of Special Collections, University of Minnesota, Minneapolis, Minnesota.

pla provided by the various characters. Its functions within the novel are multiple: the Carte's concepts provide the basis for conversation as well as behavior; its operations temper the passions of the male lover, consequently civilizing him and protecting the reputation of the female lover; the Carte furnishes the concepts and operations used by the female lover to negotiate her relationship; it provides a method for ordering violent passions; it allows one to discern the truth about the various characters, serving as a guide for going beyond appearances; and ultimately its operations work to reorder the nation.

As it pertains specifically to the love relation, the Carte redefines male–female relations in terms of negotiation and reciprocity, and not conquest or domination—a model of relations relevant as well to the situation of the Roman people of the novel. However, the female lover has the upper hand in the love relation: the male lover must obey her, albeit on the condition that, like a good Prince or Consul, she governs the relation justly, according to reason and duty. Like the reconceptualization of *gloire*, whose value is displaced from the domain of the martial arts and reinvested in the liberal arts and acts of virtue, the Carte serves as the basis for reconceptualizing the love relation, privileging a civil, bourgeois, contractual model of male–female relations over a more traditional chivalric or courtly one. Although I suggested above that through *Clélie* Scudéry engages in political debates of her time, she also advocates for more general cultural changes regarding what constitutes appropriate interpersonal relations.

The Carte de Tendre is introduced in the story of Aronce and Clélie, the story that serves as the novel's frame narrative, opening with their deferred wedding and closing with their final reunion. Although Aronce comes to represent, along with characters like Brutus and Herminius, the ideal lover, he nevertheless lacks a certain degree of self-control, as the opening pages of the novel would suggest. Whereas Clélie's calm is expressed in the tranquility of the Capuan countryside ("Clelie . . . avoit dans le coeur, et dans les yeux, la mesme tranquilité qui paroissoit estre alors en toute la nature" ["Clélie . . . had in her heart and eyes the same tranquility that appeared to be in all of nature"]), Aronce's worry and excessive joy can no longer be contained with the appearance of his rival Horace. An earthquake strikes that creates such chaos that it seems to "remettre la Nature en sa premiere confusion" ["put Nature back in its original confusion"] (1: 12). That Aronce's inner turmoil, not to mention jealousy upon seeing his rival, triumphs over his more rational faculties is expressed in terms of natural disaster: the eruptions emitted from the bosom of the earth can be read as manifestations of Aronce's terrestrial passion, the fire exploding from the earth's crevice an expression of his excessive joy. Natural disaster takes the form of fire (passion) and water (bodily fluids), which betray Aronce's lack of self-control ("il n'avoit pas esté Maistre de ses actions" ["he had not been Master of his actions"]). If gone unchecked by the rational elements of the universe, unbridled passions, corresponding here to natural phenomenon, create chaos.[7] Aronce will have to pay for such disorders by having to wait some seven thousand pages to finally marry Clélie.

It becomes clear in the unfolding of the plot that Aronce's disorders are analogous to those of his society. Though the novel opens with Aronce's immoderate desires and the chaos, which thus ensues, we soon discover that Roman society as a whole was upset around the time of Aronce's birth. The first main societal disorder introduced at the beginning of the novel immediately concerns Aronce. Mézence, king of Pérouse, imprisons Aronce's father, Porsenna, the king of Clusium. Porsenna falls in love with Galerite, daughter of Mézence, and they secretly marry. Galerite gives birth to Aronce and, in order to avert her father's wrath, sends Aronce off to Syracuse with Marcia and Nicius. While crossing the sea, their ship gets caught in a storm and capsizes at the same time that another ship overturns, carrying the Roman citizen Clélius and his wife Sulpicie, future parents of Clélie, along with their newborn son. With the confusion of the two shipwrecks, Marcia and Nicius lose Aronce, believing him dead, and Clélius and Sulpicie find Aronce, but not their own son. Clélius and Sulpicie raise Aronce as their own son, unaware of his noble origins, along with their daughter, Clélie.

The second and more significant societal disorder, which traverses the entire novel, concerns the usurpation of Tarquin Le Superbe. The king Servius Tullius had married his eldest daughter Tullie to Prince Amériole, and his youngest daughter to Amériole's younger brother, Tarquin. Wishing to become king of Rome, Tarquin conspires with the evil Tullie. They both poison their spouses, and then manage to get Tullius's consent to marry. After their marriage, an impatient Tullie and Tarquin have the king killed. Now king, Tarquin has many Roman citizens executed, and forces Clélius, Horace, Herminius, and others into exile. It is when Clélius is fleeing from Rome that he gets shipwrecked and adopts Aronce. Thus the two stories, that of Aronce's private familial disorders, which also have political undertones, and that of Rome's public or political disorders, which are at the same time familial disorders, intersect and are confused in the two shipwrecks.

Whereas in the opening pages of *Clélie* personal disorders are reflected in natural disaster, for the most part such disorders play out in terms of political chaos. What is important to retain here is the centrality of chaos to the novel's structure, the source of which is worldly or terrestrial passions, which themselves reveal the individual's failure to control or master the self. As we will see, the Carte de Tendre provides the theory for mastering the passions as it relates to both the love relation and political relations. Scudéry uses the love relation, which we will examine shortly, to highlight how the individual can be ordered by means of the Carte de Tendre. Regulating relations between individuals at the level of the microcosm provides a paradigm for regulating relations within the body politic, or macrocosm.

Scudéry was not the only early modern writer preoccupied by the question of chaos. According to Clarke, a "sense of traditional order in peril was common in the first half of the century, as belief in the ordered and purposive security of an Aristotelian interpretation of the world was increasingly shaken by the confusion of contemporary events" (13). With the Religious Wars at the end of the sixteenth century, the war against Spain and its surrounding controversies, the Fronde, and a shaken social hierarchy, it should come as no surprise that seventeenth-century writers sought to determine the causes of such disorders and to establish new foundations for universal order. Whereas Descartes, for instance, does not directly refer to contemporary events in the *Discours de la Méthode* (1637), his text nevertheless reflects in abstract terms the more general preoccupation with bringing order to chaos. In the fifth section of the *Discours*, Descartes imagines the possibility of God recreating original chaos, only in order for him to reorder it according to the laws of nature.[8] Similarly, at the beginning of *Clélie* Scudéry establishes a situation of chaos and instability more directly related to the disorders of her society that will eventually be reordered in accordance with the "laws" of Tendre.

Significantly, Scudéry at times refers to different characters' troubled psychological state in terms of *guerre civile*. Wishing to "possess" Clélie but feeling a certain obligation towards Aronce in volume 3, the state of Horace's emotions is described in these terms: "la generosité et l'amour faisant un combat continuel dans son coeur, la raison au lieu de terminer un si grand differend, prend tantost un party, et tantost un autre, et entretien plustost cette *guerre civile* qu'elle ne l'apaise" ["generosity and love continually were combating each other in his heart; reason, instead of stopping such a great dispute, at times took one side, at times the other, and thus maintained this *civil war* rather than appeased it"] (3: 105; my emphasis). Although Horace had learned the precepts of the Carte de Tendre in volume 1, here he seems to have failed the test. However, by volume 5 Horace attempts to adhere to its precepts in order to be more virtuous than Aronce. Rivalry is no longer played out in the duel (as was the case in volume 1), but rather in a competition for virtue defined by the terms of the Carte. That Horace is commemorated at the end of the novel, having overcome his private civil war just as Rome overcomes its public civil war, shows that over time, the Carte's precepts can give form to chaos.

As we have noted above, Aronce is not himself a perfect hero; nor is Horace the most despicable character in the novel. Basically the characters are organized according to a "virtue–vice spectrum," fitting within one of the following three categories: 1) total self mastery, or virtue incarnate (Clélie, Lucrece, Brutus); 2) relative self-mastery, with occasional lapses in judgment or temporary loss of reason; relatively virtuous characters to varying degrees (Aronce, Artemidore, Horace; fathers, including Clélius and Lucretius; Titus and Tiberius); 3) total lack of self-control, or vice incarnate (Tarquin, Tullie, Sextus). Such distinctions are important to keep in mind. In the following discussion of the "good" and the "bad" lover, I do not mean to suggest that the bad lover is necessarily a thoroughly negative character (although this, too, can be the case). Despite his lack of total self-mastery, Aronce plays the role of the good lover within the story of Aronce and Clélie.

Like the interspersed stories, of which theirs serves as a general paradigm due to its status as frame narrative and also to the fact that it introduces the Carte de Tendre, the story of Aronce and Clélie is structured according to triangular relations. Aronce and Clélie love each other, but Horace, who has the support of Clélie's father, disturbs their bliss. Triangular relations in the novel are organized around the civil or more virtuous lover (Aronce), and the chivalric or less virtuous one (Horace), the first adhering to the precepts of the Carte de Tendre, the second taking a more "military" approach to the love relation. Other

stories structured according to this paradigm include that of
Herminius and Valerie, with Spurius and then Mutius playing the
role of the chivalric lover; and that of Artemidore and Berelise,
based in part on the rivalry between Artemidore (civil lover) and
Terille (chivalric lover). Triangular relations, however, are not
stable but constantly shifting: at times Aronce's rivalry with Horace is highlighted, at others his rivalry with the Prince de Numi-
die or Tarquin. In the story of Brutus and Lucrece, Collatin,
favored by Lucrece's father and who eventually marries Lucrece, is the first to play Brutus's rival. Later in *Clélie* it is implicitly Sextus who occupies the position of Brutus's rival.
Characters like Sextus, referred to in the novel as "Amans brutu-
aux" ["brutal Lovers"] (4: 640), mark the extreme limits of the
chivalric or courtly lover, whose violence can potentially lead to
rape. Generally speaking, though, even the mildest form of the
chivalric lover can endanger his mistress's reputation.

As it becomes clear in the story of Aronce and Clélie, and more
generally in the novel, the Carte de Tendre provides both the
methodology for forming the good lover, and a guide for discerning the bad. Celere, who recounts the story of Aronce and Clélie
to the princesse des Leontins, introduces the Carte de Tendre
after having provided some background to the rivalry between
Aronce and Horace. The structure of this part of the story is significant. Upon the request of Hermilius, Clélie lays out the theory
behind the Carte and its operations. Then the two rivals put the
Carte's theory into practice, illustrating by means of example
and counterexample the map's precepts and operations. Unambiguously depicted as Clélie's friend, Herminius—not one of Clélie's suitors—requests the Carte, clearly situating the Carte
within a context of friendship and not love.[9] This suggests that
the love relation is modeled on friendship, further emphasized in
the association Scudéry creates between *amitié* or friendship
and *tendresse* or love. Serving as the basis for the love relation,
friendship also marks its limits in such a way as to protect the
female lover's reputation for, as Clélie remarks, "il est assez
dangereux à une Femme, d'aller un peu au delà des Bornes de
l'amitié" ["it is rather dangerous for a Woman to go beyond the
limits of friendship"] (1: 405).

According to Clélie, in order to reach either Tendre-sur-Estime or Tendre-sur-Reconnoissance, the prospective lover or
friend (*ami*) must submit himself to the object of his inclination
by adhering to the towns/operations leading to Tendre. Although
the various operations leading to the female friend's *estime* and

reconnoissance often overlap, they may be distinguished in the following way. On the one hand, those operations moving toward Tendre-sur-Estime (*Grand esprit, Jolis Vers, Billet galant, Billet doux, Sincerité, Grand Coeur, Probité, Generosité, Exactitude, Respect, Bonté*) are on the whole activities or traits that exhibit the male lover's social prowess and essential character. On the other, those leading to Tendre-sur-Reconnoissance concern specifically his submission to the female friend (*Complaisance, Soumission, Petits Soins, Assiduité, Empressement, Grands Services, Sensibilité, Tendresse, Obéissance, Constante amitié*). Overall, the operations serve to reinvest the male lover's terrestrial desires into activities that first, allow the female lover to better negotiate her relationship with him; and second, serve to prepare him for a "civil" society closely resembling the seventeenth-century salon. (A translation of the Carte's terms can be found in the Notes.)[10]

Important skills in seventeenth-century high society, letter writing and writing verse (*Jolis Vers, Billet galant, Billet doux*) were concrete means for the male lover to demonstrate his valor or *esprit* which, as Scudéry has noted elsewhere, always finds a way to reveal itself: "l'esprit est comme le feu . . . il faut absolument qu'il paroisse, de quelque maniere que ce soit" ["wit is like fire . . . it necessarily appears, in some way or another"] (*Choix*, 31). At the same time that writing allows the male lover to demonstrate his wit, it also serves as a way to mediate or temper his passions. Writing implies separation or absence. It establishes a physical distance between the two lovers, putting the male and female lover on equal footing by curtailing the male lover's potential recourse to physical aggression. Through writing, both lovers have equal access to the power of persuasion, and their letters furthermore serve to negotiate the terms of their relationship. Letter writing exemplifies the contractual nature (versus relations based on conquest or domination) of Scudéry's model of gender relations.

Operations like *Complaisance, Soumission, Petits Soins, Assiduité, Empressement,* and *Grands Services* all concern how the male lover serves his mistress, and the fact that these towns lead to Tendre-sur-Reconnoissance suggests a type of relations recalling that existing between a king and his subjects. When discussing *Obéissance*, Clélie remarks: "n'y ayant presque rien qui engage plus le coeur de ceux à qui on obeït, que de le faire aveuglément" ["there being nothing more that engages the heart of those whom we obey, than to do so blindly"] (1: 403). Although this statement seems to justify a relation of domination, the obedience a lover owes his mistress is qualified later in the novel. Comparing the relation between the lover and his mistress to that of sovereign and subject, the good prince d'Agrigente states: "je croy qu'un homme d'honneur qui se voit dans la necessité de faire une lasche action, ou de desobeïr à sa Maistresse, doit ne faire pas ce qu'elle commande; mais il doit aussi sortir de son empire, et tascher de se guerir par la connoissance qu'il a de son injustice . . . qu'on a le malheur d'aymer une personne peu genereuse, il faut renoncer à son amour" ["I believe that a man of honor who finds himself in a situation where he must choose between committing a cowardly action or disobeying his Mistress must not do as she commands; but he must also leave her empire, and try to heal himself with the knowledge of her injustice . . . and having the misfortune of loving an unkind person, one must renounce her love"] (5: 702–3). The potentially negative consequences evoked in this "maxim" cannot be demonstrated better than by the story of Brutus's sons, Titus and Tiberius. After Brutus leads the revolt against Tarquin and Tullie and the Roman Republic is tentatively established, Tarquin tries to undermine the Republic by sowing disorder from within Rome. He has Ocrisie and Teraminte, mistresses of Titus and Tiberius, respectively, write to their lovers, insisting that the brothers will no longer have a place in their hearts unless they conspire against their father and help reestablish Tarquin on the throne. In the end, Titus and Tiberius are executed for treason, a consequence for privileging love over duty, and for having the misfortune of loving unjust mistresses.[11] Just as a virtuous and generous king respects his people, so a virtuous and generous mistress respects her lover by not forcing him to forgo his obligations to duty and reason. In effect, the contractual relation between lover and mistress must be respected by both parties: the terms of the Carte function not only to "civilize" the male lover, but also to establish the conditions for the male lover's submission to his mistress.

Whereas the Carte's positive operations serve to negotiate the relationship between the male and female lover as well as to guide the male lover in his obligations and behavior towards his mistress, the negative operations, diametrically opposed to the positive ones, lead to his mistress's indifference or aversion. Arguably the lesser of two evils, the path leading to the *Lac d'Indifférence* (*Négligence, Inesgalité, Tiédeur, Légèreté*, and *Oubli*) are qualities characteristic of a mediocre lover, one who fails to be *sensible, assidu, empressé* when serving his mistress, or one who has a tendency towards fickleness, failing to maintain a *Constante Amitié*. The path leading to *La Mer d'Inimitié*, however, includes operations that pose potential threats to the female lover's reputation. A male lover's *indiscrétion* shows his lack of respect for his mistress, to be contrasted with positive operations like *probité* and *exactitude*; *médisance*, or badmouthing one's mistress (the use of "bad" words), can be opposed to *jolis vers*, *billet galant*, and *billet doux* (the use of "good" words); *perfidie* and *meschanceté* reveal the male lover's lack of *sincerité* and *bonté*. (A translation of the negative terms can be found in the Notes.)[12]

Located in the bottom left-hand corner of the map is the town called *Orgueil* [Pride]. While the other negative operations are represented as so many wanderings from the "right path," *orgueil* is practically off the map, as if, upon reaching *orgueil*, the male lover has no chance of recovering his way, immediately finding himself on the coast of the *Mer d'Inimitié*. Rather than desire the female lover's *reconnoissance* or *estime*, the male friend who is *orgueilleux* is concerned only with self-satisfaction, paying no heed whatsoever to the Carte's precepts. Being *orgueilleux* precludes the possibility of engaging in a relationship based on reciprocity, on *sensibilité, obéissance*, and *tendresse*. We might read into this conceptualization of *orgueil* a critique, again, of a military model of the love relation and more generally of social relations. For *orgueil* connoted in the seventeenth century both amour propre and a sense of military aggressiveness.[13] It should come as no surprise, then, that the name of the most demonized character in the novel, Tarquin le Superbe, can be translated as "Tarquin l'Orgueilleux" ["Tarquin the Proud"].

Immediately following the scene where the Carte is introduced and explicated, the positive suitor, Aronce, and the negative suitor, Horace, activate the Carte's operations. Our two rivals play out the distinction between the civil lover (Aronce), ready and willing to negotiate his relationship with Clélie, and the chivalric or courtly one (Horace), whose more rational faculties are overtaken by his terrestrial passion to "possess" Clélie. In the first scene of the novel Horace clearly exhibits his will to possess Clélie when, taking advantage of the confusion created by the earthquake, Horace abducts Clélie, further adding to the sense of chaos and disorder with which the novel opens. In some respects Horace plays the role of Aronce's negative double, an idea already suggested by their names: "Aronce" and "Horace" are virtually anagrams of each other. In his account of their rivalry, Celere paints Horace as clearly lacking the self-restraint of Aronce in his approach to loving Clélie:

> Horace prit celle [la résolution], apres luy avoir descouvert son amour, de la presser continuellement de luy vouloir estre favorable: et Aronce au contraire se resolut de dire à Clelie qu'il ne vouloit rien; qu'il n'esperoit rien; et qu'il ne demandoit autre chose que la seule grace d'estre creû son Amant, quoy qu'il ne pretendist d'en estre aimé, que comme le premier d'un petit nombre de Gens que Clelie apelloit ses tendres Amis.

> [After revealing his love to her, Horace was determined to continually pressure her to be favorable to him: and Aronce on the contrary decided to tell Clelie that he did not want anything; that he did not hope for anything; and that his only request was to be believed her Lover, although he did not claim to be loved except as the first among a small group of people Clelie called her tender friends.] (1: 385).

Horace's approach resembles that of the traditional courtly lover who begs for his lady's love, whereas Aronce satisfies himself with Clélie letting him believe that he is her *tendre ami*. While the courtly lover is dependent on his lady for happiness, the *tendre ami* contents himself with his own thoughts of love, taking a more stoic approach to the love relation. Aronce displaces his love from the physical Clélie to thoughts of her, an operation that tempers his terrestrial passions, allowing him to behave in a civil manner and to control himself before her.

Like the traditional courtly lover, Horace overwhelms his love with lamentations, continually expressing the physical suffering her resistance causes him, and declaring the terrestrial passion he feels for her: "helas Madame . . . je suis bien plus malheureux que tous ceux qui vous aprochent: puis qu'il est vray que je ne voy point de Route qui me puisse conduire où je veux aller, dans cette ingenieuse Carte" ["Alas, Madame . . . I am more unfortunate than all those who approach you: since it is true that I see no Path that will lead me to where I want to go on this ingenious Map"] (1: 410–11). Rejecting the terms of the map, Horace soon finds himself in *Indiscrétion*: "je suis persuadé que bien loin de pouvoir passer Tendre, je n'y arriveray jamais: eh veüillent les Dieux que quelque Inconnu [Aronce], ne soit pas desja trop prés des *Terres inconnuës*, pour pouvoir l'empescher d'y aller: et que vostre cœur ne soit pas aussi déja trop engagé à aimer celuy dont. . . ." ["I am persuaded that far from going beyond Tenderness, I will never arrive there: may the Gods make it such that a certain Stranger [Aronce] find himself too close to the Unknown Lands to prevent him from going there: and that your heart is not already too engaged to love the one of whom . . ." (1: 412). The Carte provides the conceptual framework for interpreting Horace's behavior. Indeed, Horace's rejection of the Carte's terms is a sign of his *négligence* and failure to obey (*obéissance*) or submit (*soumission*) to Clélie's conditions for maintaining a relationship. Not only does Horace fail to adhere to the Carte's precepts, but he also attacks Clélie herself by committing an indiscretion. Suggesting that Aronce has gone beyond the limits of *tendresse* or friendship puts Clélie's reputation at risk. Through Horace's example, Scudéry demonstrates for her female readers the dangers of a jealous lover who fails to master his desires and to respect the contractual terms of the Carte de Tendre.

Horace further illustrates his lack of self-control when he begins to hate Aronce, who had previously saved his life: "il sentit une disposition estrange dans son ame, à oublier ce qu'il devoit à Aronce, et à le haïr. Sa generosité naturelle s'opposa pourtant d'abord à l'injustice de son amour: mais elle fut à la fin contrainte de luy ceder" ["he felt a strange disposition in his soul to forget what he owed to Aronce, and to hate him. His natural generosity opposed itself to the injustice of his love: but finally it was forced to surrender to the latter"] (1: 428). Again, the Carte de Tendre provides the key to interpreting Horace's behavior: he demonstrates *inégalité*, *oubli*, a lack of generosity and gratitude, all of which is due to his inability to control his passions. These passions will eventually lead him to commit a *perfidie* or *méchanceté*: he challenges Aronce to a duel, which eventually results in Clélie's father, Clélius, discovering their rivalry, consequently blaming the duel on Clélie, and accusing her of loving a social inferior.[14] In *Clélie*, Scudéry seems to take a position against duels for at least two reasons. First, as exemplified above, rivals that engage in duels bring to the fore relations that, in order to preserve the female lover's reputation, must remain concealed until sanctified by marriage. Generally speaking, it is the chivalric lover, lacking the skills of negotiation and self-control, who challenges the civil lover to a duel.[15] Second, Scudéry's implicit position against duels conforms to her more general model of interpersonal relations, which should be regulated according to civility and not physical aggression.

Because of his "sentimens tumultueux" (1: 430) Horace strayed from the path leading to Tendre, an idea which takes concrete form when the reader visualizes Horace's position on the Carte de Tendre in relation to its various towns/precepts. Aronce, on the other hand, closely adheres to the laws of Tendre. After Clélie scolds Horace for his indiscretions, Aronce arrives on the scene. Whereas Horace accosted Clélie with self-pity, Aronce greets her with an account of all the *petits soins* and *grands services* he carried out for her, telling her about a party she missed, finding her flowers to make a garland, and translating from Greek the verses of Sapho she demanded. After reciting the *jolis vers* of Sapho, Aronce tries to situate himself on the map: "me permettrez vous d'esperer que pourveû que je continuë je seray bien tost au delà de cét agreable Village qui s'apelle Petits Soins: et que si je ne puis aller à Tendre sur Estime, je pourray arriver un jour à Tendre sur Reconnoissance" ["would you permit me to hope that, provided that I continue, I will soon be beyond this agreable Village called Petits Soins: and if I cannot make it to Tendre sur Estime, then I could arrive one day in Tendre sur Reconnoissance"] (1: 416–17). Shortly thereafter Clélie, expressing her *tendre amitié* and *reconnoissance*, suggests to Aronce that indeed he has arrived in Tendre-sur-Reconnoissance, upon which Aronce promises his *obéissance*: "Je suis pourtant resolu . . . de tascher de vous obéir" ["I am determined . . . to try to obey you"] (1: 419). Upon reading this segment of the story of Aronce and Clélie, it is easy to imagine Aronce's progression on the Carte, whose terms are elicited both directly and indirectly in the narration. Through such examples and using the map as an aid, the reader is able to form a concrete idea of how to apply the principles of the Carte to his or her own relationship.

The opposition between Horace's terrestrial passion and Aronce's tender one is manifest in their desires to reach, in the first case, the *Terres Inconnues*, a sort of wild frontier to be conquered or possessed; and in the second, Tendre, a clearly *civil* location, in both the sense of qualifying a city (Tendre is figured as a city), and of describing polite behavior.[16] This opposition furthermore highlights the historical shift from the chivalric conqueror (Horace) to the new civil or intellectual breed of aristocrat (Aronce). This is not to say that Aronce is an inept fighter. The novel clearly makes of Aronce the best of all swordsmen. But much like those members of the newly rising French gentry, Aronce privileges *esprit* over physical force. Even if we read into the character Aronce a figure for one of the noble *frondeurs* or more generally a member of the nobility of the sword, he nevertheless embraces the values of the rising gentry. Aronce marrying Clélie, a member of the Senatorial class, parallels the social fusions occurring in seventeenth-century France—particularly within the salons—whereby generally women from wealthy *parlementaire* or Robe families married into traditional noble families.[17] Aronce's ability to adhere to the precepts of the Carte de Tendre as well as he can brandish a sword suggests that he embodies one type of social fusion rarely referred to in seventeenth-century literature: a traditional noble embracing what some would consider to be bourgeois values. Bellicose characters like Horace and Mutius, however, adhere to a world-view that was disappearing, mainly that of a feudal culture based on military prowess. It is no wonder, then, that such characters have difficulty adhering to the terms of *bienséance* as established by the Carte de Tendre, and consequently fail to acquire the hand of a woman from the Senatorial class.

A close reading of *Clélie* with the Carte de Tendre reveals that, at every moment in the novel, the characters activate the operations inscribed in the map. For instance, many of the Carte's terms are used to describe Herminius, who has noble inclinations and a tender heart, who is generous and writes galant letters (3: 99–100). Likewise, the Carte's terms serve to qualify the young Brutus, who writes everything from friendship poems to *Billets doux* and *Billets galants* (3: 239). Even Horace is described on more than one occasion in terms of the Carte's positive operations. In order to merit Clélie's esteem, Horace praises Aronce out of *reconnaissance* (5: 32). The fact that Horace learns to adhere to the Carte's principles over time highlights the novel's pedagogical function: Horace is the textual *destinataire*, demonstrating for the extratextual *destinataire* how to modify one's behavior to conform to the laws of Tendre. As the character Raclia puts it, "je puis persuadée que quelquefois les exemples corrigent plus que les raisons" ["I'm persuaded that sometimes examples correct more than explanations"] (3: 275).

Within the context of the novel, the map makes behavior transparent: discerning readers and characters (who are also at times readers) are able to see through the ruses of Tarquin and Tullie, the perfidy of Horace, and are thus capable of discriminating between the good and the bad by means of the Carte de Tendre's precepts. It is interesting to note that mothers are particularly adept at discerning true merit. In both the story of Aronce and Clélie and that of Brutus and Lucrece, fathers tend to choose their daughters' future husbands based on appearances, their own passions, or simply to punish their daughters, whereas

mothers tend to recognize the true merit of their daughters' pre-
ferred suitors. Clélius, for instance, favors Horace for his daughter's hand first, because Horace is a Roman citizen, and second,
because Clélius had had an inclination for Horace's mother. Clélius's preference is based on the appearance of merit (i.e., Horace's status as a Roman citizen) and a former passion, not on
reason and the precepts of the Carte de Tendre, which clearly
indicate the moral superiority (read: true versus apparent merit)
of Aronce.

In the case of Lucretius, his choice of Collatin for his daughter
Lucrece's hand reveals his wish to please Tarquin as well as his
somewhat vengeful nature. Earlier in the story, Lucrece's
mother had opposed her daughter marrying Collatin because the
latter was an ally of Tarquin, which could only come to no good.
Before the events leading to Lucrece's marriage to Collatin, however, Lucrece's mother dies. After finding tablets written by Lucrece's lover (whom the reader knows to be Brutus), which
reveal that Lucrece is in love with someone who is conspiring
against Tarquin, Lucretius forces Lucrece to marry Collatin precisely because of her aversion for him, and out of his own fears
of having anything to do with an enemy of Tarquin.[18] Lucretius's
full realization of his mistake in closely allying himself with Tarquin comes only too late. He makes the following statement just
before discovering that Tarquin's son, Sextus, had raped his
daughter:

> la Mere de Lucrece avoit autrefois raison, lors qu'elle vouloit m'emp-
> escher de m'attacher fortement aux interests de Tarquin . . . il est
> ennemy declaré de tous ceux qui ont de l'ambition, ou de l'amour
> pour la gloire: aussi ma femme me disoit-elle toûjours que Tarquin
> vouloit estre le seul ambitieux de son Estat, qu'il ne luy falloit que
> des Esclaves au lieu de Sujets; qu'il seroit tousjours l'ennemy de tous
> les gens d'honneur: et que je me trouverois un jour accablé sous les
> ruines de sa Maison"

> [Lucrece's mother was right when she wished to prevent me from
> closely allying myself with Tarquin's interests . . . he is the declared
> enemy of all those with ambition, or love of glory: my wife also used
> to tell me that Tarquin wished to be the only ambitious one of his
> State, that he needed only Slaves rather than Subjects; that he would
> always be the enemy of all honorable people; and that one day I
> would find myself overwhelmed under the ruins of his Household.]
> (4: 1367–68).

Ruin comes to his household in the form of Lucrece's rape and
subsequent suicide, an act she commits out of her love of glory

which, as Lucrece's mother had discerned, would be impossible to maintain under the regime of Tarquin. Realizing that his wife *avoit raison* shows the ultimate lack of reason on the part of Lucretius in his choice of a spouse for his daughter, but also and quite consequently in the political choices he has made thus far.

Lack of reason means essentially a failure to understand the truth that is largely accessible in the novel through the Carte de Tendre and its precepts. Using the Carte de Tendre to measure a suitor's value keeps at bay irrational reasons—on the part of the female lover or her parents—in the choice of a spouse. In many respects Scudéry's Carte functions like Descartes's method in that it serves to ward off unreason, allowing the subject to discern "objectively" between the true and the false.[19] Together the Carte and its operations indicate that relationships require both a physical distance between the two lovers (implicit in the very idea of writing *billets doux* or *billets galants* to one another) as well as time (the time it takes to move from *Nouvelle Amitié* to *Tendre*). As such Scudéry is no advocate for the *coup de foudre* [love at first sight] theory of love. Instead, love is a rational affair, the Carte de Tendre allowing one to objectively "quantify" the value of a suitor by providing a methodology to discern real from apparent merit and by concretely situating him on the Carte de Tendre. For Scudéry love, much like politics, is something to be negotiated and is of a contractual nature.

ORDERING THE STATE

As we have noted above, the Carte de Tendre performs several functions in the novel, notably those of negotiating the terms of the relationship between male and female lover, ordering the individual, and ultimately discerning the truth about the various characters. These functions can be applied as well to questions pertaining to the situation of Rome and the Roman people. The novel abounds in analogies between the state of the individual and the state of the state, exemplified by the use of expressions like "guerre civile" (civil war) and "tyrannie" to refer to characters' psychological conditions, and by analogies such as the one discussed above concerning the terms of the male lover's obedience to his mistress. Moreover, the consequences of tyranny in love often play out at the political level. Sextus's rape of Lucrece, for instance, is symbolic of his family's rape of Rome, at that same time that it impels Brutus to lead the uprising against the

Tarquins—for both personal and political reasons. Motivations on the part of both good and bad characters constantly blur the boundaries between what constitutes private and public interests. As the final resolution of the novel suggests, so long as the private interests of individual subjects are sacrificed to the public interests of the state or king (which are at the same time private interests), order within the body politic cannot be maintained.

Like the bad lover, the bad leader is governed, even tyrannized, by his passions. On several occasions the narrator describes the psychological condition of both Tarquin and his son and heir Sextus in terms of tyranny. For instance, Tarquin, who has captured Clélie, is overcome by both love and hatred for her: "l'amour et la haine tyrannisoient tousjours son coeur" ["love and hate always tyrannized his heart"] (4: 1120). Likewise, Sextus feels a tyrannical passion for Lucrece: "l'amour de Lucresse tirannisoit si fort son ame, qu'il n'en pouvoit estre le Maistre" ["his love for Lucrece so strongly tyrannized his soul that he could not be its Master"] (3: 97–98). On the level of the love relation, characters like Tarquin and Sextus desire the unconditional surrender and possession of their mistress, which takes the form of abduction and rape. As Tarquin states regarding Clélie, "il faut que ce coeur, tout fier qu'il est, soit un jour en ma possession" ["this heart, with all its pride, must one day be in my possession"] (3: 77). At the political level, this type of tyrannical passion for a woman translates into usurpation, or the unconditional possession of Rome.

Creating such analogies between the body politic and the female body was not unique to Scudéry. In his "Politique du Prince" ("The Politics of the Prince"), for instance, La Mothe Le Vayer describes usurpation in the following terms: "Car quoiqu'il y ait bien du vice et de l'injustice parfois dans le commencement d'une Souveraineté usurpée, et que tout y paroisse plein de tumulte et de criéries; si est-ce qu'à la longue, comme un feu de bois verd qui fait bien de la fumée d'abord, devient clair avec le tems, ces bruits pleins d'agitations cessent à la fin, et cette femme ravie avec violence changeant de volonté devient legitime" ["For although there is sometimes vice and injustice in the beginning of a usurped Sovereignty, and that everything seems full of tumult and cries; it is such that in the long run, like a fire of green wood that makes a lot of smoke at first, becomes clear with time, these cries full of agitation finally cease, and this woman, ravished by violence and changing her will, becomes legitimate"] (315). Evidently the tutor of the young Louis XIV had a very different approach to violence against the body politic, not to mention against the female body, from the one proposed by Scudéry in *Clélie, Histoire Romaine*. In fact, Scudéry conceptualizes the situation of the tyrant in rather ironic terms. Although the tyrant (Tarquin, Sextus) possesses or holds captive the object of his desire, whether that be Clélie or Rome, he nevertheless is held captive by his own passions, never truly being master of himself.

This leads us to one of the major themes that traverses the novel, that of captivity, which plays out at multiple levels. Clélie, along with other Roman women, are referred to as Tarquin's captives; Rome itself is figured as being Tarquin's captive; Brutus's reason is also Tarquin's captive, for he must feign stupidity in order to protect himself from Tarquin's wrath; finally, Roman women, cloistered by their families, are described as being so many captives.[20] With the exception of Roman women, all the other cases of captivity are directly tied to the usurpation of Tarquin, who is himself tyrannized by his own passions. One might summarize the plot as follows: Tarquin, slave to his own passions, has enslaved Rome and the Roman people, who are consequently subjected to Tarquin's passions. Ultimately the tyrant of the story is not Tarquin himself, but the passions that rule through him. Disorder at the level of the macrocosm (Rome) is clearly related to disorder at the level of the microcosm (Tarquin), and it is not until reason reigns supremely—a reason largely and ironically embodied by the character Brutus—that the captives can regain their freedom and civil society can be reestablished.

As we noted earlier in the discussion of Scudéry's notion of the fable, love serves as the organizing principle for her model of history. At the level of the microcosm, which primarily concerns the paradigmatic pool of exempla, appropriately loving one's mistress, in other words, adhering to the precepts of the Carte de Tendre, orders the individual. At the level of the macrocosm, which primarily concerns the syntagmatic movement of the narrative, love serves as the motor that propels the overall narrative toward order, ultimately toward the solid establishment of the Roman Republic. Love serves as the unifying force that brings together the private and public interests of various characters, fusing together disparate motives in the common cause of defeating Tarquin, and consequently, of founding the Republic.

In volume 3, for instance, several characters become aware of their common interest: "Brutus et Valerius souhaitant que Rome

fust delivrée de la Tirannie de Tarquin, ne songeoient qu'à luy
oster la puissance qu'il avoit usurpée: Herminius avoit le mesme
interest, et en avoit encore beaucoup d'autres: et Aronce voulant
delivrer Clelie . . . ne pouvoit mieux faire reüsir son dessein,
qu'en destruisant celuy qui tenoit sa Maistresse Captive"
["Wishing that Rome be delivered from the Tyranny of Tarquin,
Brutus and Valerius thought only of taking away the power he
had usurped: Herminius had the same interest, and many others: and Aronce, wishing to free Clelie . . . could not have his plan
succeed better than by destroying the one who held his Mistress
Captive"] (3: 144). Although Aronce himself is not Roman, he assists his friends in their enterprises against Tarquin in order to
free Clélie from a tyrant. And while Brutus's initial motivation behind conspiring against Tarquin had to do with his noble ambition of becoming "le Liberateur de sa Patrie" (3: 262) as well as
his desire to free his reason, he is finally pushed to action after
Lucrece's rape. Thus in a single character, private and public interests, love of country (*amour de la patrie*) and love of Lucrece
(*amour de Lucrece*), come together: "il ne songeoit à la liberté
de Rome, que pour vanger la mort de l'innocente Lucrece: et ne
se servoit de l'interest de sa Patrie, qui luy estoit si cher, que
pour celuy de sa passion" ["he only thought of the freedom of
Rome to avenge the death of the innocent Lucrece: and was
serving the interest of his Homeland, which was dear to him,
only out of the interest of his passion"] (4: 1384). Similarly, private and public interests come together in the Roman citizen
Herminius's motives to topple Tarquin. Tarquin prevents Herminius from marrying Valerie and then exiles Herminius from
Rome. As long as Tarquin reigns, Herminius cannot legally reside in Rome, nor can his love of Valerie be sanctified by marriage. Love of Valerie combined with love of country fuel
Herminius's desire to free Rome from Tarquin (see 5: 378–89).

The good characters who carry out the revolt against Tarquin
are not inconsequentially good lovers. And like good lovers, who
negotiate their relationship with their mistress according to the
Carte de Tendre's precepts such as reciprocity, respect, goodness, and generosity, characters like Brutus and Herminius lead
the revolt and the Republic according to similar virtues and principles. For instance, Brutus uses the power of speech, rather
than threats or other physically aggressive forms of persuasion,
to incite the Roman people to revolt against Tarquin. In the
speech he gives before the Roman people, Brutus asks them to
revolt against an illegitimate king, not only in the name of Lu-

crece and all that her rape represents, but also and more generally in the interest of public good, justice, glory, and love of
country.[21] Brutus appeals first and foremost to the Roman people's reason, not their fears, passions, or pure self-interest, and
lays out arguments concerning the public and private good that
will result from the overthrow of the usurper. After the success
of the revolt, the Roman people insist that Brutus serve as Consul for one year. Exercising the sovereignty granted to him by
the Roman people, Brutus establishes a Senate of three hundred
men, and then forcefully insists on electing a second Consul in
order to completely dissociate the emerging Republic from the
tyrannical rule of Tarquin. (Although monarchy here does not directly come under attack, Brutus fears the Roman people may
have associated one-man-rule with tyranny.) It is the Roman
people who elect Collatin to be second Consul, and although Brutus rightly disagrees with this choice, he nevertheless respects
their will. That the liberation of Rome is so closely related to Brutus recovering his reason indicates that the reestablishment of
the Senate, with Brutus at its head, essentially signifies the reestablishment of reason in the Roman body politic.

Like the good lover, the good prince or consul reasons and negotiates with his subjects rather than dominates or enslaves
them. He resorts to words rather than physical aggression. In
some ways, a Republic or democratic society exemplifies the
idea of "government by negotiation," for such types of governments, at least theoretically, do not rely on the will of a single
leader, but rather depend on successful negotiations between
the elected leader, parliament, and the people. Of all the kingdom's described in Clélie, that of the Prince d'Agrigente receives
the highest praise. Interestingly, what makes it a particularly admirable kingdom is the respect Agrigente receives from his subjects, due in part to his character as well as to his Republican
style of governing: "il gouverne presque la Ville comme si elle
estoit en [sic] Republique" ["he governs the City almost as if it
were a Republic"] (4: 682).

In many respects, the principles of the Carte de Tendre governing the love relation are the same as those governing a republic or republiclike kingdom: the reciprocal relation between male
and female lover translates into democratic relations within the
state. In both cases, the relationship between lover and mistress,
between subject and ruler, is based on negotiation of a verbal
sort, and more generally on principles based on reason, not passion. Scudéry thus establishes a relation of continuity between

how a character behaves in love and in politics. As the examples
of Tarquin and Sextus exemplify, the passionate or mad lover at
the level of the microcosm becomes a usurper or tyrant at the
level of the macrocosm. In Herminius's words, "quand on se fait
une habitude de n'estre point exact dans les petites choses, il est
fort aisé de ne l'estre pas dans les grandes" ["when one habitu-
ally is not at all exact in small matters, it is easy not to be so in
great matters"] (9: 82). In contrast, the good lover Brutus brings
to politics the sense of respect, reciprocity, and negotiation he
already demonstrated in his relation with Lucrece.

In the same way that the Carte de Tendre mediates the relation between the male lover and his mistress, so laws based on
reason should mediate the relation between subjects and ruler.
In both cases, ideal relations are mediated by an "objective" (in
the sense of "detached," "impersonal") set of rules applicable to
all parties. The tyrannical lover or ruler, however, obeys only his
or her own passions, in other words, an irrational and "subjective" (in the sense of being attached to the self, "personal") law
that is nothing more than the will of the tyrant. As Tarquin explains to Clélie, "J'ay presupposé que ceux qui ont la souveraine
puissance, ont tousjours raison de faire leur volonté" ["I assumed that those who have sovereign power always have the
right to do as they will"] (3: 54).

In her depictions of Tarquin and the manner in which he conceives of his power, Scudéry seems to be drawing from Jean
Bodin's notion of "absolute power" as it regards the sovereign
prince. According to Bodin, a prince with absolute power is neither subject to the laws of his predecessors nor to those he establishes himself. Although Bodin believes that the laws established
by the sovereign prince should conform to natural and divine
law, he nevertheless concedes that, in the final analysis, they are
based on the will of the prince: "Aussi voyons-nous à la fin des
édits et ordonnances ces mots: CAR TEL EST NOTRE PLAISIR,
pour faire entendre que les lois du Prince souverain, [bien] qu'elles fussent fondées en bonnes et vives raisons, néanmoins qu'elles ne dépendent que de sa pure et franche volonté" ["And so we
see at the end of edicts and ordonnances these words: FOR
SUCH IS OUR PLEASURE, to make it understood that the laws
of the sovereign Prince, although founded in good and strong
reasons, nevertheless depend only on his pure and free will"]
(121). Through the figure of Tarquin, Scudéry demonstrates the
potential dangers of absolute power: when law depends solely on

the will of the sovereign, and the sovereign's will does not conform to reason, this results in tyranny.[22]

In many instances, *Clélie, Histoire Romaine* pauses to reflect on the question of sovereignty, its legitimate exercise and overthrow, whether in conversations concerning the justice of destroying Tarquin's power, or in more general conversations on the contractual (and thus conditional) relation between subject and sovereign.[23] The syntagmatic narrative itself invites the reader to consider various types of governments and their corresponding practices of exercising sovereignty. Before Tarquin's coup d'état, Rome was governed more or less as a constitutional monarchy, meaning that the king had to be elected or approved by the Senate. This is one of the facts Brutus uses to incite the Roman people to rebellion: "Cét injuste Prince est monté au Throsne contre les Loix fondamentales de nostre Estat; il n'a point esté esleu ni par le Senat, ni par le Peuple" ["This unjust Prince took the Throne against the fundamental Laws of our State; he was elected neither by the Senate, nor the People"] (4: 1398). Thus sovereignty resided with the Roman people and the Roman Senate, who temporarily granted it to the elected king for a life term. When Tarquin seizes the throne, Rome is transformed from a constitutional monarchy into an (albeit illegitimate) absolute one, in which sovereignty "belongs" to Tarquin, and upon his death would be transferred to Sextus without confirmation from the Senate or any other governmental body. Finally, with the overthrow of Tarquin, Rome is ruled democratically as a Republic, sovereignty residing with the people who elect consuls for limited terms to carry out their will. Each form of government is based on a different balance of power. With the constitutional monarchy of Servius Tullius, a balance existed between the king and the Senate; with Tarquin's rule of tyranny, the king's absolute power negated the authority of all other institutions or individuals; with the Republic, a balance of power is restored, and the potential threat of tyranny is eliminated with the regular election of consuls.

In these different forms of government, sovereignty translates into different conceptions of the law. With the establishment of the Republic, for instance, law becomes an "objective" set of rules applicable to all Roman citizens, irrespective of their particular family alliances or social status—much in the same way that the Carte de Tendre is an objective set of rules applicable to all suitors. This cannot be demonstrated better than in the episode leading to the execution of Brutus's sons. Upon being chosen Consul, Brutus, in the name of the Roman people, declares that anyone found guilty of conspiring against the newly founded Republic be executed. Little did he know that his own sons would be implicated in Tarquin's plot to overthrow the Republic. Evidence in the form of letters signed by his sons promising their allegiance to Tarquin proved irrefutable. Despite the fact that their story provides mitigating circumstances, suggesting the sons were pushed into the conspiracy and were not aware of the plot to kill their father, they nevertheless are executed according to the will of the people, in other words, according to common law. Of course Scudéry's Brutus, a *tendre père*, hoped he could find a way to clear his sons of treason. In the end, though, he chose not abuse the power granted to him, and did not prevent the sentence from being carried out. It should be noted that Scudéry writes this scene with a great sense of ambivalence towards the Roman people, who could have exercised more leniency towards Titus and Tiberius. In episodes such as this Scudéry points to the potential dangers of a democratic "mob rule" by the populace.[24]

This episode can be directly contrasted with the one concerning the rape of Lucrece. In his speech to the Roman people, Brutus characterizes the regime of Tarquin in terms of irreverence towards natural and divine law: "ni les droits du sang, ni ceux de l'hospitalité, ni les Loix humaines, ni les Loix divines, ni le respect des Dieux domestiques, témoins de l'audace et de la fureur de Sextus, n'ont pu l'empescher de commettre un crime si effroyable qu'à peine le peut-on dire" ["neither the rights of blood, nor those of hospitality, neither human Laws, nor divine Laws, nor the respect of domestic Gods, witnesses to the audacity and fury of Sextus, could prevent him from committing such an appalling and unspeakable crime"] (4: 1395–96). Because of the Tarquins' disregard for the law, he contends, Collatin and Lucretius cannot demand justice from Tarquin and Tullie, despite their family ties and fidelity to the regime. Only the Roman people can grant them justice by partaking in the rebellion. Tarquin and his immediate family members are depicted unequivocally as being above the law, whereas within the Republic, common law regulates the relation between the people and its leaders, both parties having obligations to respect a common contract that protects all members of the body politic. Without this type of contractual relation, public order is at risk, because the private interests of individuals can be sacrificed to the whims of the king and his family.

It would be difficult to say with great certainty whether

Scudéry was critical of absolutism in general, or the reign of ministers like Richelieu and Mazarin, construed by many as usurpers of the king's authority, in particular.[25] For instance, the following passage from Brutus's speech recalls many of the criticisms of Richelieu's *politique de gloire*, continued by Mazarin: "Il [Tarquin] a mis des Esclaves dans le Senat: il a apouvry tous les riches; opprimé tous les pauvres; exilé ou fait mourir tous les gens d'honneur qui n'ont pas caché une partie de leur vertu pour sauver leur vie; entrepris la guerre pour vous affoiblir; supposé des crimes pour avoir le bien de ceux qu'il a accusez" ["He [Tarquin] put Slaves in the Senate: he impoverished the wealthy; oppressed the poor; exiled or killed honorable people who did not conceal a part of their virtue to save their life; waged war to weaken you; made criminal allegations to take the wealth of those he accused"] (4: 1398). For a seventeenth-century reader, these remarks might well have brought to mind Richelieu's strategy of populating the royal administration with his "creatures," or the execution of Cinq-Mars, whose trial Richelieu completely manipulated.[26] The idea of Tarquin going to war to weaken the Roman people might have made one think of the war against Spain, which was controversial for many reasons, among them the way in which the war had impoverished so many French subjects. It is notable that later in his speech, Brutus elaborates on the notion of just war, arguing that this war of liberation is far more just than all the previous wars waged for the glory of Rome. In one of the scenes of the rebellion, the Roman people pillage the palace of queen Tullie, which recalls seventeenth-century pillages of tax collectors' houses by the people.[27] (Scudéry's depiction of the vengeful nature of many of the pillagers again reveals her ambivalence towards the Roman populace.) Brutus's speech must also have brought to mind the recent events of the Fronde, and like the *frondeurs* of the Parlement de Paris, Brutus is highly critical of Tarquin's oppression of the people.[28]

We might view the Roman Senate as a figure for the Parlement de Paris, whose members considered themselves to be "the heirs of the Roman Senate" and who constantly opposed the encroachments of absolutism on their own authority. Much like seventeenth-century *parlementaires*, members of the Senatorial class like Brutus, Clélius, and Herminius oppose Tarquin's dismantling of the Roman Senate. It is interesting to note that the seventeenth-century jurist Loyseau conceptualized the sovereignty of the Parlement de Paris as being contiguous with that of the monarch: "This nobility enjoyed by the officials of the Parlement de Paris is not founded solely on the fact they are the heirs of the Roman Senate or the Council of State of France, but also because they are the judges of the King, and exercise with him his sovereign justice" (quoted in Hamscher, 33–34). The fact that Scudéry depicts the more constitutional monarchy of Servius Tullius and the Roman Republic in positive terms, and that both forms of government grant much more sovereignty to the Senate than does the monarchy of Tarquin, suggests that she is taking a position with which many French *parlementaires* would identify. Whereas Scudéry's *Le Grand Cyrus* has generally been recognized as an allegory of the Fronde, scholarship on *Clélie, Histoire Romaine* has all but ignored the political connotations of the novel, with the notable exception of Marlies Mueller.

However, I would tend to disagree with Mueller's assessment of Scudéry's political position. Emphasizing Scudéry's ambivalence towards the Roman people and the instability of the Roman Republic throughout most of the novel, Mueller concludes that Scudéry implicitly laments the absence of a king who could reconcile the diverse factions vying for power (*Idées*, 159–63). Scudéry's critique of the people notwithstanding, she clearly valorizes the rule of the Roman Senate, both in her depictions of its leaders, particularly Brutus and Valerius, and in the association she makes between the reestablishment of the Senate and the reign of reason in Rome—not to mention in the novel's final resolution where the authority of the Republic is decidedly established. It is clear, as Mueller has argued, that Scudéry creates a rift between the "people" and members of the Senatorial class that does not exist in Livy's account; this does not necessarily mean, however, that Scudéry is antirepublican. We might think of Scudéry's model of republicanism as being akin to that of Plato, in which an intellectual elite (i.e., properly civilized leaders) rules over all other classes. As such, the Roman Republic à la Scudéry could be characterized as an aristocracy. Although the people represent a force to be reckoned with and are invested with limited authority, for all intents and purposes it is the Senators who govern Rome. Mueller's analysis of the novel furthermore fails to account for the numerous implicit and explicit critiques of monarchy, and especially of the ideology propagated by the king's ministers.

At the basis of Richelieu's and later Mazarin's policies was the conceptual separation between public and private moralities. According to William Church, Richelieu "found that the criteria of justice which prevailed in private affairs could not be applied to

public . . . because of the special nature of the latter" (496).
Through *Clélie*, Scudéry criticizes a model of government that
privileges the glory or interests of the state over the glory or interests of its subjects. In one of Brutus's remarks, the *compati-
bility* between private and public interests is plainly emphasized:
"Croyons que l'amour de la Patrie, et l'amour de la gloire [perso-
nelle] ne sont point incompatibles" ["We must believe that love
of Homeland, and love of [personal] glory are not incompatible"]
(3: 366). The analogies Scudéry creates between the state of the
individual and the state of the state, between gender relations
and political relations, and the unifying morality that binds them,
clearly indicate that Scudéry was opposed to the ideology of the
monarchy. She seems to explain the causes of her society's disorders at least in part in terms of the opposition or rupture between public and private interests. In other words, the cause of
civil disorder lies in the political ideology and practices of the
king's ministers, and the only way order can be restored is when
a constitutional government of some sort that protects the private interests of French subjects is reestablished; that is, when
private and public interests can be reconciled.

On the one hand, in *Clélie* Scudéry seems to criticize the bellicose attitude of the nobility of the sword through characters like
Horace, Mutius, and the heads of small kingdoms like Porsenna,
all of whom adhere to a more feudal worldview. On the other, she
saves her most scathing criticisms for the usurpers who believe
in nothing more than their own sovereign power and personal
ambitions. It is significant, then, that Horace and other chivalric
lovers only *abduct* the object of their desire, whereas Sextus
goes so far as to *rape* Lucrece.

I do not mean to suggest that Scudéry was outrightly opposed
to monarchy as such. Many a French subject made the distinction between the ministers and the Most Christian king. I would
argue, rather, that Scudéry, much like her contemporaries issuing from the *parlementaire* milieu, regretted the monarchy's infringement on the traditional authority the parliaments once
wielded. Through the figure of Tarquin, Scudéry indicates that
absolute power that goes unchecked can lead to tyranny and political disorder. As Mueller argues in a later piece (and apparently against her earlier thesis), *Clélie* indeed has Republican
overtones: "*Clélie* marks the emergence of an ideological movement radically opposed to the aristocratic [i.e., noble, feudal]
ethic. Madeleine de Scudéry not only demands that women
sheath their swords, and tame aggressive impulses (their own

and their suitors') but, in addition, she accredits an ideology *en petite mélodie* that would have to wait until the French Revolution for full orchestration" ("Taming," 228).

The overarching syntagmatic framework of *Clélie* does suggest that the model of state advocated by Scudéry is indeed a Republic. Like the classical medical and Platonic historiographic progressions, the syntagmatic framework of *Clélie* moves from 1) an initial state of vulnerable stability, or the constitutional monarchy of Servius Tullius, to 2) a moment of crisis or degradation, taking the form of the usurpation and tyranny of Tarquin le Superbe, to finally 3) a return to health, manifested in the foundation of the Roman Republic. Taking the form of tyranny, the historical moment of chaos parallels that of the terrestrially inclined individual subject: Tarquin's worldly lust for power overcomes the more rational principle of public good. The establishment of the Republic, however, marks the return to order and recovery of reason in Rome, which coincides with Brutus freeing his reason from Tarquin's grip. Thus the political progression of the narrative from chaos (tyranny) towards order (Republic) is also an ontological one: in overcoming its passion (Tarquin), the Roman body politic is reordered according to the principles of reason (Brutus, and after his death a Roman Senate headed by Clélius). The Republic, then, is legitimated on both pragmatic grounds, as a strategy to avoid tyranny, and on philosophical grounds: it is the most reasonable form of government.

Given the analogies between the body politic and the individual, between public and private interests, it should come as no surprise that the restoration of order in the novel's grand finale takes the form of multiple marriages. Marriage as a contract binding mutually consenting adults serves as the symbolic representation and the real manifestation of peace and order in Rome. This is particularly clear in the marriage between Clélie and Aronce, in which Clélie serves as the "lien de la paix" or link of peace between the Roman Senate, headed by her father Clélius, and the kingdom of Etruria, with whom Rome had been at war, ruled by Aronce's father Porsenna. Just as political disorder prevented the union of Aronce and Clélie as well as that of Herminius and Valerie, so political order is manifested in their union, along with that of Artemidore and Berelise, Lysimene and Zenocrate, and Clidamire and Meleonte. It is important to note here that, although the novel closes with marriage, elsewhere in the novel Scudéry legitimates divorce. In the "Histoire de Cesonie" (4: 1152–1343), for instance, private marital disorders affect public order. By allowing two couples to divorce and remarry, order in Ardée is reestablished. The multiple marriages in the grand finale, then, must be read in light of the "Histoire de Cesonie" and in terms of the mutual dependence between and the reconciliation of private and public interests.

Upon serious consideration of her works it becomes evident that Scudéry was not at all a frivolous or amateur writer. In *Clélie* she masterfully manipulates the historical discourses available to her to create the fable, a pseudohistorical genre that is structurally and thematically ordered by a concept of love recalling that of Plato and the neo-Platonists. At the syntagmatic level love provides the organizing principle of the narrative, ordering the potentially chaotic elements constitutive of descriptive history, and solidifying the various characters' motives propelling the narrative forward. At the paradigmatic level love allows the reader to "get inside" and, with the theoretical guide of the Carte de Tendre, "to know" the various characters through their portraits, conversations, and letters. Love is also the basis for the novel's exempla, ordering the individual and eventually the state by means of the Carte de Tendre's precepts. The narrative's correspondences and back-and-forth movement between the syntagmatic and the paradigmatic, between the nation-macrocosm and the individual microcosm, are indicative of Scudéry's skill as a writer to weave together and synchronize the novel's form and content, its thematics and its structure.

In seventeenth-century France, the use of history was ideologically charged. The very fact that Scudéry appropriates historiographical models to write her *romans à clé* marks her engagement in larger debates concerning the future of the French nation. Like many intellectuals of her time, Scudéry was preoccupied by the idea of political and social chaos, as well as the infringement of the monarchy on the traditional authority of the parliaments. That order can only be reestablished in Rome with the restoration of the Senate indicates Scudéry's *parlementaire* sympathies. In *Clélie* Scudéry seems to be less concerned, however, with legitimating the traditional authority not to mention the ethos of the feudal nobility. While she draws from humanist discourse to validate a more bourgeois or civil model of government, she also transforms humanist discourse to include female protagonists within universal history. Although female characters seem somewhat passive in the novel, with the exception of Lucrece and Clélie who actively defend their honor, they nevertheless are instrumental in civilizing male characters, and are generally represented as being more reasonable than their male counterparts. Female characters provide exemplary models for proper behavior, and much like national heroes, the model of subjectivity they embody is at the origin of the Roman Republic. That the love relation, mediated by the Carte de Tendre, provides the paradigm for relations at the political level also demonstrates the necessary role of women within the emerging Republic.

The models of subjectivity and social relations propagated in *Clélie* reproduce those generated in Scudéry's salon, as will become clear in the next chapter. Modifying the discourse of history to include heroines and bourgeois or robe heroes is a way to integrate contemporary cultural changes into the discourse of universal history, and consequently, to legitimate those changes by situating them in a more perfect past. By redefining notions like glory and heroism in line with how those same concepts were being defined in the salon, Scudéry recognizes the centrality of the salon in the formation of a new elite, as well as the roles women were actually playing in the constitution of ideal French subjects.

3

Adults at Play: *Les Chroniques des Samedis de Mademoiselle de Scudéry*

Often cited as a secondary source in scholarship on the seventeenth century, the *Chroniques des Samedis de Mademoiselle de Scudéry* [The Chronicles of Mademoiselle de Scudéry's Saturdays], known since Emile Colombey's 1856 edition as the *Chroniques du Samedi*, have received little critical attention in their own right.[1] A register of the various salon "events" and communications between the members of Scudéry's salon (referred to by Scudéry and her entourage as "Samedis" [Saturdays] due to the day of the week they met), the *Chroniques* provide keen insights into the ways in which Scudéry's salon functioned as a locus for the development and promotion of a new elite—not to mention for the production of texts. Parts of *Clélie* grew out of salon games and writing, as evidenced in the *Chroniques*. It is one of the few documents of the period that allow us to study the salon from the perspective of insiders. Although the abbé de Pure's *La Prétieuse* (1656) and Baudeau de Somaize's *Grand Dictionnaire historique des Précieuses* (1660) do provide us with some understanding of the internal workings of seventeenth-century salons, their depictions at times border on parody and exoticism. They both write from the perspective of the outsider, and their taxonomies of the salon world resemble those of early modern ethnographers, which makes them all the more comical. The *Chroniques*, however, allow us to examine how Scudéry and her entourage constructed themselves and defined their relationships to each other through a language that at first glance appears frivolous, but upon closer examination proves to draw from more serious types of discourses of the period. We must ask ourselves why influential men like Valentin Conrart, Jean Chapelain, and Paul Pellisson, all of whom exercised most "unfrivolous" positions in the administration of government and culture, found it necessary to frequent Madeleine de Scudéry's Samedis.

In the previous chapter we looked at the ways in which the precepts of the Carte de Tendre operated to establish the contractual relation between mistress and lover, and by extension, between king (or ruler) and subject (or citizen). In this chapter we will look at the ways in which these same precepts play themselves out primarily at the level of social relations. As we will see, the Carte's precepts serve as the criteria according to which people are included in or excluded from Tendre (or the salon), and they structure interpersonal relations in terms of "friendship." It is important to note that the terms of the Carte de Tendre were first worked out within the salon before the Carte was integrated into the narrative of *Clélie*.[2] More generally, we will look at how Scudéry's *habitués* or salon members engaged in salon games (including role play; poetry games such as anagrams, acrostics, and madrigals; and the general use of playful language demonstrated in their letters) to create for themselves new identities, to legitimate themselves as nobles, and to gain practical experience in skills and behaviors that could allow them to advance socially and professionally. We will consequently look at how relations within the salon were modeled—wittingly or unwittingly—on those structuring patronage, and how the salon generally allowed people to network and form professional alliances.

Overall it might be argued that Scudéry and her salon's sociopolitical ideals support a *parlementaire* or Robe agenda, already suggested in my reading of *Clélie*. Most of Scudéry's *salonniers* issued from Robe and High Bourgeois families: Pellisson and Samuel Isarn were from parliamentary families of Castres; Jacques II de Ranchin was from one of the wealthiest families in Castres and was himself a *conseiller à la Chambre de l'Edit*; Donneville was from a distinguished parliamentary family of Toulouse; Mademoiselle d'Arpajon, daughter of Louis Arpajon made *duc et pair* in 1650, was also from Toulouse; Jean-François Sarasin's father was a *trésorier de France* in Caen; the Parisian Conrart, whose father was a merchant, purchased in 1627 the office of *conseiller-secrétaire du roi*; Chapelain, also born in Paris, was the son of a *notaire*; Madame Aragonnais was the daughter of a financier and the widow of a *conseiller du roi*; Angélique Robineau was from a family of financiers and government tax collectors; and De Raincy was the son of the financier Bordier. Angélique Boquet and her sister Catherine were the only members of Scudéry's salon not issuing from the High Bourgeoisie or Robe.[3] (It should also be noted that Pellisson, Isarn, Ranchin, Conrart, as well as the marquis de Montausier and Tallemant des Réaux who also frequented Scudéry's salon, were all from Protestant backgrounds.)

The noble status of the Robe was not always self-evident in early modern France and came under particular attack in the seventeenth century.[4] As George Huppert has shown, many members of the Robe originally issued from bourgeois families and, after having acquired enough wealth, slowly moved away from commerce to the more noble or ennobling Robe professions and became officeholders.[5] The philosophical underpinnings of the Robe recall those propagated in *Clélie*: stoicism, proto-republicanism, and a secular asceticism that valorized self-restraint and mastery over the passions in order to maintain peace and order.[6] Such concepts were at the forefront of new definitions of nobility, particularly of *honnêteté*, and they allowed the Robe to conceive of their identity and value in terms of the intellect or the soul, as opposed to the body, which located them in the world in terms of their *condition*. Robe and High Bourgeois alike made attempts to efface a *roture* or "common" background that prevented them from attaining social legitimacy as a new aristocracy, and this required in part the creation of an identity that was discontinuous with their birthright. Scudéry's salon served as a matrix through which her members could raise their self-esteem by creating noble identities for themselves. It provided a support system by means of which they could gain practical experience in techniques of networking and self-promotion that would allow them to solidify claims of being noble, not only within the salon, but more importantly in society at large.

SALON AS GAME SPACE

Games create spaces independent from the "outside" world and are governed by their own rules and reality. Games allow one to break with this outside world, which often entails assuming another identity, such as Colonel Mustard or Miss Scarlet in the game "Clue." As contemporary board games would suggest, games nevertheless are intricately connected to the society in which they emerge: *Clue*, for instance, grew out of a particular culture fascinated by Agatha Christie–like books and films; *Monopoly*, by a stock-market culture; whereas games like *Trivial*

Pursuit test people's cultural competence in upper-middle class American trivia. Such games allow the average middle-class American to become momentarily a British aristocrat suspected of murder, or a big-time entrepreneur, or in the case of *Trivial Pursuit*, an intellectual. Based on these familiar examples, we can deduce several things about games: first, they are culturally specific; second, upon entering the closed space of the game, players shed their outside identity to become someone else; third, games can allow players to transcend their actual social status; and fourth, particularly in the case of *Monopoly* and *Trivial Pursuit*, games participate in the inculcation of rules and values that pertain to this outside world.[7] As such, play is not simply opposed to the outside world. Although occupying a space delimited from that of the everyday, games both constitute (in the inculcation of values, in providing practical experience) and are constituted by (due to their cultural specificity) this outside.

In what follows we will examine how the space of the salon is a space of game. As if playing a game, *salonniers* assume fictional names, accept certain rules, especially regarding the nature of their conversation, and exclude certain behaviors, all of which delimits the space of the salon from the outside world. A space of play, the salon is also an ideal space constitutive of and constituted by ideal subjects. It is a site for the production of elite subjects. The games Scudéry and her *salonniers* choose to play help define the group that constituted the Samedis as an exclusive one, and the salon itself as a utopic space, an alternative Ile de France. Like other games, however, the activities that take place in the insulated salon space are not unrelated to the outside world. These activities center on skills that potentially enhance those necessary to maneuver the early modern system of patronage, and more generally, skills necessary to "arrive" in seventeenth-century Paris.

Role Play

Upon reading the *Chroniques*, one is struck by the use of Greek and Persian pseudonyms Scudéry and her *salonniers* use to refer to each other in their letters, poetry, and accounts of salon games such as the "Journée des Madrigaux" and the "Gazette de Tendre." In Scudéry's salon, the overall pool of references for setting up the space and characters for the games of her Samedis comes from *Le Grand Cyrus*, whose portraits were inspired by *habitués* of both Rambouillet's and Scudéry's salons.

The *roman* (romance, novel) has a long history of serving as the inspiration for noble games. Michel Stanesco has shown that as early as the thirteenth century knights would hold tournaments called "Round Tables" in which each knight would play the role of a particular character from the King Arthur cycle. Over the course of the thirteenth to the fifteenth centuries, he argues, tournaments moved away from being physically aggressive competitions, becoming "fictions" in their own right, due in part to the fact that the traditional nobility were no longer regularly engaged in warfare (Stanesco, 94–123). In the early seventeenth century, twenty-nine aristocrats formed the *Académie des parfaits amants* and used *L'Astrée* as the code of rules for their games (Jauss, 166). As the abbé de Pure's *Prétieuse* and Somaize's *Dictionnaire* would suggest, pseudonyms were widely used in Parisian salons, making of the salon, generally speaking, a "fictional" space or space of game, in the sense that assuming a new identity, signaled by the pseudonym, was the passport to the world of play.

Within the context of Scudéry's salon, pseudonyms allowed the *salonniers* to break with the outside world, and in several respects. First, assumed names allowed women to break with a masculine order in which they were defined by their roles as mothers and wives, roles largely determined by their bodies (Pessel, 22). With assumed names, women could redefine themselves within the space of the salon in terms of intellectual and cultural pursuits, rather than be defined within the structure of the family. Like the Robe and High Bourgeoisie, women had an interest in an idealist (neo-Platonic, Cartesian) philosophy that privileged the mind over the body. By sublimating the body, women would no longer be different from men, for "the mind has no sex." Idealist philosophy provided arguments that could legitimate the equality of the sexes, just as it could be used to legitimate a new, intellectual elite. Pseudonyms marked a break from the material world, allowing women to enter the realm of the ideal where they could be men's equals, even their superiors.[8]

Second, this renaming could abolish distinctions such as bourgeois, robe, and noble, allowing the *salonniers* to transcend social *differences* of the outside world to create within the salon a democratic space of the *same*, a space of equals—of noble equals. Such names effaced social distinctions of the outside world by equally investing all *salonniers* with nobility: the noble remained noble, and the *robin* or bourgeois was ennobled. For instance, when Acante (Pellisson) writes Sapho (Scudéry) about returning

home from a particular Samedi, he "ennobles" the other, bourgeois women of the Samedi by referring to them as Sapho's
"princesses" (58). In the *Chroniques* Madame Aragonnais is
generally referred to as "Philoxène," even "la Princesse Philoxène" (166), a name that permits her to transcend her actual
status as a member of the High Bourgeoisie. After Acante writes
a witty acrostic to Sapho, Théodamas (Conrart) refers to him as
the "chevalier de l'Acrostiche" ["knight of the Acrostic"] (106),
"chevalier" also being a signifier that ennobles. This particular
example points to the fact that for Scudéry's *salonniers*, clever
poems are like so many *lettres de noblesse*. At one point Acante's
nobility is signaled by qualifying him as "le Berger Acante" (167),
recalling the shepherds of *L'Astrée* who were in fact nobles in
disguise. Acante is also compared to a great prince: "Acante qui
avec l'habit et la fortune d'un simple berger avait le courage d'un
grand prince" ["Acante, who with the attire and fortune of a simple shepherd had the heart of a great prince"] (172). When Pellisson is not referred to as Acante, the noble particle is added to
his name, and "Mr. **de** Pellisson" is used. The same is true for
Donneville, referred to either as Méliante or "Mr. **de** Donneville."

Within the space of the salon, nonnobles ennoble themselves
by taking on new, fictional names. Outside the space of the salon,
they try to acquire new names *legally*. Aspiring to legal nobility
entails a transformation of one's name. De Raincy was the son of
the financier Bordier, who built the château de Raincy and whose
son could legally adopt the name of the domain. Receiving his
lettres de noblesse in 1659, Donneville officially became the
marquis de Miremont. Arguably the assumption of pseudonyms
that ennoble within the space of the salon points to the *salonniers'* desire to acquire such names in "real life."

Third, assumed names marked a break more generally with
the order of the *particular*, already suggested by their function
in allowing *salonniers* to transcend their gender and social positions into which they were born, to gain access to the order of
the *universal*. We might think of these names as functioning like
condensed verbal portraits, an idea supported by the fact that
these names were directly related to the verbal portraits in
Cyrus, for it was through these portraits that Scudéry's readers
could identify a Samuel Isarn behind the character Trasile, or a
Madeleine de Scudéry behind the Greek poetess Sapho. Essentially the association created by the keys served to universalize
those *salonniers* portrayed in *Cyrus* by presenting them as An-

cients of the present, incarnating timeless examples of virtue. It is precisely this virtue that qualifies them as *heroes and heroines*, as they are referred to by Pellisson, the salon's chronicler: "il n'y eût là que des héroïnes et des héros de roman" ["here there were only heroines and heroes from novels"] (166). To the extent that the portrait privileged *l'esprit*, the intellect, in short, the "universal" of its subject over any "particular" determinants such as physical appearance or *condition*, it can be characterized most succinctly as a mirror of the soul.[9] As condensed portraits, the *salonniers'* Greek and Persian names signaled their value as universal subjects, sublimating their connection to the material world. Thus *salonniers* were heroes and heroines in the sense of being fictional characters taken from a novel, on the one hand, and in their status as exempla, incarnating timeless examples of virtue, on the other.

The Space of Conversation and Leisure

The constitution of *salonnier* subjectivity is inseparable from the constitution of the space of the salon, which is delimited by *conversation*. Elizabeth Goldsmith emphasizes the sense of space implicit in the concept of conversation: "In the seventeenth century the verb 'converser' retained its Latin sense of 'to frequent' or 'live with,' and the noun 'conversation' conveyed a sense of place that it no longer has today. Conversation created its own social space with carefully marked boundaries" (2). As Goldsmith maintains, the space of the salon coincided with the space of conversation. Encompassing all linguistic (oral or written) activities issuing from the salon, conversation could be characterized as the "archi-genre" of all salon writing. That is to say, letter writing and poetry could be considered ways of continuing conversations outside the physical space of the salon.[10] The space of the salon, as the space of conversation, thus transcended the physical space of either Philoxène's "palais" or Agelaste's (Madame Boquet) home, where Samedis usually were held.

Consequently, time was also transcended. Because letter writing meant that *salonniers* could communicate outside the physical space where Samedis were held, it also permitted members to "converse" on days other than Saturday. In effect, this potentially made every day a Samedi, since Samedi was synonymous with Scudéry's salon, with the virtual space of conversation. In a poem to Sapho in which every one of forty-three lines rhymes with "samedi," Trasile (Isarn) concludes that in an ideal world (or *paradis*), every day would be Saturday: "Et j'oubliais qu'en paradis / Tous les jours seront samedis" ["And I forgot that in paradise / Every day will be Saturday"] (91). Every day being Saturday means the abolition of time, itself characteristic of paradise. It is interesting to note that the chevalier de Méré also associated ideal conversation with the heavens: "il seroit à souhaiter de sçavoir comme on s'entretient dans le Ciel" ["one should wish to know how one converses in Heaven"] (2: 103). Letter writing, of which the *Chroniques* provide numerous examples, created a virtual space where *salonniers* communicated with each other in the guise of ancient heroes and heroines, constituting a sort of "virtual community."[11] In the same way that pseudonyms allowed *salonniers* to detach themselves from material reality, conversation and/as letter writing situated the salon beyond space and time.

In any game, rules establish what can or cannot be said or done. The same is true for salon games and conversation. Before engaging in games, the space of the salon, in other words, the space of conversation, had to be clearly defined. While the very names of our *salonniers* mark a break with the outside (the particular) world and permit them to enter the ideal world of play, the nature of their conversation furthermore delimits a space of the universal from a space of the particular. This is particularly clear in the "Journée des Madrigaux" (166–82), in which the space of conversation unfolds in a veritable mise en scène:

> Alors commença la plus agréable conversation qu'on saurait s'imaginer. Car Philoxène et Telamire faisaient aussi bien qu'il était possible l'honneur de leur maison, et afin que tout le reste de la compagnie fût de belle humeur, Polyandre avait oublié en entrant la négociation, et les affaires d'Etat, le berger Acante des choses à la vérité de moindre importance, mais qui ne lui touchaient pas moins au coeur, Méliante sa fièvre, Thrasyle ses constants amours et ses longs voyages, et la divine Sapho regardant le siècle, la cour, sa propre fortune comme des choses au dessous d'elle ne se souvenait pour être contente que de son esprit et de sa vertu. En cet état leurs âmes étaient sans doute bien disposées pour recevoir les inspirations d'Apollon . . . (167)

> [Thus began the most agreeable conversation one could imagine. For Philoxène and Telamire did all they could to honor their house, and so that the rest of the company would be of good humor, Polyandre had forgot business and state affairs upon entering, the shepherd

Acante things truly of less importance but that affected him nonetheless, Méliante his fever, Thrasyle his constant loves and long trips, and the divine Sapho, regarding the century, the court, her own fortune as things below her, only recalled her wit and her virtue in order to be content. In this State their souls undoubtedly were well disposed to receive the inspirations of Apollo . . .]

The space of conversation is constituted by the systematic inclusion and exclusion of certain topics. Excluded are those topics that deal with the body and material life, in other words, the particular: fortuitous state affairs, bodily sickness, physical desire, the accidental occurrences of the century, the court, and fortune. Like salon names, salon conversation functions in such a way as to constitute subjectivity in terms of universality by virtue of what is and what is not discussed, dissociating the *salonniers* from the outside world and from their very bodies. As such, they establish a utopic space that transcends the conflicts, the contradictions, the *differences* of their world to create a space of the *same*.[12] It is important to note, however, that the "Journée des Madrigaux" provides an example of an ideal conversation. In the *Chroniques*' letters, the *salonniers* at times step out of their roles to complain about migraines, toothaches, gout, and fevers. We might characterize this slippage in terms of a "return of the repressed," the sublimated physical body intruding momentarily into the space of the ideal.

This process of including the universal inside the space of the salon and leaving the particular outside of the salon points to a larger opposition structuring the Samedis: a space and time of work as opposed to a space and time of leisure. Anything having to do with work or business, be it affairs of state (Polyandre), or similar such matters (Acante), or in the case of Doralise (Angélique Robineau), working out the taxes on her father's revenues, is officially and quite consciously excluded from conversation. (Doralise could not attend this particular Samedi due to the tax business; the *salonniers* all agreed without directly referring to her situation that it would not be appropriate to write a madrigal about such matters.) A utopic space, a space of conversation, the salon was also and quite consequently a space of leisure. Historically and etymologically, leisure (*otium*) was opposed to commerce (*negotium*). In early modern France, in order to legitimate claims of being noble it was necessary to show that one had "lived nobly," meaning that one did not engage in commerce and led a leisurely lifestyle. More generally, leisure marked the time one did not engage in utilitarian activities like business or politics, activities essential to collective life. Leisure situated a person "above" the human condition and outside temporal constraints, allowing a person to "cultivate" her- or himself by acquiring manners that functioned as so many signifiers of one's superiority (Lanfant, 23–30; Stanton, 2–5).

At the same time that leisure itself was a sign of nobility, it also marked the time dedicated to the "production of the self" as value (Baudrillard, 39), particularly as *noble* value. As leisure space, the salon could be characterized as noble space as well as a space where one becomes noble, in other words, where one produces oneself as noble. An outside observer of the salon, the abbé de Pure, conceived of the formation of *précieuses* very literally in terms of the production of the self:

> [C]omme la perle vient de l'Orient, et se forme dans des coquilles par le ménage que l'huitre fait de la rosée du Ciel; ainsi la Prétieuse se forme dans la Ruelle par la culture des dons suprêmes que le ciel a versé[s] dans leur âme. . . . [P]army les Pretieuses, il est impossible de sçavoir comment le debit s'en est fait, et comment la chose s'est renduë si commune. Cet ouvrier du Temple qui a si bien contrefait les diamans, et qui a rendu ses copies si communes, n'a jamais tant fait d'hapelourdes comme il s'en voit, sur tout depuis six mois. (1: 63)

> [As the pearl comes from the Orient, and is formed in shells by the oyster who cultivates the Heaven's dew, so the Precious woman forms herself in the Salon by cultivating the supreme gifts that Heaven poured into her soul. . . . Among Precious women, it is impossible to know how the traffic came about, or how it became so common. This artisan of the Temple who counterfeited diamonds so well, and who made imitations so common, never fabricated as many false gems as we've seen, especially for the last six months.]

Despite the fact that de Pure pokes fun at salon women in this passage by suggesting that many of them are fakes, the analogy he makes between the *ruelle* or salon and the Temple, a place where false gems were manufactured, nevertheless is revealing in the way that it depicts the salon as a site for the production of subjects. Whether the *précieuses* "naturally" acquire value, as in the analogy with the creation of pearls, or whether their value is manufactured, in both cases de Pure associates the salon with the (natural or counterfeit) production of elite subjects.

Mapping Value

An integral part of the production of elite subjects within Scudéry's salon entails adherence to a set of precepts that eventually get systematized, over the course of the *Chroniques*, into the Carte de Tendre. Whereas pseudonyms and conversation delimit the space of play, precepts like "reconnaissance," "respect," "sincérité," "estime," and "tendresse" govern salon behavior, functioning like the rules of the game. At the same time that such precepts serve as measures to determine the value of each *salonnier*, they can also be used to include and exclude people from Tendre. At one point in the *Chroniques* Sapho categorizes hierarchically the value of different types of friends in terms of "nouveaux amis," "particuliers amis," and "tendres amis" (see 126–28), each of which is measured in relation to one's adherence to what will become the Carte's precepts. Those closest to being a "tendre ami" are those who have best adhered to the Carte's precepts. When determining the value of a person or thing, it is necessary to establish a standard against which value is determined, as well as measures that differentiate between these values. If the Carte's precepts measure the differentiation between the *salonniers*, Sapho serves as the ultimate standard against which their value is measured. As the standard, it is Sapho who ultimately gives value to her *salonniers*: she is the *caution*, the guarantor, of their value. It is perhaps for this reason that both Théodamas and Acante compare Sapho to Midas.[13]

In the *Chroniques'* "Gazette de Tendre" (306–29) the idea of becoming a "tendre ami" takes the form of something resembling a board game. Each *salonnier* moves across the Carte de Tendre with the goal of reaching the City of Tendre, which is synonymous with becoming Sapho's *tendre ami(e)*—and arguably, with becoming more like Sapho. We follow their every move across the Carte, from the game's starting point at *Nouvelle Amitié*, to their meanderings through towns like "Négligence," "Grand Service," and "Complaisance," to their arrival in "Tendre," through the "Gazette de Tendre." The "Gazette" imitates the style of Théophraste Renaudot's official *Gazette*. Like Renaudot's *Gazette*, which is structured according to columns headed by the names of various provincial and European cities including Paris, the columns of Scudéry's "Gazette" are headed by the provincial towns leading to the capital, Tendre.[14] In the same way that Paris metonymically came to represent France, so the city of Tendre metonymically represents the Empire of

Tendre. There is clearly a parallel being established, then, between being a provincial moving towards the capital, and being a *nouvel ami* moving towards Tendre. In both cases, a certain education, which translates in the "Gazette" as adhering to the Carte's towns or precepts, allows one to "arrive" in the capital. The value of each *salonnier* is visualized by situating them on the map in relation to Tendre, which parallels the value of the individual in France, determined by his or her distance from Paris. It is not inconsequential that several of Scudéry's *habitués* (Pellisson, Isarn, and Donneville), are all Gascons who fairly recently arrived in Paris.[15]

Naturally, Tendre is also the allegorical space of the Samedis centered around Sapho. Adhering to the Carte de Tendre's precepts thus also allows one to be "received" as a *tendre ami*, as a full-fledged member of Sapho's Samedis. The "Gazette" playfully reproduces real or imagined quarrels about who can or cannot be admitted into Tendre/Samedis. Those of the *Ancienne Ville* (Madame Aragonnais, her daughter Madame d'Aligre, and Angélique Robineau, referred to in the "Gazette" as the *Dames exilées*) seek to limit the number of *étrangers* or foreigners who can be received in Tendre (in the Samedis) by demanding that they show "des preuves très exactes sur toutes les choses nécessaires" ["exact proof of all the necessary things"] (315). The system of inclusion and exclusion of *people* at the level of Tendre is exactly isomorphic to the process of inclusion and exclusion of *topics* of conversation constitutive of the space of the salon. Agathyrse (De Raincy) may be refused because he is incapable of submitting to the laws of the land; in other words, he is incapable of *soumission*. Like Trasile, who may also be refused, Agathyrse has more of a penchant for love than *amitié tendre*. Méliante may be refused for having an unclear relation between his appearance and his being, that is, for not being *sincère* (this is also an allusion to his double identity as Artimas and Méliante in the *Grand Cyrus*). In the case of Acante, he must be quarantined in order to dissipate the rumor that he had caught a contagious disease before arriving in *Nouvelle Amitié* (315–18).

In the same way that references to the particular, such as bodily sickness and physical desire, are excluded from the space of conversation, *salonnier* subjects attached to the particular and unable to adhere to the rules of the game are excluded from the city of Tendre. (Of course, the "Gazette" is only a game: Acante, Trasile, Méliante, and Agathyrse are allowed to frequent the Samedis.) This selection process results in the creation of a homogeneous, exclusive group whose value and identity are drawn from the group's organizing principle: Sapho. Whereas in the "Journée" certain topics are excluded from the *social* space of the salon, in the "Gazette" certain people are excluded from the *political* space of the capital. In both cases, the process of inclusion and exclusion results in the creation of a universal, utopic space of the same.

Insular Spaces

Samedi or Tendre as a political allegory weaves its way throughout the *Chroniques*. Like other utopias, Samedi/Tendre is an Other France, an inverted, at times carnivalesque version of the French nation. On the one hand, Sapho describes Samedi as a Republic: "c'est une petite république où l'état monarchique n'a jamais été établi" ["it is a small republic where the monarchical state never was established"] (109). On the other, it is often suggested that Sapho is queen of Tendre. When Sapho orders Trasile to return from Le Havre, she writes: "Car tel est le plaisir d'une personne qui fut reine [de la fève] hier au soir" ["For such is the pleasure of the person who was Queen [of the charm] yesterday evening"] (217), parodying the monarchical "Car tel est notre plaisir."[16] Perhaps Tendre could best be characterized as a "republican queendom"—the inverted double of France's monarchical kingdom—where women are superior to men and members of the High Bourgeoisie are of higher quality than countesses. (In the "Gazette," the *Princesse nouvelle-venue* [La comtesse de Rieux] may be refused entry due to her unworthy *condition*.) Like other utopias, Samedi is an insular space, an island. Given the fact that Sapho is from the island of Lesbos, Samedi could be described as a utopic, feminocentric Ile de France. In the *Chroniques*' "Nouvelles de l'Ile de Delphes" (81–85), Sapho goes to the island to consult Apollo's oracle. Upon her arrival, she is celebrated, and Apollo inspires her to write *Le Grand Cyrus*. Delphes could be read as a figure for either Madame de Rambouillet's salon or her own Samedi, for Scudéry's texts clearly grew out of her salon gatherings. It is also a utopic space, where Aristée (Jean Chapelain) becomes young and handsome, Théodamas is cured from gout, and the mage de Sidon (Antoine Godeau) is no longer so short. The salon-as-island is a perfect place where its members are perfected.

The insularity of the salon is guaranteed by the systematic inclusions and exclusions of topics and people. Its insularity is reinforced by creating a sense among *habitués* that one is a member of the initiate. Inside stories constantly referred to directly and allegorically set up codes that only an insider could know. Fully aware of this, Pellisson and Scudéry made numerous annotations in the margins of the original manuscript to shed light on some of the *Chroniques'* references. Anagrams, acrostics, and enigmas, all of which require the deciphering of hidden messages, make of the salon a secret society with hermetically sealed codes. In a letter to Acante, Sapho indirectly refers to herself as "une savante magicienne" ["a knowledgeable magician"] and to the Samedis as "jours destinés au sabbat" ["designated days of the Sabbath"] (101). Playing on the double meaning of Sabbath as both Saturday and the witches' Sabbath, the passage suggests the salon is a mysterious cabal of some sort. The references to witchcraft seemed to have bothered Pellisson, who wrote back that she is rather a "sainte Déesse," or "saintly Goddess."[17] That many of the *salonniers* were Protestants might well have strengthened the bonds of the group, its sense of insularity, and its cabalistic nature.

The Value of Friendship

Structurally, the bonds and ideal image of the group grew out of the specific types of relations members of the Samedis maintained with each other. The overarching bond between *salonniers* is one of friendship, based on reciprocal exchange of "gifts," the value of which is determined by the conventions of the salon. As such, it might be said that the salon has its own economy, its own system of value and exchange. Whereas the concept of friendship grew out of humanist tradition, it also was associated with the relation binding client and patron in the early modern patronage system. These different connotations of friendship are brought to the fore in the Samedis in the *salonniers'* correspondence and games. As we will see, the reciprocal exchange that binds friends resembles the type of exchanges characteristic of patronage, at the same time that such exchanges reinforce the *salonniers'* identity as nobles.

Of Friendship

Scudéry was not the first French writer to classify and define different forms of friendship. Drawing from Aristotle and Cicero, among others, Montaigne discussed the four general categories of friendship (natural, social, hospitable, venereal) and the different motives behind forming friendships (sensual pleasure, profit, public or private need) in his essay, "De l'Amitié" ["Of Friendship"]. Despite the fact that Montaigne rejects most forms of friendship as being imperfect, his text nevertheless points to the preoccupation in humanist literature with the classification of different modes of friendship. Borrowing from Montaigne, Pierre Charron similarly created a taxonomy of friendship according to general types of relations (husband–wife, parent–child, prince–subject; friendship between equals versus unequals; voluntary versus involuntary), along with a classification of motives, in his *De la Sagesse* [Of Wisdom] (1601). In both texts, words like "inclination," "respect," "reconnaissance," "constance," and "obéissance" are used to qualify different types of friendship.[18] Scudéry's vocabulary of friendship was grounded in both the theory and practice of a humanist-inspired model of friendship. The correspondence of Jean Chapelain to the Dutch humanist Nicolas Heinsius, for instance, is replete with expressions like "Amy particulier," "Amis familiers," and "tendre" (*Heinsius*, 193–211). Overall, the style and vocabulary of Chapelain's letters resemble that of the letters exchanged between Sapho and her *habitués* in the *Chroniques*.

Traditionally ideal friendship was viewed as a relation between equals endowed with reason, which explains why humanists like Montaigne believed women to be incapable of it: humanists viewed women neither as men's equals nor as reasonable beings. Many humanist writers likened marriage to the "unreasonable rule" of the political tyrant, and opposed to both the voluntary nature of true friendship (Shannon, 657). In *Clélie*, Scudéry similarly opposes the contractual relations established by the Carte de Tendre and its model of friendship to the general oppression of women in family and in marriage (Roman women being the "captives" of their society), but puts forth a more feminist version of friendship. Early on women writers were critical of an exclusively male model of friendship. In 1540, Marguerite de Navarre proposed a model of female friendship in *La Coche ou le Débat de l'Amour* [The Coach or the Debate about Love], opening up friendship to include relations between women.[19] Although Scudéry borrows terms from humanist tradition to define and qualify relations between her *salonniers*, and in particular their relation to Sapho, she moves beyond previous notions of friendship to include relations binding men and women. That is, she proposes a mixed gender model of friendship. As such, Scudéry transposes the scope of friendship from the personal or private to the social or public, blurring the boundaries, like she does in *Clélie*, between private and public spheres. In the *Chroniques*, friendship ultimately is a social affair.

In the early modern period, the reciprocal exchange of gifts, services, and honors was deemed necessary to maintain friendships. According to Natalie Zemon Davis, true friendship "was born of love and sympathy . . . but it was sustained by mutual services, benefits, and obligations. . . . Gifts were part of this rhythm, nourishing amitié and acting as its sign" (*Gift*, 20). Books in particular were exchanged as gifts, for it was believed that knowledge could not be sold. Among writers, books naturally were a privileged gift signaling friendship. Davis cites a letter Erasmus wrote to Pieter Gillis in 1515 in which he explains that the book he is sending makes up "not without interest" for the loss of enjoyment they would experience due to their separation. The book Erasmus sends quite literally becomes a token of his friendship.[20] Thanking Heinsius on behalf of the marquis de Montausier for the "gift" of his dedication in his book of poems in 1652, Chapelain indeed views such a gift as a sign of Heinsius's friendship: "un si glorieux tesmoignage de vostre amitié" ["such a glorious testimony of your friendship"] (*Heinsius*, 191). Likewise, Sapho thanks Acante in the *Chroniques* for his gift of his book on the history of the Académie Française: "je ne regarde aujourd'hui le présent que vous me faites, que comme une preuve de votre amitié" ["I regard your present as proof of your friendship"] (62). Early modern friendship required confirmation in the form of gift exchange.

As the example of Heinsius's dedication to the marquis de Montausier might suggest, given the inequality of their *conditions*, the language of friendship was caught up in the language of patronage. Potentially Heinsius could have become Montausier's client. Patrons—the greatest being ministers of state like Richelieu, Mazarin, and Colbert, along with *les Grands*—took into their ministries and households humanist-educated men of the robe as clients who managed their affairs. Often clients were skilled writers who could furthermore glorify and immortalize their patrons through their writing. In sixteenth- and seventeenth-century France, patrons and their clients repeatedly used words like "friendship, loyalty, zeal, esteem, and affection" with each other in their correspondence, as Sharon Kettering has established (12). Whereas friendship between equals was maintained by the reciprocal exchange of gifts and services, friendship between patron and client similarly was sustained through a form of reciprocal exchange: "The patron–client bond is a reciprocal exchange relationship in which patrons provide material benefits and protection, and clients in return provide loyalty and service" (Kettering, 13). One wonders if, in the intersection of humanist and patronage notions of friendship, it was not the former that brought about the use of "votre humble serviteur" and "votre humble servante" ["your humble servant"] in the formulaic closings of letters exchanged between friends.

In the *Chroniques du Samedi* we find evidence of both traditions. On the one hand, the salon chronicles provide numerous examples of reciprocal exchange of gifts and/as words characteristic of friendship between equals. On the other, *salonniers* often relate to one another in ways that seem to mimic the relation between client and patron. Generally speaking, women play the role of patron, whereas men play that of the client who glorifies and immortalizes them in writing. Roles, however, are unstable: Sapho plays the role of patron in one instance and client in another. In the end, each (male) *salonnier* and Sapho reciprocally glorify each other through their "gifts" at the same time that they all practice skills useful in attracting a patron and in sustaining a patron–client relation. Although the Carte de Tendre contains precepts that support a humanist model of friendship between equals, precepts like "soumission," "probité," "respect," and "obéissance" would be qualities particularly relevant to maintaining "friendly" relations with one's patron.

The Economy of Reciprocal Exchange

Within the context of the salon, reciprocal exchange is above all an *exchange of words* in the form of books, poems, letters, and conversation. Such exchange has two interconnected functions: that of maintaining reciprocal relations among the *salonniers*, and that of (reciprocally) upholding ideal images of each other. As Elizabeth Goldsmith has argued, "[t]he classical ideal of civility . . . depends on a kind of perpetual verbal potlatch within a circumscribed social circle. Social contact is a kind of constant circulation of verbal gifts" (11). Reciprocal exchange as verbal potlatch means that *salonniers* must outdo each other in the game of reciprocation; they must be "more generous" with their words than the others. At the same time that exchange should be reciprocal, then, one must also give (compliments, praise, poems, letters) more than one receives. That a gift can be qualified as having more or less value further suggests that the *salonniers* have a way to evaluate, to determine the value of the verbal presents exchanged.

The overriding law governing the salon's economy of gifts is reciprocation. The very first letter of the manuscript is written by Sapho to Théodamas, praising Pellisson's verse and asking Théodamas to offer Acante "incense" (figuratively speaking) on her behalf. Fearing he cannot adequately reciprocate, Acante nevertheless writes to Théodamas that not responding, "c'est être non seulement incivil, et rustique: mais même ingrat, et brutal" ["it is not only uncivil and rustic, but even ungrateful and brutal"] (50). "Rustic," as Orest Ranum has established, was used to refer to someone who failed to know the rules of courtesy ("Courtesy," 429). Not reciprocating plays out here on the level of both the personal and the social. It is a sign of being ungrateful in friendship, at the same time that it is a sign of incivility or lack of sophistication in social matters.

In one instance not reciprocating is described in terms of failure to pay. One day Sapho complained to Théodamas that "Mr. de Donneville" came to see her less ever since her brother (herself) included his portrait as Méliante (and as Artimas) in *Le Grand Cyrus*. Moreover, Donneville never thanked her brother (nor herself) for the portrait.[21] Sapho compared the situation to people who went to get their portraits painted by Juste or Beaubrun, "qui n'en bougent pendant qu'on travaille à leur portrait, mais qui n'y retournent plus dès qu'il est achevé" ["who do not budge while one works on their portrait, but who never return as soon as it is finished"], an analogy completed by Théodamas, who adds: *"et qui oublient à payer"* [*"and who forget to pay"*] (52–53). Here a thank you is conceived of, and unambiguously so, as *payment* for a verbal gift, Méliante's portrait in *Cyrus*. Gift exchange is expressed in terms of an exchange of commodities, where the "seller" (giver) presents a product (gift) to a buyer (friend), who must pay (reciprocate) immediately. As we might expect, when compensation is not immediate, "interest" is due. When Acante sends Sapho an enigma, Sapho hesitates to (ap)-praise it immediately, and asks for six months to judge its value before responding. Because Sapho refuses immediate reciprocation, she promises to give Acante praise with interest: "je vous rendrai alors *avec usure* toutes ces louanges que je vous refuse aujourd'hui" ["I will give you all the praises I refuse you today *with interest*"] (my emphasis; 68). As noted above, Erasmus already used economic analogies and even the notion of interest to refer to gift giving between friends in the early fifteenth century.

In the *Chroniques*, reciprocal exchange typically is cyclical: A gives a present to B who reciprocates with a thank you letter or poem, to which A responds with another thank you of some sort, which might also merit a response, and so on and so forth. As exchange is cyclical, it potentially can go on *ad infinitum*. In the process, value is attributed to each gift by the parties involved in exchange, generally as being more or less equal to the original gift that originated the process. For instance, Théodamas sends Sapho a crystal *cachet*. Sapho responds with another "present," a poem thanking him for the gift. Théodamas thanks Sapho for her generosity in a madrigal that attributes value to Sapho's poem in relation to the original gift: "Le présent que vous m'avez fait / A bien surpassé mon souhait. / Je ne prétendais autre chose / Qu'un petit compliment en prose" ["The present you gave me / Well surpassed my wishes / I was not expecting anything more / Than a short thank you in prose"] (87). For Théodamas, a thank you in prose would have been a sufficient token of exchange for his crystal *cachet*. Writing in verse, Sapho reciprocated generously, which implies that the value of prose is less than that of verse in the market of words. In the *Chroniques*, poetry is considered the language of the gods (*le langage des dieux*) and prose that of men (*le langage des hommes*). Poetry's superior *ontological* value translates within the salon into a superior *economic* value of exchange.

The value of a particular gift is determined within the context of the salon. That is to say, value attributed to something outside the space of the salon might not correspond to the "rate of exchange" within the salon's borders. Acante gives Sapho a gift of his book on the Académie Française. In return, Sapho writes Acante in prose asking him to accept "toutes les grâces" (62) that she offers him. Acante's reply gives more value to Sapho's thank you than to his own book, remarking that now he owes her so much. Although one would assume the book would hold more value than the thank you, in the end it is Acante who, figuratively and literally, is indebted to Sapho. The cycle of exchange ends with Sapho's letter, in which she states that Acante's "reconnaissance" is like a second present: "c'est me faire un second présent que de m'en remercier comme vous faites" ["it is like giving me a second gift, thanking me the way you do"] (63). Later in the *Chroniques* Acante states that he would give "cent volumes" ["a hundred volumes"] for one of Sapho's *billets* (104). Within the gift economy of the salon, it is possible for a thank you, even in prose, to have more value than an entire book, or a letter to have more value than a hundred volumes. In her letters to the marquis de Sévigné, Ninon de Lenclos foregrounds the conventions of value and exchange that differentiated the salon from other spaces of French society. She advises the marquis to exchange certain "qualités" used in the "commerce" of men for "agréments," the currency of the salon. Because value is conventional, she argues, what might be "fausse monnaie" or counterfeit in one domain or country can be legitimate currency in another (120–23). The idea that the salon had its own "economy" was not foreign to seventeenth-century writers.

Words indeed function like currency. When Méliante wishes to "pay" Sapho for her portrait of him in *Cyrus*, he decides to write a poem that he recites to Pellisson and Conrart to get their opinion or "appraisal." Before Méliante can revise the poem, Pellisson memorizes it, and unbeknownst to Méliante, gives a copy to Sapho, who in turn writes Méliante, enclosing a bad copy of the poem. Méliante responds, stating that he never believed he could "s'acquitter d'une aussi grande dette avec d'aussi méchante monnaie" ["release himself from such a great debt with such inferior currency"] (57). Literally indebted to Sapho for his portrait in *Cyrus*, Méliante is not sure that his words (his poem) would be legal tender (*avoir cours*) "chez Sapho," whose words/currency consist "d'un si bon alloi" ["of such a good alloy"] (57).

The economic value of verbal currency is determined by its ontological value—its value as pure "being," as "spirit," as something universal and timeless. In his poem, Méliante compares Sapho painting his image in the novel to him painting Sapho's image in his heart. He suggests that this exchange is equal, if not unfair, for "Donneville" is not necessarily recognizable in the portrait of "Méliante." In her response, Sapho disagrees with Méliante about the value of the two portraits. Whereas her image is merely inscribed in Méliante's (mortal, inconstant) heart, his image in *Cyrus* will survive a thousand years or more (55). The value of the two portraits is determined in relation to their duration, and implicitly in relation to their diffusion: a work that endures is also one that is diffused from generation to generation. In other words, the value of each portrait is determined *ontologically* in terms of duration and diffusion, in the way that the image—and by extension, the person represented—goes beyond space and time, attaining the status of universal. Méliante notes that his portrait was painted "d'un trait immortel" ["with an immortal stroke"] (54). Given that the portrait of Méliante in *Cyrus* is "immortal" and that of Sapho in Méliante's heart is limited in time means that Sapho's portrait of Méliante carries more (onto-logical, economic) value than Méliante's portrait of Sapho.

The *Chroniques* go so far as to suggest that there are different types of immortality, each of which carries more or less value. Writing to Doralise, Théodamas mentions that Monsieur Chapel-ain or "M. de Scudéry" could immortalize her. Although "Mon-sieur de Pelisson" could also grant her immortality, it would not be "de la bonne, car il y en a de plusieurs sortes et celle de Lan-guedoc ne vaut guère et se pourrit en moins de rien" ["the good kind, for there are several types and that of Languedoc is not worth much and goes bad in no time at all"] (150). Théodamas implicitly opposes Languedoc immortality to Parisian immortal-ity (it should be recalled that Pellisson is a relatively recent ar-rival in Paris). The value of Parisian immortality resides in its duration: whereas Languedoc immortality *se pourrit en moins de rien*, Parisian immortality is *de bon aloi*, it is genuine and last-ing. Value, then, is also determined with respect to proximity and distance from Paris. From Paris, one can gain universal celebrity facilitated by the diffusion in space and time of one's image. From Languedoc, however, the extent to which one can become renowned is limited. As such, the value of Parisian immortality resides in its affiliation with the universal, whereas Languedoc immortality is of the particular. Parisian immortality is worth more because of its ontological value, because in Paris one "is" more than in the provinces.[22]

Within the salon, the value of verbal gifts is conventional, resid-ing in the gift's ontological value, specifically its proximity to the universal. Value is also determined in relation to the person who bestows the gift. We have already noted that Sapho is described as a sort of Midas who gives value to everything she touches: she turns everything into *gold*. Her words are worth a thousand books, her generous compliments make every *salonnier* in-debted to her, for their currency (words) carries less value. The notion of being indebted to Sapho is expressed quite literally in Acante's *récépissé* [receipt, IOU], in which he declares: "Je soussigné reconnais et confesse avoir reçu de Mlle de Scudéry tant de grâces qu'on n'en peut faire la somme et que je ne les lui rendrai jamais" ["I the undersigned recognize and concede having received from Mlle de Scudéry so many graces that can-not be added up and that I will never return to her"] (132). Within the gift economy of the salon, *reconnaissance* or gratitude takes

on financial dimensions, translating into either the acknowledge-
ment of a debt or a payment (a thank you). Although exchange
between *salonniers* theoretically is a reciprocal exchange between equals, the fact that everyone is *redevable* or indebted to
Sapho would suggest that she occupies the position of a superior:
everyone owes her gratitude. When discussing gift exchange
between unequals, Davis cites a French proverb that would
apply here as well: "A pere, à maistre, à Dieu tout puissant, / Nul
ne peut rendre l'equivalent" [To father, to master, to God
omnipotent / No one can return the equivalent] (*Gift*, 17). If no
one can reciprocate or "pay back" one's master, then we might
assume that everything the master gives is worth more than
what his dependents could offer, regardless of the "objective" (if
such a thing is possible) value of the gift.

Just as the master can give value to things, he can also give
value to his dependents. In the same way that Sapho guarantees
the alloy of her verbal gifts, she is also the guarantor of her *salonniers'* value as the standard against which the relative value of
her *salonniers* is determined. In other words, Sapho functions as
their *caution* [security, guarantee, backing]. This is clearly expressed in one of the *Chroniques'* letters where Acante asks
Sapho to vouch for his friend, M. de Saint Hipoly, on his behalf.
Saint Hipoly is seeking a position with the duc de Conti, and
Acante needs to speak with Sarasin, Conti's secretary, to attest
to Saint Hipoly's honor, virtue, and general character—in other
words, to certify his value and the potential value of his service.
However, Acante is unable to meet with Sarasin, and asks Sapho
to confirm the good character of his friend in a letter to Sarasin.
Acante remarks that, had he known about this earlier, he would
have spoken to Sarasin himself in Sapho's presence, and he adds:
"je m'assure que vous auriez eu la bonté de cautionner sinon
pour le principal payeur, du moins pour une mauvaise caution
comme moy" ["I am sure you would have been so kind as to back
if not the principal payer, then at least a bad security like my-
self"] (230).

Ideally, Sapho would have served as the *caution* or guarantee
for Acante, who in turn would have served as the *mauvaise caution*, as he humbly puts it, for his friend Saint Hipoly. What
makes Saint Hipoly the principal payer is that if Conti were to
take Saint Hipoly into his household, the latter would have to
"pay back" Conti for his gratitude. In other words, Saint Hipoly
would be indebted to the prince for allowing him to serve in his
household. By taking Saint Hipoly into his household, Conti is in

fact granting a favor, which must be reciprocated through service, the value of which needs to be guaranteed, like a loan, by the good word of Acante, which is in turn guaranteed by Sapho's *crédit*.[23] Ultimately Sapho confers value onto her *salonniers* as their *crédit* or *caution*, which essentially makes their value a reflection of her own. At the same time, however, her *salonniers* are a reflection of her own worth in the way that they serve and pay tribute to her (much like good debtors). The extent to which they obey, respect, and serve her (recalling precepts from the Carte de Tendre like *obéissance, soumission, respect*, and *petits soins*) contributes to her own value and glory.

Patrons and Clients

Within the context of the Samedis, friendship and the reciprocal relations that support it often mimic the type of relations characteristic of patronage. In many respects Sapho plays the role of patron within the salon, already suggested at the beginning of the *Chroniques* when Acante refers to her as "ma protectrice" (58). According to Kettering, the reciprocal relation between client and patron resides in part in the reciprocal ways they give value to each other. While the patron's reputation and prestige reflects on his clients, the loyalty of good clients can increase the prestige and reputation of the patron (Kettering, 28, 73). Likewise, Sapho's (real or imaginary) prestige extends to her *salonniers*, as noted above, and their loyalty (submission, obedience, service) is a measure of her glory and power.

On two occasions Sapho orders Trasile to abandon travel plans to prove his loyalty to her and her Samedis. On the first occasion, Trasile was about to leave for England when he received Sapho's letter ordering him not to go. His compliance is described as a "petite preuve d'obéissance" ["small proof of obedience"] and as a demonstration of Sapho's "pouvoir si absolu" ["absolute power"] over him (110–11). On the second occasion, Sapho, on the advice of Théodamas, orders Trasile to immediately leave Le Havre and return to Paris. For Théodamas, Trasile's compliance would again be a proof of her power over him, and furthermore, a measure of her own glory (147–48). Sapho also tests Acante's loyalty, ordering him to be unfaithful to the Académie Française by missing a session to join her and other Samedi *habitués* that same afternoon. The objective of this exercise is to see if "mon pouvoir s'étend jusques à vous faire infidèle" ["my power extends as far as to make you unfaithful"] (252). Obedience, submission, and loyalty on the part of the client/*salonnier* are so many measures of the power and glory, the prestige and value, of the patron/Sapho.

Generally speaking, it is the women of the Samedis who act out the role of patron, while the men perform the role of client. The ways in which patron–client relations play themselves out recall the ways in which the language and relations of vassalage were used metaphorically to characterize the love relation in medieval courtly literature, with the lady occupying the position of the lord and the poet or knight that of the vassal.[24] Just as feudalism "was transformed into clientalism," so the vassal–lord relation evolved into the client–patron relation, and by the seventeenth century, political and administrative service replaced the more feudal notion of military service (Kettering, 207–9). The games of the Samedis show that this social transformation could indeed be recuperated and used to characterize relations within the salon.

Reciprocal exchange between patron and client entailed, on an abstract level, the exchange of the patron's *crédit* to give value to the client, for the loyalty of the client to the patron. On a more concrete level, exchange meant the provision of material and professional benefits by the patron, and the provision of services by the client. One important service was writing, which also was one way a client could secure the attention of a patron.[25] Ambitious members of the High Bourgeoisie and the Robe could move up in the world through their writing. Writing was a way to get noticed. As such, it was an instrument of social promotion.

Several Samedi members did in fact advance their careers through writing. In 1633 Chapelain wrote an *Ode au Cardinal Richelieu* that got the cardinal's attention, launching his long career as a dedicated servant of the state. Already a client of the comte de Chavigny, one of Richelieu's creatures, Sarasin gained the attention of Chapelain by writing the introductory "Discours" to Georges de Scudéry's *Amour Tyrannique* (1638). When Sarasin hit hard financial times in the late 1640s, Gilles Ménage, Madame de Rambouillet, and her daughter Madame de Montausier basically lobbied the duc de Condé to take Sarasin into his household. Notably, the request was made in a poem written by Ménage. Eventually this led to Sarasin acquiring the position of secretary for the duc de Conti by 1653. Soon after settling in Paris, Pellisson wrote his *Relation contenant l'histoire de l'Académie Françoise*, which secured his reception to the Académie in 1653. Although Madame du Plessis-Bellière was the Samedi's connection to Nicolas Fouquet, Pellisson's book on the Académie and status as academician—not to mention his poem, *Remerciment du siècle à M. le Surintendent Fouquet*—must have made him an attractive client in the eyes of Fouquet. Even a highly respected writer like Racine launched his career by writing a flattering poem to a person of power. In honor of the marriage of Louis XIV and Marie-Thérèse, Racine wrote *La Nymphe de la Seine*. Addressed to the new queen, Racine submitted a copy to Chapelain, who in turn granted the young writer a state pension. As Boileau laments in his seventh satire, it was not through satirical writing that one advanced in the world, but through writing that flattered its addressee.

   The importance of writing was twofold. On the one hand, writing could be used to glorify, to increase the prestige value of the patron, and grant him or her "immortality." On the other, through writing a potential client could demonstrate skills that could also prove necessary in the performance of administrative and political duties where rhetorical skills of persuasion and negotiation might be useful. Richelieu noticed something in Chapelain's ode that led him to give Chapelain a role to play in his administration. To some degree it was through his writing that Richelieu discovered in Chapelain one of the most loyal cultural ministers of the French monarchy. Whereas the feudal knight had to demonstrate his military prowess to advertise his ability to protect his lord's seigneurie or kingdom, the early modern client had to demonstrate writerly skills that publicized his (or her) ability to bolster the patron's reputation or even manage a patron's affairs. Although many factors must have gone into the choice of a client, writing was among the more significant ones.

   One place a person could develop and perfect his or her writerly skills (besides, of course, the *collèges*) was the salon. By and large Scudéry's salon was a place of self-promotion. Here one could "produce" oneself as noble, as well as acquire skills, not to mention personal connections, useful in maneuvering within the system of patronage. Salon games and activities centered predominantly on written and verbal tests of wit and exercises in flattery, leisurely recreations that would have been advantageous to those *salonniers* whose social advancement depended on such skills. This is not to suggest, however, that *salonniers* consciously played salon games or engaged in activities that would educate them in the ways of self-promotion, any more than the makers or players of games like *Monopoly* or *Trivial Pursuit* are fully conscious of the complicated interplays between these games, our society, and ourselves. Nevertheless, games and leisure activities maintain a complicated relation with the society in which they emerge. They often reinforce certain values, behaviors, and skills that can enhance one's performance within a particular society.

In the Samedis, reciprocal exchange is based in part on the exchange of idealized images of each other. Madeleine de Scudéry becomes Sapho the Greek poetess, Madame Aragonnais the princess Philoxène, and Paul Pellisson the chevalier de l'Acrostiche through the flattering portraits Scudéry disseminates in her novels, through salon conversation, and through the exchange of letters and poems, in which each *salonnier* maintains the fiction of the others' greatness.[26] Although this type of exchange serves to idealize or ennoble members of the salon, these same skills could be used to flatter a potential patron. The practice of reciprocal exchange in the salon might thus be viewed as a way for potential clients to practice the skills of artful flattery that could be used to attract and maintain a patron. Role-play also gives *salonniers* practice in the ways of patronage, allowing them to master the language of friendship and the "rhetoric of gifts" that, according to Davis, supported the system of patronage (*Gift*, 37). Finally, the salon was a place where its members could legitimate the nobility of their profession as writers, clients, academicians, and jurists. Exercising the profession of writer or secretary of a noble household or even of the state did not ennoble the way that knighthood and vassalage had in the past. Yet *salonniers* used military metaphors to refer to and legitimate their literary exploits within the salon, creating analogies between the knight of times past and the secretary of the present.

Virtual Reality

The "Journée des Madrigaux" is exemplary in the way *salonniers* play out relations characteristic of patronage and create analogies between the knight and the poet–client. The context of the "Journée" is one of gift giving: Théodamas gives the Princess Philoxène a crystal *cachet* similar to the one he had earlier given Sapho. Because of her status as "princess," Philoxène believes it is below her to respond directly to Théodamas and decides to employ Acante as her secretary. In the end, both Acante and Polyandre (Sarasin) play the role of secretary or client, while Philoxène plays that of patron. That Sarasin is actually the secretary to the duc de Conti only reinforces the illusion of reality the game creates. Referring to Philoxène as "princess" associates her with ducal households like that of Conti. As the "real" client of the Prince de Conti, Sarasin/Polyandre himself becomes a signifier of nobility, indicating the status of Philoxène. In the game, Philoxène is represented as noble not only through her title, but also by virtue of having a secretary.

When Acante and Polyandre engage in a virtual duel, the patron–client relation takes on the guise of feudal relations. Assuming the role of Philoxène's secretary, Polyandre plays the role of her vassal ("*La fureur le saisit, il mit la main aux armes*" ["*Seized by fury he took up his arms*"]), taking up the pen instead of the sword (171). Competing with Polyandre for the "vassalage" of the princess, Acante "tira deux autres madrigaux de sa tête presque en même temps" ["drew two Madrigals from his head practically at the same time"] (172), as if he, too, were drawing his sword.[27] Their arms, of course, are their words and their pens, and the space of the combat is that of conversation, which is nevertheless referred to as a *lice* or arena: "Polyandre et Acante rentrèrent encore deux fois dans la lice" ["Polyandre and Acante entered the arena two more times"] (179).

The use of the term *lice* is significant. Whereas for the feudal nobility the *lice* was a "real" space in which physical activities such as jousts and tournaments took place, for the newly-forming nobility the *lice* has become the virtual space of conversation, defined in terms of verbal activities. In fact, the duel of madrigals is described in terms of conversation, as "une espèce de dialogue" ["a type of dialogue"] (178). Just as feudal nobles performed feats in an actual space with arms made of steel, so our *salonniers* joust in a virtual space created by conversation, arming themselves with rhyme. Such a joust is nevertheless considered by the *salonniers* to be a true combat: "On donna à Polyandre l'honneur de ce combat, car pour Acante il n'était que trop content de l'honneur d'avoir combattu" ["We gave the honor of this combat to Polyandre, for Acante was only too pleased by the honor of having fought"] (181). Whereas the outcome of the traditional joust was based on the physical domination of one's opponent, that of the *salonniers*' verbal combat is decided by the quality and quantity of verbal gifts produced. A couple of Polyandre's madrigals are considered "par dessus le marché" ["above the market"] (180), suggesting the *lice* is also a marketplace of words. What once was a physical competition between two noblemen becomes a verbal game between two *robins*, an appropriate leisure-time activity for Pellisson, the future right-hand man of Fouquet and historiographer of Louis XIV.

Like the ladies of courtly literature, the women of the Samedis rather passively witness the deeds of men and serve as their inspiration. As the narrator of the "Journée" informs us, Philoxène and Telamire did in fact compose madrigals in both French and Italian, but were reluctant to "go public" with them, and they are not reproduced in the *Chroniques*. It would seem that even within the space of the salon, norms of female modesty limited their scope of action. Salon activities gave especially male *salonniers* the opportunity to practice types of writing and behavior that could potentially prove useful in acquiring patrons, which many of them, especially Pellisson, were successful in doing. For women, they momentarily played the role of patron, a role they could play to some extent in reality, often "brokering" a relation between a writer and a male family member or intimate, as we saw in the case of Madame de Rambouillet and her daughter lobbying the duc de Condé on behalf of Sarasin, or in the case of Scudéry vouching for Saint Hipoly. In other words, women did have some degree of *crédit* within the system of patronage, although they rarely found themselves in the position of independent patron or of client, with a few exceptions. For the most part, this rather passive role assigned to women outside of the salon seems to go unchallenged in the *Chroniques* and apparently in the space of the salon.

Sapho, however, provides the exception to the rule. In the *Chroniques*, Sapho is the only woman who plays both patron and client, and she competes with the men of the "Journée" much like an Amazon warrior: "l'incomparable Sapho qui semblait ne devoir que juger des coups et donner le prix avec le reste des dames, sentit je ne sais quelle émotion dans son courage, qui ne lui permit pas d'en demeurer là, et [elle descendit] du théâtre pour se mêler parmi les combattants" ["the incomparable Sapho who, it would seem, should only judge the blows and hand out the prizes with the rest of the ladies, felt a certain emotion in her heart that did not allow her to remain there, and she descended from the theater to join the combatants"] (175–76). Incarnating both male and female virtues, Sapho appears to be somewhat androgynous, something also suggested in her portrait in *Le Grand Cyrus*.[28] As a writer and as an unmarried woman without much wealth, Madeleine de Scudéry had to compete with men in the *lice*, in the marketplace of words. Although she had a difficult time mustering support in the early part of her career, eventually, and with the help of Pellisson, Scudéry was successful in acquiring influential patrons such as Fouquet and later Louis XIV. Of course, her role as client was limited to writing, without exercising other administrative duties. Nevertheless, Sapho/Scudéry provides a counterexample to the other female members of the salon, not to mention to upper-class women outside the space of the salon.

Implicitly figured in the *Chroniques du Samedi* as an island, the Samedis were constructed as an insular space, an "other" Ile de France with its own laws and economy. Basically members of Scudéry's salon created a space of play, an ideal or utopic space, through the assumption of pseudonyms and through the systematic inclusion and exclusion of words, topics, and behaviors associated with the particular, to create a space of the universal. Such inclusions and exclusions are based largely on the terms of the Carte de Tendre that function simultaneously to 1) create the exclusive space of the Samedis; 2) produce elite subjects; and 3) regulate relations between *salonniers*. Because the space of the salon was contiguous with that of conversation, the Samedis could be described as a virtual space that transcended physical space and time. Samedi marked the "un-time" of leisure, the time of the production of the self as universal hero or heroine. It marked the time of the production of the self as noble.

Scudéry's salon was the site for the production of elite subjects, in at least two respects. First, salon members created themselves as noble through their language and through the reciprocal exchange of verbal gifts, especially the mutual exchange of idealized images of each other. Second, *salonniers* could acquire skills useful to their real advancement outside the space of the salon. In the *Chroniques*, reciprocal exchange of gifts often is expressed in terms of an exchange of commodities, the value of which is based on the gift's proximity to the universal and on the value of the giver. Although the type of gift exchange carried out in the Samedis is characteristic of a humanist model of friendship, it also recalls the type of exchange—not to mention system of determining value—emblematic of patronage. At the same time that Scudéry's *salonniers* seek to ennoble themselves, they also attempt to ennoble their profession as writers and clients by appropriating signs associated with activities representative of the feudal nobility to qualify those of the robe. The pen becomes an allegorical sword and the secretary a modern-day vassal.

It is interesting to note that the salon's refiguring of the client–

patron relation could be recuperated to qualify the relation between men and women of the salon in ways that recall the poet
and the lady of courtly literature. As such it would seem that, although the Samedis transcend space and time, they fail to transcend the limits of gender. However, the Amazonian Sapho does
descend into the ring and compete with men in the marketplace
of words. Sapho is the only woman who truly "goes public" in the
Chroniques, and her character arguably indicates the direction
Scudéry wanted to take the "woman question." As Marlies Mueller has maintained, Scudéry sought to tame both the male and
female warrior ("Taming," 223). Nevertheless, the figure of
Sapho would suggest that she did not wish women simply to play
passive roles in society. Through her fictional alter ego Sapho,
Scudéry proposes, as she does more explicitly in the earlier
Femmes Illustres, that women indeed should take up the pen.

4

Boileau and Perrault: The Public Sphere and Female Folly

MADELEINE DE SCUDÉRY'S WORKS AND THE IDEAS DIFFUSED IN THEM were well received by many members of Parisian high society. Her novels influenced writers like Lafayette, Philippe Quinault, fairy-tale writers of the 1690s like Marie-Catherine d'Aulnoy, and even English writers of the period, such as John Dryden and Nathaniel Lee. However, literary critics historically have focused on the poor reception of her works by canonical writers like Molière and Boileau, often failing to take into account the ideological positions underlying their assessment of her oeuvre. Scudéry, her works, her style, and her entourage have gone down in literary history as notorious targets of satire, whether we think of Boileau's *Les Héros de roman* [Heroes of Novels] or Molière's *Les Précieuses Ridicules* and *Les Femmes Savantes* [The Learned Ladies].

By midcentury, Scudéry and the modern salon and literary culture she and other *salonnières* fostered became the focal point of an attack on what more generally could be called, in Lewis Seifert's words, "mondain culture," a culture located somewhere between erudite and popular culture (69). As *mondain* culture was closely associated with the salons, with the cause of the Moderns, with "feminine" genres, and more generally with women, Scudéry served as a perfect target, being a prolific and popular writer, as well as a celebrated salon woman. In this chapter, we will consider the ways in which Boileau and Perrault responded negatively to the types of cultural change promoted by writers and *salonnières* like Scudéry. Although the two academicians have been studied almost exclusively in terms of what opposes them, I will illustrate here how they come together in their attack on the emergence of the "public," *mondain* woman.[1] Despite aesthetic and political differences, Boileau and

Perrault both sought to extricate women from the sociocultural public sphere that women indeed helped create.

MAD HEROES

For Boileau, Scudéry became a particularly ideal target since his hostility towards her was also personal. Along with Gilles Ménage and Paul Pellisson, Scudéry tried to block his election, not to mention that of his brother Gilles, to the Académie Française, both of whom nevertheless were elected, in 1684 and 1659 respectively. That Boileau somehow privileged Scudéry and her works above all other symbols of *mondain* culture is evident in his preoccupation with them from at least 1665 until his death. Implicit or explicit references to her and her works are found scattered throughout Boileau's oeuvre: in Satires II, III, IX, and especially the Satire X; in the third canto of the *Art Poétique*; in the fifth canto of *Le Lutrin*; and in *Les Héros de roman*. In a letter written to his friend Claude Brossette in January 1703, two years after Scudéry's death, Boileau evidently felt compelled to pronounce as well the death of all that she represented: "Le temps a fait voir que la Scudéry était un esprit faux. C'est à elle qu'on doit l'institution des Précieuses. Le fameux Hôtel de Rambouillet n'était pas tout à fait exempt de ce jargon, qui a, Dieu merci, trouvé sa fin" ["Time showed that Scudéry was a false wit. We owe her the institution of Precious women. The famous Hôtel de Rambouillet was not fully exempt of this jargon which, thank God, came to an end"] (*Héros*, 30). One gets the sense that Boileau wished for all traces of Scudéry's literary, social, and cultural influence on seventeenth-century French society to disappear. Given the associations he made between Scudéry, salon culture, and Modern writers, we can speculate that Boileau sought more generally the end of women's sociocultural influence—their "feminization" of French literature and culture—within the public sphere.

Boileau obviously was preoccupied by the "Scudéry question." This is nowhere more evident than in *Les Héros de roman: Dialogue à la manière de Lucien*, in which Boileau ridicules the various heroes of popular novels of the period. Although Boileau makes sport of characters in works by Quinault, Chapelain, de Pure, and La Calprenède, the overwhelming attack falls on Scudéry (six out of the eleven characters are taken from Scudéry's novels). Even if Boileau criticizes the novelistic tradition in general, Scudéry's novels constitute the particular example that serves as the general rule for the genre. Boileau himself singles out Scudéry in his introductory "Discours," in which he notes that her *Cyrus* and *Clélie* "s'attirèrent le plus d'applaudisse-mens" ["attracted the most applause"] and argues that Scudéry, more than any other novelist, pushed the genre towards greater puerility (284).[2] For Boileau, Scudéry's works are perfect examples of the genre because they epitomize all that he finds objectionable about it.

First composed in 1665, Boileau considered publishing *Les Héros de roman* as early as 1674. Unauthorized editions of the dialogue appeared in 1687, 1688, 1693, 1697, and 1706. The proliferation of unauthorized versions pushed Boileau to revise the piece in 1704, for which he composed an introductory "Discours" in 1710, only to have his version published posthumously in 1713 (Crane, 33–44). Boileau often recited the piece, which explains the unauthorized versions, many of which can be attributed to Saint-Evremond. According to Antoine Arnauld, Boileau apparently read the dialogue to the duchesse de Longueville and the princesse de Conti, both of whom encouraged Boileau to publish it. This would have been sometime before 1672, the year of Conti's death (Arnauld, 334; Crane, 35). Although we may never know why Boileau hesitated to publish the dialogue—Did he think it too offensive to publish while Scudéry was alive? Did the king, influenced by Madame de Maintenon, prohibit Boileau from publishing it?—the dialogue nevertheless did circulate through Boileau's readings and through unauthorized versions for some three decades.

It is indeed a clever text. Pluto, king of the underworld, calls upon the dead heroes of the Champs Elysées to protect his kingdom from the criminals of Tartar, who are threatening to revolt. In the beginning of the dialogue Pluto refuses to believe Diogène, the inscribed satirist of the piece, who describes these heroes as "une troupe de fous" ["a troupe of madmen"] more prepared to go dancing than to wage war. Furthermore, they are described as *damaret*, or effeminate (289). One by one the great heroes of Antiquity appear before Pluto and Minos, including Cyrus, Horace, Clélie, Brutus, Lucrèce, Sapho, and Joan of Arc, with Diogène sarcastically making wisecracks on the side. As they pass in review before Pluto, the incongruousness between the situation (a threatened kingdom) and the heroes' language (they speak only of love) creates quite a comic effect. In interview after interview, Pluto comes to the conclusion that these heroes are

all "mad," just as Diogène had described them at the beginning
of the dialogue. Finally a Frenchman unmasks the false heroes,
stating that "ce sont tous la plupart des bourgeois de mon quart-
ier" ["most of them are bourgeois from my neighborhood"] (309).
In the end, we discover that the real heroes are preparing for
battle, while "ces impertinens usurpateurs de leurs noms"
["these impertinent usurpers of their names"] (310) are whipped
and thrown into the river of oblivion.

Clearly the overall objective of the dialogue is to show how "un-
heroic" novelistic heroes are and to write them into literary
oblivion through a process of unmasking and delegitimation.
Boileau accomplishes this in two ways: 1) by maintaining that the
characters usurped names to ennoble themselves; and 2) by representing them as mad. The notion of usurpation in the text plays
itself out on two levels. On the level of fiction, Boileau contends
that novelists have their characters usurp the names of heroic
characters in order to ennoble their amorous ones. In his "Discours" Boileau maintains that novelists like Scudéry are bad imi-
tators of Honoré d'Urfé, because instead of taking as their heroes
lovesick shepherds, they make of great princes, kings, and famous captains of Antiquity lovesick shepherds, and even worse,
"des bourgeois," in order to embellish them (284). In other
words, novelists create characters that in essence are frivolous
shepherds, and they give them names of Ancient heroes in order
to make them appear more noble and dignified than they indeed
are.

On the extra-textual level, usurpation characterizes the novelist's move to ennoble through fiction members of his or her
"real" entourage, who served as keys to the novel's characters.
Boileau notes: "Les auteurs de ces romans, sous le nom de ces
héros, peignaient quelquefois le caractère de leurs amis particuliers, gens de peu de conséquence" ["The authors of such novels
sometimes painted the character of their intimate friends, people
of little consequence, under the name of these heroes"] (285). As
such, usurpation not only pertains to the fictional use the novelist
makes of "noble" names of heroes from Antiquity to refer to their
"frivolous," even bourgeois characters. Usurpation also refers to
the practice of creating associations through the novel's keys between members of the novelist's entourage and heroes from Antiquity, a practice that ultimately served to ennoble them, and
illegitimately so, from Boileau's perspective.

It is interesting to note that Boileau himself was investigated
in 1697 for usurpation of nobility, particularly his family's use of

the title "ecuyer" ["squire"]. During the investigation Boileau hired the genealogist Haudiquer to back up his family's false claim, as it turns out, to have descended from Jean Boileau, ennobled in 1371. It is nonetheless possible that Boileau paid Haudiquer twenty louis d'or in good faith to support his claim. His noble status was maintained in 1699; Haudiquer, however, was arrested in 1701 for fabricating genealogies (Clarac, 4–7). In spite of his somewhat skewed social identity, Boileau evidently viewed himself as issuing from a noble family some three hundred years old, which explains his conservative position with respect to the traditional social hierarchy.[3] In the *Dialogue*, the perhaps inadvertent usurper ardently criticizes the efforts on the part of people like Scudéry and her *salonniers* to legitimate themselves as noble through fiction, for such "imposters" destabilize the traditional social hierarchy and put the entire body politic at risk by usurping the names of competent defenders of the state.

Boileau also delegitimates the novel by representing its most famous characters as being completely mad. Their madness is signified 1) directly, in declarative statements made particularly by Pluto and Diogène; 2) in their incoherent language; and 3) in the general incongruousness of their behavior, that is to say, in their inadequate or inappropriate responses to the specific situation. After each character appears before Pluto and Minos, the latter simply declare them mad in statements like: "Il est fou" ["He is mad"] (291), "Le fou! Le fou!" ["The madman! The madman!"] (295), and regarding Sapho, "celle-ci est la plus folle de toutes. Elle a la mine d'avoir gâté toutes les autres" ["this one is the maddest of them all. She seems to have spoiled all the others"] (300). Having Minos remark not only that Sapho was the maddest of them all but also that she spoiled all the others is about as close as Boileau could get to saying—without actually saying it—that Scudéry was the most deranged novelist of the time.[4] She was to blame for the degradation since d'Urfé of an already problematic genre.

The incoherence of the characters' language takes the form of a precious jargon Pluto finds totally incomprehensible, a "langage inconcevable" (296). It is a limited language in which each word can only connote things that are related somehow to love. For instance, "enemy" does not and cannot signify a political enemy, but refers to the person with whom one is in love. When Clélie hears of mutiny, her only geographical reference is the kingdom of Tendre, and she fears there is trouble in her imaginary world. Every utterance gets recontextualized by the *héros de roman* and has meaning only in relation to the novelistic discourse of love. In his anger and frustration with Clélie's incessant talk about the Carte de Tendre and the towns that lead there, Pluto insists that such towns take one instead to "des petites maisons" (296), a reference to the Parisian insane asylum known as Hôpital des petites maisons (*Héros*, 193n.). Pluto's message is clear: those who speak such a jargon should be locked up, as the jargon itself is a sign of madness. Making of precious language a sign of madness and characterizing it as unreason, Boileau attempts to delegitimize and marginalize preciosity as a sociocultural movement.

In the scene where Lucrèce and Brutus each present Pluto with a tablet, the incoherence of the heroes' language is pushed to an extreme. First Pluto reads Lucrèce's tablet: "Toujours. l'on. si. mais. aimoit. d'éternelles. hélas. amour. d'aimer. doux. il point. seroit. n'est. qu'il" (297). Then he reads Brutus's tablet: "Moi. nos. verrez. vous. de. permettez. d'éternelles. jours. qu'on. merveille. peut. amours. d'aimer. voir" (298). One can easily imagine the comic effect this passage would have had as Boileau recited it before his friends. Reading the lines aloud, the fragmented, nonsensical, disordered sentences sound like baby talk, or the words of a madperson. Boileau faithfully reproduces the words on the tablets from *Clélie, Histoire Romaine*, only to mock them as another example of the incoherence of precious language.[5] Ironically, the purpose of the scene in *Clélie* is to allow Lucrèce to penetrate Brutus's feigned appearance of stupidity: that Brutus responds to Lucrèce's enigma with his own enigma is a sign of his intelligence. Taking a scene that originally revolved around the revelation of Brutus's wit and transforming it into one that would legitimate sending both Brutus and Lucrèce to the Hôpital des petites maisons, actually suggests that Boileau carefully read Scudéry's novel. His rewriting of the scene qualifies precious games as madness, for characters and loyal readers embrace falsity for truth; they accept signs of madness (the enigmas) for signs of intelligence. As Michel Foucault has argued, madness was associated in the early modern period with all that was false: unreason, false science, unregulated imagination, and trompe l'oeil. Basically, madness meant taking what was false, or illusion, for what was true, or reality (see Foucault, 8–49).

The incoherence of the characters' language overlaps with their incongruous responses to the specific situation. Whereas the context in which the heroes appear before Pluto demands a military discourse, the characters mechanically respond with the language of love. When Clélie appears before Pluto, she confuses trouble in Hades with trouble in Tendre, which leads to her digression on the Carte de Tendre that completely loses Pluto. When Sapho appears before him, she does not simply talk about love, like the other characters, but wishes to "divert" Pluto by asking him to comment on friendship and love, rather than discuss military strategy. Mocking the structure of novels like *Cyrus* and *Clélie*, Diogène informs Pluto that such heroes spend their time listening to stories about the various other characters right before leading a battle, "au lieu d'employer le temps à encourager les soldats et à ranger leurs armées" ["instead of making use of this time to encourage the soldiers and organize their armies"] (300). Such scenes from the dialogue oppose the feminine love ethic of novelistic heroes to the more virile war ethic of "true" heroes of Antiquity in order to highlight the superiority of the latter and the absurdity of the former. In his depictions of the incoherence of their language and the incongruousness with which they respond to the situation at hand, Boileau foregrounds the *invraisemblance* of novelistic heroes.

In the *Dialogue*, Boileau upholds the traditional notion of the hero-as-soldier against the type of redefinition of heroism we saw in *Clélie*. By situating novelistic heroes within the "real" context of imminent warfare, Boileau shows them to be incapable of defending Pluto's kingdom precisely because they are mad. Madness takes the form of an incoherent, disordered precious language and irrational behavior that, we are to deduce, are completely opposed to reason. In his defense of a virile, masculine, and rational model of heroism and subjectivity, Boileau associates mad, disordered, irrational novelistic characters—male and female—with all that is feminine. The three figures of male authority—Pluto, the king; Minos, the judge; and Diogène, the philosopher—are not only protectors of the kingdom, but also defenders of reason, giving new meaning to *raison d'état*. In the final analysis, the order of Pluto's kingdom is maintained by the inclusion of what male authority determines to be reason and by the exclusion of a feminized unreason or folly. Epitomized by Scudéry/Sapho, this feminine needs to be locked up, whipped, and thrown into the river of oblivion in order to preserve order in Pluto's kingdom, which could be read as a figure for the French nation.

PRECIOUS WITCHES

Pluto attributes the primary cause of this novelistic madness to Sapho, who "spoiled them all." Sapho/Scudéry is one of the principal forces behind the deception of making readers believe the illusion of Clélie's or Brutus's heroism, just as she can make what is in fact ugly appear beautiful to them. Her novels disturb the order of signification by leading her readers to take false illusions for authentic reality. That her perception and representation of the world is distorted is epitomized in the scene where Sapho paints for Pluto the portrait of the fury Tisiphone, who arguably becomes the figure of the *précieuse* in general, and of the female writer in particular. Boileau's parody of Scudéry's use of the portrait goes beyond simply an attack on the aesthetics of the Moderns and a defense of classicism. It brings together and conflates the image of the woman-as-witch, the woman-as-Amazon, and the mad woman writer who throws together heterogeneous elements that combine to form not so much a work of art, but rather something resembling a witch's brew.

Given that the portrait is the polar opposite of satire, we can only imagine the pleasure Boileau must have taken in writing this satirical portrait of Tisiphone. The very idea of doing a portrait of a fury is counter to the rules *vraisemblance*. As the principal objective of the genre is to flatter, a portrait is supposed to emphasize the beauty and virtues of the person represented. Because she is a fury, Tisiphone should not be represented by the genre at all, for a woman/witch steeped in ugliness and vice essentially has no virtues, which explains the humor and absurdity of the scene. By extension, Boileau suggests that the women of Scudéry's entourage never should have been represented in portraits. When Pluto expresses his surprise that Sapho was going to do the portrait of Tisiphone, Diogène explains that she similarly painted many of her female friends, "qui ne surpassent guère en beauté Tisiphone" ["who hardly surpass Tisiphone in beauty"] (300). Boileau compares Scudéry's *salonnières* to Tisiphone to emphasize what he viewed as the gap between the reality of the model and the ideal representation of the model in the portrait. His antiportrait works to unmask the "witches" who usurped the names of virtuous heroines of Antiquity to represent themselves in novels.

Read as a general example of Scudéry's portraits of women from her entourage, Boileau's antiportrait makes of them so many Medusas, given the fury's serpentine hair. Although Tisiphone is compared to Amazons, the potentially threatening image of the woman warrior is undone by the emphasis on her ugliness, signified by her dark skin and her mutilated and monstrous bosom. In some respects Boileau's attack on the *précieuses* resembles contemporary attacks on feminists, who are represented by some as ugly man haters, and whose political agenda is merely a pretext to unleash their resentment. In Boileau's antiportrait, the potential threat salon women represent, as expressed in the implicit comparison between the *précieuse* and Medusa or the Amazon, is negated by ridiculing the symbols of feminine power. His antiportrait enacts a sort of symbolic castration of all that makes women threatening to men, namely, their beauty, hair, and breasts; their magical and even their physical power. It is important to note here that partisans of the Counter-Reformation typically viewed women's hair as a sign of impiety, of sociopolitical and sexual disorder, and of seduction. Writers and moralists described courtesans who curled their hair as furies, whose hair resembled "venomous serpents." Laywomen convicted of sexual deviancy had their heads shaved as a "symbolic execution" (Farr, "Pure," 401–5). In his antiportrait, Boileau clearly draws from the pool of Counter-Reformation symbols used to express the immorality, power, and threat associated with the female body.

Although we might also read the portrait of Tisiphone specifically as a parody of Scudéry's own portrait of Sapho,[6] more important is the analogy Boileau seems to create between the woman writer and the fury. In Ovid's *Metamorphoses*, Tisiphone carries out the vengeance of Juno against Ino and her husband Athamas. The fury combines the froth of Cerberus, the venom of Echidna, fresh blood, and hemlock to create a brew that poisons the mind, not the body. Athamas's distorted mind leads him to take his wife and children for a lioness and her cubs. What brings their destruction is the illusion, the distortion of reality caused by Tisiphone's brew (see Ovid, 105–8). By the same token, as Boileau seems to suggest, Scudéry/Sapho's novels poison the mind with distorted notions of heroism that could have resulted in the disorder and destruction of Pluto's kingdom. Like a witch's brew, the novel makes one delusional. And like a Tisiphone, the woman writer Scudéry/Sapho poisons the minds of her readers through her books, driving them to madness, leading them to see things that are not real, only fantasy. Just as Ino and her children were not in reality a lioness and her cubs, so Sapho and Tisiphone are not beautiful, nor Brutus and Lucrèce heroic.

Boileau's antiportrait of Tisiphone, in which he sarcastically represents the fury as virtuous and beautiful, goes so far as to suggest that novelistic portraits of women, whom contemporaries recognized as specific Parisian socialites, in fact conceal so many witches. Thus the portrait of Tisiphone functions to qualify as witches both the woman writer, if we take the antiportrait to parody that of Sapho, and *mondain* women in general, if it is understood to parody the portrait of salon women. At the end of the dialogue, when the false heroes are unmasked, punished, and replaced by authentic ones, the order of signification is reestablished. It is the novel, women writers, women, and the feminine that disturb the order of signification by distorting the reader's sense of reality, by enchanting the reader into taking so many false illusions for authentic reality.[7] As the dialogue implies, trouble in the order of signification can lead to trouble in the political order, for belief in false heroes could have led to the destruction of Pluto's kingdom. For this reason, Pluto not only punishes the *héros de roman*, but also takes them completely out of circulation by casting them into the river of oblivion.

SATIRE X

With the Satire X, Boileau moves away from a specific attack on Scudéry and novelists to a more general condemnation of marriage, women, and especially the role of women in the sociocultural public sphere as adherents of the Modernist cause. Although Boileau based this satire on Juvenal's Satire VI, the misogyny expressed in Boileau's version cannot be attributed to his model alone. Boileau chooses not to include, for instance, Juvenal's attack on husbands who approve of their wives' whoring if it brings them financial gain. He does, however, condemn religious directors for debauching zealot wives, only to emphasize the victimization of husbands. Overall, Juvenal's satires attack sexual transgressions and excesses on the part of both men and women. Boileau's satires, however, contain few references to men's sexual behavior. This suggests, on the one hand, that in writing his Satire X Boileau drew from several literary traditions, and on the other, that an essential feature distinguishing women from men in the satire is the former's sexual depravity, itself linked to the bestial and even diabolical nature of women.

In his celebrated book *Medieval Misogyny*, R. Howard Bloch situates Boileau within the tradition of *molestiae nuptiarum*, literally the "pains of marriage," of which the fifteenth-century *Les Quinze Joies de Mariage* [The Fifteen Joys of Marriage] is exemplary in its depiction of adulterous and tyrannical wives (Bloch, 15). This tradition was still alive at the beginning of the seventeenth century, epitomized in the *Querelle des Alphabets*, initiated by the violently antiwoman pamphlet by Jacques Olivier, entitled, *L'Alphabet de l'imperfection et malice des femmes* [The Alphabet of Women's Imperfection and Malice], first published in 1617 and reprinted no less than eighteen times by 1650. As Linda Timmermans has documented, the defenders of women were more numerous than their detractors, and the *Querelle* died down by 1625, after which there were few straight-out antiwomen tracts circulating in France until roughly the 1670s (241–44). In the latter part of the century, such tracts generally targeted upper-class women's supposed depravation and luxurious tastes, with a more veiled critique of the "inherent" vices of feminine nature than in earlier treatises. For instance, Jacques Chaussé's *Traité de l'Excelence du mariage* [Treaty on the Excellence of Marriage] (1686), presents itself as a defense of marriage, and Fénelon's *Education des filles* [The Education of Girls] (1687), a defense of women's education. However, both texts are infused with attacks on the negative influence of *mondain* culture on women, who are particularly vulnerable to its sway due to the fact that they are, as Chaussé puts it, "des créatures infirmes et pécheresses" ["weak and sinful creatures"] (186). That the second major *Querelle des femmes* of the seventeenth century was building up over the 1670s and 1680s, at a time when Louis XIV was consolidating the sociocultural public sphere through the proliferation of academies, is not inconsequential. The attack on *mondain* culture and on women can very well be read in terms of a backlash against salon culture and the privileged role women played within it as writers, critics, and arbiters of taste.

For his tenth Satire, Boileau weaves together an antifeminism directly tied to the *Querelle des Anciens et des Modernes* with the traditional gaulois *molestiae nuptiarum* and the emerging critique of the "depravities" of what I call "public women," that is, upper-class women active within the sociocultural public sphere. The satire consists of several portraits, including: the dishonorable woman, the coquette, the miser, the quick-tempered woman, the hypochondriac, the learned lady, the precious woman, and, last but not least, the zealot.[8] Despite their apparent diversity, each portrait characterizes women in terms of first, their deception (that is, they are not what they appear to be); and second, their monstrosity, which they conceal through their deception (in the same manner that the dialogue's Sapho conceals the monstrosity of Tisiphone in the portrait). As we might assume, it is the art of the Moderns—Scudéry's novels and Lully's operas—that draws out women's innate monstrosity which, in the satire, takes the form of female sexuality and excess. In his depictions of women and modernism, Boileau ends up making of the culture of the Moderns a sort of heresy, and women its irrational followers.

Images of woman-as-monster abound in the satire. On several occasions Boileau uses the direct approach, referring to the miser as "un monstre affreux sous l'habit d'une fille" ["an awful monster under the clothes of a girl"], or to mothers who beat their children out of spite for their husbands as "[c]es monstres pleins d'un fiel que n'ont point les lionnes" ["these monsters full of a rancor unknown to lionesses"] (109, 119).[9] At other times Boileau uses more poetic devices to evoke women's monstrous side. In his description of the miserly woman, whom readers recognized to be Madame Tardieu (murdered with her husband in 1665), Boileau describes her as having turned out eyelids and a "masse de chair bizarrement taillée" ["bizarrely shaped mass of flesh"] (109). (Tallemant des Réaux notably describes Madame Tardieu as being good looking, at least in her youth [1: 657].) Given her hump, often indicative of ogres in seventeenth-century fairy tales, Boileau's physical description makes of Madame Tardieu an ogress, an appropriate image for an avaricious woman who hoards money and completely dominates her husband. The *coléreuse* or the quick-tempered woman also enslaves her husband and has him "vivre de couleuvres" ["live on grass snakes"], a play on the expression "avaler des couleuvres" ["swallow grass snakes"], meaning "to suffer insults without protest." Boileau describes the *coléreuse* as having "les cheveux hérissés" ["bristly hair"] which, given her snakelike tongue, suggests that beneath her womanly appearance lies a monstrous Medusa.

Both the image of the ogress and that of the Medusa connect women to animality, an association well established in Antiquity and in Western Europe, especially with the publication of Heinrich Kramer and James Sprenger's influential *Malleus Maleficarum* (1486), reprinted in France throughout the seventeenth century.[10] From beginning to end Kramer and Sprenger allude to women's animal nature, which takes concrete form in their comparison of Woman to the Chimera, a monster with the face of a lion, the belly of a goat, and the tail of a viper (46). In the same vein Olivier describes women as "Bestiale barathrum," in other words an abyss of stupidity or *bêtise*, etymologically related to the word "beast." According to Olivier, women, like beasts, lack reason, which explains their lasciviousness: "Or il est hors de controverse que la femme ne soit plus lascive et plus insatiable de l'impure volupté que l'homme, et par consequent moins judicieuse et moins capable de raison en tous ses comportemens" ["Now it is undoubtedly the case that woman is more lascivious and insatiable with respect to impure sensuality than man, and consequently less judicious and capable of reason in her behavior"] (quoted in Timmermans, 245). Likewise, Boileau associates the image of the beastly woman with that of the lustful one in his Satire X.

Women's innate lustfulness is particularly highlighted in the discussion of opera's overpowering effect on even what might appear to be the most saintly of women. As his nephew Alcippe insists that his bride-to-be is virtuous, the satire's narrator responds:

> Par toi-même bientôt conduite à l'Opéra,
> De quel air penses-tu que ta sainte verra
> D'un spectacle enchanteur la pompe harmonieuse,
> Ces danses, ces héros à voix luxurieuse,
> Entendra ces discours sur l'amour seul roulants,
> Ces doucereux Renauds, ces insensés Rolands;
> Saura d'eux qu'à l'amour, comme au seul dieu suprême,
> On doit immoler tout, jusqu'à la vertu même . . .
> Et tous ces lieux communs de morale lubrique
> Que Lulli réchauffa des sons de sa musique?
>
> (105–6)

> [Soon you yourself will take her to the Opera,
> How do you think your saint will view
> The harmonious pomp of an enchanting spectacle,
> These dances, these heroes with luxurious voices,
> How will she receive these speeches on love,
> These suave Renauds, these foolish Rolands;
> Will she learn from them that for love, like to a supreme god,
> One must sacrifice everything, even virtue . . .
> And all these common motifs of lecherous morality
> That Lully rekindles with the sounds of his music?]

With its luxurious voices and lustful morality, opera enchants women, eliciting, to use Olivier's words, their "impure volupté."

Men, on the other hand, apparently remain unaffected by it: the narrator is not worried that opera will have the same effect on his nephew. In the same way that Boileau implicitly compares novels to poison in *Héros de roman,* Arnauld explicitly associates opera with poison in his defense of the Satire X, when he speaks of "le poison de ces chansons lascives" ["the poison of these lascivious songs"] (333) that insidiously insinuates itself in the female listener.

Like Boileau, Fénelon condemns opera, associating it with a disruptive, disorderly feminine threatening to Republics. He states: "les anciens croyoient que rien n'étoit plus pernicieux à une Republique bien policée que d'y laisser introduire une mélodie effeminée: elle énerve les hommes, elle rend les ames molles et voluptueuses: les tons languissants et passionez ne font tant de plaisir qu'à cause que l'ame s'y abandonne à l'attrait des sens" ["the ancients believed that nothing was more harmful to a well-ordered Republic than to allow for an effeminate melody; such music disturbs men, renders their souls soft and voluptuous: the languishing and passionate tones are pleasurable only because the soul is taken by the attraction of the senses"] (247).[11] Underlying the assumptions of each author is that what is qualified as feminine music renders the listener soft and malleable, which translates into becoming morally unsound. By contrast, the supposed solidity and sturdiness of masculine music upholds not only morality but also the state. Of course, none of our authors associate this masculine military music with the rape, pillage, and political disorder characteristic of war, much of which was going on right under their noses with the dragonnades against the Protestants.

Taking into account the associations Boileau creates between women, animality, and sexuality, it should come as no surprise that he furthermore associates women with the devil. Easily swayed by Satan, Lucifer, and the "démon du jeu" ["gambling demon"], women bring hell itself into the home: "Vrais démons [qui] apporte[nt] l'enfer dans leurs ménages" ["True demons who bring hell into their households"] (111). Within the specific context of his satire of the flirtatious coquette, Boileau's use of the rather innocuous term "cornettes" (107), referring to a woman's nightcap, takes on heightened meaning. The "corne" ["horn"] of "cornette" evokes images of both the devil and the cuckolded husband, and is reminiscent of late medieval texts that similarly associated women's hairstyles with the devil and the cuckold.[12] Connecting women with demons, hell, and the horns of Satan, Boileau depicts Woman as the devil's harpy, in line with demonologists from Kramer and Sprenger to Pierre de Lancre.

Although opera, novels, and a popular science that leads the overly curious learned lady to observe dissections are not the same thing as witchcraft, they nevertheless represent new, "heretical" forms of art and knowledge propagated by the Moderns. (Depicting a woman observing a dissection does recall images of witches and sorcerers cutting up human hearts at the Sabbath.) In the satire, Boileau's use of terms and analogies drawn from the discourse of the Counter-Reformation ends up equating the knowledge of the Moderns with heretical knowledge, often associated with witchcraft in the seventeenth century. The Counter-Reformation discourse on witchcraft and on heresy mutually reinforced each other. Among other things, they shared the topos of a dangerous and insatiable curiosity that led believers to abandon the "true" faith (Jacques-Chaquin, 109). In the same way that witchcraft and heresy divert the faithful from God and the Catholic Church, so novels, opera, and all that is modern draw people away from the "true" art, literature, and culture of the ancients and their heirs, so Boileau seems to suggest. Fénelon believed that attention to fashion and *nouveautés* had the effect of a "charme" (192) on girls and distracted them from attending to their salvation. Boileau similarly paints fashion and new trends, including the novel and opera, as destructive (the coquette ruins her husband in the name of fashion) and as vehicles of bad taste, rather than bad faith.

In the Satire X Boileau draws an implicit parallel between women as partisans of modernism and women as advocates of heresy (in the form of Protestantism or witchcraft). The figure of the false director who, "aidé de Lucifer" ["with Lucifer's help"], has his zealot taste in paradise "les plaisirs de l'enfer" ["the pleasures of hell"] (117), recalls renegade priests like Mariette and Tournet, both of whom were tried and executed for sorcery in 1668 and 1677 respectively (Mossiker, 128; 139–40). Although Boileau is attacking here the casuistry of the Jesuits, he nevertheless creates an analogy between the order, which he demonizes in the satire as apologists of sin, and abjured priests engaged in what was believed to be heretical—in other words, sinful—acts of witchcraft. Like the sorcerer-priest, Boileau's Jesuit casuist implicitly makes a pact with the devil and tempts the vulnerable (i.e., women) into following the ways of hell.

That readers of the satire associated Boileau's depictions of women with contemporary ideas about women and witchcraft is evident in the case of François Gacon. In his *Apologie pour Mr. Despreaux, ou Nouvêle Satire contre les Femmes* [Defense of Mr. Despreaux, or New Satire Against Women], published anonymously in 1695, Gacon defends the satire by making reference to contemporary cases of "witches" like the marquise de Brinvilliers and la Voisin, maintaining: "Qu'auroit-ce donc été si ta plume hardie, / Peignant *la Brinvilliers* des traits de *Canidie*, / Eut fait voir tout Paris en proye à ses poisons; / Sçavante en ce bel art, cheri de-là les Monts; / N'a-t-elle pas commis par *la Voisin* aidée, / Tous les maux dont la Fable a noirci sa *Medée*" ["What would have happened if your bold pen, / Depicting *la Brinvilliers* as *Canidie*, / Would have shown all Paris in the grips of her poisons; / Knowledgeable in this beautiful art cherished beyond the Mountains; / Did she not commit, with the help of *la Voisin*, / All the legendary evil acts that defamed *Medea*"] (2–3).[13] Wondering what would have happened had Boileau depicted Brinvilliers as Canidie (perhaps Brinvilliers would have had fewer victims?), he seems to suggest that Boileau's satire contains real and practical warnings about women and the potential danger they pose to social and especially to familial order.

In the end, Boileau depicts women as irrational, mad handmaids to heretical movements, using metaphors of witchcraft to express what he viewed as transgressive literary and social practices. At face value a satire against marriage, the Satire X is at heart a treatise against women's active or passive participation in literary, cultural, scientific, or even religious affairs. Although some scholars have argued that criticizing women in the Satire X was only a pretext to criticize the Moderns,[14] one wonders if the proposition needs to be reversed. In other words, perhaps Boileau's attack on the Moderns is just a pretext to condemn women, their tastes, and their general influence in society. For Boileau, women not only support the Moderns; they also shape their style, and are their primary devotees. In fact, male Moderns are practically women themselves: they are *damarets* or effeminate, and everything they produce smacks of the feminine. Using women or the feminine to discredit a movement, and particularly one that has made a place for women within it, ultimately is an attack on women themselves. It seems to me that Boileau would have defined his opposition to the Moderns much differently if women had not been implicated in the quarrel as writers, partisans, and *salonnières*.

THE *QUERELLE*

Although Charles Perrault's *Apologie des femmes* is the best-known response to the Satire X, it is perhaps not the most favorable to women. Whereas Perrault privileges a defense of marriage in his response to Boileau, other writers tend to privilege a defense of women. Writers like Jacques Nicolas Pradon, Pierre Bellocq, Jean-François Regnard, and Jean Donneau de Visé all reject the notion that women should somehow be "removed" from the sociocultural public sphere, and they bring to the fore ways in which women were victimized in late seventeenth-century French society. Before we examine Perrault's *Apologie*, let us first briefly examine the lesser-known responses in order to better assess the position Perrault took within the quarrel.

In his *Réponse à la Satire X du Sieur D**** (1694), Pradon proves to be closest ideologically to Perrault in his concern for the institution of marriage, and in particular, marriage as the vehicle for reproduction. Drawing on arguments that seem to come directly from Chaussé's treatise on marriage, Pradon contends that attacking marriage is like taking subjects away from the king, and faithful away from God (30).[15] Also borrowing from arguments Perrault presented in his *Parallèle des Anciens et des Modernes* (1688), Pradon further maintains that the refinement and politeness of the French court and of Paris are all due to the influence of women. Indeed, it is what makes France distinct from and serve as a model for other nations. Pradon's most crucial critique of the satire resides in what he perceives to be Boileau's agenda for women. He sees in Boileau's satire a justification for excluding women from the public sphere, even locking them up, stating: "Sans se servir icy [en France] comme en d'autres climats / De grilles, de verroux, de clefs, de cadenats, . . . L'honneur et la vertu servent icy de guides" ["Without using here [in France] as in other climates / Bars, bolts, padlocks, . . . Honor and virtue are our guides"] (35).

Perrault's *Parallèle* also provides inspiration, at least in its basic form, for Bellocq's response to the Satire X. In his *Lettre de Madame de N . . . A Madame la Marquise de . . . Sur la Satyre de M. D*** contre les Femmes* (1694), Bellocq has a lady, a knight, and an abbot discuss the Satire X. Notably, Bellocq replaces Perrault's president, a partisan of the ancients, with a lady of quality, thus including a woman in the debate. Taking a literary approach to their reading of the satire, the three characters criticize it for its stylistic and semantic shortcomings, as

well as its overall lack of verisimilitude. The three characters
find particularly troubling Boileau's discussion of the effects of
opera. First they wonder what the effect of opera would have, in
Boileau's view, on fathers and husbands. Then the abbot contests
the idea that a young, well-raised woman would simply throw
herself at a man the first time she went to see an opera, a ridiculous not to mention *invraisemblable* idea (9–10). By taking the
terms of the satire literally, Bellocq is able to poke fun at the satirist. In a similar move, Pradon concludes that Boileau must be
"un vray fils de P . . ." ["a true son of a W[hore]"] if all women
are as unfaithful as he claims (36).

Essentially a pastiche of Boileau's satire, Regnard's *Satire
contre les Maris* [Satire against Husbands] (1694) is perhaps the
most radical response in its depiction of the actual institutional
mechanisms that oppressed women. The satire's narrator tries
to dissuade his niece (we are to assume) Eudoxe from marrying
Alcippe, the nephew from Boileau's satire. He begins by discussing the inherent injustice of marriage between a young woman
raised in a convent, and a much older man whom she meets from
behind a grate and with whom she shortly thereafter must share
a bed (437).[16] From the gambler to the miser, the satire moves to
focus on the most abusive husbands: Alidor is so jealous of his
wife he mistreats her and locks her up with him; Licidas interned
his wife in a convent "par arrêt du sénat" ["by judgement of the
senate"], only to take a second wife three months later; and in
his rage Lisimon beats his better half (443–44). Regnard highlights the very real helplessness of women by underscoring the
institutional and legal advantages of husbands, making Boileau's
parallel representations look like what they are: base attacks on
women.

In his play *Les Dames Vengées* [The Avenged Ladies], first
staged in 1695, Donneau de Visé also takes the name Alcippe
from Boileau's satire, to whom is opposed his alter ego Lisandre.
Whereas we are to assume Alcippe resisted the lessons from his
uncle (he ends up happily married to Lisandre's sister Henriette), Lisandre is a philandering good-for-nothing whose negative views on women are simply a reflection of his own bad
behavior. His condemnations of women as superficial and deceitful justify his own chameleonlike behavior. At the same time that
the play's objective is to paint the woman-hater as a hypocrite
and to show that he might regret all he had said and done if he
falls in love one day, the play also is critical of the common practice of sacrificing daughters to consolidate the wealth and posi-

tion of the son. Lisandre falls in love with Hortense, not knowing that she was destined for the convent so that her brother Alcippe could marry Henriette. Her sacrifice is rendered unnecessary when Lisandre's miserly and sickly unmarried uncle (a figure for Boileau?) dies, leaving Alcippe everything. In the end, however, Hortense confines herself to the convent in a rather uneasy vengeance for women.

Although I do not wish to suggest that the positions of these writers are not unproblematic, they nevertheless present much stronger defenses of women and their role in society than does Charles Perrault, as we will see. For the most part these writers refuse the terms themselves of Boileau's characterization of women in the Satire X, and tend to question and relativize his representation of women's faults by bringing to the fore similar imperfections to be found in men. As such, they reject the notion that women need to be cloistered in order to protect social order. Donneau de Visé and especially Bellocq give voice to women and inscribe them into contemporary debates by including female characters in their apologies. Both Regnard and Donneau de Visé bring up the very real practices of marriage, supported by social and political institutions, that put women in a disadvantageous position with respect to men. Overall, each of these writers refuses the essentialist dichotomy Boileau sets up between male reason and female folly. Perrault, however, never refutes the underlying definition of women constitutive of Boileau's satire. Instead, he creates an opposition between bad public women and good domestic women, an opposition that takes women out of the public sphere.

From "Griselidis" to the *Apologie*

Perrault's *Apologie des femmes* can be read in conjunction with his earlier piece, "Griselidis," which the abbé de Lavau recited before the Académie Française on 25 August 1691.[17] "Griselidis" was published that same year in the *Recueil de plusieurs pièces d'éloquence et de poésie présentées à l'Académie française pour les prix de l'année 1691* [Collection of Several Pieces of Eloquence and Poetry Presented at the French Academy for the Prizes of the Year 1691] as well as in a separate edition. It was republished again in another collection in 1694 before it finally appeared in his *Contes en vers* [Fairy Tales in Verse] in 1695. In both "Griselidis" and the *Apologie* Perrault stresses the need to reproduce for familial, religious, and political reasons, and reaffirms the superior role of the husband and the subservient role of the wife in marriage. Women are limited to the domestic sphere, where they must nurse their children and attend to household duties. "Bad women" are located in the public sphere where they engage in leisure activities that endanger their reputation, not to mention their sanity. Ultimately, however, husbands are responsible for their wives behavior, and must know how to govern them properly. As such, Perrault's "Griselidis" and *Apologie* can be situated within the tradition of moralist writings about marriage, recalling works by writers like Jean Bouchet, Jacques Chaussé, and Fénelon.[18]

Boccaccio's "Griselda," the final story of his *Decameron* (1349–53), was translated into Latin by Petrarch in 1374, whereby the latinized name "Griseldis" came into being. Petrarch's version was diffused throughout France by Philippe de Mézières, who produced the earliest French translation of the tale around 1384, soon to be followed by Christine de Pizan's rendition, published in *Le Livre de la Cité des dames* [The Book of the City of Ladies] (1405). Primarily published within the genre of the *Miroir des dames mariées* [Mirror of Married Ladies], the tale was widely distributed in Paris as well as the provinces, with both a noble and bourgeois readership, throughout the fifteenth century (Golenistcheff-Koutouzoff, 131–32). It was still being republished in the seventeenth century. Editions of *Le Miroir des dames, ou la patience de Griseldis, autrefois Marquise de Saluces. Ou il est rémontré la vraye obéissance que les femmes vertueuses doivent à leurs maris* [The Mirror of Ladies, or the Patience of Griseldis, Formerly Marquise de Saluces. Where True Obedience Virtuous Wives Owe Their Husbands Is Demonstrated] were published, for instance, in Limoges (1660) and in Troyes (1690). Boccaccio's tale quickly became a widely disseminated handbook on how wives were suppose to conduct themselves in marriage. As the full title of the popular versions of "Griselidis" would suggest, the tale unambiguously equated feminine virtue with wifely obedience.[19]

From Petrarch to Perrault, authors and critics have highlighted allegorical readings of the tale. Griselidis subjecting herself to the marquis (or the prince, in Perrault's version) is read as an allegory of the faithful subjecting herself or himself to God, or as an allegory of patience (Griselidis) and wisdom (the marquis or prince), or one highlighting the relation between Christ and God.[20] However, the very idea that allegories of faith are expressed in terms of wifely submission only strengthens the imperative of the latter. It is difficult to imagine the possibility of there existing a widely accepted text in which a positive allegory of faith would be expressed in terms of husbandly obedience to his wife. The very implausibility of the idea is a sign of the cultural imbalance that existed (and that still exists) concerning the relation between the sexes. Moreover, the continuous reprinting of "Griselidis" as a *Miroir des dames mariées* from the fifteenth to the seventeenth centuries would suggest that, allegory or no allegory, the general public viewed the story as an exemplary one to which wives should adhere. Perrault says as much when he states: "la Morale de Griselidis . . . tend à porter les femmes à souffrir de leurs maris, et à faire qu'il n'y en a point de si brutal ni de si bizarre, dont la patience d'une honnête femme ne puisse venir à bout" ["the Moral of Griselidis . . . encourages wives to endure their husbands, and there is none so brutal or bizarre that the patience of an honest wife cannot overcome"] (*Contes*, 51). Although written within the specific context of his quarrel with Boileau, Perrault's *Apologie* is in many respects a reiteration of the central points of "Griselidis."

Both "Griselidis" and the *Apologie* open with a male character who refuses to marry. Whereas the tale's prince believes all women to be deceitful, vain, and hypocritical, the *Apologie*'s misanthropic son believes women to be unfaithful and worthy of scorn. Both characters are critical of such figures as the zealot, the coquette, the *précieuse*, the gambler, and generally speaking women who seek to "donner la loi" ["determine the law"] (*Contes*, 62; "Apologie," 259–62). Arguably, Perrault parodies the misogyny of La Bruyère in "Griselidis," and that of Boileau in the *Apologie*.[21] That being said, Perrault never puts into question their negative stereotypes of women. On the contrary, he leaves them fully intact. The *Apologie*'s narrator Timandre concedes: "Il est, j'en suis d'accord, des femmes infidèles, / Et dignes du mépris que ton coeur a pour elles" ["I agree, there are unfaithful women, / Worthy of the contempt your heart has for them"] (260).

In the *Apologie*, bad, disobedient women clearly are located in the public sphere, spaces Timandre refers to as "des lieux de plaisir" ["places of pleasure"] (262). Timandre's portrait of the coquette is exemplary in its depiction of the public woman: "A toute heure, en tous lieux, la coquette se montre; / Il n'est point de plaisirs où l'on ne la rencontre: / Allez au cours, au bal, allez à l'Opéra, / A la foire, il est sûr qu'elle s'y trouvera. / Il semble, à regarder l'essor de sa folie, / Que pour être partout elle se multiplie" ["At all hours, in all places, the coquette displays herself; / There are no amusements where one does not find her: / Go to the races, to the ball, go to the Opera, / She undoubtedly will be at the fair. / Seeing the flight of her folly, it seems / That she multiplies herself to be everywhere"] (261). Bad women are constantly seen and talked about, they are omnipresent, which explains why men take them to represent all women. A good woman, however, is one "dont on ne dit rien" ["about whom nothing is said"] (261). Because the public sphere is described in terms of pleasure, women's desire to participate actively within it takes on sexual overtones, which explains why one cannot find here "des femmes d'honneur" ["honorable women"] (262). By sexualizing their participation in public spaces, by suggesting the circulation of their images within public spaces negatively affects their reputation, Perrault implicitly associates such women with whores.[22]

When we consider that Perrault must have been influenced by Tertullian, whose *De l'Habillement des femmes* [The Apparel of Women] Perrault translated with his friend Beaurain around 1643, the associations he creates in both "Griselidis" and the *Apologie* between *mondain* women and whores come as no surprise. Tertullian argues that women should not dress ostentatiously, but rather should go about "in mourning garments . . . acting the part of mourning and repentant Eve in order to expiate more fully by all sorts of penitential garb that which woman derives from Eve—the ignominy, I mean, of original sin and the odium of being the cause of the fall of the human race" (117). On several occasions Tertullian likens "care of hair, and of the skin and of those parts of the body which attract the eye" to "prostitution" (123). Adorning oneself with fashionable clothes, styling or dying one's hair, and wearing makeup all are viewed as practices that corrupt nature, and as such, they are of the devil.[23] It is no wonder, then, that the prince of "Griselidis" immediately regrets the simplicity of his shepherdess after she is dressed in royal attire. Unlike other versions of the story, the prince takes back the pearls, rubies, and jewelry he had given her as presents, well before he takes away her daughter. The scene seems to allude to Tertullian's denunciation of women's worship of pearls and other gems—some of which are taken from the heads of dragons, which he associates with serpents—all of which is the work of the devil, and built on "this silly admiration of women" (Tertullian, 124–25). That Griselidis remains indifferent to such *mondain* concerns is a sign of her virtue and distinguishes her from all other women represented in the story.

Where Perrault differs with Boileau, then, is in his conviction that "good women" indeed exist. In the *Apologie*, Timandre explains to his son that it is only the women we see, in other words, women who are out in public, that are of questionable morality. In order to find an honorable woman, one must go to more obscure places:

> Va dans les hôpitaux, où l'on voit de longs rangs
> De malades plaintifs, de morts et de mourans . . .
> Descends dans des caveaux, monte dans des greniers,
> Où des pauvres obscurs fourmillent à milliers . . .
> Entre dans les réduits des honnêtes familles,
> Et vois y travailler les mères et les filles,
> Ne songeant qu'à leur tâche et qu'à bien recevoir
> Leur père ou leur époux quand il revient le soir.
>
> (262)

> [Go to the hospitals, where one sees long rows
> Of mournful sick people, of dead and dying . . .
> Go down into cellars, climb up into attics,
> Where the obscure poor swarm by the thousands . . .
> Enter the shacks of honest families,
> And see mothers and daughters working,
> Thinking only of their task and of receiving well
> Their father or husband, when he returns in the evening.]

Good, honorable women are located in domestic and abject spaces such as hospitals, attics, and hovels, which Perrault opposes to the *mondain* and secular spaces making up the sociocultural public sphere.[24] Death and poverty, rather than the potentially corruptive forces of pleasure and opulence, surround these women. Within such spaces women preoccupy themselves with domestic labor—feeding, cleaning, and caring for others—and do not concern themselves with more public and intellectual forms of activity such as judging and writing literary works. Such places not only are far removed from the sociocultural public sphere, but they also are hidden from public view, which explains why Timandre's son is unaware of the existence of such women. Not surprisingly, the prince of "Griselidis" finds his ideal woman, the daughter of a poor peasant, spinning in a remote part of the forest, far from the luxury and leisure of "corrupt" city women. At heart Perrault shares Boileau's ideas concerning women's innate immorality. However, by situating his ideal women in such abject conditions, Perrault shows that women can be restrained and redeemed through a life built on penance. Griselidis is exemplary in this matter.

In the previous chapter we noted that leisure time could be conceived of as the time for the production of the self. In both Boileau's satire and in Perrault's tale and apology, it is implicitly suggested that men have a right to leisure time, whereas for women, leisure leads to idleness and folly. Perrault's prince, for instance, can rationally enjoy "les beaux Arts," whereas the *précieuse*, "des beaux Arts follement curieuse" ["madly curious about the Arts"], can only irrationally engage in intellectual pursuits (*Contes*, 59, 62). In effect, Perrault denies women the right to cultivate, in other words, to "produce" themselves, which is particularly clear in "Griselidis." The prince's cruelty towards his wife is legitimated in terms of the "crowning" of Griselidis's virtue: "Je veux que plus encore on parle de la gloire / Dont j'aurai couronné sa suprême vertu" ["More than anything I wish people to speak of the glory / With which I crowned her supreme virtue"] (*Contes*, 86). At one point the prince is described as a "Forgeron" ["Blacksmith"] (*Contes*, 79), suggesting that he is indeed her creator. In other words, the prince produces or gives form to Griselidis as the supreme example of feminine virtue. Feminine virtue, then, is the creation of Man.

In the tale Perrault reproduces the idealist (Christian, Platonic) dichotomy equating women with matter and the body (sites of passion and sin), and men with form, the soul, and the mind (sites of reason). Left to their own devices, women can only construct themselves as insatiable and irrational monsters, for how can matter form itself? Men, however, can make of them virtuous and obedient wives. The idea of the husband molding his wife recalls the 1660 print, created in response to the salon movement, of the doctor Lustucru, who hammers wives' heads on an anvil to make them "good" (Warner, 27–29). Associating man with form and making of them the smiths of women's virtue lead writers like Perrault and Chaussé to assert that men, therefore, are the principal cause of their wives' misconduct. As Perrault remarks in the *Apologie*, husbands who fail to properly govern their wives cause female folly "par le dur excès de leur sévérité" ["by the harsh excess of their severity"] or "par leur indolence et leur trop de bonté" ["by their indolence and excessive goodness"] (263). Just as the mind must rule over the body, and reason over passion, so the husband must govern his wife.

In his *Pensées chrétiennes* [Christian Reflections], Perrault maintains that disorder, the result of sin, occurs when the inferior part, or the senses, goes against the superior part, or reason (70). Thus disorder in the family occurs when wives rule over or disobey their husbands.

Griselidis provides the perfect example of matter (or the inferior wife) completely subjugating itself to form (or the superior husband). This is emphasized early on in the tale, when Griselidis swears not to have another will than the prince's own; she is to *con-form* herself to him. In his *Pensées* Perrault states that the "péché d'Adam consiste principalement en ce qu'il a voulu avoir une volonté autre que celle de Dieu" ["sin of Adam principally resides in his wish to have a will other than that of God"] (18). Griselidis obeys and conforms herself to her husband in a way that Adam failed to obey and conform himself to God. If we accept that Griselidis is to the prince what Adam is to God, then wifely disobedience of the husband is constructed by Perrault in terms of sin, and as such it goes against the rational, not to mention Christian, order of things. As the very choice of the tale would suggest, Perrault defines feminine virtue in terms of wifely obedience, which is only reinforced in the *Apologie*.

In both "Griselidis" and the *Apologie*, women ultimately serve as the material base for the reproduction of patriarchal society. While "Griselidis" opens with the problem of the prince's political succession, the *Apologie* concerns the problem of familial succession and one's religious duty. The fact that the prince of "Griselidis" is both lord and husband brings together the political and the familial. In the tale, it is the prince's political duty to furnish his people with a successor.[25] In the *Apologie*, the very first issue raised is related only marginally to a defense of women; it concerns Timandre's desire to have heirs. Immediately after a description of the son, line 7 begins with: "Le père . . . voulait qu'une suite d'enfans / Pût transmettre son nom dans les siècles suivans" ["The father . . . wished that a succession of children / Could pass his name on into the following eras"] (259).

Reproduction means specifically reproduction of the male line, of the name of the father. Women are the material support, but it is men who provide the form.[26] Timandre entreats his son to reproduce "de toi . . . un autre toi-même" ["from yourself . . . another you"] (260), which suggests that the father "imprints" the form of his self onto the children in the same way that they are marked by his name. That this child would be born "from yourself" sounds as if Timandre's son were to bear his own child. The passage reads like a fantasy of male auto-reproduction, which highlights the fate Perrault reserved for women in marriage, limiting them to being the material support of the family. It is interesting to note that Perrault named his first two sons Charles-Samuel and Charles, clearly signaling Perrault's own need to reproduce his self. His wife, whom Perrault married when he was forty-four and when she was only nineteen, died some six months after the birth of their third son Pierre, living just long enough to furnish him with three sons, whom he took great care in raising himself. Perrault notably never remarried.

Marked by the name of the father, children are also his property. In "Griselidis," the daughter belongs to the prince, who may dispose of the child as he wishes. Whereas Griselidis performed her motherly (natural, material) duty by nursing the child herself, the father forms her by deciding to send her away to be educated. Although this is only a pretext to take the child away from Griselidis, the girl nevertheless is raised in an austere monastery of his choosing, from behind a grate. (Pradon and Regnard notably regard the grate as a sign of women's oppression.) In other versions of the tale, the children are entrusted to a female relative of the marquis; neither the daughter nor the son is raised within the Church. Rather than have the daughter be brought up by a female relative, Perrault has the daughter educated by an abbess, a cloistered and docile woman married to the Church and to God, the ultimate Father who forms the child. (Interestingly, Perrault's own wife, whom he saw only once outside the convent before marrying, was raised in a convent from the age of four.)[27] As the tale suggests, the prince has the right to dispose of the life of "his" child, and Griselidis's virtue resides in her accepting with constancy the fate he reserves for her own daughter.

In his *Apologie* Perrault fails to refute anything Boileau says about women in the Satire X, except that virtuous women indeed exist. However, the fact that Perrault situates virtuous women in such abject conditions, in spaces of internment, and defines their virtue in terms of total, even masochistic submission to men, makes his defense of women hardly comforting. Ultimately Perrault defends marriage more than he defends women in his *Apologie des femmes*, and a type of marriage based on a patriarchal authority that views itself as being akin to the authority of God. In the end, Perrault defends women only to defend the institution of marriage as a vehicle for social, political, and religious reproduction, much in line with the ideas of Jacques Chaussé. What

distinguishes the positions taken by Boileau and Perrault in relation to women is above all the traditions from which they write.
Whereas Boileau's satire can be located within the gaulois tradition of *molestiae nuptiarum*, Perrault's works set the groundwork for and anticipate the bourgeois misogyny of the eighteenth
and nineteenth centuries that sought to circumscribe women's
activity to the domestic sphere of the patriarchal family. Basically, Boileau and Perrault share similar views of women, but
they write from different perspectives and traditions, the Ancient
drawing from medieval and humanist stereotypes of women, and
the Modern formulating new notions of the domestic and subservient housewife.[28]

Both Boileau's Satire X and Perrault's *Apologie* were written
in response to the overwhelming influence of upper-class women
in Parisian society, exercised through the cultural institution of
the salon. Both Boileau and Perrault were academicians, and as
active defenders of the authority of the Académie Française, they
had good reasons to put into question the legitimacy of women's
cultural activity and authority within the sociocultural public
sphere. In order to delegitimate women's intellectual pursuits,
both writers portray women as being incapable of conducting
themselves properly in the public sphere—and Perrault furthermore puts them in their "rightful" place. The acerbic tone
Boileau takes in his satire has led some critics to make excuses
for Perrault's kinder, gentler approach to misogyny. Opening up
the terms of the quarrel to its minor participants like Pradon, Bellocq, Regnard, and Donneau de Visé, however, makes us realize
that we do not need to settle for what some critics have viewed
as the "lesser evil" in this debate.

THE ABJECTIFICATION OF WOMEN IN THE TALES

Female characters of Perrault's tales can be divided into obedient, submissive, patient women, on the one hand, and disobedient ones, the most extreme of which exhibit traits that recall the
figure of the witch, on the other.[29] Witchcraft and madness went
hand in hand in the early modern period. As Nicole Jacques-Chaquin has argued, satanic knowledge was perceived to be a disordered knowledge (111), much like the disordered thoughts of a
mad person, or the disordered thoughts, as described by Fénelon, of women: "elles ne choisissent point entre leurs pensees;
elles n'y mettent aucun ordre par rapport aux choses qu'elles ont

a expliquer" ["they do not chose among their thoughts; they apply no order to the things they have to explain"] (180). Women, the satanic, and the mad were viewed as bestial, which justified the abusive treatment of the latter in asylums: "Unbridled animality, they can only be controlled by *taming them and dulling the mind*" (Foucault, 94). Eve's association with the serpent, sexuality, and sin haunts the literature on demonology, not to mention treatises on marriage and on the education of girls.

Such associations underlying the belief in the "inherent" bestial, disorderly nature of women provide insights into Perrault's treatment of women in his tales. While "good women" seem to be kept in check by the abject conditions that make their virtue shine, "bad women" display transgressive behavior that leads to their fall—or close to it. Perrault's depictions of women justify, much like Boileau, the need to take women out of the public sphere, including positions of authority, in order to maintain not only social and political order, but religious order as well.

Exemplary in her submission, suffering, and patience, Griselidis serves as the model for all positive heroines in Perrault's tales. In the same way that Griselidis subjects herself to an abusive, tyrannical husband, Donkey Skin is reduced to cleaning rags and pigpens under the skin of a domestic animal in order not to disobey her incestuous father, and Cinderella is given the responsibility for the "plus viles occupations de la Maison" ["the most vile household chores"] before being rewarded with a prince (171). With the exception of Sleeping Beauty, who only attempts to spin, each of Perrault's heroines occupies herself with domestic labor, which would be most uncommon for the upper-class women of the salons Perrault frequented, not to mention for a princess. Each of the heroines shares the quality of patience: Cinderella "souffrait tout avec patience" ["suffered everything patiently"] (171), and Sleeping Beauty, unlike most women, could wait a hundred years to marry. They are all blindly obedient, illustrating the moral of "Peau d'âne" ["Donkey Skin"]: "il vaut mieux s'exposer à la plus rude peine / que de manquer à son devoir" ["it is better to expose oneself to the harshest difficulties / than to neglect one's duty"] (115). Perrault's tales attempt to lure women into submission, suggesting that if they subject themselves to pain and hardship—without resistance and with absolute constancy—they will be rewarded with a prince.

Considering the social status of positive heroines, it is curious that Perrault subjects them to such abject conditions. Donkey

Skin not only covers herself in a "vilaine crasse" ["vile filth"] (105); she must also put up with people well below her actual status calling her "noire Taupe" ["black Mole"], identifying her with an animal that lives underground, and "Marmiton" or "kitchen hand," associating her with the lowliest of domestic positions (109). Her Italian counterparts were not reduced to being the absolute lowest person, a "sale guenon" ["dirty monkey"] (112), within the social hierarchy. To escape her incestuous father, Straparola's Doralice takes a magic potion that allows her to forego eating, and she locks herself up in a chest that subsequently is sent to England. Although she does do some domestic chores and at one point is tortured, she ends up marrying a prince without her father's consent, and her deceptive father is quartered and his flesh thrown to the dogs (*Great Fairy Tale*, 27-33). Basile's Preziosa is given the ability to turn herself into a bear; she then flees into the forest to escape her perverse father and eventually marries a prince (*Great Fairy Tale*, 33–38). Whereas Doralice cleans a prince's room, Donkey Skin cleans pigpens. While Preziosa is turned into a bear, Donkey Skin is forced to wear the dead, excremental skin of a donkey. Both Doralice and Preziosa are active and sexual beings without being demonized, whereas Donkey Skin is the desexualized object of contemplation for the prince.[30]

It is significant that Donkey Skin, like Cinderella, is reduced to being a "souillon" ["dirty servant"], etymologically related to "souillure," meaning "stain" or "sin." Marked by the stain of Eve, Perrault's positive heroines must be purged of that which makes them sinful and threatening: their feminine will and their sexuality. Each of these heroines descends into a veritable hell, into absolute abjection, becoming socially marginalized objects of disdain. If they are to be reintegrated into society, all that makes them socially and even politically dangerous must be sublimated or repressed. Taking them through insult, abuse, the basest forms of work, and death in the case of Sleeping Beauty, their penance is a process of purification. Their abject nature is exteriorized in the visible vileness of their lowly occupations and dirty faces, which is eventually expelled from their being by the end of the tale. As a result, the power and threat of the feminine is subdued.

Julia Kristeva has argued that the abject "would be, then, the object of primary repression" (20). In Perrault's tales, the feminine is the abject, taking concrete form in all that is dirty, excremental, and animal-like. Herself an uncontrollable beast, Woman can only be mastered by the taming and dulling that eventually expurgates any threat the feminine might pose. That Perrault's sadistic male characters are ambivalent figures of power, that he parodies everyone from La Bruyère, Boileau, and Louis XIV, does not take away from the role he reserves for his female protagonists as their designated and sanctioned victims. Maybe Griselidis's prince went too far, but Griselidis is glorified all the more for having submitted to his albeit sadistic will that ultimately served to purify her virtue. Although the king of "Peau d'âne" is perverse, and his incestuous desires should release the princess from any obligation to obey him, the tale's moral insists that she unconditionally honor her father, which ends up bringing her glory. Moreover, the beginning of the tale intimates that the princess herself bears some of the responsibility. She possesses "certains tendres appas" ["certain tender charms"] (100), so many lures ["appâts"] that solicit the perverse and dangerous love of her father. After her trajectory, moving from abjection to purification, she no longer inspires such criminal flames in her father who, far from being quartered and thrown to the dogs as in Straparola's tale, is welcomed into the family at the end of the story. In the end, feminine will and the lure of female sexuality are put in check; they are controlled and dominated, through a process of abjection.

If we resituate the analysis within the sociocultural domain, we could read Perrault's "abjectification" of women in terms of his desire to purge the public sphere of influential women. With few exceptions, most female characters are princesses or upper-class women with significant power in society. Whereas the positive heroines all are reduced to the lowest positions within the social hierarchy at one point in each tale before their virtue is rewarded, the negative ones similarly are humiliated and either must repent or be killed off. In Perrault's dedicatory epistle of "Griselidis," the narrator clearly expresses disdain for Parisian women, whom he sarcastically describes as so many queens: "Les femmes y sont souveraines, / Tout s'y règle selon leurs voeux, / Enfin c'est un climat heureux / Qui n'est habité que de Reines" ["Women are sovereign here, / Everything adheres to their wishes, / At last it is a happy climate / Which is inhabited by Queens"] (57). In his dedicatory epistle to "Les Souhaits ridicules" ["Foolish Wishes"], the *précieuse*, who would judge a story about a sausage to be "une horreur" and who only values stories about love, similarly is mocked for her pretensions of literary authority (119). Perrault singles out *mondain* women for reproach in the prefaces to his tales.

Much like Boileau, Perrault constructs women as creatures who wish to dominate and judge literary matters (among other things), and much like Boileau, Perrault views female domination as tyranny, and feminine judgement as faulty. Through his tales, Perrault "abjectifies" potentially powerful and influential women in order to symbolically exclude them from or at least circumscribe their influence within the public sphere, consequently consolidating male authority. In her discussion of the abject, Judith Butler maintains: "the repudiation of bodies for their sex, sexuality, and/or color is an 'expulsion' followed by a 'repulsion' that founds and consolidates culturally hegemonic identities along sex/race/sexuality axes of differentiation" (133). Purging the public sphere of women, of the feminine, makes of women "excrement," the abject from which the male subject differentiates himself and which he attempts to repress and dominate. Erica Harth has argued that in seventeenth-century France, the "salon and the academy entered into a gendered competition with each other for intellectual space" (*Cartesian*, 17). It is this competition that explains Perrault's implicit and explicit condemnations of *mondain* women in his tales. As a Modern, Perrault signals his supposed support for women by giving them marginal importance in his *Parallèle* and by writing his *Apologie des femmes*. As an academician, however, he clearly upholds the ultimate authority of men in cultural and political affairs.

DISOBEDIENT WOMEN

Feminine disobedience takes several forms in Perrault's tales, including transgressive or uncivil speech, transgressive eating habits, and female curiosity, or transgressive knowledge. As the father of the *Apologie* maintains, good women are women who are neither seen nor spoken about, and we might add: who do not speak. Mistreated by her widowed mother and abused by her sister, the Cinderella-like unnamed heroine of "Les Fées" ["The Fairies"] comes upon a poor woman—in reality a fairy—who asks for something to drink. In a most unprecious manner, the girl answers: "Oui-da ma bonne mère" ["You bet, my good mother"] (165), and serves her some water. Consequently, she is rewarded with the gift of emitting roses, pearls, and diamonds with each word she pronounces. Given her speech acts thus far in the tale, we can imagine that she would accumulate only a modest fortune. Her sister Fanchon, however, does not fare so well.

Upon learning of her daughter's gift, the mother orders a reluctant Fanchon to seek out the same poor woman in hopes that she too would receive such a gift. However, "la brutale" (166) cannot contain her hostility in serving the fairy, who appears before her as a beautiful princess. Fanchon's negative passion overflows in her words: "Est-ce que je suis ici venue . . . pour vous donner à boire? Justement j'ai apporté un Flacon d'argent tout exprès pour donner à boire à Madame! J'en suis d'avis, buvez à même si vous voulez" ["Did I come here . . . just to give you something to drink? As it happens, I brought a silver flask just to fetch Madame a drink! You know what I think, get your own drink if you would like one"] (166). Her bad nature is expressed not only by her refusal to serve, but also in the sarcastic, insolent nature of her speech. The nameless sister's simple, naive, and obliging speech is opposed to Fanchon's complicated speech that moves from artifice, also signaled by the silver flask she unnecessarily brought to serve the woman, to insolence. The fact that Fanchon talks too much only serves to enhance her negative traits. As such, her punishment is to emit toads and serpents with each word she pronounces. In the end, the unnamed, anonymous girl marries the prince, and Fanchon, abandoned by her own mother, dies alone in the woods.

Whereas positive female characters bear original sin like a cross in order to purify the soul, unrepentant female characters must be made to see their sin through such punishments. Like the donkey of "Peau d'âne," the unnamed heroine of "Les Fées" emits a purified excrement. Through the process of abjectification and purification, shit is turned into gold, and the *souillon* becomes a princess. However, unrepentant women who fail to tie their tongues and fulfill their destiny of serving others are made to wear a scarlet letter. Fanchon is forced to display through her body toads and serpents, symbols of witchcraft and externalized signs of her own sin and vice that lead to her ostracization and death.

It should come as no surprise that the badmouthing wife of "Les Souhaits ridicules" also is named Fanchon. Though the husband of the story is indeed foolish, it is perhaps less for his wishes than for not knowing how to control his wife, who yells at him using foul language when he inadvertently wishes for a length of sausage. Unable to take his wife's abuse, Blaise, the henpecked husband, uses his second wish to hang the sausage from his wife's nose, thus impeding his wife from speaking. The serpentine sausage comes to signify the use of her tongue for vulgar words, speech acts that Chaussé refers to as fornication of the mouth: "O langues serpens qui répandent par tout le mortel venin de leur soûillûres! O langues de Démons, qui ne se plaisent que dans l'impureté, et qu'à parler le langage des Enfers!" ["O serpent tongues that spread everywhere the deadly venom of their sins! O tongues of Demons that only take pleasure in impurity and in speaking the language of Hell!"] (89). Such images bring to mind the serpent in the garden of Eden, and Eve's own loose tongue that brought the fall of humankind.[31]

Given the specific context of the tale, we might also read the scene as one in which the disobedient wife grows the phallus that she has already usurped in usurping the husband's authority. In other words, her transgression is made visible through the sausage. Finally in a position of power, Blaise is caught in a dilemma: he can either remove the sausage and return Fanchon to her former beauty, or become king and share the scepter with an ugly queen. He consults Fanchon, who decides to renounce the scepter and regain her beauty. Ridding herself of the sausage means giving up the scepter, both of which can be viewed as Fanchon's symbolic castration. Already roles have begun to be reversed (in other words, brought to "normal") when Blaise has the power to remove the sausage, and Fanchon is at his mercy. We can safely assume by the end of the tale that the humiliated Fanchon takes her "rightful" place beside—not above—her husband, and that Blaise has regained some control in the home. Unrepentant of her feminine nature and daring to usurp male authority, Fanchon is made to bear the sign of her sin: the sausage. The fact that Fanchon renounces the phallus—that is, she renounces her authority in the home and relinquishes power to her husband—means that she can be reintegrated into, in this case, the order of the family.

In "La Belle au bois dormant" ["Sleeping Beauty"], it is the queen mother who represents feminine transgression, this time in the form of transgressive eating habits. Although we know that the mother of the prince who awakens Sleeping Beauty is of the race of ogres, she does not act upon her ogress instincts until she becomes regent; that is, until she is in a position of political power. While the king is alive and while her son rules, she can repress her ogress desire to consume children. (That she wishes to eat Sleeping Beauty, then, puts the princess in the category of children.) But the minute masculine authority is suspended, her perverse impulses can no longer be kept in check.[32] The very first action she takes as regent is to send her daughter-in-law Sleeping Beauty and her two grandchildren Jour and Aurore to a country home "pour pouvoir plus aisément assouvir son horrible envie" ["to more easily be able to satisfy her horrible craving"] (137). Female rule is made monstrous in the association Perrault creates between the queen mother's regency and her cannibalism. In other words, female rule is a transgression of political order in the same way that cannibalism is a perversion of alimentary order.

Despite the fact that masculine authority can keep the queen's desires at bay, she nevertheless always represented a potential threat. Overcoming any disgust he might have had about her ogress nature, the king married her for "ses grands biens" ["her great riches"] (137), meaning that the queen possesses considerable independent wealth. Well before she becomes regent, people at court suspect her of having ogress inclinations, and her son the prince fears her. Upon becoming regent, no longer restrained by masculine authority, the queen's malevolent power is unleashed. It manifests itself in her cannibalistic desires and takes on witchlike dimensions when she prepares the pot of toads and vipers she intends to use to execute her son's family after discovering her Maître d'Hôtel saved their lives. Her witchlike nature is alluded to already at the beginning of the story. Before discovering the truth about Sleeping Beauty and her castle from an old peasant man, the prince hears rumors that Spirits live there. Others believe that "tous les Sorciers de la contrée y faisaient leur sabbat" ["all the Witches of the region held their Sabbath here"] (134), and yet others are convinced that an ogre inhabits the castle, where he carries off children to devour. The rumors are rather ironic, for Sleeping Beauty is completely and utterly harmless. Given the fact that the queen is an ogress, however, it is as if the rumors about Sleeping Beauty's castle refer instead to the queen. They prepare us for the end of the tale, when the queen's ogress and witch nature are given free reign in the absence of male authority. In the end, female political authority is conflated with cannibalism and witchcraft; it is delegitimated as tyrannical and perverse.

It is important to note that transgression of parental, even political authority and moral norms is to some degree permissible for male characters. For instance, in "La Belle au bois dormant," the prince first marries the princess without parental consent and then has two undeclared children. Both of these actions were illegal throughout the seventeenth century.[33] Even though Sleeping Beauty arguably committed the same transgressions, she has no parents to speak of, she exists in and is from another world, and she plays such a passive role in the story that it would be difficult to say that she does anything at all but wait for her prince. Whereas Donkey Skin must endure great hardships so as not to directly disobey her incestuous father, Sleeping Beauty's prince can be somewhat carefree in his disobedience, particularly since he will himself "become the law" when he takes over his father's throne. Likewise, the prince of "Peau d'âne" can peek through the keyhole and spy on the princess with impunity, while the heroine of "La Barbe bleue" ["Bluebeard"] nearly loses her life for peering into the forbidden chamber. In "Le Petit Poucet" ["Little Thumbling"], the title character implicitly disobeys his parents in his constant attempts to outwit them, and the cat in "Le Chat botté" ["Puss-in-Boots"] goes so far as to fool even kings. In the Italian versions by Straparola and Basile of this last tale, the trickster-cat notably is female, suggesting that Perrault, who probably was familiar with at least Straparola's version, consciously substituted a male for a female cat.[34]

Positive male characters in Perrault's tales are enterprising and often challenge authority. Positive female characters' sphere of action, however, is highly restricted, limited to passive actions such as patience (waiting, sleeping) and obedience (adherence to the will of husbandly or parental authority). That Perrault changed the sex of the cat in "Le Chat botté" clearly shows he did not wish to depict his positive female characters as clever and resourceful. The morals of the tales consistently reiterate the theme of feminine submission to male authority, regardless of the specific situation in which the heroine finds herself.

THE STRANGE CASE OF MR. AND MRS. BLUEBEARD

One tale stands out in its highly ambivalent representation of feminine disobedience and male authority: "Barbe bleue." Whereas the prince of "Griselidis" and especially the father of "Peau d'âne" can be viewed as somewhat problematic male characters, they nevertheless are redeemed by the end of the tale. Ultimately their sadism—especially that of the prince— serves to underscore the virtue (measured in terms of the servility) of the heroines in question. Bluebeard, on the other hand, is monstrous in a way that goes beyond redemption. Compared to Bluebeard, the prince of "Griselidis" represents a tempered, almost rational sadism in the way that he calculates the effects of his actions on the crowning of his wife's virtue. Whereas the prince's severity stresses the extent to which Griselidis is virtuous, which is determined by the extent to which her will conforms to his own, Bluebeard represents an extreme, negative form of husbandly authority that exceeds coercing the wife into passivity to actually rendering her lifeless. Naturally, Perrault situates such terrible husbands in the past, humorously declaring that modern husbands now do the knitting, thus exculpating his male contemporaries from the tale's reproof of bad husbands.

In effect, "Barbe bleue" could be read as the parallel opposite of "Les Souhaits ridicules." In both tales, the wife transgresses husbandly authority, either verbally, as in the case of "Les Souhaits ridicules," or impelled by excessive curiosity, as in the case of "Barbe bleue." In both tales, the wife appropriates the husband's phallus or authority, symbolized by the sausage, in the first tale, and by the fairy key, in the second. And in both tales the husbands are imperfect, Blaise representing the weak husband, and Bluebeard the tyrannical one. As such, they implicitly are to blame for their wives' transgressions for, as Perrault already stated in the *Apologie*, husbands often are the principal cause of their wives' follies by reason of their hard and excessive severity, or their indolence and being too good natured. Neither Fanchon nor Bluebeard's wife is fully responsible for their misconduct, due to the fact that their husbands are too weak or too tyrannical to provide good examples and properly mold them. Moreover, both husbands to some degree are "feminized." Blaise allows his wife to wear the pants in the house, and Bluebeard embodies artifice, counternature, and seduction—concepts generally associated with women.

At the very beginning of Perrault's tale, Bluebeard is portrayed first in relation to his belongings. Whereas the wealth of male characters usually is described in general terms, the narrator of Bluebeard goes into some detail, listing not only his estates but also his household furnishings, like silver and gold dishes, and embroidered furniture, belongings typically associated with or of interest to women. Then he is described by his physical appearance, in particular his blue beard. As Marina Warner explains, beards evoked the image of goats, viewed as lustful and diabolical in their association with Pan and the Devil (242). In Counter-Reformation France, such a beard likely would have been read as a sign of male debauchery, in the same way that certain female hairstyles were viewed as impious. Warner notes that beards were far from fashionable at Louis XIV's court, meaning that a beard would have been the mark of an outsider, in other words, a "barbare," which recalls the word "barbe." Warner maintains that Bluebeard "is represented as a man against nature, either by dyeing his hair like a luxurious Oriental, or by producing such a monstrous growth without resorting to artifice" (242–43). The orientalist association is implied in the 1695 illumination, in which Bluebeard was represented as a pirate (see Velay-Vallentin, 71), the most notorious of the period being the Barbary pirates of Ottoman North Africa. In the 1695 illustration, Bluebeard is notably darker than his wife, and both characters are dressed in red, underscoring the role of passion in the tale. Although Perrault's 1697 edition represents Bluebeard as a bourgeois, the earlier image of the pirate suggests that Perrault imagined his character to have criminally acquired his wealth, and that he intended Bluebeard to exhibit the luxurious tendencies and even the tyranny believed to be characteristic of Orientals—traits also associated, as we have seen, with women.[35]

Described in terms of artifice and counternature, Bluebeard also is characterized by seduction. By holding festivities for eight days and displaying throughout his enormous wealth, Bluebeard ends up seducing the youngest daughter of an impoverished noblewoman, who finally agrees to marry him. After the eight days are up, Bluebeard no longer disgusts her, but rather has become "un fort honnête homme" ["quite an honest man"] (149) in her eyes. Like a witch, Bluebeard can "poison the mind" of vulnerable young women, leading them to take the devil for an *honnête homme* through a show of artifice. In the tale, seduction is also linked to the secret knowledge with which Bluebeard seems to intentionally tempt his young bride into disobedience. Secret knowledge is the knowledge of witches and sorcerers; it is ungodly knowledge, as Bluebeard's wife and the reader are to discover as the plot unfolds. And it is secret knowledge in particular that elicits female curiosity.[36]

When Bluebeard's wife invites her neighbors (*les voisines*) and friends (*les bonnes amies*) to the house after Bluebeard's departure, they all seem driven by a curiosity to examine his treasures: "tant elles avaient d'impatience de voir toutes les richesses de sa Maison, n'ayant osé y venir pendant que le Mari y était . . . Les voilà aussitôt à parcourir les chambres, les cabi-

la Barbe bleüe

Conte

Il estoit unefois un hom-
me, qui auoit de belles maisons a la ville, et a la
campagne, dela vaisselle
d'or et d'argent des meubles
en broderie, et des carosses
tout dorez mais qui par
malheur auoit la barbe bleüe

Illustration of Bluebeard from the 1695 edition of Charles Perrault's
Contes de ma Mère l'Oye. Courtesy of the Pierpont Morgan Library.

L A
BARBE BLEÜE

IL eſtoit une fois un homme qui avoit de belles maiſons à la Ville & à la Campagne, de la vaiſſelle d'or & d'argent, des meubles en broderie; & des ca-

Illustration of Bluebeard from the 1697 edition of Charles Perrault's *Histoires ou contes du temps passé: avec des moralitez* (Amsterdam: Jacques Desbordes). Courtesy of the Pierpont Morgan Library.

nets, les garde-robes. . . . Elles montèrent ensuite aux garde-meubles, où elles ne pouvaient assez admirer le nombre et la beauté des tapisseries, des lits, des sofas, des cabinets" ["they were so impatient to see all the riches of her Home, not daring to come when the Husband was there. . . . There they were going through the rooms, closets, wardrobes. . . . Then they went up into the storerooms, where they could not admire enough the quantity and beauty of the tapestries, beds, sofas, cabinets"] (150). The impatience of the wife to examine the contents of the forbidden chamber is matched by that of her female guests, who behave like ransacking thieves as they go through Bluebeard's riches. Again, female disobedience—here taking the form of excessive curiosity—occurs when male authority is absent. Both the "hidden" treasures of Bluebeard's home and the contents of the forbidden chamber are implicitly and explicitly the booty of a crime, suggesting the object of female curiosity is somehow criminal or taboo.[37] While the other women's curiosity leads to a covetousness bordering on idolatry in their admiration of Bluebeard's criminal riches, the unnamed heroine's curiosity leads her to disobey, to sin against her husband. That she indeed sinned is emphasized in the scene where she asks her husband's forgiveness "avec toutes les marques d'un vrai repentir de n'avoir pas été obéissante" ["with all the marks of true repentance for not having been obedient"] (152). From the parallel Perrault establishes between the friends' curiosity and that of the heroine, we can safely deduce that any one of these women would have violated the prohibition to enter the forbidden room. In effect, they are all guilty.

Behind the moralizing discourse on feminine curiosity lies the will to exclude women from knowledge in order to better keep them in line: "Pour les filles, dit-on, il ne faut pas qu'elles soient sçavantes, la curiosité les rend vaines et precieuses, il suffit qu'elles sçachent gouverner un jour leurs ménages, et obeïr à leurs maris sans raisonner" ["Regarding girls, it is said that they should not be knowledgeable, curiosity makes them vain and affected, it suffices that they know how to run their household one day, and obey their husbands without thinking about it"] (Fénelon, 2).[38] Restricting knowledge makes for docile wives. Keeping novels away from girls, for instance, is a way to get them to accept the menial chores of domestic life.[39] Curiosity exposes women to forms of knowledge and to information—from witchcraft to Cartesianism to discovering the neighbor's new coach—

that in turn lead them to be disobedient, thus disturbing domestic order and hierarchy.

In the case of "Barbe bleue," female curiosity ends up being less transgressive or at least more complicated than it might seem at first glance. As critics from Philip Lewis and Jean-Marie Apostolidès to Patricia Hannon have remarked, the status of Bluebeard's wealth is problematic, for no one knows exactly its source. Unlike other heroes, whose wealth is explained through the story or by virtue of their status, the source of Bluebeard's wealth remains dubious. From the very beginning of the tale Bluebeard's wealth solicits the readers' as well as the other characters' curiosity. Although the heroine could have avoided the trauma of nearly being beheaded had she respected her husband's command, the enigma Bluebeard represents lessens the crime of female disobedience. He bears some of the blame for having such an ambiguous status that demands explanation. Moreover, Bluebeard himself is a primary source of household disorder in his tyranny that leads him to kill his wives.

Well before opening the door to the secret chamber, the heroine already made her pact with the devil by marrying Bluebeard for his wealth. Although the pact could be read in terms of the youngest daughter voluntarily sacrificing herself to consolidate the wealth of the family, it is nevertheless a Faustian deal. We might even think of Bluebeard as metonymically representing the tyrannical passion of covetousness, exemplified in his hoarded wealth and collection of dead wives he completely possesses; or that of luxuriousness, exhibited in the parties given to seduce the heroine. He could well be read as the beast of the heroine's own passions that nearly brought about her death. Whereas the "good husband" is associated with God and positive virtues, the "bad husband," the false *honnête homme*, is a sort of devil figure who is characterized by negative passions.[40] In "Barbe bleue," the disobedient heroine does not betray the order of the Christian family, but rather infringes on the mock order of the devil's. Philip Lewis compares Bluebeard forbidding his wife to enter the secret *cabinet* to God forbidding Adam to eat from the tree of knowledge (*Seeing*, 221). To modify this affirmation slightly, we might read the scene as a "mock fall," where it is the devil and not God who issues the prohibition, only to conceal his true identity from the heroine.

At the same time that the scene of interdiction plays on the theme of female curiosity, it also highlights the tyranny of Bluebeard. The apparent arbitrariness of his command not to open the room is doubled by the underlying tyranny of a character who has murdered several women. In and of itself, the order is an absolute one with no apparent justification. Some critics have suggested that the wife somehow is guilty of adultery, whether early on in the tale, at Bluebeard's lavish parties, or while he is away on business.[41] The violation of the prohibition not to enter the room and the blood on the key, then, signal her infidelity, and provide some justification for Bluebeard's reaction. However, in the early modern period feminine disobedience in general and female curiosity in particular were expressed in terms of sexual transgression. Adultery served as a metaphor for female disobedience, regardless of the specific form it took.[42] Thus the heroine's excessive curiosity to peer inside the room, described as a temptation to which she succumbs, is merely *figured* in terms of adultery, but *it is not adultery.* Yet the act nearly is punished as such by a barbaric husband, who takes the figurative literally, signaling a lack of subtlety that would pass for barbaric in Parisian high society. In order to represent Bluebeard as the tyrannical husband, the punishment must exceed the crime, so the ungodly husband is prepared to execute his wife for simply opening a door he forbid her to open. As Lewis contends, "the truth of the secret is that there is no secret . . . the victim's ordeal was essentially a test of her obedience" (208). The law of the false father is the law of literal and brute force.

However, the heroine does in fact discover a secret. By disobeying her husband she finds out that he is not an *honnête homme* at all. Like a second Eve, the heroine learns the difference between good and evil upon opening the door to the forbidden chamber. Behind Bluebeard's great riches, wealth, and opulent festivities that seduced her into accepting him as an *honnête homme*, his wife discovers the devil himself. Bluebeard's status is no longer problematic or ambiguous: he clearly and unambiguously is evil. The knowledge the heroine has gained can potentially allow her to unmask her husband and thus destroy him, which explains why he must destroy her first. Though guilty of transgression herself, due to her feminine weakness (as many Christian moralists would argue), her sin is practically effaced, eclipsed as it is by the monstrosity of her husband and his actual identity. Can one truly sin against the devil?

Nevertheless "Barbe bleue" is a warning tale, demonstrating the potential deadly consequences of curiosity and wifely disobedience. It also suggests that women should be careful when choosing a husband, and must not be swayed by external appearances or by lust for material wealth. Having learned her lesson, now able to distinguish between good and evil, the heroine ends up marrying a true *honnête homme,* and we can easily imagine that she will prove to be an obedient wife. Although the heroine distributes the booty at the end of the tale, she does so only to strengthen the position of her family—particularly her brothers—which is why she married Bluebeard in the first place. As the youngest daughter of an impoverished noble family, she likely would have ended up in a convent had she not married the wealthy Bluebeard who, dead or alive, would have bolstered her family's situation. As Lewis notes, masculine authority is reestablished at the end of the tale, with the heroine's brothers consolidating their positions in society, while she puts herself under the tutelage of another man *(Seeing,* 234–44). In the end, the false masculine order of Bluebeard is replaced by the Christian patriarchal order of the brothers and new husband, and wifely disobedience is subdued.

Rather than dismiss women altogether, as Boileau seems to do in his writings, Perrault seeks to "reform" them. Through a process of "abjectification," Perrault puts *mondain* women through the wringer in order to extract obedience from them, and takes them out of the sociocultural public sphere. Both writers drew from the overlapping discourses of demonology, folklore, the Christian moralists, and Greco-Roman texts that defined women in terms of the Fall, witchcraft, monstrosity, and ultimately unreason.[43] Whereas Boileau explicitly makes of (virile) men the keepers of reason in *Les Héros de roman,* Perrault does so implicitly in his tales. In the Satire X, Boileau's women are simply mad. In Perrault's tales, however, women are kept in check by a masculine authority that restrains them from acting upon their passions. In the absence of genuine male authority, female folly is brought to the fore and disorder ensues, taking the form of insolence, henpecking, cannibalism, and excessive curiosity. In some respects Boileau gives more power to women than Perrault. For the satirist, women are simply uncontrollable monsters. Perrault, on the other hand, views men as their tamers, capable of reducing the female beast into submission.

The discourse on women by the defender of the Ancients and that by the defender of the Moderns ultimately come together in their attack of "public women" or the women of the salons, the cultural emergence of which threatened the masculine monopoly over literature, culture, and social mores. Taking different approaches, two of the most influential academicians of the period sought to delegitimate *mondain* women by representing them as mad, incapable of reason or judgement, in order to strengthen male authority in general, and arguably, the Académie Française in particular. Perrault goes even further than Boileau. His reflections on the position of women concern not only the sociocultural public sphere, but also the institution of the family, where the *pater familias* rules supremely. At the same time that Perrault defends male authority within the public sphere, he also legitimates a rather absolute rule of the father and husband within the private sphere.

5

The Tyranny of Patriarchs in *L'Histoire d'Hypolite, Comte de Duglas*

IN THE 1650s, WHEN SCUDÉRY ADDRESSES THE QUESTION OF POLITICAL tyranny in *Clélie, Histoire Romaine*, she is able to imagine the possibility of a more just society, evidenced in the novel's rather utopic conclusion. By the time Marie-Catherine d'Aulnoy published her first novel in 1690, however, many people had become disillusioned with the regime of the now autocratic and staunchly pious Louis XIV. Real alternatives must have felt impossible in a nation where the king had recently abolished Protestantism, and repression in all areas of life was on the rise. Already with Nicolas Fouquet's arrest in 1661, Louis XIV demonstrated that he would not tolerate any potential threat to his regime or symbolic challenge to his political or even cultural supremacy. Absolutism entrenched itself in the capital and the provinces through political institutions like the parliament, through the Catholic Church that had been evangelizing the countryside since the beginning of the century, and most recently through the proliferation of government-sanctioned academies. Both the monarchy and the Catholic Church increasingly focused their attention on the family and viewed the father as an agent of centralization, in whom was mirrored the authority of God and king (Muchembled, 198). It is important to note that relations of authority within the family differed from region to region, although the general tendency was towards some degree of patriarchal authority.[1] The centralizing efforts of the government and the church served to universalize, standardize, and reinforce existing patriarchal practices. As it played itself out in both the public and private spheres, absolutism favored the authority of men.

With respect to the sociocultural public sphere, the proliferation of academies had a negative effect on the role of elite women in French society. Between 1663 and 1671 six of the eight major Parisian academies were established, and between 1669 and 1706 nine out of twelve provincial academies received their letters of patent (see Table 2, chapter 1). Such institutions began to assume the function of salons and unofficial academies as centers for literary and cultural production, and they notably excluded women from their ranks. At the same time that the establishment of official academies allowed Louis XIV to consolidate and control the intellectual activity of the sociocultural public sphere, it gave men exclusive rights over literary and cultural production.[2]

With respect to private life, the parliaments reinforced over the course of the century edicts first passed between 1556 to 1639 regarding clandestine marriage, in which consensual marriage without parental consent was defined legally as "consensual rapt" and viewed to be as criminal as forced abduction (Hanley, 9–10; Haase-Dubosc, 114–18). Missionaries of the Catholic Reformation communicated to their flocks a conception of the passions as something sinful and even criminal, and they emphasized the importance of the fourth commandment, all of which served to support the need for parental consent in marriage, ultimately for financial, not moral, reasons (Farr, *Authority*, 93). Marriage as a vehicle for social stratification and the transmission of patrimonies was particularly exacting on women, as James Farr notes: "patriarchy demanded female chastity and fidelity unconditionally, and female purity was carefully guarded, hedged about with boundaries of honor and shame and locked within the institution of marriage, even to the literal extent of the house or the bedroom" (*Authority*, 50). The absolute rule of the father in the family corresponded to that of the king within the state, and women were losing out on all fronts. However, they were writing, and writing like never before.[3]

In her works Marie-Catherine d'Aulnoy challenges the tyranny of patriarchs within both the private and the public spheres. As we will see in the following chapter, d'Aulnoy defends the *mondain* culture condemned by writers like Fénelon, Boileau, and Perrault by inscribing elements characteristic of this culture (i.e., the salon, opera, and romances) into her fairy tales. In this chapter, however, we will focus on the ways in which d'Aulnoy's first novel, *L'Histoire d'Hypolite, comte de Duglas* [The Story of Hypolitus, Earl of Duglas] (1690), provides a critical response to both absolutism and the patriarchal family. Through her representation of the oppressive English monarchies of Henry VII, Henry VIII, and Mary Tudor, d'Aulnoy allegorically attacks French society under Louis XIV, particularly with respect to religious persecution, the assault on the feudal nobility, and the repression of women. Although d'Aulnoy uses this historical backdrop to question absolutism and its effect on the traditional nobility, she concentrates her attention on the cloistering of women, as well as how women psychologically cloister themselves by interiorizing norms of feminine decorum or *bienséance.*

HISTORICAL HOUSE OF MIRRORS

In many respects the history of the reign of Henry VIII serves as a perfect allegory for the reign of Louis XIV. Indeed, even twentieth-century historians have remarked upon the similarities between the two kings, especially regarding their mutual "achievements" of political centralization and religious persecution. Given the system of censorship under Louis XIV and the fact that seditious material was severely punished, it seems only natural that writers would find historical parallels that would allow them to speak about contemporary issues and people without worrying about the social or political repercussions.[4] D'Aulnoy herself implicitly invites the reader to make associations between the English court of Edward IV and that of Louis XIV in her preface to her last novel, *Le Comte de Warwick* [The Earl of Warwick] (1704), in which she states: "on a trouvé que les évenemens étoient trop recens et trop connus. Je vous avoue que cette objection m'a jettée dans un grand embarras. J'ay été obligée de chercher dans les siècles passés, une Cour et des noms qui convinssent à ceux dont je parlois. Il a fallu suivre le Regne d'Edoüard d'York Roy d'Angleterre, sans m'éloigner de la verité" ["some found that the events were too recent and well known. I admit that this put me in an awkward situation. I was obliged to find in past periods, a Court and names that were appropriate to what I was talking about. It was necessary to follow the Reign of Edward of York, King of England, without straying from the truth"] (3–4). English history could serve as a mirror, doubling the events and even the gossip of seventeenth-century French court society.

In 1674 Claude Barbin published a book attributed to d'Aulnoy, entitled *Les Nouvelles d'Elisabeth, reine d'Angleterre* [The Novels of Elizabeth, Queen of England], republished in 1680. Whether or not d'Aulnoy wrote the book, it is likely that she read it, given her obvious interest in English history, as well as certain incidents she seems to borrow and incorporate into the narrative of *L'Histoire d'Hypolite*. One of the stories, that of Henry VIII and Anne Boleyn, is particularly conducive to creating parallels with louis-quatorzième France.[5] For instance, much like a young Louis XIV, Henry VIII is an inconstant monarch with several mistresses who neglects his Spanish queen. Henry VIII's principal mistress at the beginning of the story, Elizabeth Blount, likely would have brought to mind for a seventeenth-century reader Louise de La Vallière or Madame de Montespan, given the issue of legitimating bastard children and the imminent menace of a new rival, in the English case, Anne Boleyn. The Cardinal Woolsey might have made one think of the cardinal ministers Richelieu or Mazarin, or, given his low birth, Jean-Baptiste Colbert. That Woolsey causes the demise of the Duke of Buckingham by accusing him of treason just after the duke demonstrated his greatness and generosity at the Camp of the Cloth of Gold, recalls Colbert's role in the fall of Fouquet soon after Fouquet gave a lavish party at Vaux-le-Vicomte.

Although I do not wish to suggest that the author of *Les Nouvelles* created precise keys between English and French personalities, I do wish to demonstrate the ease with which readers could move between the two periods and courts to discuss the very contemporary issues of ambition, betrayal, passion, and tyranny. As Buford Norman has shown with respect to French opera, seventeenth-century spectators (and readers) perceived analogies between characters and their contemporaries. For instance, Montespan believed Quinault intentionally represented her as a vindictive Juno in *Isis* (1677), and Sévigné refers to her as such in her correspondence. After the performance of *Prosperine* (1680), Sévigné remarked to her daughter that people were comparing them to Cérès and Prosperine (Norman, 33, 186, 223). Creating analogies and understanding events allegorically were as much a part of late seventeenth-century culture as they were a part of earlier decades, when readers delighted in finding correspondences between characters from *Le Grand Cyrus* and *Clélie* and personalities of *la cour et la ville*. However, later readers were more active in creating such "keys" that authors like Quinault or d'Aulnoy arguably did not spell out as unequivocally as did Scudéry. In the case of d'Aulnoy, moreover, the strategy of projecting French political leaders and problems onto England had little to do with glorifying the real individuals who were fictionalized, as in the case of Scudéry's keys. Such a mirroring effect served the purpose of creating a space of contestation that evaded the censors.

Throughout her career d'Aulnoy moves between situating her stories in Spain and situating them in England. Whereas her use of Spanish settings must have appealed to her readers' sense of the exotic, the use of a very unexotic England, which she comes back to in *Les Mémoires de la cour d'Angleterre* [Memoirs of the Court of England] (1695) and *Le Comte de Warwick*, can be explained in terms of creating a double or mirror image of France. Yet the historical references constitutive of this doubling are often polyvalent, pointing to people and events in modern France and/or modern England, and as such evoke or suggest more than they denote. For instance, Shirley Jones Day remarks that d'Aulnoy's assertion in *Hypolite* that Mary Tudor and Philip of Spain outlawed duels may be historically accurate. However, Day argues that "it is more likely that she is referring to William and Mary," who were crowned in 1689 and who took strong measures against duels. Day further proposes that d'Aulnoy might also be referring to Louis XIV, who "had issued the severe Edit des Duels in 1679" (*Hypolite*, n.147). That correspondences between people and events are not unequivocal creates a mirror effect that is polyvalent, allowing d'Aulnoy to treat in general and even ambiguous terms the themes of absolutism and religious persecution without directly referring to any specific events in France, or even clearly defining her own position.

In *Hypolite*, religious persecution is discussed primarily in relation to the story of the comte de Warwick, which we will examine in more detail shortly. A Catholic in Protestant England, the count suffers great hardships and lives much of his life in misery because of the monarchy's intolerance. Without considering d'Aulnoy's strategy of mirroring, the novel could well be read as a defense of Catholicism and of Louis XIV's policy towards the Huguenots. However, as she later implies in *Le Comte de Warwick*, d'Aulnoy expects her audience to read the text allegorically. Certain factors suggest that d'Aulnoy was in fact critical of religious intolerance. First, d'Aulnoy dedicated her first collection of tales in 1697 to Charlotte Elisabeth de Bavière, the Princesse Palatine, who was, in Emmanuel Le Roy Ladurie's words, "categorically allergic to pure and simple acts of intolerance, like the revocation of the edict of Nantes" (133). "La Palatine" herself was a former Calvinist, forced to convert to Catholicism in order to marry the duc d'Orléans. Second, d'Aulnoy was friends with Anne-Marguerite Petit Dunoyer, a Protestant writer and the first

woman journalist in western Europe. Forced to flee France for
Amsterdam during the dragonnades, Dunoyer was openly critical of Louis XIV's monarchy.[6] Although it is not clear when d'Aulnoy made Dunoyer's acquaintance, we can safely deduce that
had d'Aulnoy been ardently pro-Catholic, she would not have af-
filiated herself with a scandalous Protestant personality like Dunoyer.

Finally, the novel itself suggests that d'Aulnoy was against religious intolerance. Most of the frame narrative concerns the persecution of Catholics under Henry VII and Henry VIII. However,
persecution does not end when the Catholic Mary Tudor takes
the throne. The queen unjustly torments the marquise de Northampton, whose Protestant husband was killed with the duc de
Northumberland in conjunction with the controversy over the
reign of Lady Jane Grey.[7] Though this episode is referred to only
briefly in *Hypolite*, it implies that d'Aulnoy was critical of all
forms of religious persecution. In fact, religious intolerance on
the part of rulers becomes a sign of their tyranny. Clearly d'Aulnoy's decision to frame *Hypolite* with a story of religious persecution was a calculated one that encouraged readers to make
associations with the current situation in France. In the words
of Jean Mainil, "[f]ive years after the Revocation of the Edict of
Nantes, the argument undoubtedly was a burning issue" (96).

POLITICAL TYRANNY, OR THE COUNT'S TALE

Like other historical novels of the period, *L'Histoire d'Hypolite*
consists of historical figures that are fictionalized, on the one
hand, and fictional characters that are historicized, on the other
(see Harth, *Ideology*, 195). D'Aulnoy weaves her fictional comte
de Warwick into the fabric of sixteenth-century English history
by inserting him into the Warwick-Pole family, one of the last ves-
tiges of the feudal nobility, and the greatest menace to the Tudor
monarchy of Henry VII and Henry VIII. However, the ways in
which d'Aulnoy modifies the nature of the relations between the
nobility and the monarchy serve to stress the tyranny of the latter, and the innocence of the former. Much like the noble *frondeurs* of the 1640s, the Warwick-Pole family represented a
potential threat to the authority and legitimacy of the newly
emerging Tudor monarchy. Yet d'Aulnoy represents the members of the Warwick household chiefly as innocent victims of an
arbitrary power. Through Warwick d'Aulnoy depicts a dispos-

sessed nobility, whose only options are dishonorable submission to a despot or life as an adventurer. Although d'Aulnoy paints Warwick primarily as a victim, she is also somewhat critical of the model of masculinity he represents, which becomes clear when his story is read against that of Julie and Hypolite and the inserted tale "L'Ile de la Félicité" ["The Island of Felicity"].

Indeed, the name "Warwick" is legendary one, recalling Richard Neville, Earl of Warwick, dubbed "the kingmaker." D'Aulnoy later wrote a novel based on the gallant exploits of her fictional Warwick's illustrious ancestor, who rivals king Edward IV in both love and glory. In her works a general pattern emerges according to which a loyal and worthy nobleman is unjustly persecuted by his king for the potential threat he represents, usually in love or gallantry, and in the case of *Hypolite*, due to family ties and religion.[8] The fact that *Hypolite*'s comte de Warwick is believed to have been killed but actually is a prisoner in the corsair Dragut Rais's galley suggests that d'Aulnoy is playing on the story of Edward Plantagenet, Earl of Warwick and grandson of the kingmaker. Edward spent much of his life in prison; he was rumored to be dead, which sparked a rebellion; and finally he was executed for posing a purely symbolic threat to the crown.[9] *Hypolite*'s fictional comte de Warwick bears traces of his historical ancestors in his fighting ability, his supposed death, as well as his persecution by the monarchy. The very name Warwick, then, evokes both the dignity of the traditional nobility, as well as the injustices it endured.

Although Warwick is essentially a fictional character, he lives among historical figures, like his paternal uncle George Neville, Lord Abergavenny, whom d'Aulnoy refers to as George de Neuilly, comte de Burgen; Edmund de la Pole; the duc de Buckingham; Henry Courtenay, Marquis d'Exeter; and Henry Pole, Lord Montague. Situating Warwick within an actual noble household not only contributes to establishing his historical authenticity. It also allows d'Aulnoy to write her version of the history of the nobility through that of a single family. In the first few pages of *Hypolite*, d'Aulnoy relates their story of imprisonment, execution, and exile, themes her readers could easily associate with contemporary events. The family's story is structured around three instances of wrongful or unjust accusations that lead to the supposed death of the comte de Warwick, the source of his daughter Julie's own troubles.

In the first instance, Georges de Neuilly, the comte de Warwick's guardian, is arrested and imprisoned in the Tower of London by Henry VII due to his association with Edmund de la Pole, in accordance with his historical counterpart, George Neville. In fact, the novel opens with this incident, the very first lines of which read: "Sous le regne de Henry VII. Roy d'Angleterre, George de Neuilly, Comte de Burgen, eut le malheur d'estre soupçonné d'avoir eu part à la conduite criminelle d'Edmond de la Poole. Le Roy le fit arrester, et conduire dans la Tour de Londres: Il y resta long-temps; mais ayant fait connoistre son innocence, il obtint enfin sa liberté" ["Under the reign of Henry VII, King of England, George de Neuilly, Earl of Burgen, had the misfortune of being suspected of taking part in the criminal conduct of Edmond de la Poole. The King had him arrested and brought to the Tower of London: He remained there for a long time; but having his innocence discovered, he finally obtained his freedom"] (5). *Hypolite* begins with a tale of false accusations and innocence wronged. Although the historical George Neville probably had something to do with Pole's rebellious activities, and himself was fined for having illegally retained some 470 men between 1504 and 1506 (Pugh, 71), d'Aulnoy depicts Georges de Neuilly as unquestionably above suspicion. Knowingly or unknowingly, d'Aulnoy skips over the precise details of the affair, with the effect of making her Georges de Neuilly look totally innocent, and of amplifying the tyranny and injustice of Henry VII.

The second incident occurs under the reign of Henry VIII, who is depicted by d'Aulnoy as being completely blind to the intentions of the Cardinal Volsey, which recalls seventeenth-century French perceptions of the relation between kings and their ministers. D'Aulnoy reproduces the story of the duc de Buckingham's fall, and paints the cardinal as being particularly vengeful in the satisfaction he takes in the duke's execution and in the imprisonment of Georges de Neuilly, Buckingham's son-in-law, whose wealth also was confiscated, "malgré son innocence" ["despite his innocence"] (7). However, the historical Neville's land never was seized, nor was he thrown in the Tower of London on the occasion of Buckingham's demise. As for the historical Duke of Buckingham, he was believed to have voiced his desire to make a claim for the throne, thus representing a threat, but there is no proof that he ever actually plotted against the king (Williamson, 98). Even though Buckingham's sentence was unmerited, d'Aulnoy completely downplays the real threat Buckingham posed to Henry VIII. Both Buckingham's and Neuilly's situations bring to mind that of Fouquet, whose wealth was confiscated and who was imprisoned after Colbert accused him of financial misdeeds. By juxtaposing the story of Neuilly, imprisoned merely for being the duke's relative, with that of the duc de Buckingham, d'Aulnoy magnifies the arbitrary nature of monarchical judgments, at the same time that she strengthens analogies to be made with seventeenth-century France.

In the third example of Tudor injustice, three members of the comte de Warwick's family, Edoüard de Neuilly, the Marquis d'Exeter, and the brother of the cardinal de la Poole, are executed for having spoken out against Henry VIII, who had declared himself head of the Anglican Church and launched a reign of terror: "on voyoit chaque jour des personnes de tous sexes et de toutes qualitez punis du dernier supplice à cause de la Religion" ["one saw everyday people of all sexes and positions executed because of Religion"] (8). Indeed, the historical Edward Neville, the marquis of Exeter, and the cardinal's brother Lord Montague all were executed by Henry VIII for religious activities deemed seditious (they defended Roman Catholicism and the pope), as well as for being members of the Warwick-Pole family, the last potential rivals for the English throne (Elton, 155; Williamson, 161). In an episode of her own invention, d'Aulnoy frames their persecution not in terms of opposition or rivalry, but as a collective and disinterested protest of the king's injustices: "animez de zele, [ils] voulurent representer au roy le tort qu'il avoit, ils payerent de leurs testes la sainte liberté qu'ils avoient prise" ["animated by zeal, they wished to speak to the king about his wrongs, they paid with their heads the saintly liberty they had taken"] (8). It is interesting to note that d'Aulnoy fails to mention the well-known story of Sir Thomas More and Bishop Fisher when speaking of religious persecution under Henry VIII. In fact, the way in which d'Aulnoy describes the Warwick-Pole encounter with the king brings to mind the truly "zealous" opposition to the Act of Supremacy expressed by More and Fisher. It is as if d'Aulnoy has fused together the two events, which actually occurred around the same time (More and Fisher were executed in 1535; Neville, the marquis, and Lord Montague were executed in 1538), in order to depict the members of the Warwick-Pole family as noble martyrs.

After the first two instances of monarchical injustice, the comte de Warwick finds himself in France. Georges de Neuilly sends his nephew across the Channel to protect him from the wrath of first Henry VII, and then Henry VIII. In the third case, Warwick exiles himself, fearing that his ties of kinship to Edoüard de Neuilly would be cause for Henry VIII to execute him as well. The idea of Englishmen taking exile in France was a familiar one to French audiences, with the English kings Charles II and James II having been raised at the French court during Oliver Cromwell's regime, and with the return of James II to France in 1688 after being dethroned by William and Mary. Since the Revocation of the Edict of Nantes in 1685, however, the flow of refugees was moving primarily from France to England. Eventually ending up a galley slave, Warwick's fate, moreover, recalls that reserved for Protestant men in France who refused to abjure and failed to flee the country.[10] Throughout the novel, the back-and-forth movement between France and England strengthens the doubling or mirror effect suggested by the novel's timely theme by practically blurring the distinction between the two countries. And although England is specified as the site of persecution in the case of Warwick, France certainly is no safe haven for his daughter Julie.

ADVENTURERS, LOVERS, AND TRAITORS

Through the story of Warwick, d'Aulnoy indicates that the nobility had two choices before them: "une soûmission rampante à toutes les volontez du Roy" ["a groveling submission to all the wishes of the king"] (9), or the life of an adventurer. Recalling how some viewed court at Versailles under Louis XIV, the first choice results in the loss of honor, at least from the narrator's perspective. The second option points to a more feudal notion of nobility. Warwick decides to join the knights of Malta, who were fighting the Turks in a modern "crusade." Indeed, the knights were considered to be modern-day crusaders well into the eighteenth century (Bamford, 8; Engel, 21). With the renewed interest in the 1680s in chivalric romances like *Jerusalem Delivered* and *Orlando furioso*, not to mention the fact that Louis XIV was leading a European coalition against the Turks, Warwick certainly would have been an appealing character for French audiences. Nevertheless, d'Aulnoy implicitly questions such a model of male subjectivity, which becomes clear when Warwick's story is considered within the context of the novel.

Warwick's desire to join the knights of Malta and fight against Soliman is propelled by his desire to obtain honor and glory, even if this means separation from his beloved wife and leads to his own death: "c'estoit un lieu propre pour acquerir de l'honneur ou pour trouver une mort glorieuse" ["this was a proper place to acquire honor or find a glorious death"] (9). Honor and glory are attained through military prowess, and are opposed to the more "feminine" qualities of leisure and love: "comme il estoit dans l'âge où un homme de coeur se reproche de passer sa vie dans une molle oisiveté, sa vertu et son courage l'emporterent sur son amour" ["as he was in an age where a brave man reproaches himself for spending his life in a soft idleness, his virtue and courage overtook his love"] (9). Love is associated with *molle oisiveté*, sensual and leisurely pleasures that Warwick rejects to assume the hard masculinity of the warrior. In the end, his quest for glory results in his presumed death, which causes the death of his wife, the comtesse de Warwick, and leaves his daughter Julie, now orphaned, vulnerable and defenseless.

In many respects Warwick resembles Adolphe, the hero of the fairy tale Hypolite recounts later in the novel to the abbess who guards Julie. In the tale Adolphe has found perfect happiness with princess Félicité. However, when Adolphe discovers that three hundred years have gone by since he has arrived on the island, he reproaches himself, much like Warwick, for having spent too much time engaged in pleasurable activities, and regrets the glory he might have attained had he died: "si j'estois mort à présent j'aurois peut-estre fait de si grandes actions qu'elles auroient éternisé ma memoire: je vois avec honte ma Vertu sans occupation et mon nom sans éclat" ["if I were dead at present, perhaps I would have undertaken great actions that would have immortalized my memory: I shamefully see my virtue without profession and my name without renown"] (133). Adolphe's words ring with irony, for he prefers to die and have his glory live eternally, rather than live eternally himself and enjoy life with Félicité. At the end of the story, Adolphe dies most ingloriously, suggesting such a quest for glory is futile and leads only to death, destruction, and unhappiness.

Like Scudéry, d'Aulnoy criticizes the masculine warrior model of subjectivity. Unlike Scudéry, she does not open up the concept of glory to women or those engaged in nonmilitary exploits, but rather, she exalts the principle of love over glory, and highlights the pointlessness of sacrificing one's life and happiness for empty visions of grandeur. Representing the perfect lover who would not let something like glory take him away from his mistress, Hypolite presents a contrast to both Warwick and Adolphe. When he disguises himself as Hyacinthe and pretends to be the painter Cardiny's assistant in order to see Julie in the convent at Saint Menoux, Hypolite aspires to nothing more: "il n'auroit pas changé son sort à celui du plus grand Monarque" ["he would not have changed is destiny for that of the greatest Monarch"] (138). His highest ambition is to love and be loved by Julie. As the narrator notes: "c'est un des secrets de l'amour de guerir de l'ambition, et de mille autres passions dont les ames sans tendresse sont tiranisées" ["one of the secrets of love is to cure ambition, and a thousand other passions that tyrannize souls without tenderness"] (140). Although toward the end of the novel Hypolite fights with the knights of Malta against the Turks, he does so only because he believes Julie to be dead. For Hypolite, military glory takes on the guise of a death wish that compensates for the loss, through forced separation or death, of his beloved. Military prowess and glory are only the secondary effects of his death wish, and love always takes precedence over glory.

Despite the fact that d'Aulnoy is critical of the warrior model of male subjectivity as represented by Warwick, she nevertheless represents his character overall in a positive light, and as a victim of tyrannical forces. In many respects the marquis d'Yvrée of Catherine Bernard's *Eléonor d'Yvrée* (1687) prefigures *Hypolite*'s comte de Warwick and presents an interesting contrast to d'Aulnoy's character. In both novels, the father character represents a real or imagined threat to the monarchy or emperor, they both engage in military actions that lead either to their civil or presumed death, which consequently results in the death of their wives, leaving their children orphaned. The differences between the two characters are quite telling. In *Eléonor d'Yvrée*, the marquis, unlike Warwick, poses a very real threat to the emperor. He leads troops against the emperor and even is proclaimed king of Italy, but eventually the emperor defeats him. While Warwick is believed to have been killed by Dragut Rais when he is in fact a galley slave, d'Yvrée confines himself to a monastery in Besançon, renouncing civil life for good. Upon the news of Warwick's presumed death, his wife the countess dies out of her love for him, whereas the marquise d'Yvrée dies out of shame for her husband's disgrace.

Bernard's narrative implicitly condemns the marquis d'Yvrée for challenging the authority of "le plus juste et le plus puissant de tous les Princes qui jusque-là estoient parvenus à l'Empire" ["the most just and powerful of all the Princes who had acquired the Empire"] (1–2). That d'Yvrée is somehow guilty is expressed both in the attitude of his wife towards his revolt and in the marquis's decision to retire to a monastery, itself an act of penance. Ideologically, Bernard and d'Aulnoy take quite different positions with respect to their representation of the emperor/king and the nobility. D'Aulnoy depicts the members of the Warwick-Pole family as victims of a tyrannical power, whereas Bernard implies that it is the emperor/king who is just, and members of the nobility who take advantage of "sa douceur et sa moderation" ["his gentleness and moderation"] (2), repaying his kindness with rebellion. As a Protestant who recently converted to Catholicism with the Revocation, Bernard was not in a position to challenge Louis XIV's monarchy, and as René Godenne remarks, she actively was seeking to gain royal favor (viii). In writing *Hypolite*, d'Aulnoy contests Bernard's portrayal of the emperor, arguably a figure for Louis XIV, in part by representing the nobility as innocent victims of an arbitrary and jealous power. As we will see later in the chapter, d'Aulnoy revises other aspects of Bernard's plot, which suggests that her differences with Bernard are not limited to political matters.

Prominent figures of the feudal nobility, honorable men who exercise largesse and defend the Christian faith in the tradition of the crusaders, Warwick and his kin are contrasted with the interested and faithless monarchs who torment them. In a similar manner, the virtuous Julie is persecuted by adoptive parents and a husband, all of whom, much like the Tudor monarchs, prove to be self-interested, jealous, and use morality to further their own interests. Warwick's tale takes us through the public history of politics, whereas Julie's story leads us through the private history of the family. In many respects Julie represents the feminine double of Warwick, evident in the basic elements constitutive of their respective stories: both were orphaned as children; both were exiled from England, ending up in France and Italy; and both were imprisoned and believed to be dead. What makes their life experiences different is their gender. Whereas noble men are executed, imprisoned, forced into exile, or humbled into servile submission primarily by kings, noble women are locked up in homes and convents, subjected to the surveillance of parents, husbands, and abbesses. Through Warwick and Julie, d'Aulnoy can address the tyranny of the patriarchs in both the public and private spheres.

FAMILIAL TYRANNY, OR THE STORY OF JULIE

Most of the novel is concerned with the trials and tribulations of the lovers Julie and Hypolite. Although Hypolite figures prominently in the scheme of things, it is the situation of Julie that structures their love story. Julie's status constantly changes, from dependent daughter to adopted orphan, from married woman to a forcibly cloistered one, Julie even occupies momentarily the position of widow. As her status changes, so do the prospects that Julie and Hypolite can marry and live happily ever after. Each of these positions allows d'Aulnoy to explore the restrictions placed on women's sphere of action, restrictions enforced by parents, husbands, and even women themselves. The changes in Julie's status come about through the various machinations on the part of Milord and Madame de Duglas (Julie's adoptive and Hypolite's biological parents), and later the comte de Bedfort, to separate the two lovers for reasons of personal (financial, social, emotional) interest.

In many respects we can read into *L'Histoire d'Hypolite, comte de Duglas*, a critique of the ideology of the Counter-Reformation, which reinforced parental and above all paternal control over the marriage of children. Marriage was the vehicle for the social and economic reproduction of society through the maintenance and extension of family networks (see Hanley, 8–9; Farr, *Authority*, 97). Legally, parental/paternal control over marriage was supported by both the parliament, whose interest resided in the preservation of the parliamentary class, and the monarchy, whose absolute rule was legitimated by and reflected in the absolute authority of the father within the family (see Haase-Dubosc, 112). As James Farr has argued, values promoted by Catholic Reformers, like the reaffirmation of the fourth commandment concerning obedience to parents, the contempt for worldly and especially sexual pleasures, the equation of sin with disobedience, and the criminalization of sin, worked together to legitimate the supposed need for parents to intervene and rationally decide their children's fate (*Authority*, 33–43, 90–97). Of course, such values served to morally legitimate the parents' very worldly concerns about the social and economic advancement of their particular family or household. If parents and priests could inculcate upon the minds of the young the idea that passionate love, not to mention disobedience of one's parents, was in and of itself a sin and a crime, then parental control over marriage would be nearly absolute. The early modern preoccupation with controlling sexuality cannot be separated from the efforts on the part of parents and legislators to exercise an absolute control over the marriages of their children.

Julie and Hypolite's story brings to the fore many of the anxieties surrounding sexuality and parental control over marriage. Already before any character is fully aware that Julie and Hypolite are in love, Madame de Duglas scolds the adolescent Hypolite for spending too much time in his sisters' bedroom: "Vous estes bien matinal . . . et vous devriez bien-plûtost employer vostre temps à apprendre les choses que vous estes obligé de sçavoir, qu'à venir dans la Chambre de vos soeurs" ["You are up early . . . and you should rather spend your time learning things you are obligated to know, than to come into the Room of your sisters"] (17). Madame de Duglas seems to reprimand him for using his time inappropriately. Clearly, however, this is only a pretext concealing her real fear that Hypolite might be in love with his adoptive sister, while she and her husband have already begun arranging for Hypolite to marry Mademoiselle d'Argille. As Jean-Louis Flandrin has shown, there was an increased concern for familial sleeping arrangements over the course of the sixteenth and seventeenth centuries (98–99). Whereas previously entire families could share a bed without any moral implications, now the idea of brothers and sisters or parents and children sleeping together was viewed as a situation that gave rise to, in the words of a sixteenth-century bishop, "an infinite number of horrible sins" (quoted in Flandrin, 98). Although this scene in *L'Histoire d'Hypolite* is not about sleeping arrangements per se, it does point to the emerging preoccupation with separating male from female children within the home, as well as the moralization of this separation. The scene also introduces the problem of parental surveillance, which cannot be separated from parental concern over children's sexual behavior, nor ultimately parents' will to determine their children's future spouse.

In seventeenth-century literature, ideal love often was expressed in terms of brother–sister relations. In Scudéry's *Artamène, ou le Grand Cyrus*, the lovers Cyrus and Mandane were keys for the Grand Condé and his sister the duchesse de Longueville, and in *Clélie*, Aronce and Clélie were raised as brother and sister, always aware, however, that they were not blood related. In her analysis of *Les Mémoires de Madame de La Guette* (1681), Danielle Haase-Dubosc observes that Catherine Meurdrac de La Guette probably was influenced by literary representations of pure love expressed in terms of brother–sister relations in her account of her marriage (119). Referring to the love between her and her husband, whom she secretly marries against the wishes of her father, La Guette describes it as "ce bel amour chaste et pudique" ["this beautiful love, chaste and modest"] and maintains that her husband assured her "que nous vivrions comme frères et soeurs" ["that we would live like sister and brother"] (29). As the above examples suggest, pure love was also transgressive, in the sense that it went against the will of the parents. However chaste this ideal love might have been, it was propelled by a strong, unrelinquishing desire that could lead to disobedience if not checked by so-called moral considerations. In the words of La Guette, "La forte inclination que j'avois pour le sieur de la Guette me porta à la désobéissance, ce que les filles bien nées ne doivent jamais faire" ["The strong inclination I had for Sir de la Guette led me to disobey, something well-bred girls must never do"] (17).

Some Medieval and Renaissance theologians believed that incestuous passion was dangerous precisely because it manifested itself more violently than passion directed outside of the nuclear or extended family. Natalie Zemon Davis cites the Jesuit Emond Auger, who argued that carnal desires "are by nature strongest toward those closest to us and would be boundless if we married them," and she goes on to argue that such moral considerations only upheld socioeconomic ones: "Marrying outside the prohibited degrees, then, enables us both to enlarge the circle of our alliance with more people and to be more virtuous at the same time" (Davis, "Ghosts," 102–3). A century later d'Aulnoy's Julie remarks upon the strength of her presumed incestuous love for Hypolite: "je vous aime, et je vous aime trop, puisque vous estes mon frere" ["I love you, and I love you too much, because you are my brother"] (19). Excessive desire meant lack of control and consequently failure to obey, and even if such desire technically was not incestuous, it is as if it were, given the intensity of the desire. The incest taboo serves as a mechanism to channel the passions within the limits of a particular kinship system; it is part of a moral code that reinforces the social norms constitutive of that particular society. The ways in which brother–sister or incestuous relations are used in seventeenth-century literature suggest that we might view incest as a figure for what was considered more generally to be transgressive sexual behavior, transgressive in the sense that it went against the social and religious norms (obedience to parents, criminalization of the passions) that upheld the kinship system of seventeenth-century France.

Unlike Clélie and Aronce, Julie and Hypolite fall in love fully believing they are blood related. Tormented by such feelings, Hypolite is prepared to kill himself: "Julie, ma chere Julie! . . . puisque la passion que j'ay pour vous ne m'est pas permise, puisque je commets un crime lorsque je vous adore . . . il m'est plus aisé de cesser de vivre, qu'il ne m'est aisé de cesser de vous aimer" ["Julie, my dear Julie! . . . since the passion I have for you is not permitted to me, since I commit a crime by adoring you . . . it is easier for me to cease living than to stop loving you"] (18). Both Julie and Hypolite refer to their love as a "crime," and Julie is prepared to "sacrifice" her passions and freedom by locking herself away in a convent in France. However, even after the revelation that Milord and Madame de Duglas adopted Julie, their love continues to be viewed as criminal because it goes against the wishes of their parents. Ironically, the marriages the Duglas want to arrange for their son and adoptive daughter are more biologically "incestuous" than the "criminal" love of Julie and Hypolite. While they hope to marry Hypolite to Mademoiselle d'Argille, a cousin on the paternal side, they wish to marry Julie (or possibly Lucile) to the comte de Bedfort, a cousin on the maternal side. Both Mademoiselle d'Argille and Bedfort are wealthy, and such marriages would only strengthen alliances with maternal and paternal family networks.

By the late sixteenth century, marriage was not permitted within four degrees, that is, "one was forbidden to marry any of the descendents of one's sixteen great-great grandparents" (Davis, "Ghosts" 101). Nevertheless, families could obtain official dispensations from the Catholic Church when such prohibitions went against the interests of the family. In *Hypolite* d'Aulnoy repeatedly points to the fact that socioeconomic considerations outweigh moral ones, whether in relation to the politics of the kingdom or the politics of the family. Although in the beginning of the novel Julie and Hypolite's love is criminal because it is incestuous, it remains criminal throughout the novel because the real taboo does not have to do with consanguinity, but rather with the fact that Julie is not rich and has no family with which the Duglas can ally themselves. In marrying Hypolite to Julie, there is no financial, social, or political gain to be had, and therefore the union is deemed forbidden or taboo.

In early modern France, disobedience on the part of children (many of whom were indeed adults)[11] regarding marriage was constructed in terms of seduction and incompetence, in the legal sense of the term. It is worth recalling that traditionally the Catholic Church recognized consensual marriages contracted without parental consent. In the evolution of the concept of clandestine marriage and its reconceptualization as "consensual rapt," however, jurists found ways to discredit children's ability to contract their own marriages and consequently to criminalize marriages contracted without parental/paternal consent. Essentially jurists argued that children were incompetent, that they only believed to have consented to marry, when in fact they were somehow seduced into it and were unable to exercise their free will (see Haase-Dubosc, 116–118). Because jurists denied children their status as reasonable beings, they took away the possibility for them to position themselves as subjects before the law, at least in matters regarding marriage. In effect, the status of children was reduced to that of objects of exchange, with parents and ultimately the father functioning as the subjects or agents regulating that exchange. In the eyes of parents, priests, and jurists, the very idea that two people, impelled by their "strong inclination," in other words, by their "criminal" passions, would defy family and law, already suggests they are unfit to contract such an affair. Legalistic and religious discourses mutually reinforced each other to discredit marriages of love in favor of *mariages de raison*.

In the novel, such questions eventually come to the fore when Madame de Duglas realizes the extent to which Hypolite and Julie are attached to each other. After Julie discovers she is not Hypolite's biological sister, she no longer wishes to confine herself to a convent, and pretends to be sick in order to postpone her trip to France, which raises Madame de Duglas's suspicions. A vigilant mother, Madame de Duglas closely watches her children, and follows Julie and Hypolite into the grotto where they first declared their forbidden love to each other. Her suspicions regarding their love are confirmed, which leads the Duglas to separate Julie and Hypolite by giving Julie the option of marrying Bedfort or going to a convent, and by sending Hypolite abroad. D'Aulnoy depicts surveillance as a mechanism of control that leads to either confinement or exile, and as such parallels mechanisms of control within the public sphere.

When Madame de Duglas surprises the lovers, she first reminds Julie that she does not have the right to dispose of her own heart, and later accuses her of having seduced Hypolite into disobedience. Her words to Julie, "je ne pensois pas . . . qu'une fille si bien née deût disposer de son coeur sans l'aveu des personnes de qui elle dépend" ["I did not think . . . that such a well-born girl should dispose of her heart without the consent of the people on whom she depends"] (31), recall La Guette's similar remark from the *Mémoires*. (La Guette is somewhat ironic, however, for she did marry against her father's will and managed to live happily ever after.) Madame's statement takes away the possibility for Julie to act as a subject or agent of her own will or desire without damaging her reputation as a well-bred young woman. Although "bien née" has both social and moral connotations, the ultimate value of such a reputation is measured on the marriage market. As Farr has argued, women often conformed to the restrictive moral standards of Counter-Reformation France in order to compete for husbands, their honor being their main commodity ("Pure," 407–12). In a society where paternal authority was being reinforced like never before, disobedience in a woman was highly discouraged. As we have seen in Perrault's tales, feminine obedience was viewed as a measure of a woman's morality, which in turn was constitutive of her honor or reputation. Parents naturally were interested in their daughter's obedience precisely because they functioned as the agents of the exchange of this "commodity," at the same time that they wanted their daughter to comply with their choice of spouse.

Much like Dona Juana of "Don Gabriel Ponce de Leon" and the comtesse de Fuentès of "Don Fernand de Tolède," characters from d'Aulnoy's later Spanish novellas, Madame de Duglas functions as an agent of patriarchal ideology, playing the role of informant, prison guard, and spokesperson. Embracing notions of women reminiscent of Boileau, Perrault, and Fénelon, Madame de Duglas goes so far as to suggest that Julie pushed Hypolite to disobedience by seducing him: "vous voulez ruïner la fortune d'Hypolite et révoltant son coeur contre l'obeïsance qu'il nous doit, vous allumez une passion que vous sçavez bien qui peut nous déplaire" ["you wish to ruin the fortune of Hypolite, and having his heart rebel against the obedience he owes us, you light up a passion that you know well can displease us"] (32). Such words make of the most innocent Julie a sort of Eve, whose seduction has blinded Hypolite to his duty and taken away his free will: thus the need for parental "protection" in matters of consensual rapt. Within the context of the novel, Madame de Duglas's statement appears ridiculous, if not absurd, even without considering the fact that Julie is supposed to be four years younger than Hypolite, who is in his early twenties at this time in the narrative. In effect, d'Aulnoy highlights the Duglas's rather hypocritical use of morality to manipulate their children into submission.

Disobedience on the part of daughters is unacceptable, nor is it tolerated on the part of sons. Madame de Duglas considers Hypolite's love for Julie as transgressive, given the arrangements for his marriage to Mademoiselle d'Argille : "vous estes bien téméraire d'oser vous attacher à Julie, dans le temps où nous sommes sur le point de conclure vôtre Mariage avec Mademoiselle d'Argille" ["you are most bold to dare attach yourself to Julie, at a time when we are about to conclude your marriage with Mademoiselle d'Argile"] (31). In order to punish his disobedience, the Duglas attempt to "exile" him in France. However, Hypolite only feigns his departure, all the while remaining in England and making nocturnal visits to Julie. Hypolite is finally caught, only because he stops the comte de Bedfort from abducting Julie against her will. Yet Milord de Duglas defends Bedfort, accusing his son Hypolite of having injured a family friend, a relative of his mother, and a man who is "riche et puissant" ["rich and powerful"] (47). Despite the fact that Bedfort's actions would have been deemed illegal had Milord de Duglas decided to pursue him in the courts, Duglas aims his attack at Hypolite, criticizing him for failing to obey. In fact, if Bedfort had succeeded in abducting Julie, it would have served Duglas's intentions of marrying her to the wealthy count. In the end, Milord sends his son off to Florence under careful guard, warning Hypolite that if he returns before three years are up, he will have him arrested and imprisoned. Meanwhile Milord and Madame de Duglas decide they cannot sent Julie to a convent in France, fearing that Hypolite will take her away. They leave Julie with the choice of remaining in the paternal home or marrying Bedfort. The strategy to "exile" Hypolite and "imprison" Julie ultimately serves to avert the possibility of a clandestine marriage or consensual rapt, although even forced rapt would have been tolerated in the case of Bedfort.

In order to take control of his son's life, Milord de Duglas resorts to professional connections in England and Italy, as well as legal support in England. His threat to imprison Hypolite brings to mind the use of *lettres de cachet* in France, increasingly used to control family members deemed violent, debauched, or insane. In the novel, d'Aulnoy points to the type of networks parents could utilize to exercise their authority over their children. (Interestingly, the story of La Guette shows the ways in which disobedient couples also could tap into networks to get their marriages legitimized, and subsequently, to reconcile with angry fathers.) In fact, moral arguments concerning the alleged transgressions of children only served to legitimate the actions taken through recourse to such networks, actions that functioned primarily to assert parental rights over their children. Eventually the Duglas use such networks to take control of their children's correspondence. A scene reminiscent of an episode of Anne Boleyn's story, the Duglas circulate counterfeit letters and succeed in convincing Julie that Hypolite had betrayed her, which leads Julie, out of desperation and pride, to finally consent to marry Bedfort.[12] And while Anne Boleyn's marriage to Henry VIII eventually leads to her death, Julie's wedding is described as *"un jour de pompe funebre"* ["a day of funeral ceremonies"] (80).

PERSPECTIVES ON FORCED MARRIAGE

One could argue that in depicting the extremely jealous and eventually bigamous comte de Bedfort, d'Aulnoy draws to some extent from the *Nouvelles*'s portrait of Henry VIII. Indeed, Bedfort is represented unequivocally as a tyrant.[13] He is described as being of "une jalousie effroyable" ["an appalling jealousy"] (85), which impels him to keep Julie at home under lock and key, and he takes over the parental role of surveillance: "le Comte de Bedfort la veilloit de si prés" ["the Count of Bedfort monitored her closely"] (104). When he discovers that Julie is in fact in love with Hypolite, he secretly steals her away to a convent in France, where the abbess assures him that Julie "seroit plus soigneusement gardée qu'une prisonniere d'Etat" ["would be more carefully guarded than a prisoner of the State"] (106), and that she will neither see nor write to anyone. D'Aulnoy's representation of Julie's marriage to Bedfort clearly puts into question the practice of forced marriages. Marriage based on free choice is an affair involving two active subjects whose desire is reciprocal. In the case of Julie's forced marriage, however, Bedfort is a desiring subject, who desires Julie as one desires a possession. Consequently, the relation between husband and wife is constructed in terms of husband/subject and wife/object, and thus takes on sadomasochistic traits. Immediately after their wedding, Bedfort begins to play the role of Julie's accuser, judge, and jailer, while Julie is reduced to being his passive victim. As Julie remarks: "vous serez toûjours en estat de me punir" ["you will always be in a position to punish me"] (105). First out of unfounded jealousy, then out of the realization that Julie has feelings for Hypolite, Bedfort can only treat Julie like a prisoner, a treasure he must lock up and keep away from the covetous eyes of others.

That Julie's wedding day resembles a funeral is symbolic of

the internment and passivity to which she is condemned by marrying Bedfort. Through her depiction of Bedfort, d'Aulnoy indicates the potential dangers of marrying one's daughter to an unsuitable husband at a time when French law gave husbands the right to cloister their wives indefinitely on mere allegations of sexual misconduct. As a matter of fact, towards the end of the novel Bedfort attempts to kidnap Julie in order to confine her to a convent for the rest of her life, after having married the wealthy marquise de Becarelly.[14] Just as law gave parents control over their children's lives, so it gave husbands control over their wives' lives.

D'Aulnoy's account of forced marriage in *Hypolite* differs significantly from Catherine Bernard's portrayal of Eléonor's marriage to a man at least the age of her father in *Eléonor d'Yvrée*. As d'Aulnoy clearly drew from Bernard's novel, it comes as no surprise that Eléonor's story closely parallels that of Julie. Like Julie, Eléonor, for all intents and purposes, is orphaned (her father has retired to a monastery). Eléonor is raised conjointly by the comtesse de Tuscanelle and the duchesse de Misnie, while her brother grows up in the household of the comte de Retelois, their father's friend. Falling in love with her adoptive brother, the duc de Misnie, Eléonor finds herself to be the rival of her adoptive sister, Matilde, the daughter of the comtesse de Tuscanelle. In the meantime Eléonor's absent father wishes her to marry the comte de Retelois, whose intentions are presented as most noble: he wishes to marry in Eléonor the daughter of an unhappy friend.

Bernard only evokes the count's age, stating that it impeded him from undertaking long trips, which suggests that he is significantly older than Eléonor. Unlike Bedfort, Retelois is most patient and does not wish to rush Eléonor in her decision, which "luy auroit paru tirannique" ["would have seemed tyrannical to him"] (92). In fact, he actually begins to fall in love with her and hopes to merit her "par son respect et par ses soins" ["by his respect and consideration"] (93). In the end, Eléonor fulfills her duty to her albeit absent father and respects the wishes of her dying friend Matilde, and "elle vécut avec le Comte comme une personne dont la vertu estoit parfaite, quoy qu'elle fust toujours malheureuse par la passion qu'elle avoit dans le coeur" ["she lived with the Count like a person of perfect virtue, although she was always unhappy due to the passion she had in her heart"] (236–37). Although Bernard does not exactly present us with a happy ending, she does depict the husband of the forced marriage, the comte de Retelois, in favorable terms.[15]

At the same time that d'Aulnoy streamlines the story by having a single family adopt only the daughter of the absent father, she also organizes the characters more clearly in terms of positive and negative characteristics. Bernard's Yvrée obliges his daughter Eléonor to marry Retelois, but neither Yvrée nor Retelois merit the title "maître absolu" ["absolute master"] or "tyrant" that d'Aulnoy uses to characterize the Duglas and Bedfort. Even Matilde, who resorts to emotional blackmail in an attempt to convince Eléonor to renounce her love for the duc de Misnie, is forgiven in the end, due to the fact that she thus pushes Eléonor to obey her father. By contrast, d'Aulnoy associates the very idea of forcing one to marry against one's will with despotism. D'Aulnoy also has her Julie mockingly ridicule the attempts on the part of the old to seduce the young as Julie tries to ward off the Senator Alberty who wishes to marry her, a scene that indirectly denounces the common marriage practice uniting a younger woman and a much older man, which goes unquestioned in Bernard.[16] As Patricia Hannon has argued, Bernard's pessimistic view towards love was influenced by Jansenism (128–29). Taking this into account, *Eléonor d'Yvrée* could be read in terms of the impossibility of reconciling one's various obligations, one's virtue, and one's passion, making it impossible to live happily in the world. Basically, no one in the story is "guilty" (with the exception, perhaps, of the self-interested duchesse de Misnie). The problem lies in the incompatibility of the different characters' desires and mutual obligations.

While Bernard's novel reads like a philosophical tale, d'Aulnoy's *Hypolite* deals with the more material and legal realities pertaining to domestic life and particularly the distribution of power within the family. Through Julie's story, d'Aulnoy explores how first parents and then husbands have recourse to moral discourses, familial and professional alliances, and institutions like the convent, to control the sexuality and life choices of children and wives, and more generally, to dominate them. D'Aulnoy puts into question the morality that traps characters like Julie into submission by revealing the hypocrisy of other characters who use morality to further their own personal interests. The very idea that obedience to parental or husbandly authority is a virtue and must be respected unconditionally is seriously problematized in the novel. In the same way that Scudéry justifies overthrowing political tyranny in *Clélie, Histoire Romaine*, so d'Aulnoy legitimates opposing the domestic tyranny of parents and husbands in *L'Histoire d'Hypolite*.

OF *BIENSÉANCE*

The dilemma in which characters like the Princesse de Clèves, Eléonor d'Yvrée, and Julie find themselves exists only to the extent that they insist on adhering to notions of virtue, honor, and *bienséance*.[17] Whereas Lafayette's Princesse de Clèves and Bernard's Eléonor fully accept the validity of such principles, Julie's closest companions, notably Hypolite and Lucile, push Julie to question them, ultimately so that Julie can free herself and become the agent of her own desire. Through the telling of Julie and Hypolite's story, d'Aulnoy problematizes the concepts of virtue, honor, and *bienséance* by highlighting how characters in positions of power use them to subjugate those characters, that is, women and children, in positions of powerlessness.

As the novel makes clear, *bienséance* or decorum imposes quite different, even opposing, norms of behavior on young men and women. In the case of men, *bienséance* means traveling and gaining worldly experience. In the case of women, it means remaining cloistered in the parental or marital home, or in the convent. In other words, masculine *bienséance* has to do with the conquest of space, and feminine *bienséance* with containment within a space. Although norms of decorum are quite severe for women, men who go against masculine norms also are reprimanded, particularly when their transgressions threaten parental control over marriage.

When Milord and Madame de Duglas discover Julie and Hypolite are in love, Milord tries to call his son to duty, insisting that he adhere to norms of masculinity: "vous estes dans un âge auquel il n'est pas séant de rester dans la Maison paternelle; il faut que vous voyagiez mon fils, il faut que vous alliez dans d'autres pays pour vous façonner, pour en prendre les belles manieres, et pour vous polir; nous sommes persuadez que vous allez estre ravi que nous secondions le desir que vous avez sans doute de voir le monde" ["you are at an age where it is not appropriate to remain in the paternal Home; you must travel, my son, you must go to other countries to develop yourself, to take on good manners, and to polish yourself; we are persuaded that you will be delighted that we second the desire you undoubtedly have to see the world"] (35). Whereas *bienséance* requires women to remain in the closed space of the home, it compels men to leave the home to enter the open space of the world. Milord invokes *bienséance* in order to "interpellate" his son into the world of masculinity, evident in his use of an imperative form (*il faut que*), and the way he shapes his son's responses (*vous allez estre ravi; le desir que vous avez sans doute*).[18]

At the same time that Hypolite is encouraged to travel the world, to conquer space, Milord usurps, in a sense, Hypolite's agency, not only by ordering him to travel, but also by inciting him to respond according to the norms of masculine *bienséance*. The father attempts to "recruit" his son into the patriarchal ideology he upholds, demanding that Hypolite recognize himself in such values. Of course, Hypolite consistently rejects such interpellation, for the recognition of his father's values would result in his separation from Julie, which he categorically refuses.[19] It is important to keep in mind that the Duglas's insistence on decorum in dealing with Hypolite and Julie cannot be separated from their will to determine their children's destiny. Morality is invoked for the purpose of exercising authority over the children.

Disguise becomes a means for characters to transgress norms of *bienséance* appropriate to their gender. For instance, when Julie finally decides to take action toward the end of the novel, she first disguises herself as a lower-class woman and travels to Italy accompanied by her maidservant in order to flee from the convent. Later, after having been the victim of two attempted kidnappings and fearful of being abducted again by Alberty, Julie disguises herself as a male pilgrim, which allows her to travel without escort to Boulogne. Whereas Julie disguises herself to move out of spaces, Hypolite disguises himself to enter spaces. When Hypolite returns to the paternal home after his father attempted to send him to France, he disguises himself in a wig and strange clothes for his nocturnal visits to Julie. Later, when he manages to see Julie at her husband's home, Hypolite dresses as an Italian merchant. Finally, in order to gain access to the convent in which Julie is incarcerated, Hypolite pretends to be Hyacinthe, the painter Cardiny's assistant. Disguise allows characters to temporarily abandon their identity and to transgress the norms that define that identity. However, resorting to the strategy of disguise implies that the particular character already has questioned the norms of *bienséance*. Transgression means that, to some degree, one has rejected or refused to adhere to social norms. That Julie does not resort to disguise until the end of the novel, which allows her to move freely out of spaces of confinement, suggests that it took extreme circumstances and much persuasion for her to reject the social norms that coerced her into passively accepting her subjugation. To some degree *Hypolite* can be characterized as a *roman de désapprentissage* [a novel of unlearning] in which Julie learns to undo her moral education.

In many ways, Julie is a heroine reminiscent of Lafayette's Princesse de Clèves, whose precedent also clearly marked Bernard's Eléonor. In each case a virtuous heroine is caught between her love or passion, her duty to her family, and her concern for her virtue and reputation, all of which provides a pretext for dramatic tension and melodrama. As in the case of the Princesse de Clèves, the imperative that Julie be singularly virtuous comes from beyond the grave. On her deathbed, Madame de Warwick implores the Duglas to continue to raise Julie in the ways of virtue, Madame's principal legacy to her daughter, and to have her pay respects to the memory of her parents: "comme le plus solide bien consiste dans la vertu, [j'espère] qu'elle sera toûjours suffisamment riche, et qu'elle n'en pourra manquer, Madame, estant élevée auprés de vous. . . . veuillez l'engager, Madame, à rendre des devoirs à nostre Memoire, qu'elle nous auroit sans doute rendus à nous-mêmes si Dieu ne nous avoit pas retirez à lui" ["as the most solid riches consist in virtue, I hope that she will always be sufficiently rich, and that she cannot lack any, Madame, being raised by you. . . . I wish you to incite her, Madame, to render duties to our Memory, that she undoubtedly would have rendered to ourselves if God had not taken us away"] (13). Although Julie's mother dies when Julie is only two years old, d'Aulnoy seems to play on Madame de Chartre's last words to Madame de Clèves, which primarily serve to inculcate and solidify the daughter's attachment to virtue and *bienséance*. Much like Lafayette's princess, Julie moves from parental to husbandly supervision, which keeps her virtue in check. And like the princess, Julie is prepared to reject marrying her true love for reasons of virtue and decorum when she finally has the opportunity to marry according to her inclination. This "fantôme de devoir" ("phantom of duty" [Lafayette 229]) that ensnares the princess also traps Julie into accepting her suffering.

After Hypolite gets seriously injured when he is forced to fight as a gladiator, a scene recalling the one in the *Princesse de Clèves* where Nemours is injured in a tournament, Julie must be persuaded by Lucile to visit Hypolite: "vous estes trop timide répondit Lucile d'un ton impatient, allons allons ma chere soeur, allons n'hesitez plus. Julie se leva en tremblant" ["you are too timid, Lucile responded impatiently, let's go, let's go, my dear sister, let's go, do not hesitate any longer. Trembling, Julie got up"] (101). Questions of decorum not only impede Julie from visiting a wounded Hypolite. They also discourage her from fleeing a tyrannical husband, even after she discovers that her father is indeed alive and will annul her marriage with Bedfort and consent to her marriage with Hypolite. She declares to Hypolite: "Il faut Hypolite, il faut nous résoudre à cette cruelle nécessité que mon devoir m'impose. La mort me seroit préferable à une vie honteuse: et n'y eût-il que moy dans le monde, je voudrois agir comme si toute la terre me voyoit" ["Hypolite, we must reconcile ourselves with this cruel necessity my duty imposes on me. Death would be preferable to me over a shameful life; and if there were only me in the world, I would want to behave as if all the earth could see me"] (102). Julie has interiorized the notion of *bienséance*, which prevents her from taking initiatives to free herself from her oppressors. Whereas Milord de Bedfort tries to call Hypolite to his duty, Julie interpellates herself into adhering to her duty to a husband and parents who think only of their personal financial and emotional interests, and at Julie's expense. Like Madame de Clèves or Eléonor, Julie naively takes notions like *bienséance*, virtue, and duty as absolute and universal values, unaware of the manipulative ways in which parents and husbands use such values to their own ends.

For instance, when the Envoy to Florence arrives at the house of the Duglas, Julie wishes to retire to her room. However, the Envoy is part of the "play" Milord and Madame de Duglas set up to make Julie believe Hypolite is going to marry the fictional Mademoiselle de Néry. In order to get Julie to remain in the room with the Envoy, Madame de Duglas appeals to her sense of *bienséance*: it would not be appropriate for Madame de Duglas to be with the Envoy and Monsieur de Duglas unaccompanied by other women. Decorum is invoked to force Julie to be witness to the Envoy, who speaks about the wonderful qualities of Néry and authenticates the fiction that Hypolite intends to marry her. Earlier in the novel, the idea that it is not *bienséant* for a brother to spend time in his sisters' room is just an excuse to keep Julie and Hypolite separate from one another. Madame de Duglas also suggests that it is not *bienséant* for a girl to dispose of her own heart, ultimately because Madame wants to determine Julie's fate in marriage. That Bedfort decides to intern Julie in a French convent presupposes she committed some sort of moral trans-

gression like adultery, when Julie's only crime is having inappropriate feelings for Hypolite. Bedfort locks her up out of jealousy,
Julie's supposed infidelity or transgression of husbandly authority serving as a pretext for Bedfort's own covetous behavior. With
the example of Bedfort, the novel suggests that even when wives
are virtuous and adhere to social and moral conventions, husbands can still accuse them of being unfaithful, clearly highlighting the arbitrary use of moral principles in practice. Through the
story of Julie, d'Aulnoy demonstrates that *bienséance*, not to
mention justice or virtue, is a concept invoked only when it
serves those in positions of authority.

Social norms operate in such a way as to maintain the position
of those in power, mainly fathers and husbands, as well as female
agents of patriarchy. This is particularly clear in d'Aulnoy's
Spanish novellas. Dona Juana of "Don Gabriel Ponce de Léon,"
for example, is neither pretty nor young, and one gets a sense
that it is out of spite that she guards so carefully her nieces Isidore and Mélanie. As a matter of fact, she is most overzealous in
enforcing norms of decorum, to the extent that Isidore and Mélanie's father is himself critical of her extremism. While she uses
and abuses social norms to oppress her nieces, she proves to be
hypocritical and most ridiculous when she wishes to pursue ro-
mantically the young comte d'Aguilar, who is in love with Mélanie. Already her name signals the incongruence between her
pious appearance and her albeit ridiculous amorous desires:
"Dona Juana" is the feminine for "Don Juan." When Dona Juana
realizes that the count loves her niece, she steals Isidore and Mélanie away to a convent, and like the comte de Bedfort, she does
not allow them to speak or write to anyone. Dona Juana uses her
authority as their guardian to take revenge on her nieces by denying them what she herself cannot have. In "Don Fernand de
Tolède," the comtesse de Fuentès, a jealous wife and social
climber, similarly locks up her daughters Léonor and Mathilde
at home. The two sisters are in love with Don Jaime and Don
Fernand, but fear speaking to them due to their mother's threats
that "elle les mettrait en religion pour le reste de leur vie" ["she
would put them in a convent for the rest of their lives"] (*Contes
I*, 475). D'Aulnoy provides many examples in her stories and tales
of how characters use virtue and *bienséance* to further their own
ends, as well as examples of women who use social norms to oppress those below them, namely their children, and especially
their daughters. As such, d'Aulnoy problematizes the imperative

to adhere to so-called moral precepts that only reinforce existing relations of power.

At the same time that those in positions of authority co-opt concepts like *bienséance,* virtue, and duty for their own ends, female characters in positions of victimization also resort to such concepts to give themselves value. When Julie considers her options, she hesitates to leave Bedfort for Hypolite: "elle pensoit que puis qu'elle étoit mariée elle devoit rester avec son époux; qu'enfin on n'avoit usé d'aucune violence pour l'obliger à faire cét hymen, elle faisoit reflexion sur ce que le monde en pourroit penser, et tout cela l'empeschoit de répondre" ["she thought that since she was married she had to remain with her husband; that finally no one had used any violence to oblige her to agree to this marriage, she reflected on what people could think, and all of this prevented her from responding"] (103). Later she remarks: "et ma gloire, cher Hypolite; ma gloire" ["and my glory, dear Hypolite, my glory"] (138). In the same way that Julie's father Warwick privileges military glory over love, so Julie privileges feminine glory (chastity, obedience, virtue) over her love for Hypolite: "Je suis encore cette même Julie . . . qui aime plus la vertu et son devoir qu'elle ne vous aime, et qu'elle ne s'aime elle-même" ["I am still this same Julie . . . who loves her virtue and duty more than she loves you, and more than she loves herself"] (139). Not unlike the Princesse de Clèves, Julie rejects the idea of taking a second husband out of an abstract notion of virtue, which both heroines accept at face value. Clearly Julie refuses to be reduced to an object of exchange, evident in her desire to go to a convent (meaning that she would take herself out of social circulation), and in her desire to marry Hypolite (meaning that she would be the subject of her own desire). However, Julie fails to reject the very concepts that reduce her to an object of exchange, and until she can transgress the norms of her society, she will remain the possession and in the possession of others.

On several occasions, Hypolite and Lucile push Julie to violate the rules of decorum and present compelling arguments that put into question *bienséance.* When Hypolite strategizes his feigned trip to France so that he can return home at night to see Julie, Lucile comes up with a plan that would allow the two lovers to see each other without Milord and Madame de Duglas finding out. Julie's first reaction is: "il me semble que la bien-séance n'est pas tout-à-fait gardé dans cette conduite" ["it seems to me that decorum is not fully respected in this conduct"] (38). Lucile argues that there is no need to be so exact under the circum-

stances, and that she herself risks the wrath of her father in as-
sisting the two lovers. Julie finally gives in, saying: "vous sçavez
bien l'un et l'autre . . . que vous n'avez que trop le pouvoir de me
persuader" ["you both know very well . . . that you have the
power to persuade me"] (39). Later Lucile persuades Julie, now
the wife of Bedfort, to go see Hypolite after he has been injured:
"Il faut vaincre vos scrupules et vos allarmes, ma chere soeur . . .
il y va de la vie de mon frere" ["You must overcome your scruples
and fears, my dear sister . . . this is about the life of my brother"]
(100). It should be noted that going to Hypolite's room also gives
Lucile the opportunity to see Léandre, with whom she has fallen
in love. For Lucile, considerations of love and friendship far outweigh those of *bienséance*. Unlike Julie, Lucile never hesitates
to transgress social norms in order to help a friend or lover.

In a similar manner, Hypolite tries to convince Julie that her
freedom is more important than her glory or duty. When Hypolite finds Julie at the convent in Saint Menoux, he pleads with her
to flee to Florence, and exasperated, declares:

> Que vous avez d'injustice pour vous-même et pour moy, Madame . . .
> pourra-t'on trouver mauvais que vous rompiez vos chaines, que vous
> abandonniez une indigne prison, où l'on vous a mise sans sujet? si
> vous ne voulez pas que je vous accompagne, je partiray aprés vous.
> Est-il rien au monde plus naturel, et plus ordinaire que de chercher
> sa liberté quand on l'a perdüe? . . . je ne puis vous persuader, vous
> aimez vos peines; vous refusez un remede qui seroit aprouvé de
> toute la terre.
>
> (139)

> [How you are unjust towards yourself and towards me, Madame . . .
> could one find reproachful that you break out of your chains, that you
> flee an indignant prison, where you were put for no reason? if you do
> not want me to accompany you, I will leave after you. Is there any-
> thing in the world more natural, more ordinary than to seek one's
> freedom when one has lost it? . . . I cannot persuade you, you love
> your suffering; you refuse a remedy of which the entire world would
> approve.]

Although Julie does not act immediately upon hearing these
words, she does seem to consider them later, when she discovers
that Bedfort is prepared to hide her in yet another convent after
learning that the comte de Warwick is indeed alive and well. In
order to persuade Julie to "break her chains," Hypolite legiti-

mates resistance to oppression by naturalizing the pursuit of freedom. His words point to the idea that if notions like *bienséance*, virtue, or duty prevent Julie from being free, then such concepts must not be natural, meaning that she is entitled to infringe upon them. Hypolite's declaration seriously questions the extent to which one should adhere to social norms, and certainly argues that one has a right to disregard them when one's freedom is at stake. In the end, however, a frustrated Hypolite advances the idea that Julie "loves her pains," suggesting that her behavior is somewhat masochistic. As Mainil has argued, "Julie announces Sade's Justine" (86) in the depiction of the misfortunes of virtue. Given that Julie fails to act out of anxiety over her virtue and reputation, as well as the masochistic overtones of her behavior, I would have to disagree with Shirley Jones Day's assessment of Julie as a heroine. Arguing that Julie is "strong and courageous" whereas Hypolite is "weak and helpless" (79), Day disregards Julie's timidity to take action, a timidity constantly challenged by Lucile and Hypolite over the course of the novel.[20]

Contrary to Julie, both Lucile and Hypolite place love and friendship above decorum or duty to parents. Lucile notably does not fear transgressing social norms or disobeying Milord and Madame de Duglas. Far from being punished for such behavior, she is in fact rewarded, marrying Hypolite's Italian friend Léandre without any complications. As we might expect, Hypolite finds this highly annoying: "Helas! . . . vous n'avez pas esté troublez un moment dans vostre passion, l'hymen [a] couronné vostre amour; vous n'avez point eu le temps de craindre, d'esperer, d'avoir des soupçons, des rivaux, des traverses et des peines: mais pour moy que n'ay-je point souffert" ["Alas! . . . you were not disturbed for a moment in your passion, marriage crowned your love; you did not have the time to fear, hope, have suspicions, rivals, obstacles, and pains: but for me, how I have suffered"] (118). Hypolite's words are almost comical in the enumeration of what he must go through in order to gain Julie's hand, which is due in part to Julie's insistence on protecting her virtue and glory. The opposition between the two couples gives a slightly humorous tone to the melodramatic pair of Julie and Hypolite. And if Julie anticipates a Justine, then Lucile might be viewed as a precursor to Juliette.[21]

Interestingly, d'Aulnoy later uses the name Lucile for one of her characters in "Don Gabriel." At the beginning of the story, the Spanish Lucile is Louis's fiancée. When her brother dies, however, Lucile becomes a wealthy heiress, and her father insists on marrying her to one of his friends rather than to Louis. In order to avert an unwanted marriage, Lucile runs off with Louis and they secretly marry. In the end, Lucile is reconciled with her father, her story recalling in many ways that of the non-fictional La Guette. In the same vein, the enterprising Léonor and her sister Mathilde of "Don Fernand" run off and marry Don Fernand and Don Jaime without parental consent, and again, everything works out for the best. In the latter novella, d'Aulnoy obviously draws from the story of Bernard's tragic friends, Eléonor and Matilde. In rewriting their story, d'Aulnoy eliminates the rivalry that divides Bernard's Eléonor and Matilde, and she satisfies both women by uniting them with their true love. D'Aulnoy also and quite consequently removes the psychological barriers, such as the moral imperative to obey one's parents, which prevent Bernard's Eléonor from marrying the duc de Misnie. By privileging "true love" over obedience to parents, d'Aulnoy makes love a moral imperative superior to all others, implicitly writing against the predominant ideology of the Counter-Reformation.[22]

CHALLENGING THE WISDOM OF WOMEN WRITERS

Taking into account d'Aulnoy's tolerant position vis-à-vis consensual rapt in the two novellas, we might read *Hypolite* as a critique, if not a burlesque imitation, of the sentimental novel à la Lafayette. From Madame de Villedieu to Bernard, women writers insisted upon the incompatibility of passion, love, *bienséance*, and *repos*, evident in titles like *Les Désordres de l'amour* [The Disorders of Love] and *Les Malheurs de l'amour* [The Misfortunes of Love]. But this incompatibility is based first, on the acceptance of received notions of virtue and morality; second, on a tragic view of love and life; and third, on the belief that men are naturally inconstant. From *L'Histoire d'Hypolite* to "Don Fernand de Tolède," d'Aulnoy proves to be a skeptic in her assessment of conventional moral principals. Through the examples of Milord and Madame de Duglas, Bedfort, Dona Juana, and the comtesse de Fuèntes, d'Aulnoy demonstrates how morality or *bienséance* becomes a pretext for such characters to control and even abuse others. If morality and *bienséance* are problematized, then love and morality are no longer necessarily incompatible. If disobedience towards parents is not viewed as being immoral, then clandestine marriage becomes unproblematic, and couples in love can embrace rather than reject the world. To give another example, if a woman is pushed into marrying a man she does not particularly care for so that her parents can profit socially and financially, then when given the opportunity to annul the marriage, or upon the death of an unwanted husband, she has no reason to reject a marriage offer from the man she truly loves. In her works in general, and in *L'Histoire d'Hypolite* in particular, d'Aulnoy questions the "conventional wisdom" communicated by the women novelists of her generation, particularly with respect to love, fate, and men's capacity to be faithful.

Women writers from Scudéry to Lafayette express in their works the fear of male inconstancy. In Scudéry's novels, male characters are subjected to many trials in order to prove their fidelity and steadfastness. Villedieu's marquise de Termes is betrayed by Bellegarde, who tires of her as soon as they are married, and Lafayette's princess fears the same fate with Nemours. Similarly, Julie believes early on in the novel that Hypolite is capable of infidelity: "vostre raison vous r'appellera à vostre devoir, vous m'oublierez quand vous ne me verrez plus" ["your reason will call you to your duty, you will forget me when you no longer see me"] (21). It is perhaps this belief that leads Julie to fall into the trap set by her adoptive parents. The inscribed tale, "L'Ile de la Félicité," also concerns the issue of male inconstancy, for Adolphe leaves Félicité to make a name for himself. After noting that Bedfort quickly forgets Julie after the abbess informs him that she died, the narrator remarks upon "l'inconstance naturelle des hommes" ["the natural inconstancy of men"] (145). However, Hypolite is always constant in the novel, never doubting Julie for a minute, and he remains faithful even after learning about Julie's marriage to Bedfort and her supposed death at Saint Menoux. Léandre and the comte de Sussex also represent loyal male lovers. At times d'Aulnoy inserts contradictory morals or morals that present a contrast with the general narrative, with the result that the universal validity of statements like "all men are inconstant" is relativized.

In d'Aulnoy's works, such universal statements can lead female characters to misread their situation. For instance, in the tale "Gracieuse et Percinet," Gracieuse fails to trust Percinet, and like Julie, unnecessarily undergoes masochistic ordeals until Percinet's mother orders Gracieuse to marry her son: "Il est temps de rendre mon fils heureux et de vous tirer de l'état déplorable où vous vivez sous la tyrannie de Grognon" ["It is time to make my son happy and to take you out of the deplorable state where you live under the tyranny of Grognon"] (*Contes I*, 55). Overly concerned about questions of decorum, Gracieuse entreats Percinet to leave her room, even though he has just saved her from being torn apart by four furies. Like Julie, Gracieuse is "fort obéissante" ["most obedient"] and believes that "il vaut mieux souffrir que manquer à mon devoir" ["it is better to suffer than to fall short of my duty"] (*Contes I*, 34, 46), even if this means obeying her immoral and sadistic stepmother. Again, considerations of *bienséance* and conventional morality prevent the heroine from taking initiatives to free herself from the tyranny of others.

"Gracieuse et Percinet" is perhaps the fairy tale by d'Aulnoy that best approximates the story of Julie and Hypolite, but other tales, like the "Le Prince Lutin," also treat the question of women being unduly cautious of worthy men. D'Aulnoy, however, does not simply reverse the terms of the maxim "all men are inconstant." Rather, she shows that there exist inconstant and constant men, as well as inconstant and constant women. In "Le Mouton" ["The Ram"], for instance, Merveilleuse forgets to return to her Ram, which leads to his death, while the rather naive princess of "La Princesse Printanière" is betrayed by the most inconstant Fanfarinet, with whom she runs off to marry. Although the moral of the latter story communicates the message that children should obey their parents regarding marriage, read within the context of d'Aulnoy's oeuvre, we could take the moral to mean "sometimes parents know best" or "parents are not always wrong." Arguably, the contradictory messages proliferated in d'Aulnoy's stories and tales suggest that there are no universal maxims that can explain every situation, and what is true in one instance may not be true in another. As there are no absolutes, characters must deduce from their own particular situation whether or not someone is constant, just, honorable, or not. Characters who resort to universals in trying to understand their situation end up misunderstanding it.

Julie's failure to fully trust Hypolite could very well derive from the fact that she spent too much time reading Villedieu, Lafayette, and Bernard, learning their lessons all too well. In their novelistic worlds, love cannot flourish due to 1) arranged marriages; 2) love's incompatibility with morality, duty, and *bienséance*; or 3) because love is viewed in and of itself as an ephemeral passion that eventually extinguishes itself, leading to inconstancy or ennui. As the titles of Villedieu's and Bernard's texts would suggest, love is doomed to failure, destined to create disorder and unhappiness. The unhappy fate of love is depicted as inevitable. In *Hypolite*, however, d'Aulnoy plays with the notion of fate, problematizing the rather Jansenist perspective of her contemporaries, who seem to embrace—at least in their novels—the Counter-Reformation's condemnation of the passions.

Whereas in the *Princesse de Clèves*, the tragic deaths of characters like Elisabeth de France, Chastelart, and Marie Stuart are presented in terms of an inevitable destiny, d'Aulnoy tends to render the notion of fate unstable, for characters' perceptions of their destinies change and evolve over the course of the novel. For instance, when Hypolite is prepared to kill himself, believing his feelings for Julie are incestuous, he blames the "Astre fatal" ["fatal Star"] (18) under which he was born. Overhearing her brother, Julie complains about this same unlucky star. But as the narrative progresses, their luck changes when they realize they are not blood related. Although at one moment destiny demands that Julie depart for a convent in France, a moment later Julie plans to remain in England. Destiny also refers to one's fate in marriage. Julie reminds Hypolite: "vous estes destiné depuis long-temps à Mademoiselle d'Argille" ["you have been destined to Mademoiselle d'Argille for a long time"] (28). Of course, there is no mention of Mademoiselle d'Argille after page thirty-one, meaning that destiny constantly changes. At one point Julie laments "la fatalité de mon étoille" ["the fatality of my star"] (100), believing that she is destined to suffer in life, when in the end she will marry Hypolite and live happily ever after. In *Hypolite* d'Aulnoy presents a changing destiny that depends as much on external circumstances as it does on personal decisions. In the final analysis, what is destined to happen is what the characters will themselves. As Hypolite says to Julie, "si vous ne m'estes point contraire, qui pourra séparer nos coeurs?" ["if you are not contrary to me, who will be able to separate our hearts"] (34). It is only when Julie breaks from the prison of *bienséance*, freeing herself from the tyranny of others, that she finally is rewarded with marriage to Hypolite.

Perhaps the only predestined occurrence in the novel is Julie and Hypolite's love for one another. And although love might be fated, it need not be fatal. Arguably, the central problem in the novel is not love, but those obstacles, most of which could be attributed to the tyranny of Henry VIII, that prevent Hypolite and Julie from uniting their hearts. Had the comte de Warwick not been forced into exile, Julie's mother never would have died, and consequently Julie never would have been orphaned. If love is fate, Julie still would have fallen in love with Hypolite, but she could have married him without having to go through so many trials and tribulations. Her father would not have lost his wealth to the monarchy nor would he have been exiled, meaning that Julie would have been an acceptable match for Hypolite in terms of wealth and status. In spite of all the obstacles to their love caused by the political tyranny of Henry VIII, Julie and Hypolite nevertheless could have been united sooner if Julie had been more skeptical about the principals that psychologically trapped her into accepting submission to parents and especially to her husband, the comte de Bedfort. For d'Aulnoy, true love, unconstrained by social and moral conventions, can overcome all other obstacles. As such, d'Aulnoy clearly challenges the condemnation of love, so much a part of Counter-Reformation France and often reiterated in the woman-authored novel of the 1670s and 1680s.

Just as England mirrors France, so the politics of the family mirror the politics of the kingdom. Henry VIII uses the pretext of religious disagreement to break with the pope and Roman Catholicism in order to divorce Catherine of Aragon and marry Anne Boleyn. Similarly, Milord and Madame de Duglas, along with the comte de Bedfort, implicitly and explicitly play on social and moral conventions in order to control and separate Hypolite and Julie. Whereas kings arbitrarily imprison and persecute members of the nobility, parents and husbands arbitrarily imprison and persecute children and wives. But sometimes women play a role in their own victimization. By taking social and moral conventions at face value, women psychologically cloister themselves, making it impossible for them to take action. D'Aulnoy rewrites the sentimental novel in the tradition of Villedieu, Lafayette, and Bernard in such a way as to reject their pessimistic views of love and the world, and to highlight how one's blind attachment to virtue can become a mechanism of self-inflicted oppression. Indeed, the Catholic Reformation's focus on obedience to fathers and husbands and the criminalization of the passions only served to uphold the patriarchal authority of the father, and by extension, that of the king. In subtle ways, then, d'Aulnoy challenges the authority of both the absolute monarchy and the institution of the family. Finally, d'Aulnoy problematizes the values embraced by women writers of her generation, values that only reaffirmed the submissive, even nihilistic roles reserved for women in absolutist and Counter-Reformation France.

6

Fairy Tales and *Mondanité*

MANY OF THE SOCIAL AND POLITICAL ISSUES D'AULNOY ADDRESSES IN *L'Histoire d'Hypolite* are carried into her fairy-tale worlds. Parental domination, political tyranny, and forced marriage are themes taken up in practically every one of her tales. Perhaps even more pronounced in her tales than in her novel is d'Aulnoy's opposition to Counter-Reformation ideology, and particularly its assault on *mondain* culture. As we might expect, then, the ideology communicated through d'Aulnoy's tales contrasts with that of tales written by her contemporary, Charles Perrault. D'Aulnoy and Perrault frequented the same circles in which fairy tales were told as salon games, which explains the many intertextual references present in tales by writers of the first fairy-tale vogue.[1] As the comparative studies of different versions of "Riquet à la houppe" ["Riquet with the Tuft"] by Lewis Seifert and Patricia Hannon suggest, fairy-tale writers of the 1690s used the genre to debate contemporary issues through the use of allegory, a privileged form of expression in the age of absolutism.[2] At stake in the implicit debate between Perrault and d'Aulnoy, the larger context of which included other writers we will not discuss here, are the issues of class, gender, and more generally *mondanité*. As suggested in the previous chapter, d'Aulnoy is a skeptic: her apparently contradictory maxims function to deny the universality of moral precepts. However, the ways in which she responds to Perrault's tales and worldview demonstrate that d'Aulnoy indeed defended a particular vision of French society.

The main ideological difference between the two writers can be summed up in terms of their respective positions on *mondain* culture, particularly on *mondain* women and their role in society. As we saw in chapter 4, both Boileau and Perrault condemn *mondain* women, in large part on moral grounds, in order to exclude them from the sociocultural public sphere. The fact that d'Aulnoy problematizes the universality of moral maxims and that, in *Hypolite*, she highlights the ways in which powerful characters use and abuse morality to establish their power over others, represents one strategy for responding to the moralist critics of *mondain* women and culture. In the second part of this chapter we will focus on another strategy d'Aulnoy uses to defend *mondanité*: the incorporation of operatic elements into her tales. Arguably, it is the influence of opera, the *mondain* genre par excellence, that differentiates d'Aulnoy's tales from the ostensibly more folkloric and classical tales of Perrault, at least stylistically, if not ideologically.[3] Despite the fact that d'Aulnoy embraces opera in her tales, she also is implicitly critical of opera's representations of women and absolutism.

INTERTEXTUALITIES: RIDING HOODS AND PUMPKINS

Perrault's *Contes en Vers* appeared in 1695 and his *Histoires ou contes du temps passé avec des moralités* [Stories or Tales of Past Times, with Morals] in 1697, the same year d'Aulnoy published *Les Contes des fées* [Tales of the Fairies] (1697), soon to be followed by another collection, *Contes nouveaux ou les fées à la mode* [New Tales, or Fairies in Fashion] (1698). Given the proximity of the publishing dates of their respective collections and the references in d'Aulnoy's tales to those by Perrault, it is clear that Perrault and d'Aulnoy were familiar with each other's tales. As Jack Zipes maintains, before publishing their tales fairy-tale writers of the 1690s "first practiced them orally and recited them in the salons" (*Dreams*, 41). Moreover, their tales often were inspired by common sources, Straparola and Basile figuring prominently among them.[4] Given the intertextual environment out of which the fairy-tale vogue emerged, it should come as no surprise that d'Aulnoy integrated elements, often extracted from their specific narrative context, borrowed from Perrault's tales. What is surprising is the lack of references to d'Aulnoy's tales in Perrault. In any case, d'Aulnoy playfully integrates elements drawn from Perrault's tales in such a way as to subvert the ideology conveyed through them. Ideological differences between the two writers can also be highlighted upon considering the different ways the two writers appropriate plots and characters taken from their shared sources.

In some instances d'Aulnoy borrows specific elements from Perrault in ways that, one could easily imagine, would have provided comic relief in salon readings of her tales. D'Aulnoy plays on "Le Petit Chaperon Rouge" ["Little Red Riding Hood"] in several of her tales. In "Le Prince Lutin," for instance, a fairy gives Léandre a "petit chapeau rouge" ["a little red hat"] that allows him to become invisible. In "Le Rameau d'or" ["The Golden Branch"], the good fairy Bénigne appears before Trognon as an old lady in a "chaperon" to give her the choice of beauty or virtue; and the evil fairy of the desert in "Le Nain jaune" ["The Yellow Dwarf"] turns up at Toute Belle's wedding in "un chaperon de velours rouge." Although folklorists contend that Perrault's tale is inspired by the oral folk tradition, they also have shown that "the independent oral tales lack the motif of the red riding hood or the color red" (Zipes, *Trials*, 6). Thus d'Aulnoy's references to red hats and hoods undoubtedly constitute so many allusions to Perrault's tale.

D'Aulnoy takes what becomes in Perrault's tale the metonymic sign of a young and naive peasant girl and turns it into polyvalent sign that can refer to disparate things. Whereas the red cape of Perrault's little girl can be read as the sign of her sinful nature and future victimization, Léandre's little red hat empowers him to do good deeds for others: "il semblait que son petit chapeau rouge ne lui devait servir que pour réparer les torts publics et pour consoler les affligés" ["it seemed that his little red hat should only serve him in repairing public wrongs and in consoling the afflicted"] (*Contes I*, 129).[5] The fairy Bénigne wears the *chaperon*, considered a lower-class accessory, to cloak, so to say, her true noble identity in order to test a princess. By contrast, the *chaperon* of "Le Nain jaune" signals the evil fairy's unfashionable taste and the fact that she is out of place at a royal wedding. In effect, d'Aulnoy destabilizes Perrault's signifier by attributing to it various signifieds. In its different forms, "petit chaperon rouge" can refer to women or men, mortals or fairies, good or evil, depending on the specific context.

To a different end d'Aulnoy appropriates and modifies the use of the pumpkin carriage, rat coachman, and lizard footmen of Perrault's "Cendrillon" ["Cinderella"]. In composing "L'Oiseau bleu" ["The Blue Bird"], d'Aulnoy draws from the story of princess Zoza, which constitutes the frame narrative of Basile's *Pentamerone*. In order to approach prince Tadeo, now married to the slave Lucia who took Zoza's place as his bride, Zoza offers Lucia three presents that come out of a walnut, a chestnut, and a hazelnut. In d'Aulnoy's "L'Oiseau bleu," objects similarly emerge from four eggs, one of which contains a miniature coach drawn by four green mice, with a pink rat as coachman. Although the main narrative at the end of "L'Oiseau bleu" closely follows Basile's story, d'Aulnoy splices in a moment taken directly out of Perrault, as if winking at her audience. In another tale, "Le Mouton" ["The Ram"], d'Aulnoy again makes reference to Perrault's "Cendrillon" when she has the tale's title character transport Merveilleuse to his cave in a pumpkin drawn by six goats. What makes d'Aulnoy's allusions to "Cendrillon" particularly comical is that the objects she borrows from Perrault's tale remain anchored in the realm of the marvelous. That is to say, whereas Perrault has a fairy godmother transform the pumpkin, rat, and lizards into the more verisimilar coach, coachman, and footmen, d'Aulnoy gives marvelous properties to the objects themselves, without providing a translation for her readers from fairyland into the "real world."

D'Aulnoy modifies elements taken from Perrault's tales in order to open up the possible associations to be made between signifier and signified and to reinvest objects, to which Perrault gives mimetic value, with marvelous or nonmimetic value. Generally speaking, Perrault's tales are verisimilar, and as his succinct and more classical style would suggest, they mark Perrault's attempt to create a stable and ordered moral universe.[6] A playful relation to both signification and reality characterizes d'Aulnoy's more baroque style. As Jean Mainil has argued, d'Aulnoy constantly puts into question the meaning of particular tales, even the validity of the genre, through the interplays between frame narratives and tales, thus making univocal meaning difficult, if not impossible (224–34). Stylistic differences are often indicative of ideological ones, and this is clearly the case in d'Aulnoy's allegorical debate with Perrault. Already the idea of destabilizing systems of signification and rejecting mimetic representation for the pleasurable contemplation of the marvelous is compatible with d'Aulnoy's skeptical position on morality and rejection of Counter-Reformation ideology, with its iconoclastic tendencies.[7] D'Aulnoy's conception of and attachment to the *mondain* culture Perrault implicitly attacks furthermore leads her to turn Perrault's notions of class and gender on their head.

PEASANTS, NOBLES, AND *MÉSALLIANCE*

In "Griselidis," Perrault puts forth a peasant girl, a shepherdess, as the exemplary woman, and has her marry a prince.

Through the tale Perrault suggests that a woman of low *condition* can serve as an exemplum for women in general, and he implicitly approves of *mésalliance*, evident as well in "Le Chat Botté" ["Puss-in-Boots"], in which the son of a miller ends up marrying a princess. Such unions do not occur in d'Aulnoy's tales. Whereas Perrault retains the "rags-to-riches" motif found in Straparola, d'Aulnoy systematically modifies the *condition* of characters she borrows from her Italian source precisely in order to avoid alliances between nobles and commoners.[8] D'Aulnoy conceives of one's station in life as one's birthright, and characters of various ranks who respect the limits of their *condition* are represented in positive terms, whereas those whose behavior transgresses such limits literally are dragged through the mud. Although peasants who remain within the confines of their social identity often play positive roles, they are relegated to the margins of the story, and never perform the role of hero or heroine within d'Aulnoy's corpus.

Upon meeting a poor woman who asks her for a drink of water, the heroine of Perrault's "Les Fées" ["The Fairies"] responds in a language that identifies her as a commoner: "Oui-da, ma bonne mère" ["You bet, my good woman"] (*Contes*, 165). At the end of the tale, the polite girl of low rank ends up marrying a prince. A similar scene occurs in d'Aulnoy's "Fortunée." Believing herself to be the daughter of a poor farmer, Fortunée encounters the queen of the woods with six ladies of honor while fetching water from a fountain. As the tale unfolds, however, Fortunée discovers she is in fact the daughter of another queen, and marries the son of the queen of the woods. In Straparola's "Ancilotto, King of Provino," from which d'Aulnoy borrows to write "La Princesse Belle Etoile et le Prince Chéri," the three sisters are lowborn, and the youngest marries a king. In her version, d'Aulnoy rescripts them as daughters of a dispossessed queen. Similarly, she replaces the three daughters of a poor, lower-class widow of Straparola's "Pig Prince" with three noble daughters of an ambitious but impoverished lady who is ready to sacrifice them in order to recover her wealth and status in "Le Prince Marcassin" ["The Wild Boar"]. In Straparola's "Pietro the Fool," a poor woman's son ends up marrying a princess, whereas in "Le Dauphin" ["The Dolphin"], d'Aulnoy substitutes the peasant for a prince.

Although salon women often were accused of promoting *mésalliances*, d'Aulnoy, who ran her own salon, clearly opposes such practices. As a member of the traditional nobility, d'Aulnoy likely was sensitive to the derogation of noble status that ensued when noble women married commoners. (Noble men, however, could marry commoners without suffering derogation.) Not only did women lose their nobility, but they also were forced to pay the *taille*, which put many women in a precarious financial situation upon the death of their husbands. As Gayle Brunelle concludes, "derogation threatened a widow's income and social status" (83). Brunelle also establishes that noble women, whose families were ready to tolerate their daughters' and sisters' derogation for financial gain and "to reduce the costs of dowries" (80), were married to commoners more often than noble men. Although d'Aulnoy never suffered derogation herself, she was married for financial reasons to the lower-ranking and recently ennobled François de la Motte, baron d'Aulnoy, more than thirty years her senior. She probably experienced a sense of lost status, evident in her use of "Comtesse" rather than "Baronne" when signing her works. In her tales, d'Aulnoy promotes intermarriage within the nobility regardless of the characters' financial situation (which fairies always amend), as she consistently privileges noble status over wealth in order to avert *mésalliances* especially between noble men and wealthy women of ambiguous social status. Given the tight marriage market of the late seventeenth century, if daughters of wealthy commoners married noble men, noble women were left with few options.[9]

Like Straparola, Perrault often plays on the "rags to riches through marriage" story, which Ruth Bottigheimer contends is a thoroughly urban and early modern type of tale.[10] D'Aulnoy on the contrary reinforces traditional feudal distinctions of rank, and her tales are so many lessons on how to distinguish between true and false nobility. Such lessons take the form of, on the one hand, discerning the noble disguised as a peasant, and on the other, discerning the peasant disguised as a noble. Characters like Fortunée, Aimée, Rosette, Brillante, Sans Pair, Subtile, and Constancia all momentarily live as peasants, usually as shepherds and shepherdesses, which would immediately bring to mind for a seventeenth-century reader the pastoral—and noble—world of *L'Astrée*. However, they are never fully (mis)-taken for a person truly belonging to the lower ranks. Despite her savage surroundings and the fact that she was raised by ogres, Aimée shows signs of natural "good taste" indicative of her true noble identity in "L'Oranger et l'abeille" ["The Bee and the Orange Tree"]. In "Le Pigeon et la colombe" ["The Pigeon and the Dove"], the fairy Souveraine attempts to conceal Constancia's identity, dressing her as a shepherdess and taking her to the countryside. Nevertheless "cette charmante princesse ne pouvait être si bien couverte, que l'on n'aperçut quelques-unes de ses beautés et, malgré tous les soins de la fée, on ne parlait plus de Constancia que comme d'un chef d'oeuvre des cieux, qui ravissait tous les coeurs" ["this charming princess could not be covered well enough for others not to perceive some of her beauty, and despite the pains taken by the fairy, people spoke of Constancia as a masterpiece of the heavens, who stole everyone's heart"] (*Contes II*, 284).[11]

The very idea that a prince like Aimé would be capable of falling in love with an apparently savage Aimée, or that Brillante and Sans Pair, believing each other to be a shepherdess and shepherd, also manage to fall in love, suggests they instinctively sense that the object of their affection is indeed noble. Even so, characters are rather uncomfortable with their feelings for a person who appears to be their social inferior until the truth is finally revealed. In "Le Rameau d'or," Brillante deeply feels the loss of rank, and constantly reproaches herself for loving Sans Pair, whom she believes to be a shepherd. Constancio similarly laments the fact that he loves a shepherdess, and the resolution of the tale itself comes with the revelation of Constancia's true identity as a princess. *Mésalliance* is not tolerated on the part of male or female characters. Unlike the prince of "Griselidis," d'Aulnoy's noble characters immediately reproach themselves for the very idea of loving a social inferior, and the problem itself disappears when the identity of their true love is revealed. In the end, d'Aulnoy communicates through her tales the notion that a noble can only truly fall in love with another noble. The authenticity of noble identity coincides with and is even revealed by the authenticity of love.

When "peasant" and "shepherd(ess)" are used to qualify a noble character, such terms emphasize the natural beauty and nobility of that character, whose nobility is shown to exceed outward appearance. Just as the moon can never fully eclipse the sun, so the rays of nobility cannot be concealed beneath the attire of a peasant. Terms referring to low-ranking characters who remain within the confines of their *condition* are also without negative connotations. The "good old man" who assists Rosette is rewarded at the end of the tale, and the old shepherdess who takes in Brillante also is a sympathetic character. Peasants form the support for noble identity and background for the pastoral settings of many of the tales. The fact that fairies often disguise themselves as peasants to test the heroine emphasizes the sense of *noblesse oblige* a true noble must embrace, and as such, a peasant who knows his or her place is necessary to noble identity.

However, characters who attempt to elevate themselves through marriage or usurp in any way a noble identity are referred to pejoratively as "peasants." Thus the so-called duchess Grognon, who manages to marry a king and persecute the noble Gracieuse, whom she uselessly tries to outdo, is described as being "plus mal bâtie qu'une paysanne" ["built worse than a peasant woman"] (*Contes I*, 37). Whereas Rosette can dress like a peasant, and the good old man indeed is a peasant, the unnamed daughter of Rosette's nurse who attempts to usurp Rosette's identity and marry the king of the Peacocks is described negatively as "une laide paysanne" ["an ugly peasant woman"] (*Contes I*, 198). Both Truitonne of "L'Oiseau bleu," and the nurse's daughter of "La Princesse Rosette" probably are modeled on the slave girl Lucia, who usurps the identity of Basile's princess Zoza to marry the prince, which again associates such characters with the lower classes.[12] Just as nobles cannot conceal their birth beneath peasant garb, so the lowborn cannot conceal their identity beneath a crown.

A particular social order is established by the end of each tale, when signifiers of the various characters' rank finally correspond to their "true" *condition*, which theoretically is stable. Nobles temporarily metamorphosed into shepherds or even animals are adorned with the rich clothing indicative of their status, and the lowborn hiding behind noble attire are "defrocked" or unmasked, and often eliminated altogether. Characters like Grognon who seek to transcend their status usually are killed off by the end of the story, which allows for the transparency between noble signifiers and signifieds. By representing *mésalliance* as an impossible bond doomed to failure due to inherent differences in *condition*, and which notably does not produce any fruit, d'Aulnoy guarantees the traditional feudal order of French society, which in reality has all but disappeared by the end of the seventeenth century. As we saw earlier, d'Aulnoy often plays with signifiers borrowed from Perrault's tales in such a way as to destabilize them. Nevertheless she creates a stable social order of her own that is diametrically opposed to that of Perrault. D'Aulnoy's fairy worlds also present a contrast with the salon world of Scudéry: while d'Aulnoy advances an essentialist notion of nobility and seeks to create an absolute correspondence between noble signifiers and authentic nobility, Scudéry recombines freely circulating noble signifiers to construct her High Bourgeois and Robe *salonniers* as noble.

At the same time that we can read d'Aulnoy's critique of apparently lowborn characters who aspire to nobility like Grognon, Truitonne, and the nurse's daughter of "Rosette" in terms of her defense of a traditional nobility, we might also read this in terms of d'Aulnoy defending aristocratic women in particular. In his *Apologie* and "Griselidis," Perrault holds up domesticated lower-class women as positive examples of patience and wifely submission, to be contrasted with unruly, hypocritical, and domineering aristocratic women. Without making her noble heroines submissive, d'Aulnoy clearly depicts them as being more reasonable, kind, and sincere than their lowly and sadistic adversaries. Whereas d'Aulnoy's noble female characters seek relations of reciprocity and mutual respect with the object of their desire, her nonnoble ones instead wish to dominate (Grognon), imprison (Truitonne), and deceive (nurse's daughter) noble men, and especially kings. In fact, d'Aulnoy's critique of domineering lower-ranking women recalls seventeenth-century perceptions of Françoise d'Aubigné, the marquise de Maintenon.[13] It is their will to transcend their actual status that makes lower-class women dangerous to men in d'Aulnoy's tales: they marry out of interest, not love. D'Aulnoy's conception of ideal women presents a stark contrast to that of Perrault, not only regarding their *condition*, but also with respect to the types of trials they endure, and their relation to knowledge and power.

WOMEN, POWER, AND KNOWLEDGE

As we saw in chapter 4, Perrault views women as inherently mad and sinful, which explains the need for them to be formed, even forged, by a rational male authority that keeps them in check. Positive female characters must go through a process of abjection, usually consisting of public humiliation and the basest forms of domestic labor, in order to be redeemed. It is a process that makes of already passive female characters submissive wives, whose sphere of action is circumscribed by the patriarchal household. Like Fénelon, Perrault implicitly institutes a division of labor whereby the domain of politics, military art, jurisprudence, philosophy, theology, and mechanical arts is the domain of men, whereas the duties of women are limited to industriousness, cleanliness, and frugality (see Fénelon, 4). Such a division

of labor clearly takes women out of the public sphere and cuts
them off from centers of power and knowledge. Contained within
the narrow realm of domesticity, Counter-Reformation ideology
refused women freedom of action or thought. Playing on images
and plotlines of female submission found in Perrault, d'Aulnoy
responds to them in such a way as to resituate women in relation
to different forms of power, thus opening up their sphere of action.

In his *Apologie*, Perrault applauds lower-class women who engage in grueling domestic work, and in a tale like "Peau d'âne"
he reduces a princess to a *souillon* or scullion. *Souillon* is a term
used infrequently in the seventeenth century precisely because
it referred to the basest position within a household, which suggests that d'Aulnoy's use of the term indeed is borrowed from
Perrault, marking her engagement in an allegorical debate with
him about women's relation to work.[14] D'Aulnoy rarely has her
noble heroines engage in any type of work at all, and although
the princess Constancia leisurely takes up her spindle when disguised as a shepherdess, domestic labor generally is viewed negatively, and often is portrayed as a form of subjugation. In "La
Bonne petite souris" ["The Good Little Mouse"], the neighboring
king and enemy of pleasure takes over the kingdom of Joy and
imprisons the good queen. She is forced to knit "car le méchant
roi, qui était fort avare, la faisait travailler jour et nuit" ["because
the wicked king, who was very stingy, made her work day and
night"] (*Contes I*, 281). Her daughter Joliette is reduced to being
a *souillon*, which does not prevent her from becoming the sole
ruler of the kingdom of Joy at the end of the tale. D'Aulnoy alters
the meaning Perrault invested in the word *souillon*, not only by
downplaying the humiliation it brings to the heroine or by emphasizing the sense of oppression the status conveys, but also by
modifying its connotation altogether. In "L'Oiseau bleu," for instance, Florine disguises herself as "mie Souillon" and tricks
Truitonne into letting her speak with King Charming in order to
prevent their marriage. Here, momentarily becoming a *souillon*
empowers the heroine by allowing her to penetrate the castle
walls and outsmart the malicious Truitonne. Florine takes a sign
of powerlessness, *souillon*, and makes it into an instrument that
gives her power.[15]

In other tales, d'Aulnoy modifies the notion of feminine patience so valorized by Perrault. In "Le Serpentin vert" ["The
Green Serpent"], the evil fairy Magotine enslaves Laideronette,
informing her: "vous donnerez à tout le monde, malgré vous, des

exemples de patience qu'il sera difficile d'imiter" ["you will provide for the world, despite yourself, examples of patience difficult to imitate"] (*Contes I,* 545). Although the tale also borrows from the story of Psyché, the emphasis on patience is reminiscent of Griselidis, this model of patience Perrault offers to Mademoiselle. However, the character who tries her patience is depicted in unambiguously negative terms. Rather than have a goddess like Venus impose impossible tasks as in the story of Psyché, d'Aulnoy gives this role to the vindictive Magotine.

Again domestic work is part of Laideronette's cruel trial, and one of her tasks is to spin a spider's web, which the princess clumsily tries to do: "Lorsqu'elle voulut filer cette crasseuse toile d'araignée, son fuseau trop pesant tombait cent et cent fois en terre" ["When she attempted to spin this filthy web, her heavy spindle fell to the ground a hundred times"] (*Contes I,* 546). It is notable that d'Aulnoy focuses in particular on Laideronette's difficulty with this rather foul trial, suggesting that Laideronette indeed was not made for such work.[16] D'Aulnoy furthermore modifies the Griselidis/Psyché narrative by incorporating the story of Orpheus. After overcoming several trials with the assistance of the fairy Protectrice, Laideronette must descend into Hell and retrieve for Magotine the Essence of Long Life and save her husband, the green serpent. At the same time that Laideronette is a modern Psyché, she also plays the role of a female Orpheus. Trials of domesticity lead up to the more heroic trial of descending into Hell, as d'Aulnoy tests her heroine's patience as well as her courage. Aristocratic women in d'Aulnoy's tales recall the noble *frondeuses* like Anne Marie Louise d'Orléans, duchesse de Montpensier, who sought to display the grandeur of their lineage through chivalric exploits, much like their male counterparts.

By depicting domestic work in oppressive terms and by introducing into the classical story of Psyche a female Orpheus, d'Aulnoy distances *mondain* women from domesticity to give them more noble pursuits. In "Le Serpentin vert" as well as in "Le Rameau d'or," d'Aulnoy furthermore redefines female characters' relation to intelligence in her own renditions of "Riquet à la houppe."[17] In Perrault's version, Riquet is the brilliant but ugly son of a king and queen, and a fairy gives him the gift to bestow intelligence onto his true love. Another king and queen bring into the world two daughters, one of whom is intelligent and ugly, the other, beautiful and stupid, but who can endow the one she loves with good looks (the intelligent daughter receives no such gift).

Perrault goes on to follow the story of the beautiful but stupid sister, and as the narrative progresses, the intelligent but ugly sister falls by the wayside. While the narrative leaves open the question as to whether or not the princess made Riquet handsome, or if love alone performed this transformation, the moral of the story also leaves doubt as to whether or not Riquet actually gave the princess any intelligence at all: "Tout est beau dans ce que l'on aime, / Tout ce qu'on aime a de l'esprit" ["Everything is beautiful in what we love, / Everything we love is clever"] (*Contes*, 188). Perrault's narrator leads the reader to believe that Riquet may not have been transformed, but leaves Riquet's power to grant intelligence intact. Then in the moral of the story Perrault takes away the princess's intelligence—meaning perhaps that Riquet is a lot smarter than we initially thought in his ability to make the princess believe both that she gained in intelligence, and that she made Riquet handsome. Regardless of how we read into these ambiguities of the tale, in the end knowledge and power reside with Riquet.

Rather than pair off male and female characters in terms of masculine intelligence and feminine beauty (also the case in Catherine Bernard's version), thus giving male characters the monopoly on brainpower, d'Aulnoy portrays both the prince and the princess of her tales as ugly and intelligent. In "Le Rameau d'or," Torticolis and Trognon are equally hideous, and what they lack in beauty is compensated by their intellect and virtue. After having refused to marry each other, each believing the other to be especially unsightly, Torticolis and Trognon prove their worth and arguably are metamorphosed into their "authentic," handsome noble selves by the end of the tale, symbolized in their new names: Sans Pair [Without Peer] and Brillante.

Similarly in "Le Serpentin vert," Laideronette must overcome her aversion for the green serpent, and learns to love him despite his ugly exterior. As in Perrault's "Riquet," d'Aulnoy has a fairy interfere with the birth of a princess: Magotine maliciously makes the queen's first twin daughter perfectly ugly, but is prevented from harming the second. Consequently the queen names her daughters Laideronette (from "laide" ["ugly"]) and Bellotte (from "belle" ["beautiful"]). Unlike Perrault, however, d'Aulnoy completely ignores the story of the beautiful princess to focus on the adventures of the intelligent but ugly and sometimes imprudent Laideronette, whom a fairy—not a male character— rewards with beauty for her endurance. Taking both female and male characters through tests of wit and virtue, which eventually lead all characters to acquire beauty, not to mention love, the narrative of "Le Rameau d'or" and "Le Serpentin vert" present intelligence as well as beauty in gender-neutral terms.

Far from being the monopoly of men, knowledge in d'Aulnoy's tales is the privilege of both sexes. Female characters like Laidronette and the fairy souveraine of "Le Pigeon et la colombe" *moralisent* (moralize, philosophize) about their situation and other events, an activity writers like Fénelon reserve for men alone. Both the princess Félicité and the White Cat are described as being *universelle*, a term usually reserved for men used to qualify a person who possesses a great breadth of knowledge.[18] The White Cat furthermore is described as being "plus savante qu'il n'est permis à une chatte de l'être" ["more knowledgeable than a cat is allowed to be"] (*Contes II*, 177), pointing to the limits society puts on women's (here cats') acquisition of knowledge. D'Aulnoy rejects the gendered division of knowledge proposed explicitly by Fénelon and implicitly by Perrault, which restricts feminine knowledge to the realm of the particular or the domestic, leaving public and universal matters exclusively to men. She does so in part by responding to a tale like Perrault's "Riquet" in such a way as to eliminate the male monopoly on intelligence, and furthermore, by offering female characters like Félicité and White Cat, who demonstrate great intellectual capacities. Knowledge is power, and d'Aulnoy's universal heroines not surprisingly prove more enterprising than the submissive female characters of Perrault. They quite consequently hold more important positions within the public, political arena of d'Aulnoy's fairy worlds.

Although Joliette is reduced to a *petite souillon* in "La Bonne petite souris," she eventually becomes an independent queen after the good fairy leads a coup d'état against the tyrant and his son. Other kingdoms ruled at least for a time by kingless queens or princesses include that of Félicité, la Belle aux cheveux d'or [Beauty with the Golden Hair], Florine, the princess of the Ile des Plaisirs tranquilles [Island of Tranquil Pleasures], Merveilleuse, Babiole, and the White Cat. Female characters not only rule kingdoms, they also support them as soldiers, as in the case of the Amazon warriors who protect the kingdom of the princess of the Ile des Plaisirs tranquilles; or Belle-Belle who, disguised as the knight Fortuné, defeats the emperor Matapa and restores a "castrated" king to his throne.[19] D'Aulnoy imagines worlds in which women attain and maintain political power without the assistance of men. Perhaps "maintain" is the more appropriate term, for modifications in social or political order, including social climbing and usurpation, are depicted negatively in her tales. Whereas in Perrault's "Le Chat botté" the son of a miller usurps a noble identity and marries a princess with the aid of an enterprising male cat, in d'Aulnoy's "La Chatte blanche" a female cat, who is in fact sovereign of six kingdoms, helps the youngest son of a king claim his father's throne. In the end, however, the White Cat guarantees the stability of all royal lines by offering the king and his two older sons each a kingdom. *Largesse* on the part of sovereigns is lauded in the tale in order to guarantee the maintenance and continuity of noble lines. Revolutions occur only to reestablish reigns unjustly toppled. The revolution in "La Bonne petite souris," for instance, does not mark the foundation of a new regime; it allows Joliette to reclaim her father's usurped throne. Likewise, Belle-Belle does not conquer new kingdoms, but wins back that of her king. As rulers and as fighters, noble women preserve stability and order.

D'Aulnoy's depiction of women in positions of power and authority is a far cry from the ogress queen-mother of Perrault's "La Belle au bois dormant," or Fénelon's understanding of the roles women played in history: "Quelles intrigues se presentent à nous dans les Histoires, quel renversement des loix et des moeurs, quelles guerres sanglantes, quelles nouveautez contre la Religion, quelles revolutions d'Etat causées par le déreglement des femmes!" ["What intrigues present themselves to us in History, what toppling of laws and customs, what bloody wars, what fashions that go against Religion, what National revolutions caused by the disorder of women!"] (8). For writers like Perrault and Fénelon, women need to be confined to the particular and the domestic in order to prevent them from wreaking havoc on the body politic or defying universal, Christian morality. In her tales, d'Aulnoy contests the portrayal of women as so many perturbers of public or political order, not only by providing examples of powerful women who maintain order, but also by attributing multiple causes to the instability and downfall of kingdoms.

For instance, in "L'Ile de la Félicité," the peace and order of Félicité's kingdom is destroyed by male indifference, and in "Le Prince Lutin," the kingdom of the Ile des Plaisirs Tranquilles nearly comes under attack by Furibond, impelled by his violent passion for the island's princess. In several tales, male usurpers dethrone legitimate kings, whereas in "Finette-Cendron" the fall of the king and queen is due to their own mismanagement.[20] In a tale like "Le Prince Lutin," d'Aulnoy invents a world in which the stereotypes of her society are inverted, meaning that Léandre must convince the women of the Ile des Plaisirs Tranquilles that men are not all troublesome, and some can be admitted into their kingdom without creating disorder. His example counters the prejudices of the princess, who tries to blame national disorder on love and implicitly on men, an idea that is problematized in the tale. D'Aulnoy questions the universal validity of attributing social and political disorder to a single cause, whether that cause be unruly women, unruly men, or love.

On the question of class, Perrault proves to be much more flexible than d'Aulnoy, mixing and matching princesses and commoners, kings and shepherdesses. As viewed through Perrault's tales, the social hierarchy is malleable and can be manipulated by enterprising and clever men. However, Perrault's position on women is most inflexible, and his female characters closely adhere to norms of femininity propagated by writers like Chaussé, Fénelon, as well as Maintenon. With respect to the notion of cultural change, Perrault proves to be "progressive" with respect to class, but takes a conservative position on the roles he believes women should be allowed to play in French cultural life, which could be read as his reaction to the influential role aristocratic women were indeed playing within the sociocultural public sphere.

D'Aulnoy, on the other hand, upholds a rigid social hierarchy, conceiving of one's *condition* in essentialist terms, at the same time that she is highly critical of moralist representations of especially aristocratic women. Whereas d'Aulnoy sometimes destabilizes signs she borrows from Perrault's tales, her own narratives nevertheless attempt to fuse signs of nobility with authentic noble identities in order to repair the "damage" caused by the detachment of signifiers from their traditional signifieds, a phenomenon that has allowed for commoners to appropriate signs of nobility. Yet d'Aulnoy takes a much more progressive attitude toward women. Rather than depict domestic labor as an acceptable vehicle for female penitence and containment, as does Perrault, d'Aulnoy paints it as an instrument of torture and oppression. Through her tales she contests not only the limits placed upon women's intellectual pursuits, but she also challenges the idea that men "own" knowledge and have the power to grant it or not to women, an idea that presupposes women's inherent lack of intelligence. With her independently ruling princesses, d'Aulnoy demonstrates that women indeed can be capable and reasonable rulers who participate effectively in maintaining the stability of the public sphere. D'Aulnoy's socially conservative yet proto-feminist position reflects one of the tendencies of salon culture, and clearly presents a contrast with that of Scudéry, who takes a more progressive position on class.

SPECTACLES AND *MONDANITÉ*

At the same time that d'Aulnoy defends *mondain* culture by contesting Perrault's representations of the aristocratic women associated with it, she also does so by integrating elements of this culture into her tales in order to flout the anti-*mondain* position. Makeup, beauty, and fashion regularly come under the attack of writers from Perrault and Fénelon to Maintenon and Bossuet. Despite differences of opinion concerning the monarchy, nobility, and even religion, anti-*mondain* writers come together in their assessment of women's supposedly inherent tendency toward luxury, leisure, and pleasure, whose geographical locus within French society is the court and salons. Warning against everything from fashion to novels, they hold up theater and opera as particularly dangerous forms of entertainment that must be avoided. Rejecting the demonization of *mondain* culture, d'Aulnoy has positive characters guiltlessly adorn themselves—in good taste, of course—and engage in pleasurable *mondain* activities without falling prey to perverse and disordered passions. She especially celebrates the privileged *mondain* spectacle of late seventeenth-century France, opera, by incorporating and mimicking aspects of it in her tales.

In Tertullian's *The Apparel of Women* and *Spectacles*, one common theme brings together the self-as-spectacle and worldly spectacles: both are construed as artifice, and all artifice is the work of the devil and associated with idolatry. With respect to the self, idolatry manifests itself in the worship of physical beauty and all that entails (fashion, luxury, jewels); with respect to spectacle, idolatry concerns the worship of pagan gods, for all forms of spectacle, he argues, originates in cultish devotion to a particular god (i.e., the circus is dedicated to Circe, the theater to Venus). In both cases, the devil insinuates himself in the spectator as well as in the agents of spectacle by inspiring in them pleasure and exciting their passions, and as such distracts the Christian from thoughts of God (Tertullian, 47–107; 117–49). Such reflections are echoed in works by Counter-Reformation writers of different tendencies, including: Fénelon, Maintenon, Bossuet, and Pierre Nicole. In the society of late seventeenth-century France, when the aristocrat displayed his or her noble self through the body and its adornment (Stanton, 109), as well as by attending court ballets and opera, these moralists clearly were taking aim at *mondain* culture, and at women in particular, who were viewed to be especially vulnerable to the temptations and pleasures of artifice.

Blaming the destabilization of the traditional hierarchy on luxury and holding women responsible for promoting it, Fénelon condemns women's attachment to fashion. For Fénelon, women keen on fashion end up ruining their households, and he constructs such an attachment in terms of sin in the association he creates, like Tertullian, between fashion and idolatry (Fénelon, 199–207; see also Lougee, *"Noblesse,"* 89–91). In her lessons to her noble but impoverished girls at Saint-Cyr, Maintenon similarly uses sin to dissuade them from pursuing *mondain* interests. She cautions them against everything from curling their hair to wearing ribbons: "Toute fille qui met un ruban pour plaire à des hommes a déjà commis le péché dans son coeur" ["Every girl who wears a ribbon to please men already committed sin in her heart"]. Maintenon goes on to tell her young pupils that women who make themselves attractive in this way are guilty of their own sin as well as of leading men to sin: "une personne de notre sexe qui s'ajuste pour plaire est coupable non seulement du péché que renferme ce désir de plaire, mais encore de tous ceux que commettent les hommes qui la voient" ["a person of our sex who adorns herself to please is guilty not only of the sin implicit in this desire to please, but also of all those committed by the men who see her"] (44). Likewise, Bossuet criticizes women who adorn themselves and place value on their "superb beauty," which indicates their desire to be adored like a goddess or idol, and he considers physical beauty itself as a "deceitful mirror" (51–54). For anti-*mondain* writers, the desire to please and be adored through the enhancement and display of beauty feeds the chaotic passions, which leads to carnal sin and the ruin of households. Maintenon notably suggests to her pupils that their noble families have fallen due to the past sins of their ancestors (192).

In many respects d'Aulnoy's tales are all about worldly pleasures and men and women pleasing each other. Part of this pleasure comes from the physical beauty of the characters, enhanced by makeup, jewels, and fine clothing. In order to please her father, Gracieuse wears a green robe lined with gold and a crown of roses and jasmine with emerald leaves. Before meeting the White Cat, the prince is "poudré, frisé, parfumé, paré, ajusté et rendu plus beau qu'Adonis" ["powdered, curled, perfumed, adorned, fitted, and made more handsome than Adonis"] (*Contes II*, 168). Preparing to meet the queen Belle aux cheveux d'or, Avenant combs his hair and powders himself, while Belle puts on her satin dress and is "made up like a queen." In each instance, the character's exterior appearance is constructed in such a way as to display her or his inner nobility. Stylish and measured attention to one's appearance becomes a sign that one wishes to please without, however, connoting sinful behavior. It also signifies nobility. Nonnoble characters like Grognon or Truitonne who attempt to project a noble appearance without actually being noble end up looking tacky, even grotesque.[21]

Frequently the specular nature of such adornment is emphasized by the presence of mirrors. Passing through the halls of her palace, Belle looks at herself in her great mirrors "pour voir si rien ne lui manquait" ["to see if anything was lacking"] before meeting Avenant (*Contes I*, 63). In order to trick the fairy of the desert into believing he is in love with her, the king of the gold mines, consulting his mirror, combs his hair, powders himself, applies a *mouche*, and puts on a magnificent outfit. At one point in "Le Nain jaune" a siren of extraordinary beauty emerges from the sea, holding a mirror in one hand and a comb in the other. Such scenes recall paintings of Venus gazing at herself in a mirror held by Cupid, in the tradition of Titian, Rubens, and Velázquez. This worldly contemplation of beauty contrasts significantly with the moralistic Allegories of Vanity, in which a skull near a mirror symbolizes the ephemeral nature of physical beauty.[22] To some degree, these trends in painting illustrate well the distinction between the pleasurable contemplation of the marvelous in d'Aulnoy's tales—whether that take the form of flying chariots or great beauty—and the anti-*mondain* position that d'Aulnoy contests.

Indeed, d'Aulnoy's heroines often are equated with Venus, whether in direct references to the goddess, or by surrounding them with little *amours* or cupids. Her siren in particular emphasizes the connection with Venus in that she holds up a mirror while emerging from the sea, recalling the aforementioned paintings, as well as representations of the birth of Venus. In "La Chatte blanche," the prince is compared to Adonis, which stresses the importance of beauty in positive male characters as well. Such characters likely would have been perceived to be ef-

Jan Miense Molenaer (Dutch, ca. 1610–1668), *Allegory of Vanity*, 1633, oil on canvas, 40¼ × 59 in (102 × 127 cm); Toledo Museum of Art, Purchased with funds from the Libbey Endowment, Gift of Edward Drummond Libbey, 1975.21.

Diego Rodriguez de Silva y Velázquez, *Venus at her Mirror* (Rokeby Venus) (1649–1651). Oil on canvas, 122.5 × 177 cm. National Gallery, London.

feminate by writers like Boileau, who viewed male adherents to the Modernist cause as womanish. It should be recalled that at the beginning of the century, dandies who rejected Church doctrine and the monarchy, and who marked their opposition through nonconformist dress, were referred to as "hermaphrodites."[23] Displaying nobility through the body was practiced by men and women alike, which d'Aulnoy highlights in her tales. That positive male and female characters are intelligent and seek to please each other through their physical appearance undoes the dichotomy between male intelligence and female beauty already discussed above.[24] By making beauty both a female and a male virtue, d'Aulnoy furthermore renders gender-neutral the attachment to fashion and artifice. Whereas Fénelon and Maintenon feared fashion's economical as well as moral effect on individuals and families, d'Aulnoy upholds fashion as a visible sign of one's nobility and affection for another person. With respect to the expenses incurred in dressing fashionable, however, that is a matter for the fairies.

Besides attention to physical beauty (fashion, makeup, etc.), anti-*mondain* writers put theater and especially opera at the top of their list of harmful aspects of the aristocratic culture of the court and salons. We already have taken note in chapter 4 of the view of writers like Boileau, Perrault, Arnauld, and Fénelon concerning the allegedly insidious effect of opera on the female spectator: opera's effeminate melody, like a poison, softens the soul of its listeners, leading to everything from adultery to madness. In her lessons to the girls of Saint-Cyr, Maintenon makes explicit what is implicit in Perrault and Fénelon: as a public spectacle, opera takes women out of the domestic sphere, which in and of itself presents a danger to a woman's reputation. Maintenon very clearly opposes the public spectacle of opera to the private and virtuous domestic work within the home:

> Si vous n'avez point de vocation pour la vie religieuse, vous retournerez . . . avec un père ou une mère peut-être veufs ou infirmes . . . chargés d'enfants dont vous irez augmenter le nombre; vous passerez bien souvent vos journées à travailler dans la chambre de votre mère ou dans la vôtre, et vous ne penserez certainement pas à donner une pistole pour aller à l'opéra, vous n'en entendrez pas même parler; vous voudrez encore moins, si vous avez de l'honneur, vous y faire conduire par un homme qui, en payant votre place, vous perdrait de réputation.

(191)

[If the religious life is not for you, you will return . . . to a father or
mother, perhaps widowed or crippled . . . responsible for children of
which you will increase the number; you often will spend your days
working in your mother's or your own room, and you certainly will
not think of giving a penny to go to the opera, you will not even hear
it spoken of; if you are honorable, you will want even less to let a man
escort you there who, paying for your seat, will cause you to lose your
reputation.]

Instilling fear of sin in her girls, Maintenon makes accepting an
invitation to the opera akin to prostitution, ultimately a pretext to
keep them locked up and working in the home. Much like Perrault and Boileau, Maintenon creates an association between the
public, leisurely, *mondain* woman and women of ill repute. And
like Perrault, she makes domesticity the highest of female virtues.

Although this text was written in 1707, Maintenon was never a
fan of opera. Her morganatic marriage with Louis XIV in 1683
and her subsequent influence at court marked thereafter the
themes of opera and eventually led to opera's decline at court.
Beginning with *Amadis* in 1684, Quinault and Lully produced operas with implicitly Christian themes. Norman speculates that
Maintenon "seems to have convinced Louis not to spend excessive amounts of time and money on such lavish theatrical entertainments. In fact, 1686 marks the end of large-scale operatic
productions at Versailles" (328). As demonstrated above, Maintenon also opposed opera for ideological reasons. Opera arguably
was the privileged form of entertainment that allowed aristocrats to express and display conspicuous leisure, at the same
time that they could engage in the idolatrous contemplation of,
in the words of Sévigné, "un prodige de beauté" ["a beautiful
marvel"] (1: 661) and other "choses admirables" ["admirable
things"] (2: 285). Next to the novel, opera was one of the most
influential cultural mediums of the time, a particular opera generally enjoying three shows a week and "a run of as many as 150
performances," far outplaying the run of thirty performances
typical of a Racinian tragedy (Norman, 8). Given the frequency
of productions, going to the opera potentially could keep a well-
to-do woman out of the house on a regular basis, and along with
her weekly salon gatherings, was a sign in and of itself of a leisurely noblewoman. The *mondain* woman was diametrically opposed to Maintenon's domesticated noblewoman.

In d'Aulnoy's tales, conspicuous leisure is the rule. When Gracieuse comes upon Percinet's crystal palace, she is entertained by the opera *Les Amours de Psyché et de Cupidon*, and "Le Prince Lutin" concludes with theater, opera, and games to celebrate Léandre's marriage to the princess. At the idyllic beginning of "La Bonne petite souris," the good king and queen enjoy hunting, fishing, dancing, theater, and opera together. When Laideronette finds herself in the kingdom of Pagodie, she spends her time watching plays by Corneille and Molière (and notably not Racine), and generally being amused by the pagods, who dance and sing for her. In "La Chatte blanche," the prince is entertained by theater, ballet, feasts, and a carnivalesque hunt. Opera is one of the leisure-time activities that signals the characters' nobility.

The impact of opera on d'Aulnoy's tales, however, is not limited to establishing the noble, nondomestic identity of her heroes and heroines. Although little research has been done that closely examines the relation between opera and the tale, a relation often referred to but rarely studied in depth, scholars from Jean-Marie Apostolidès and Raymonde Robert to Jean Mainil have concurred that a relation indeed exists between the fairy-tale tradition and opera, a genre that grew out of Louis XIV's royal fêtes.[25] However, the nature of this relation is under debate. Apostolidès and Robert have focused on the ways in which Louis XIV's use of the marvelous, as manifested in opera, Versailles, and court festivals, influenced the literary fairy tale. Mainil has argued that, on the contrary, it was what he refers to as the "corpus féerique" that shaped the form the marvelous took in Louis XIV's court entertainments (52).[26] Yet Mainil's thesis cannot account for why the marvelous of the late seventeenth-century literary tale is distinct from that of medieval romance, folklore, and works by the earlier Italian fairy-tale writers, Straparola and Basile. Opera influences, I contend, the specific shape the marvelous takes in d'Aulnoy's tales. Its popularity and the frequency of productions made opera a widely accessible source of references and scenarios within *mondain* society.[27]

OPERA AND FAIRY TALES

In the 1670s and 1680s, the creation of a distinctly French operatic tradition marks the attempt by the monarchy of Louis XIV to influence the domain of *mondain* culture, constituted by the mixed company gatherings of aristocrats at salons and court,

whose members were steeped in novels and theater. For much of
the century the locus of *mondain* culture was the decentralized
networks of salons, as well as the circles that developed around
les Grands, powerful noble families like the Longuevilles and the
Condés, who served as important patrons of the arts and to
whom numerous literary works were dedicated. Upon assuming
his personal reign, Louis XIV had Nicolas Fouquet, one of the
century's greatest patrons, arrested in 1661, a decision indicative
of Louis XIV's desire to eliminate competition within the literary
and cultural field and to consolidate it as sole patron. The extent
to which the king was successful in doing so is evident in the publishing history of Scudéry's texts. Whereas *Les Femmes Illustres, Le Grand Cyrus*, and *Clélie* were dedicated to Madame de
Longueville, and Mademoiselle de Longueville respectively,
most of her post-1661 publications were dedicated to Louis XIV,
who incidentally succeeded Fouquet as her patron.

During this same period, Louis XIV accelerated the creation of
state academies in an effort to displace the cultural centrality of
the salon. As we have seen, some academicians attempted to delegitimate female authority in literary and cultural matters in
order to maintain their monopoly over knowledge, a monopoly
sanctioned by the creation of all-male academies. A genre that
emerged out of collaboration between Louis XIV, who often
chose its themes, and the Académie Royale de Musique, directed
by Lully, opera celebrated (not without some ambivalence)[28] the
glory of Louis XIV and the ultimate authority of men. Opera
could and indeed did effectively compete with the influence of
genres like the novel, and although opera's critics tended to associate the two, novel and opera often conveyed divergent ideologies. However, as Buford Norman cautions, we must be careful
not to take the ideology communicated through opera as a reflection of Quinault and Lully's personal position.[29] Opera's ostensibly pro-monarchy position and propagation of negative
stereotypes of women must be understood in terms of monarchical and academic ideology and not in terms of Quinault's own
opinions.

Before the emergence of the French literary fairy tale, opera
clearly was the genre of the marvelous par excellence, and arguably prepared the public's positive reception of the tale. The marvelous was an integral part of opera, providing a pretext for the
use of machines, not to mention, in Sévigné's words, "magnifi-
ques et galants" costumes (2: 285).[30] Lully and Quinault's operas
evolved with the monarchy, moving away from mythological

themes like *Thésée* and *Prosperine* toward stories taken from chivalric romance like *Amadis* and *Roland*, as representations of Louis XIV as Apollo came to be replaced by Louis, the defender of Christianity and Most Christian King.[31] Quinault and Lully's last operatic collaboration, *Armide*, played from 1686 to 1688. In 1690 d'Aulnoy published her first fairy tale, "L'Ile de la Félicité," in which she happens to make reference to this particular opera. That the literary fairy tale emerged as a genre soon after the production of Quinault and Lully's final opera should come as no surprise.

Louis XIV grew up listening to fairy tales, a genre that later, as Mainil contends, would define the nature of royal fêtes (52), consisting of forms of entertainment like equestrian games, ballets, and theater, referred to as *divertissements*. Whereas the various themes for the *divertissements* were taken primarily from stories by Ovid, Ariosto, and Tasso, the royal festivals shaped the spectacular and specular form the marvelous would take in seventeenth-century France. In May 1664 Louis XIV's first great festival took place, the famous "Plaisirs de l'Isle Enchantée" ["Pleasures of the Enchanted Island"], whose overall themes came from *Orlando furioso* and which consisted of three days of grand entries, machine plays, and fireworks (Marie, 1: 44–53). This first fête was to be followed by those of 1668, 1674 (which included a performance of *Alceste*), and 1678 (Marie, 2: 327–47). The spectacular/specular nature of the marvelous as performed in royal festivals would be integrated into opera, whose *divertissements*, the term also used for operatic interludes of song and dance, recall those of the royal fête (see Norman, 40–44). As its precursor, opera marks the tale of d'Aulnoy in very specific ways, including: 1) the use of supernatural means of movement borrowed from opera's machinery; 2) the inclusion of choruses; 3) the incorporation of sung verse into her tales; and 4) inscriptions of Versailles or Versailles-like palaces.

Quinault and Lully's eleven operas contain numerous examples of supernatural means of movement or transportation. In *Cadmus et Hermione*, a flying python is knocked out of the sky; in *Alceste*, Apollon and Mercure magically take to the skies, while Pluton's flying chariot carries Alcide and Alceste out of hell; Médée flees the scene on a coach drawn by dragons in *Thésée*, and numerous other female characters, such as *Prosperine*'s Cérès and Armide, are also associated with flying contraptions. Such magical ways characters in opera move about are all but absent from the chivalric tradition and from the works of the Italian fairy-tale writers, Straparola and Basile.[32] Yet d'Aulnoy uses some eight flying chariots in the fifteen tales of *Les Contes des fées*: fairies arrive at Gracieuse and Percinet's wedding in chariots drawn by dragons and swans; in "La Princesse Printanière" an aerial duel occurs between two fairies in chariots; and in "La Bonne petite souris," a fairy saves the heroine from a tower in her flying coach.[33] The lack of spectacular/specular feats such as supernatural means of transport in pre-1690 textual sources for the marvelous is clear evidence that the imagination of fairy-tale writers like d'Aulnoy was "conditioned," in Robert's words, by scenic references taken from genres like opera and machine plays.[34] Although contemporary notions of the fairy-tale tradition take for granted characters' capacity to fly or magically transport themselves in a split second to another local, it is important to acknowledge the fact that it was not until the 1690s that such incidents became common currency in fairyland.

Opera abounds in choruses and troupes of nymphs, shepherds, cupids, personified pleasures, games, and winds. Such types of stock characters are nonexistent in the chivalric and the Italian fairy-tale traditions from which d'Aulnoy draws, not to mention French folklore. Nevertheless, in "L'Ile de la Félicité," the princess's palace is filled with nymphs, and the princess herself is surrounded by little cupids. D'Aulnoy likely borrowed her zephyr that appears in the tale from *Psyché*, the opera (*tragédie-ballet*) by Molière, Corneille, and Quinault, whereas the idea of including other winds—notably Eole and the *aquilons*—brings to mind Quinault and Lully's *Cadmus et Hermoine*. In "Le Prince Lutin," the fairy Gentille appears, followed by a troupe of singing cupids, games, and pleasures. Troupes of shepherds and shepherdesses who dance, play music, and sing appear in tales like "Gracieuse et Percinet" and "Le Rameau d'or" and recall operatic scenes like *Roland*'s pastoral *divertissement* at the end of act IV, scene 2. Even the singing and dancing pagods of "Le Serpentin vert" are like a carnivalesque version of opera's choruses and troupes. By including cupids and winds as well as troupes of singing nymphs and shepherds in her tales, d'Aulnoy celebrates the fantastic extravagance of opera and of the royal fête. Rather than sing of the glories of the monarch, however, choruses tend to glorify princes and princesses who embody the aristocratic ideal of *mondanité*.

It is notable that sixteen out of d'Aulnoy's twenty-five tales contain scenes in which characters sing, and most of her tales include references to music in general, or opera in particular.[35] For instance, in "L'Ile de la Félicité" Adolphe comes upon a chorus of nymphs singing the warning of the tale, and in "La Princesse Carpillon," a troupe of shepherds and shepherdesses sing of the love between hero and heroine. In "Le Mouton," three daughters sing the praise of their father, who has just returned triumphant from war. The scene strikingly resembles the prologues to Quinault's operas, in which characters express their love for and submission to the king. Thus far critics have ignored the function of verse in d'Aulnoy's tales. When we take into account the fact that much of the verse is *sung*, we might think of these moments as *divertissements*—in all senses of the word—which connect the tales to opera in particular, and to royal fêtes in general. Clearly the marvelous deployed by Louis XIV's monarchy shaped d'Aulnoy's tales. For her part, d'Aulnoy reshapes marvelous elements borrowed from royal spectacles to subvert the absolutist ideology communicated through them to create aristocratic, feminocentric worlds.

INSCRIPTIONS OF VERSAILLES

Just as operatic prologues extol the glory of the king, they also celebrate that of his great monument to himself: Versailles. Although only two of Quinault and Lully's operas premiered at Versailles, references to the palace abound. *Thésée*'s prologue opens with the theater representing the gardens and façade of the Palais de Versailles, and the first act of *Alceste* is reminiscent of the nautical festivals held on its Grand Canal (Norman, 104). Also suggestive of Versailles are the sets of *Atys*, *Isis*, and *Roland*, in which the palace is referred to allegorically as the "Palais du Temps" ["Palace of Time"], "Palais de la Renommée" ["Palace of Renown"], and the "Palais de Démogorgon," king of the fairies. Like a fairy kingdom, Versailles is represented in opera's prologues as a timeless land of heroes and fairies, and each prologue celebrates Versailles's greatest Hero of all who, like a god, cannot be named, but whose attributes are enumerated and praised.

Louis XIV's reign, the glories of which are inscribed on the walls of Versailles, is commemorated allegorically in the prologue of *Phaéton*, whose subtitle reads "Le Retour de l'Age d'Or" ["The Return of the Golden Age"]. Notably, the opera premiered at Versailles, and although the prologue is set in the palace of the goddess Astrée [Astrea], daughter of the sun god Saturn, the plot of the story takes us into the Palace of the Sun God (incidentally not that of Saturn). Here prologue and narrative play on references to sun gods and their palaces, highlighted all the more by the fact that the opera opened at Versailles, the palace of France's modern sun god. That the prologue is set in a golden age is further emphasized by the name of Saturn's daughter, Astrée, which immediately would have brought to mind for spectators the pastoral novel of Honoré d'Urfé, whose golden age, however, was an aristocratic, not a monarchical, one. The timelessness the prologues express in terms of golden ages and fairy worlds is exemplified in *Atys*, first performed in January 1676. The opera opens with the appearance of Flore, which elicits the following words from Time: "La saison des frimas peut-elle nous offrir / Les fleurs que nous voyons paraître?" ["Can the season of frosts offer us / The flowers we see appear?"]. By this time Louis Le Vau had built in the gardens of Versailles the Bassin de Flore and the first Orangerie, whose tropical trees produced fruit in winter, only one of many signs of Louis XIV's wish to control space, time, and nature itself like a true god. Making reference to Flore and to the appearance of flowers in winter is only one example of the many instances in which prologues—not to mention moments in the principal narrative—allude to aspects of Versailles.

As in Quinault's operas, d'Aulnoy's tales contain many references to Versailles, or more precisely, to carnivalesque, feminocentric versions of it. Looking for the princess Félicité, Adolphe wanders through vast gardens with fountains, and "[il] traversa des salles, des galeries, des chambres sans nombre" ["he crossed halls, galleries, innumerable chambers"] before arriving in that of the sovereign (*Contes I*, 19). The scene brings to mind the immensity of Versailles and its grounds. Princess Félicité sits upon a throne made of a great carbuncle more brilliant than the sun, recalling the solar metaphors used to qualify Louis XIV. D'Aulnoy often employs solar metaphors to characterize the people and places of her fairy worlds. In "Gracieuse et Percinet," there emerges a crystal palace "qui brillait autant que le soleil" ["that sparkled as much as the sun"] (*Contes I*, 42). Avenant is described as being "beau comme le soleil" ["handsome like the sun"] and he finds the princess "plus belle que le soleil" ["more beautiful than the sun"] (*Contes I*, 59, 70). The fairy Gentille in "Le Prince Lutin" is described as being "plus brillante que le soleil" ["brighter than the sun"], and in "La Bonne petite souris," the queen and fairy wear crowns "qui brillaient comme des soleils" ["that shone like suns"] (*Contes I*, 155, 291). When the Amazon fairy of "La Princesse Carpillon" disappears, she leaves behind her a long trace of light "semblable aux rayons du soleil" ["similar to the rays of the sun"] (*Contes II*, 49).

In addition to solar metaphors, d'Aulnoy includes even more precise references to Versailles in her tales. For instance, in "La Belle aux cheveux d'or," the princess walks through "sa galerie aux grands miroirs" ["her gallery of great mirrors"] before meeting Avenant, and the chambers of the princess in "Le Prince Lutin" similarly are "tout entier de grandes glaces de miroirs, car on ne pouvait trop multiplier un objet si charmant" ["entirely of great sheets of mirror, for one could not multiply enough such a charming object"] (*Contes I*, 63, 136). Both scenes recall the Galerie des Glaces at Versailles, and the second points to its function in multiplying the image of the king. In tales like "Gracieuse et Percinet," "Le Rameau d'or," and "La Chatte blanche," the specific stories of the characters or references to them are inscribed on tower and palace walls, in much the same way that Louis XIV's personal history was inscribed on the walls of Versailles, as well as in the prologues of operas. D'Aulnoy proves to be attuned to the representational strategies of the monarchy and borrows from these strategies to reflect upon and subvert them. Opera's marvelous decor was intended to evoke the greatness of Versailles, and by extension, that of Louis XIV. The marvelous decor of d'Aulnoy's tales, however, evokes the greatness of so many alternative, salonlike Versailles, and by extension, that of *mondain* women.

This cannot be better demonstrated than in d'Aulnoy's frame narrative to the third volume of *Les Contes des fées*. The set of four volumes is dedicated to the Princesse Palatine, whom the author claims to be the inspiration for her fairy worlds: "Ce sont sans doute de grandes princesses comme vous, MADAME, qui ont donné lieu d'imaginer le royaume de Féerie" ["Undoubtedly it is great princesses like you, MADAME, who lead us to imagine the kingdom of Enchantment"] (*Contes I*, 30). The frame narrative of volume three is set at Saint Cloud, the residence of the Palatine and her husband, the duc d'Orléans, brother of Louis XIV. In the frame, also entitled "Les Contes des Fées," Madame D*** takes a break from strolling the grounds with her companions and sits beside a fountain. Suddenly a beautiful nymph appears, who recites a long poem about the "auguste Prince" and the "Princesse incomparable" who inhabit Saint Cloud.

Although the nymph does not sing her lines, many elements of the poem recall the tone and themes of operatic verse. As in operas like *Phaéton* or *Amadis*, "Les Contes des Fées" associates the prince and princess of Saint Cloud with a golden age, specifically "les heureux jours de Rhée" ["the happy days of Rhea"], the period in myth before Jupiter took over the throne of the gods. Here d'Aulnoy implicitly associates the Princesse Palatine and her husband with Rhea and Saturn, whose peaceful dominion contrasts with that of Jupiter—in other words, Louis XIV. As in opera's prologues, games, pleasures, and laughter are personified and enjoy the eternal springtime of the palace and its grounds from which sorrows and winter eternally are banished. Just as Versailles is constructed around the figure of Louis XIV, so Saint Cloud centers around the Princesse Palatine, "[p]our qui s'embellissent ces lieux" ["for whom these grounds embellish themselves"] (*Contes I*, 295). Like an operatic prologue, "Les Contes des Fées" establishes connections between an enchanted palace, its inhabitant(s), and a marvelous genre. In so doing, d'Aulnoy creates a string of associations (Saint Cloud–Princesse Palatine–fairy tale) implicitly opposed to another (Versailles–Louis XIV–opera). Through its connections with La Palatine and Saint Cloud, d'Aulnoy uses the fairy tale to create so many alternative, female-centered enchanted worlds that provide critical responses to Louis XIV's absolutism as represented in opera.

FAIRIES VERSUS FURIES

Unlike opera, whose manifest purpose is to exalt Louis XIV, d'Aulnoy glorifies in her tales *mondain* women, exemplified in her panygeric "prologues" (the dedication and frame narrative) honoring the Princesse Palatine. Going against opera's insistence on unconditional submission to the monarch, d'Aulnoy also tends to favor worthy noblemen over kings, which plays itself out in the ways in which rivalries with kings get resolved. Unconditional submission to kings and gods is the rule in matters of love, in earlier operas, and war, in later ones. Abduction and forced marriage consequently are made palatable, whereas later operas privilege a masculine duty to the king over the pursuit of love and pleasure, associated with deceitful seductresses. In her tales, d'Aulnoy responds to opera's narratives concerning the unconditional submission to monarchs, forced marriage, and military glory in such a way as to celebrate the pleasures of love in clear opposition to the morality of especially the later operas of

Quinault and Lully. She does so in such a way as to rehabilitate opera's furies and to relativize the authority and merit of kings.[36]

Although Quinault and Lully do not subject love to duty in their earlier operas as explicitly as they do in later ones (Norman, 328–29), love nevertheless plays a rather problematic role in most of their operas. At the beginning of *Alceste*, Alcide laments the fact that his beloved, the title character, is marrying king Admète, who later in the opera turns out to be cowardly in his willingness to let another sacrifice their life to save his own. When Alceste immolates herself to spare the life of her husband and ends up in Hades, Alcide risks his own life descending into hell to save her, only to lose her in the end to a less than glorious king. Unlike Alcide, who manages to renounce his love for Alceste and give her up to the king, Atys betrays his friend and king, Célénus, by loving the king's fiancée Sangaride. Unlike Alceste, Sangaride reciprocates Atys's love, favoring the title character over the king, and ends up disobeying her father, all of which ultimately leads to her death. Living solely for military glory, characters like Alcide and later Roland renounce love altogether, whereas Sangaride and Atys are punished for their amorous transgressions, and in particular, for rejecting the advances of a king and a goddess.

For female characters love is especially problematic. Eventually deified, Io is pursued by Jupiter, whom she rather unconvincingly and most passively loves, but can never marry. Abducted by Pluto, Prosperine reluctantly accepts her fate as a token of peace between the underworld and earth, an agreement negotiated and authorized by Jupiter. Norman observes that *Prosperine*, first represented in February 1680, was written in light of the treaty of Nymwegen, signed in the fall of 1679, which included the forced marriage of Louis XIV's niece, Marie-Louise d'Orléans, to Charles II of Spain, a marriage the princess deeply loathed (228). Marie-Louise's displacement south of the border is allegorized in Prosperine forcibly having to reside in Hades. In French opera, love can best be characterized in terms of renunciation and, in Downing Thomas's words, "dispossession."[37] In fact, most characters end up dispossessed of their power by the end of the opera. Just as worthy knights like Alcide must set aside rivalry and submit to the king, female characters who are not vilified are abducted, raped, and reduced to passivity.

Whereas Quinault's Isis passively accepts her fate as Jupiter's mistress, and Prosperine that as the wife of Pluto, d'Aulnoy's Babiole, for all the monkey she is, actively resists becoming the token of peace between her adoptive mother's kingdom and that of the ape, king Magot. Fearing Magot's people will eat up all of her subjects, the queen pleads with Babiole to marry him, but to no avail. Babiole responds: "Cela signifie, madame . . . que vous êtes résolue de me sacrifier à ce vilain monstre pour éviter sa colère" ["That means, madame . . . that you are determined to sacrifice me to this sordid monster in order to avoid his wrath"] (*Contes I*, 452). Rather than have the heroine passively accept marrying the monstrous Magot, d'Aulnoy unambiguously represents forced marriage as human sacrifice, a pact Babiole outrightly rejects. It should be noted that Charles II was viewed as monstrous himself, being physically and mentally handicapped, and endowed with an enlarged head and jaw. Only twenty-seven years old, the unhappy Marie-Louise died in 1689, poisoned by raw oysters, according to the Princesse Palatine (Orléans, 64). Through tales like "Babiole," d'Aulnoy seems to rewrite stories like that of Marie-Louise, the princess sacrificed to a monster to end a war. However, d'Aulnoy gives her princess the will to reject the proposal and to withstand the immediate consequences, and rewards her disobedience at the end of the tale.

In "Babiole" d'Aulnoy contests the use of forced marriage for political ends, and provides an example of a positive female character who resists it. In tales like "La Belle aux cheveux d'or" and "Le Prince Lutin," d'Aulnoy responds to the operatic narrative concerning the rivalry between a loyal and worthy servant to the crown and an unworthy king. Much like Alcide, who accomplishes the impossible task of descending into hell to save Alceste, Avenant of "La Belle aux cheveux d'or" successfully carries out three tasks, the last of which entails entering the tenebrous cave, an ordeal comparable to that of going to hell and back. In so doing, Avenant wins the hand of Belle for his king, who nevertheless imprisons Avenant in a tower out of jealousy. In the end, d'Aulnoy has the king accidentally poison himself with the same poison he uses to kill princes and great lords, and queen Belle takes Avenant as her husband. D'Aulnoy's story also brings to mind *Roland*'s Angélique, who flees the epic hero only to crown the Moor Médor, socially her inferior. Although Quinault's version of Angélique's story is a definite improvement on his source Ariosto, Quinault nevertheless depicts Angélique's love for Médor as a stain on her glory.[38] Moreover, in her efforts to dodge Roland, Angélique resorts to trickery and artifice, the opera ultimately suggesting she is a less than exemplary character.[39] In her revision of this type of operatic narrative, d'Aulnoy rehabilitates the heroine by demonstrating that the lower-ranking Avenant indeed is more worthy of the throne than the king, making Belle's crowning of Avenant a sign of her own good judgement and character.

Again in "Le Prince Lutin" d'Aulnoy opposes the worthy knight Léandre to the heir apparent and later king Furibond. At the beginning of the tale, foreign ambassadors mistake Léandre for the prince and Furibond for the king's dwarf, which infuriates the latter. Furibond orders Léandre never to appear before him again, essentially sending Léandre into exile in the countryside, which all the ladies at court regret. The situation of Léandre recalls that of *frondeurs* like La Rochefoucauld and Gaston d'Orléans, worthy noblemen momentarily banished from court for presenting a threat to the king. Léandre proves his worth by playing the role of the errant knight, which situates him within the tradition of chivalric romances like *Jerusalem Delivered* and *Orlando furioso*. Unlike opera's rendition of these stories, however, the figure for the king, Furibond, is represented in unambiguously tyrannical terms. Whereas Léandre proves to be a patient lover who frees women and children from the men and parents who oppress them, Furibond is prepared to take the princess of the Ile des Plaisirs tranquilles by force. Characters, male or female, who wish to abduct the object of their love are represented in categorically negative and ugly terms. In d'Aulnoy's tales, abductors never attain the dignity of *Isis*'s Jupiter or *Prosperine*'s Pluto.[40] Moreover, d'Aulnoy systematically favors the noble lord over the king, or the less powerful king over the emperor, which goes against the grain of opera's at least apparent insistence on the unconditional respect of monarchy.[41]

Whether we think of Alcide or Io, Atys or Prosperine, noble characters in opera must fully submit to kings and gods. They must also and quite consequently sacrifice love to duty. This is particularly the case, as Norman has argued, in Quinault and Lully's later operas. From *Amadis* to *Armide*, love, *repos*, and worldly pleasures are viewed as shameful and associated with women, who are represented as so many distractions that prevent men from carrying out their duty. In *Amadis*, Corisande tries to persuade her lover and Amadis's brother Florestan to remain with her rather than go off to war, to which Florestan replies: "Pouvais-je demeurer dans un honteux repos?" ["Could I remain in shameful repose?"] (1.2). When Roland is prepared to desert Charlemagne's army for Angélique, his friend Astolphe reprimands him, stating: "Le grand coeur de Roland n'est fait que pour la Gloire; / Peut-il languir dans un honteux repos? / Triomphez de l'Amour" ["Roland's great courage is made only for Glory, / Could it languish in shameful repose? / Triumph over Love"] (4.1). In *Armide*, the Danish knight complains that Renaud "Est reduit à languir avec indignité / Dans une molle oisiveté" ["Is reduced to languish indignantly / In a soft idleness"]. Just after pronouncing these words, he is seduced himself by the illusion of his mistress Lucine, who entices him with pleasure: "Voici la charmante retraite / De la félicité parfaite; / Voici l'heureux séjour / Des Jeux et de l'Amour" ["Here is the charming retreat / Of perfect felicity; / Here is the sojourn / Of Games and of Love"] (4.4). After being tricked by Armide's magic, the Danish knight and Ubalde both conclude that love is "une honte éternelle" ["an eternal shame"] and a "funeste enchantement" ["deadly enchantment"] (4.4). Although at the end of *Amadis* the epic hero is reunited with his beloved Oriane, *Roland* concludes with the title character renouncing all love to regain Charlemagne's army. Likewise, in *Armide* Renaud, Ubalde, and the Danish knight flee the illusions of pleasure to rejoin Godefroi's camp and seek their glory on the battlefield. As much as glory brings honor and is associated with men, so love brings shame and is associated with women.

In opera as in myth, women frequently are construed as so many seductresses, and the site of their seduction often is an island. Médée takes Thésée to the Ile Enchantée in an attempt to seduce him, whereas Arcalaüs brings Amadis to the Ile agréable. In *Armide*, the island itself seduces Renaud. The invulnerable hero readily succumbs to the island's pleasures: "Plus j'observe ces lieux et plus je les admire. / . . . Les plus aimables fleurs et le plus doux Zéphir / Parfument l'air qu'on y respire. / Non, je ne puis quitter des rivages si beaux. / . . . Ce gazon, cet ombrage frais, / Tout m'invite au repos" ["The more I observe these grounds the more I admire them. / . . . The most likeable flowers and the most gentle Zephyr / Perfume the air one breathes here. / No, I cannot leave such beautiful banks. / . . . This grass, this fresh shade, / It all invites me to repose"] (2.3). Of course, the pleasures that surround Renaud are only illusory, for in reality, the nymphs, shepherds, and zephyrs are so many demons. The island is a feminized, insulated, and enclosed space of *repos* and pleasure that is cut off from the "real" world in which honor is acquired through service to the king. As a space of pleasure and bliss, the island represents a sort of Eden, and the woman with whom it is associated an Eve, who tempts man to sin against his king.

In several tales, d'Aulnoy contests the idea that love and pleasure must surrender to duty. In "L'Ile de la Félicité," d'Aulnoy
signals the fact that she rewrites the story of *Armide*. As Zéphir
flies him onto the island, Adolphe remarks, like Renaud, the fact
that "L'air y était tout parfumé" ["The air here was perfumed"]
(*Contes I*, 15). On the island of Félicité, just like on Armide's island, there are flowing streams and a harmonious concert of
birds. And just like Renaud, Adolphe lies down upon a bed of
grass and falls asleep. After realizing he has spent some three
hundred years with the princess Félicité, Adolphe reproaches
himself for having yielded to such *repos*, stating: "Je vois avec
honte ma vertu sans occupation et mon nom sans éclat: tel était
le brave Renaud entre les bras de son Armide, mais la gloire l'ar-
racha de ses bras" ["I shamefully see my virtue without profession and my name without renown: such was the brave Renaud
in the arms of his Armide, but glory tore him away from her"]
(*Contes I*, 22). Unlike Renaud, however, upon leaving Félicité Adolphe finds only an inglorious death. Whereas Quinault's libretto
depicts love as illusory, d'Aulnoy's tale communicates the idea
that, on the contrary, it is glory, not love, which is deceptive.
Whereas "félicité parfaite" is rejected in *Armide* because it is associated with seduction and treachery, in d'Aulnoy's tale, "félicité parfaite" is represented as an inaccessible but desirable
ideal, inseparable from love and fidelity. That both island and
princess are given the name Félicité plays on the conflation in
myth and opera between the seductress and the space where she
leads men astray. However, d'Aulnoy does so only to valorize
pleasure, love, and women. In "Le Prince Lutin," the Ile des
Plaisirs tranquilles closely resembles the Ile de la Félicité, in
that it is defined as a feminine space and a space of pleasure, and
it similarly identifies the good princess with the island. In the
tale, love is again privileged over glory: "*Les plus beaux jours de
la vie / S'écoulent sans agrément; / Si l'Amour n'est de la partie*" ["*The most beautiful days of life / Go by without charm; / If
Love is not part of it*"] (*Contes I*, 38).

That love is more important than glory is clear in the tale
"Babiole." After the monkey Babiole regains her naturally beautiful form and becomes ruler of her own kingdom, the prince who
earlier had rebuked her comes to pay his respects. In order to
attract her attention he intends on performing several gallant-
ries. However, a fight breaks out among the knights and "le plus
fort battit le plus faible, et ce plus faible . . . fut le prince" ["the
strongest knight beat the weakest, and the weakest one . . . was

the prince"] (*Contes I*, 465). Despite the fact that the prince is the weakest knight at court, he wins the love of the princess. Propelled by his love and with the supernatural help of the river god Biroqua, however, the prince later proves courageous and gallant in saving Babiole from the fairy Fanfreluche. In effect, it is because the prince loves that he can attain glory. In turn, glory serves to reunite lovers separated by evildoers, and to reestablish pleasure and *repos*. "Babiole" seems to anticipate the morals of "La Princesse Carpillon" and "La Princesse Belle Etoile et le Prince Chéri," in which d'Aulnoy criticizes those who dismiss love and valorize only glory: *"fuyez, censeurs odieux, / qui voulez qu'un héros résiste à la tendresse: / Pourvu que la Raison en soit toujours maîtresse, / L'Amour donne l'éclat aux exploits glorieux"* [*"flee, odious critics, / who want a hero to resist tenderness: / Provided that Reason is always his mistress, / Love gives luster to glorious exploits"*] (*Contes II*, 56); *"L'amour, n'en déplaise aux censeurs, / Est l'origine de la gloire; / Il sait animer les grands coeurs / A braver le péril, à chercher la victoire"* [*"Love, whether its critics like it or not, / Is the origin of glory; / Love knows how to rouse great courage / To defy peril, to seek victory"*] (*Contes II*, 406). Such morals clearly subvert the message communicated in Lully and Quinault's later operas, especially *Armide*.

D'Aulnoy challenges notions of duty and glory as propagated in opera, which are inseparable from opera's negative representations of the female seductress and her island-lair. She does this in part by reconfiguring feminine spaces, transforming dens of sin into salonlike realms of *divertissement* and pleasure. In "L'Ile de la Félicité" and "Le Prince Lutin," the fact that both fairylands are insular spaces identified with a princess recalls the associations made in Scudéry's salon chronicles between Sapho, queen of the Samedis, and the salon itself, which is imagined in terms of an island. In both tales, men and "uncivil" people are excluded from the island in the same way that certain types of people are excluded from the space of Scudéry's Samedis. As I have argued elsewhere, "only those who conform to a particular code of behavior" are admitted onto the island, the criteria for which resemble those of "an exclusive salon" ("Feminine Genealogy," 201). This process of inclusion and exclusion that we saw at work in chapter 3 plays itself out tacitly in the tales. In "L'Ile de la Félicité," for instance, Zephyr is the only wind allowed onto Félicité, which can be explained by his civil manners that contrast with the violent behavior of his brother winds. Although men are unconditionally excluded from the Ile des Plaisirs Tranquilles at the beginning of the tale, Léandre ends up proving to the princess and fairies that certain men—those who desire to please women, who enjoy pleasure, and who are not tyrannical or violent—merit admittance onto the island. At the same time that d'Aulnoy explicitly celebrates *mondain* women in the specific figure of the Princesse Palatine, she allegorically celebrates them in her tales in implicit references to salon culture. Countering opera's positive valuation of the monarchical space of Versailles and negative valuation of insular feminine spaces, d'Aulnoy holds up as ideal the pleasurable and feminocentric spaces of both Saint Cloud and the salon.

On the one hand, d'Aulnoy drew from opera, a genre that, along with the novel, most often came under the attack of anti-*mondain* writers. Integrating operatic elements into her tales represents one strategy d'Aulnoy employed to defend *mondain* culture. As both the predecessor of and source of inspiration for the fairy tale, opera necessarily shaped the specific form the marvelous would take in d'Aulnoy's tales. On the other hand, d'Aulnoy subverted opera's representations of kings and women alike. Whether in politics or love, d'Aulnoy promoted relations freely engaged in, rejecting the legitimation, in operas like *Isis* and *Prosperine*, of forced love, or the imperative to submit unconditionally to kings. Whereas opera celebrated a glory based on physical force and submission to duty, d'Aulnoy privileged the force of love which, as in the case of Babiole's prince, could compensate for physical shortcomings. D'Aulnoy transformed opera's treacherous sorceresses and their islands of seduction into good fairies and princesses, whose islands offer guiltless pleasure and *repos* in ways that recall the seventeenth-century salon.

Through the writing of fairy tales, d'Aulnoy responds at the same time to the Christian, bourgeois modernism of Perrault, and to the *mondain*, monarchical modernism of opera. Perrault puts forth a gendered division of knowledge and power in order to limit his female characters to the realm of domesticity, ultimately governed by fathers and husbands. Opera similarly limits female characters' sphere of influence. Although Médée and Armide are never reduced to being a *souillon*, they nevertheless are rendered powerless, whereas other heroines, much like those found in Perrault's tales, passively accept their fate as ravished objects of male desire and aggression, usually that of kings or gods. King of the gods, Jupiter both abducts women, as in *Isis*, and authorizes their abduction, as in the case of *Prosperine*. Perrault's modernism privileges bourgeois *arrivisme*, in which enterprising male characters rise above their station, while opera, with some ambivalence, posits the absolute nature of monarchy by legitimating total compliance to the wishes of kings.[42]

D'Aulnoy responds to both positions by resituating female characters in relation to the sociocultural and political public sphere, and by privileging nobility over both *arrivisme* and absolutism. On the one hand, she distances aristocratic women from the domestic by showing their capacities in domains refused to them by writers like Fénelon. D'Aulnoy's heroines prove to be universally knowledgeable, and capable in war and government alike. She transforms opera's temptresses into cultured *salonnières* well-versed in the art of entertainment, and privileges love and pleasure over a duty and glory she views as vain, except in the service of love. On the other hand, d'Aulnoy rejects the *mésalliances* prevalent in Perrault's tales, as well as the absolutist position propagated in opera. Systematically replacing lower-class characters borrowed from Straparola and Perrault with noble ones, d'Aulnoy projects onto her tales a world in which nobility is a stable and absolute concept protected by fairy magic. That she dedicates her *Contes des fées* to the Princesse Palatine, whose nobility is "du plus précieux sang" ["of the most precious blood"] (30), and who virulently defended the traditional hierarchy, should come as no surprise. Implicitly opposing Saint Cloud to Versailles in "Les Contes des Fées," d'Aulnoy suggests that the duchesse and duc d'Orléans embody an aristocratic ideal the king fails to exemplify, meaning that the prince and princess are more worthy of her praise. In her tales, respect for kings or queens is relative to their character; it is never absolute. Although d'Aulnoy's position on nobility differs significantly from that of Scudéry, they come together in the problematization of absolutism, which is represented in works by both authors as a form of government that borders on tyranny.

More generally, d'Aulnoy flouts the ideology of the Counter Reformation in her tales, not only in the ways she represents women, but also in her "idolatric" celebration of artifice. Highlighting the "importance" of dressing stylishly and making oneself up as a sign of nobility as well as one's desire to please, d'Aulnoy makes of fashion and artifice gender-neutral concepts necessary to the pursuit of *mondanité*. Her tales bring out the specular nature of *mondain* culture, given the emphasis on the display of the self and on spectacles as a central form of *mondain* entertainment. As opposed to Perrault's verisimilar tales, d'Aulnoy celebrates the nonmimetic and spectacular quality of the marvelous, the sources of which can be found, not the pre-1690 fairy-tale tradition, but in French opera, the proscribed genre of writers like Boileau, Fénelon, and Maintenon. Like spectators of opera, readers of d'Aulnoy's tales are to relish in the pleasurable contemplation of the marvelous, whether that take the form of an incomparably beautiful princess, an exceptionally handsome prince, or an aerial chariot fight between two fairies.[43] Just as her fairies and princesses offer guiltless pleasure and *repos* to worthy men, so d'Aulnoy offers her readers guiltless indulgence in worldly contemplation, and at a time when orators like Bossuet were exhorting their congregations to reject "the world." In its relation to the specular and to spectacle, *mondanité* necessarily is opposed to those dark corners of penitent domesticity where Perrault locates his ideal women. By nature, the *femme mondaine* is situated within the sociocultural public sphere, where she sees and is seen. The very defense of *mondanité* d'Aulnoy undertakes in her tales, then, unambiguously marks her opposition to Counter-Reformation ideology.

Afterword

READING WOMEN WRITERS WITHIN THE BROAD CULTURAL, SOCIAL, and political context of their times not only enhances our appreciation of the highly complex ways they engaged in the issues that affected them as women and as members of a particular social group. It also elucidates our interpretations of canonical writers like Molière or Boileau, who responded to their influence in society. As I began to closely examine the works and social practices of Madeleine de Scudéry, I wondered how one could approach studying the reaction to Scudéry by canonical writers without considering—even reading—her oeuvre. Although scholars slowly are beginning to fill the gap in literary history, it seems to me that the dialogues, both implicit and explicit, that were going on between men and women writers—not to mention among women writers—need to be explored further. By examining the debates occurring between Scudéry and Boileau, between d'Aulnoy and Perrault, we situate women writers as active subjects in a dialogic process constitutive of the literary and cultural field of the period. Women writers, then, cannot simply be categorized as minor players within cultural history and thus relegated to the margins of literary history. Reading and analyzing texts by women writers, particularly those like Scudéry and d'Aulnoy who published bestsellers, indeed are necessary steps in doing justice to our readings of what are considered to be canonical writers.

Appreciating the degree to which women writers do not write beyond class and nation complicates the dialogues and debates that went on between female and male authors. What opposes Scudéry and Boileau, Perrault and d'Aulnoy, resides not only in their concepts of gender, but also in their social and political ideals, all of which shapes their responses to the cultural changes taking place in early modern France. Clearly Boileau is a misogynous writer. However, his attack on Scudéry also addresses the question of social class and models of nobility. Indeed, Boileau unwittingly gives Scudéry the credit she deserves for having contributed to reconceptualizing the models of noble subjectivity that had become predominant by the second half of the century. In her tales, d'Aulnoy responded to Perrault's degrading images of women as well as to the *mésalliance* and social climbing prevalent in the academician's tales. Both Scudéry and d'Aulnoy advocated the ideals of their gender and of their *condition*, which becomes clear upon comparing the two women authors. Whereas Scudéry puts forth a republican, robe or parliamentary model of subjectivity and state, d'Aulnoy vindicates a feudal and aristocratic one. Scudéry picks up the pieces of the crumbling social hierarchy to create a new order, whereas d'Aulnoy remains nostalgic for a time when the nobility was not threatened by the bourgeoisie, nor dominated by an absolute monarch. At the same time that these two authors respond differently to cultural changes related to class, they come together in their active participation in and promotion in their literary works of salon culture.

It is important to open up the debates between men and women writers to consider the wide range of positions they took with respect to gender, as well as class and political ideologies. I would argue that this is also true when examining debates between writers of any gender. As we have seen in chapter 4, by resituating Perrault's response to Boileau's Satire X within the larger quarrel that had transpired, it becomes clear that Perrault was not as feminist as one might want to believe—even for his time. Opening up the terms of the quarrel reveals the fact that various positions regarding women in the public sphere were available to male writers, and quite a few of them—notably Donneau de Visé and Regnard—took rather "progressive" positions on the issue. By situating Perrault's *Apologie* within the terms of the larger debate, his "defense" of women reveals its affinities with Boileau's satire, particularly regarding the critique of *mondain* women. The *Apologie* distinguishes itself from the Satire X only in that it proposes a solution to the presence of women in the public sphere: women must be put in their place, meaning the private space of domesticity, which Perrault emphasizes in his tales.

In the same vein, when considering the position of Scudéry, d'Aulnoy, and Catherine Bernard regarding marriage and norms of feminine decorum, it becomes evident that each writer took a slightly different view. Scholars generally have accepted as the only available options to women of the period the neo-Platonic, rather stoic view of love and marriage expressed in Scudéry's works, on the one hand; and the more pessimistic, fatal view of love and marriage in the tradition of Lafayette and Bernard, on the other. In her novels and stories, however, d'Aulnoy points to evidence of a "counterfeit culture," providing other options for women by questioning the universality and the moral validity of norms of decorum that other women writers seem to accept—at least in their literary works. Obviously, transgression of laws and social norms was an option only for venturesome women, like many of d'Aulnoy's heroines, not to mention d'Aulnoy herself and Madame de La Guette. Nevertheless, it should be acknowledged that characters like Clélie, the Princesse de Clèves, and Eléonor were not the only models of subjectivity available to women of the time, which d'Aulnoy emphasizes in her works. Rather than accept at face value the duty to obey parental figures and the imperative to adhere to norms of feminine decorum, d'Aulnoy highlights how female characters interiorize such norms in ways that imprison them physically and psychologically, and how characters in positions of authority enforce such norms, not for moral reasons, but to maintain their control over women.

Reading these writers together and taking account of the implicit and explicit debates they engaged in with each other furthermore elucidate our understanding of the ways in which women situated themselves and were situated within the sociocultural public sphere. Writing at the time of the growth and apogee of salon culture, Scudéry proves to be a more optimistic theorist than women writers of the late seventeenth century. Although Scudéry, like d'Aulnoy, criticized absolutism and parental tyranny in her works, she also advanced new models of subjectivity and state, imagining the possibility of a just society for women and men located in the future. At a practical level, she worked towards this goal within the context of her salon, fostering networks of patronage and providing models of subjectivity that could assist her *salonniers* in positioning themselves strategically within French society.

With the attack on *mondain* women later in the century, however, women writers like d'Aulnoy had to take a more defensive position. From Boileau and Fénelon to Perrault and Madame de Maintenon, moralistic writers, not inconsequentially partisans of the Catholic Reformation, viewed salon culture and *mondain* genres like the novel and opera as cultural practices and genres that corrupted aristocratic women who, they believed, exercised too much influence within French society. The interests of the king and academicians came together in the desire to monopolize the sociocultural public sphere. Louis XIV sought to consolidate his authority over the cultural and literary field through the proliferation of state-sponsored academies and the creation of court at Versailles. Many male academicians wished to eliminate competition from the salons in linguistic and artistic matters, and thus attempted to delegitimize female authority by associating women with madness and disorder. Whereas works by Lafayette and Bernard express the pessimism many women must have felt at the time, d'Aulnoy challenges Catholic Reformation notions of women by defending the genres and values constitutive of the *mondain* culture associated with aristocratic women. In her tales in particular, she resituates women within the public sphere and validates their public presence by demonstrating the ways in which they are necessary to a stable, peaceful, and pleasurable society, situated in an ideal, feudal past.[1]

Opening up the paradigms of early modern Women's Studies and challenging our notions of the centrality of canonical works creates a dynamism in our approach to seventeenth-century literature, a dynamism that indeed existed in the period. Literary quarrels were constitutive of that culture, and women actively took part in these quarrels through the salon and through writing, legitimating themselves as thinking subjects and agents of cultural change. Evident in the works of Scudéry and d'Aulnoy, women's engagement in these debates was not limited to issues pertaining to their gender. They also proposed and defended class interests and models of state and society that were inseparable from their gender ideals.

Notes

Unless otherwise noted, all translations are mine, including translations of secondary texts for which I have omitted the French. First epigram in French: "[N]ous crûmes que le romantisme était le genre historique ... qui, depuis peu, a pris nos auteurs d'appeler des personnages de roman et de mélodrames Charlemagne, François Ier ou Henri IV, au lieu d'Amadis, d'Oronte, ou de Saint-Albin. Mlle De Scudéry est, je crois, la première qui ait donné en France l'exemple de cette mode, et beaucoup de gens disent du mal des ouvrages de cette demoiselle, qui ne les ont certainement pas lus. ... [M]ais ils nous ont semblé aussi vraisemblables, mieux écrits, et guère plus ridicules que certains romans de nos jours dont on ne parlera pas si longtemps."

1. "Je lis maintenant les contes d'enfant de Mme D'Aulnoy, dans une vieille édition dont j'ai colorié les images à l'âge de six ou sept ans. Les dragons sont roses et les arbres bleus; il y a une image où tout est peint en rouge, même la mer. Ça m'amuse beaucoup, ces contes."

2. With respect to Scudéry, I am thinking notably of Joan DeJean's *Tender Geographies* (1991), Elizabeth Goldsmith's *Exclusive Conversations* (1988), and Erica Harth's *Cartesian Women* (1992). With respect to d'Aulnoy, Jack Zipes introduced her works to American scholars in the 1980s. Other studies that have opened up scholarship on the 1690s fairy-tale vogue in general and on d'Aulnoy's works in particular include Lewis Seifert's *Fairy Tales, Sexuality, and Gender in France 1690–1715* (1996); Patricia Hannon's *Fabulous Identities* (1998); and in France Raymonde Robert's *Le Conte de fées littéraire en France* (1982), Catherine Velay-Vallentin's *L'Histoire des contes* (1992), and Jean Mainil's *Madame d'Aulnoy et le rire des fées: essai sur la subversion féerique et le merveilleux comique sous l'Ancien Régime* (2001).

3. Scudéry published and/or republished her works regularly, almost yearly, from about 1641 until 1693. From 1690 until 1875, d'Aulnoy's *Histoire d'Hypolite* alone was republished some thirty-two times. Her tales, published collectively or as individual texts, were also regularly republished until the nineteenth century (at least twelve reprints in the eighteenth century; at least six reprints in the nineteenth).

4. The *Recueil des plus belles pièces françois* also was attributed to d'Aulnoy. Further references are made to Scudéry and d'Aulnoy in critical works like Lenglet du Fresnoy's *De l'Usage des Romans* (1734), Aubert de la Chesnaye-Desbois' *Lettres sur les Romans* (1743), and Jean-François Marmontel's *Essai sur les Romans* (1799).

5. Tracing the publishing history of d'Aulnoy's English editions, Palmer gives testimony to the great popularity of her works in England: "By 1740 at least thirty-six editions of Mme d'Aulnoy's work had been published in England.

. . . In the first thirty years of its publishing history there were more English editions of the *Travels into Spain* than there were of Galland's popular *Arabian Nights* and more than all of the editions of Mme de Lafayette's works. . . . And even excluding the *Spanish Memoirs* and *Travels*, Professor McBurney's *Check-List of English Prose Fiction, 1700–1739* . . . has more listings for Mme d'Aulnoy than for any of her French contemporaries" ("Madame" 238).

6. Inspired by Scudéry's *Les Femmes Illustres ou les Harangues Héroïques* (1642), Marguerite Buffet's *Nouvelles Observations sur la langue françoise avec Les Eloges des Illustres Sçavantes* (1668), which DeJean cites as one of the earliest worldly canons, reads like a vindication of women, arguing for the inclusion of women in universal history and their equal right to exemplarity. Buffet paints Scudéry, for example, as a writer of universal appeal whose example contributes to the glory of the French nation: "la France n'est pas plus au dessus des autres Nations par la gloire de ses Heros, que par la science et la vertu de ses Heroïnes . . . nous trouverons en la Sapho de nos jours, l'incomparable Mademoiselle Scudery, plus de science, de doctrine, et d'esprit que dans la Sapho des Grecs tant vantée dans l'Antiquité" ["France is not more above other Nations for the glory of its Heroes, than for the science and virtue of its Heroines . . . we will find in our Sapho of today, the incomparable Mademoiselle Scudery, more science, doctrine, and wit than in the Sapho of the Greeks so celebrated in Antiquity"] (245). Like the later pedagogical canons, worldly canons depicted their subjects in terms of universality and as exemplary models incarnating the spirit of the nation.

7. According to Kelly, "[u]ntil the European states were fully consolidated, women continued to exercise governing and military power in times of need" (22). Collins also notes that "[i]n the sixteenth century, noble women often ran estates and even conducted counter-seige operations" (455). See also Mueller, "Taming."

1. POLITICS, GENDER, AND CULTURAL CHANGE

1. Already in his *Le Siècle de Louis XIV* [The Age of Louis XIV], 1687), Charles Perrault's position that French culture is superior to that of the Ancients is based primarily on France's technological progress, from which Perrault infers the consequent progress made by France in the arts.

2. J. Delumeau argues that the nobility was not consolidated until the sixteenth and seventeenth centuries, with the increased gap between rich and poor (126–28). J. Batany argues the following: "social category is not designated by a name, but by a verb: 'role play' is not distinguished from the role itself. . . . As soon as a noble becomes a hermit and goes 'seeking his own bread,' he *is* poor" (61). *Fabliaux* like "Le paysan devenu médecin" ["The Peasant Who Became a Doctor"], in which a wealthy peasant marries the daughter of a poor knight, also suggest that "mixed marriages" were within the realm of possibility in the Medieval period (see Aubailly, 86–95).

3. It might be noted here that the use of grates in convents to physically separate the already cloistered women from their visitors was not universally imposed until the Council of Trent.

4. With respect to fairies at the workplace, Davis states: "[t]he women's workplace was itself open to fairies. At best they came when everyone was asleep and finish the spinning. More often they were mischievous, and would

take a spindle as their right if all the week's thread had not been properly wound on the reel on Saturday" ("Women," 179–80). With respect to fairies in peasant culture in the early twentieth century, see for instance Jalby (337–42).

5. See for instance *Les Cent Nouvelles Nouvelles* (ca.1456–1461) and Aubailly's edition of the *Fabliaux*.

6. Whether in reference to the *Chanson de Roland* (end of eleventh century, with a literary heritage running into the fourteenth with *Roland à Saragosse*) or the works of Marie de France (1154–1189), scholars tend to agree that the oral and the written traditions mutually influenced each other in the High Middle Ages.

7. Provinces like Normandy had their own charter with the king, first ratified by Louis X in 1315 and reaffirmed by Charles VII in 1458, which granted Norman subjects exemption from all extraordinary taxation, as well as the right to appeal directly to the king in cases of malfeasance or incompetence on the part of royal officers. See the entries "communal (mouvement)," "commune," "franchises," and "Normandie" in the *Dictionnaire de l'Histoire de France*. See also Clarke's excellent analysis of relations between Normandy and the monarchy (17–34).

8. With respect to Normandy's charter, Henri IV excluded it from the list of "Lois Fondamentales" at his sacre, and Louis XIII did not swear to uphold it. See Clarke (20).

9. Kelly states: "Until the European states were fully consolidated, women continued to exercise governing and military power in times of need. Indeed, as we are now beginning to rediscover, women were a normal part of European armies from the fourteenth century until well into the nineteenth century, in addition to the noblewomen who participated in positions of command. Nonetheless, by the second half of the seventeenth century, Castiglione's image of the disarmed lady excluded from functions of state prevailed throughout Europe as ideology—and increasingly as reality" (7).

10. Regarding the curialization of the nobility, see "The sociogenesis and development of French court society" (Elias, 146–213).

11. According to Huppert, these schools were open to members of the lower bourgeoisie as well as peasants, but the overwhelming majority of students issued from the High Bourgeoisie.

12. Huppert notes that "the private study . . . had replaced the private chapel in the *hôtels* of the gentry" (61).

13. For an overview of eighteenth-century debates on this question, see "Plaidoyers pour l'enfant" (Badinter, 191–254).

14. James Collins discusses the increasing limitations put on women's right to vote in guilds, and in a footnote cites the "Parlement of Paris *arrêt* depriving women of the right to sit as *maîtres-jurés* of the guild of *fruitiers-regratiers* in 1594 and the text of royal letters patent of 1608 removing their right to hire apprentices" (458). According to Davis, "royal edicts were trying to curb the use of property by widows who remarried and to constrain married women to make contracts only with their husbands' consent" ("Women," 185).

15. To this end a series of edicts were issued over the sixteenth and seventeenth centuries protecting the 1556 edict requiring parental consent: the edicts of 1556 and 1559 contained clauses associating clandestine marriage with rapt, the penalty for which was banishment; the ordinance of 1629 prohibited priests from marrying people from outside their parish without the permission of their parish priest or diocesan bishop; in 1639 priests were required to obtain written proof of parental consent from couples (see Hanley, 9–11).

16. Of course, master artisans co-existed with manufacturers until the period of industrialization, and peasants, only marginally dependent on salaried work to supplement their incomes, were largely self-sufficient; local markets continued to exist alongside national and international ones. This does not take away from the fact that entrepreneurs were consolidating economic power. See the article "industrie" in *Dictionnaire* I: 787–88.

17. According to Clark, "[state] revenues went from ten million in direct taxes in 1610 to seventy-three million in 1643" (424). Clark also notes that many merchants opposed the monarchy's protectionist policies, and mercantilists like Charles Loyseau felt that "excess domestic taxes . . . depressed incentives for production" (424).

18. See the article "manufactures royales privilégiées" in *Dictionnaire* (I:978).

19. Larry Riggs discusses the manipulative use of signs in terms of an ethics based not on essence, but on *performance*: "As Molière suggests in *Le Tartuffe* and *Le Misanthrope*, the desire to be perceived as devout, or sincere, makes devotion and sincerity performances rather than truths as it locks the pretentious self into the system of simulations" (127).

20. Although it may appear incongruous to cite Deleuze on Proust in a discussion of seventeenth-century sign systems, we cannot forget all that Proust owed to models taken from seventeenth-century authors, notably Saint-Simon and Sévigné.

21. Erica Harth puts forth the idea that the salon indeed was a *public* institution: "To the extent that the seventeenth-century salon offered its habitués— male and female—a space for speaking and writing, it was a public space" ("Salon Woman," 182).

22. For an overview of Gordon's notion of political vs. apolitical public spheres, see his "Introduction" (3–8).

23. For the salon, see DeJean's appendix in *Tender* (201–19) and Heyden-Rynsch (36–68). For dates on academies, see Viala (*Naissance*, 303–4).

24. Maclean's statement suggests that, in order to fully assess French literary history, we must take a serious look at the salon which, until the late 1980s, had been regarded as a rather "frivolous" phenomenon. Recent scholarship, such as Alain Viala's *Racine. La stratégie du caméléon* (1990), does take a serious look at the impact of salon culture on what are considered to be "classical" (read: "unfrivolous") texts.

25. In reaction to Vaugelas, Dupleix affirms in his *Liberté de la langue françoise dans sa pureté* [Freedom of the French Language in Its Purity, 1651] that women must fulfill two conditions to be considered authorities in matters pertaining to good usage: "L'une qu'elles soient bien instruites aux regles de la Grammaire, pour sçavoir sa congruité; et aux preceptes de la Rhetorique, pour juger de l'elegance et de la pureté des termes et des phrases. L'autre qu'elles soient bien versées en la langue Latine et mesmes en la Greque, afin de sçavoir la force de l'expression d'une infinité de mots que la nostre emprunte de l'une, et de bon nombre qu'elle a tiré de l'autre. Cela estant ainsi, où se trouveront des femmes qui aient ces deux conditions?" ["First, they must be well educated in the rules of Grammar, in order to understand its harmony, and in the precepts of Rhetoric, in order to judge the elegance and purity of the terms and sentences. The other is that they must be well versed in Latin and even Greek, so as to know the expressive force of an infinity of words that our language borrows from the one, and a good number taken from the other. Given these condi-

tions, where will one find women who fulfill these two conditions?"] (quoted in Maclean, 151).

26. For a discussion on the use of court at Versailles to control the high nobility, see Elias, chapters VI and VII.

27. For the dates of academies, see Viala (*Naissance*, 303–4) and Roche (I: 15–31).

28. "The academic movement of the seventeenth century presented itself as an enterprise of confiscation and transformation of knowledge by the State" (Apostolidès, 34). This project was actualized by monitoring intellectual activity and then excluding elements critical of the monarchy: "If monarchical power tends to include intellectuals in the nation, it seeks at the same time to exclude those who do not submit to reasons of State" (Apostolidès, 36). An academy such as the Académie des Sciences was founded specifically with the intention of providing the monarchy with technological experts who could erect various types of edifices to glorify Louis XIV: "Louis marshaled the forces of science and technology to support the massive edifice of absolutism" (*Ideology*, 162). Harth points out the irony of this project, for Louis XIV's support for the sciences prepared the way for the *encyclopédistes*, who would formulate a criticism of the monarchy, and announce the Revolution.

2. LOVE ORDERS CHAOS

1. In *Le Grand Cyrus*, Scudéry defines the fable as follows: "Vous pourrez, dis-je, voir qu'encore qu'une Fable ne soit pas une Histoire, et qu'il suffise à celuy qui la compose de s'attacher au vray-semblable, sans s'attacher toujours au vray" ["You will see, I said, that although a Fable is not a History, and that it suffices that the one who composes it adheres to verisimilitude, without always adhering to truth"] (1: 3).

2. On the keys in *Clélie*, see Niderst's *Madeleine* (287–302) and "Sur les clefs" (471–83).

3. Scudéry herself employs the term "maxime" to refer to the sayings scattered throughout the novel (6: 81).

4. Clarke's position is that *Horace* was not an unambiguously pro-Richelieu play, as many critics have argued. Rather, it puts into question the ethics of Richelieu's pursuit of national glory and his belief in reason of state. What makes Clarke's analysis convincing is the way in which he situates the play within a larger pool of texts on the same question.

5. One mazarinade, *Le Manifeste de la Noblesse de Normandie* [Manifesto of the Nobility of Normandy] (1652), clearly depicts Mazarin as a usurper on several occasions. He is described as "l'ennemi de l'Etat, le perturbateur du repos public et le détenteur de la personne sacrée de notre Monarque" ["enemy of the State, disrupter of public peace, and possessor of the sacred person of our Monarch"] (n.p.). The Fronde is described as a just war ("La Guerre qu'on a déclaré au C. Mazarin est pieuse" ["The War declared against the Cardinal Mazarin is pious"]) conducted against the "monster Mazarin." Mazarin was perceived to be a tyrant, whose tyranny was particularly severe in Normandy: "C'est elle [la Normandie] qui a plus souffert de la Tyrannie des Ministres, c'est elle qu'on a plus sollicitée de prendre le parti Mazarin et qui même se trouve contrainte de servir de retraite au tyran Mazarin lequel a voulu établir un Nouveau Parlement dans une de nos Villes" ["It is Normandy

that has suffered the most from the Tyranny of Ministers, it is Normandy that was most solicited to take the side of Mazarin and that even finds itself constrained to serve as the retreat for the tyrant Mazarin, who tried to established a New Parliament in one of our Cities"].

6. Inserted in her *Histoire du comte d'Albe*, Scudéry's history of French literature shows that she was strongly influenced by neo-Platonism. Her general list includes Guillaume de Lorris and Jean de Meun, Marie de France, Dante and Petrarque, and the writers of the Pléiade. Marguerite de Navarre, Montaigne, Ronsard, and Bertaut are particularly emphasized (see *De la poësie*, 42–96).

7. To create analogies between the body and its movements on the one hand, and nature and its activity on the other, was a *lieu commun* in the seventeenth century. See for instance Bayley (124–25, 153–60) and Rousset (119–23).

8. Descartes asks his readers to image in that "Dieu créait maintenant quelque part, dans les espaces imaginaires, assez de matière pour le composer, et qu'il agitât diversement et sans ordre les diverses parties de cette matière, en sorte qu'il en composât un chaos aussi confus que les poètes en puissent feindre, et que, par après, il ne fît autre chose que prêter son concours ordinaires à la nature, et la laisser agir suivant les lois qu'il a établies" ["God was creating somewhere, in imaginary spaces, enough matter to compose it [a world], and that he stirred up diversely and without order the various parts of this matter, in such a way as to compose a chaos as confused as the poets could imagine, and that, afterwards, he did no more than to lend his ordinary hand to nature, and let her move according to the laws he established"] (68). Although this passage can be situated within the larger context of Descartes defending the idea of the existence of God, it nevertheless demonstrates Descartes's preoccupation with the notions of chaos and order.

9. None of Clélie's other suitors ever suspect Herminius of being their rival. However, when Herminius's mistress Valerie learns about the Carte de Tendre and reads the letters exchanged between him and Clélie, she becomes jealous (5: 422–60). This instance provides an example of misreading, and was likely inserted in the novel to prevent the reader's own misinterpretations of the Carte.

10. Tendre-sur-Estime [Tenderness-by-Esteem], Tendre-sur-Reconoissance [Tenderness-by-Gratitude], Grand esprit [Great Wit], Jolis Vers [Pretty Verse], Billet galant [Gallant Letter], Billet doux [Love Letter], Grand Coeur [Great Heart/Courage], Bonté [Goodness], Complaisance [Obligingness], Petits Soins [Little Cares], Empressement [Eagerness], Grands Services [Big Favors], Sensibilité [Sensitivity], Obéissance [Obedience], Constante amitié [Constant/Faithful Friendship].

11. Teraminte, however, does try to dissuade Tiberius from conspiring against his father and is full of remorse when her lover is tried. She explains that Tarquin forced her to write the letter, and that if she failed to convince Tiberius to take part in the conspiracy, she would be executed. Unable to overcome his sense of pity for his mistress for the good of his country, Tiberius ends up taking part in the conspiracy. In the case of Teraminte and Tiberius, their situation is more the result of their weakness than their injustice.

12. Inesgalité [Changeability], Tiédeur [Half-Heartedness], Légèreté [Casualness], Oubli [Forgetfulness], and Meschanceté [Meanness].

13. Claude Fauchet, for instance, often uses *orgueil* to refer to military aggression: "l'orgueil et vanité d'aucuns espagnols" ["the pride and vanity of

some of the Spanish"] (72); "En mesme saison l'empereur adverty de l'orgueil et vanterie de Godefroy roy de Dannemarck, delibera d'edifier une ville ou chasteau outre la riviere d'Elbe, et y mettre garnison" ["In the same season the emperor, warned of the pride and conceit of Godefroy, king of Denmark, decided to erect a town or castle on the other side of the Elbe river, and set up a garrison"] (156). Guez de Balzac similarly refers to "l'orgueil des rebelles" ["the pride of rebels"] (53).

14. At this point in the novel, Aronce's noble birth is not yet known, thus he is referred to as the *Inconnu* or "unknown."

15. For another example of this, see the story of Artemidore and Berelise, in which Terille, Artemidore's rival, challenges him to a duel that Artemidore tries to prevent. The duel ends in Terille's death. See 4: 1055–57.

16. Tendre-sur-Inclination, Tendre-sur-Reconnoissance, and Tendre-sur-Estime are referred to as "ces trois *Villes* de Tendre" (1: 399; my emphasis).

17. On such social fusions in the seventeenth century, see Lougee, *Paradis*.

18. See 3: 497–559 for the events leading to Lucrece's marriage to Collatin.

19. Discussing Descartes' *méthode*, Timothy Reiss argues that it serves to bypass the prejudices (i.e., educational and cultural) or "unreason" inscribed in the subject that prevent it from discerning the true from the false. Method was a way to apply "objective" criteria to the analysis of the world that did not depend on the "subjective" nature of individual perception. Reiss states: "Method . . . provided something like the rules for writing. It acted by the strict organization of good sense, and entirely on its own. Its operation was always the same, ever true, general, rational, and universal. . . . Method operated not by reiterating discrete terms, not by thinking the variables of locally specific instances, but by repeating the course of reasoning itself, the constants that enabled thinking at all" ("Denying," 601). Similarly, the Carte provides "universal" guidelines to determine the merit of a suitor which do not depend on the "subjective" perception of the individual.

20. On Roman women as "captives," see for example 3: 120. Immediately after the section describing Roman women as captives, Rome is said to be "asservie" (enslaved) and must be "delivrée" (saved) from Tarquin (3: 130). As if speaking about a woman, Brutus remarks about Rome: "peut-elle estre plus mal-traitté qu'elle est?" ["can she be more mistreated than she already is?"] (3: 150). Later Brutus makes reference to "ma raison captive" ["my captive reason"] (3: 258; see also 3: 335 and 4: 1083). Clélie and the other Roman women are referred to throughout the novel as Tarquin's "captives," and on more than one occasion the struggle to free Clélie is likened to freeing Rome, exemplified in the following quote: "et la libertté [sic] de Rome, et celle de Clelie" ["and the liberty of Rome, and that of Clélie"] (4: 1082).

21. See Brutus's speech (4: 1392–1412).

22. In "La Politique du Prince," La Mothe Le Vayer similarly argues that when a monarchy or the rule of a single person is corrupt, it deteriorates into tyranny (301–2).

23. On the conversation on the justice of destroying Tarquin, see 3: 148–50. This is also touched on in Brutus's speech (4: 1398). On the contractual relation between subject and sovereign, and by extension lover and mistress, children and father, see 4: 702–5.

24. The potential danger of the mob is first evoked in the pillage of Tarquin's palace (4: 1434). Later, when the Roman people must choose a second Consul, they decide on Collatin for the sole reason that he might prove more vengeful

than anyone else because Sextus raped his wife. The narrator comments: "tant les deliberations populaires sont pour l'ordinaire tumultueuses, inconsiderées, et esloignées de la droite raison" ["so often popular deliberations are tumultuous, inconsiderate, and far from good reason"] (5: 41). In the episode where Brutus's sons are found guilty of treason, the Roman people demand they be executed on the spot, refusing to listen to evidence of any mitigating circumstances. Brutus is forced to comply, particularly when the Roman people cry out: "qu'ils meurent, qu'ils meurent" ["death onto them, death onto them"] (6: 654).

25. Gordon argues that in the pre-Revolutionary period, "French authors created a unique ideological space that was neither democratic nor absolutist" (4). Discussing Scudéry's later collections of conversations, published in the 1680s and 1690s, Gordon situates her within this democratizing yet hierarchical worldview (see 107–12). Her earlier works like Le Grand Cyrus and Clélie, however, are more politicized in content than her later work, even if the political aspects of the texts are downplayed.

26. On Richelieu's strategies to control the royal administration, see Church (283). On Richelieu's role in the prosecution of Cinq-Mars, see Church (329–32).

27. "The 'people' legitimately wished to take affairs into their own hands, which usually meant confiscating the money and furnishings found in the houses of tax collectors and partisans" (Ranum, Fronde, 55).

28. On the abundance of speeches about the poverty and oppression of the people during the Fronde, see Ranum (Fronde, 53–6).

3. Adults at Play

1. For the authorship of the Chroniques, I have listed Madeleine de Scudéry, Paul Pellisson, and Valentin Conrart, each of whom participated in putting the manuscript together. I would argue, like Joan DeJean, that Scudéry was the principle author, in the sense that she was the "director or animator" of the Samedis (Tender, 75). For the historical background of the Chroniques see Belmont and the introduction to the 2002 critical edition, from which all references to the Chroniques are taken. To my knowledge, Alain Génetiot is the only scholar who has studied the Chroniques as a literary text.

2. According to the Chroniques, the Carte de Tendre was created sometime in August or September of 1653; the first mention of the first volume of Clélie in which it appeared was after February 1654. On page 238 of the Chroniques, it is clearly February, six months since Sapho created the Carte for Acante, who hoped to reach Tendre by this time. The first mention of Aronce and Horace, two of the principle characters of Clélie, are in the letter of Acante to Sapho (253).

3. For biographies see Niderst (Madeleine 11–124 and 235–67); on Pellisson, Isarn, Donneville, and Ranchin see Barbaza; on Conrart see Mabille de Poncheville 16–70; on Chapelain see Brun; on Sarasin see Festugière.

4. During the religious wars, lawyers acquired prestigious and authoritative situations due to the disintegration of central power. With Henri IV and the return to order, lawyers came under attack, and writers like Gilles Ménage, another intimate of Scudéry's group, felt the need to write an apology for the profession. Some were criticized for being sophists due to the wealth they had amassed over the course of this period (Fumaroli, Age, 587–91).

5. Although Jonathan Dewald has tried to show that members of the Robe in sixteenth-century Rouen constituted a more heterogeneous group than once believed, it becomes clear, however, that the majority of the Parlement de Rouen's members were indeed nonnoble. Dewald shows that from 1539 to 1558 only 10% of the *parlementaires* could show four or more generations of nobility; 3% demonstrated two to three generations of nobility. Sons of high officials (sons of *parlementaires* or other sovereign courts) made up 23% of the parliament during this period, 15% were sons of lawyers, 15% were sons of lesser officials, and 15% were sons of bourgeois. One problem with these statistics is that Dewald does not account for the percentage of *parlementaire* families that moved from one category to the other over time. Nevertheless, it is important, as he argues, to note that the Robe of Rouen did not consist solely of people of bourgeois background (73–78). In Rouen each generation of *parlementaires* included a higher or lower percentage of members issuing from families Dewald categorizes as "bourgeois" (which I take to mean "merchant" as opposed to lawyers or other members of the Robe who were not technically noble) ranging from as high as 19% from 1589 to 1598, and as low as 6% from 1619 to 1638.

6. See Dewald (21–35) and Fumaroli ("Rhetoric" 253–62).

7. On notions of play and game, see Huizinga (4–13); Caillois 13–24; and Jauss (164–67).

8. Acante writes to Sapho: "votre sexe surpasse le nôtre en toutes choses" ["your sex surpasses ours in everything"] (98).

9. The genre of the portrait can be traced back to the Medieval genre of the Mirror which emerged in the twelfth century as a predominantly religious genre. Over the next centuries, the scope of the genre was extended to include natural science, history, and even social etiquette. The Mirror generally created correspondences between the physical self and the moral self, the Mirror allowing one to "see" the state of one's moral self through the example of, for example, Christ or the Virgin Mother, in order to correct one's self in the same manner that one looks into a mirror to adjust one's physical appearance. For historical background on the portrait, see Harth (*Ideology*, 69–75). For a summary of the function of the Mirror in the twelfth- and thirteenth-centuries, see Johnsson. For an example of the later secularization of the genre, see Piaget's edition of *Le Miroir aux dames: Poème inédit du XVième siècle* (1908) and Watriquet de Couvin's *Li Mireoirs as Dames*.

10. Alain Génetiot considers conversation as "the totalizing genre that encompassed all other *mondain* genres" (175). He argues that poetry doubles oral language in its strictly utilitarian purposes (171), something we will discuss in more detail below.

11. In many respects the functioning of Scudéry's salon brings to mind the ways in which Dena Goodman characterizes the Republic of Letters. For Goodman, the Republic was constituted by the reciprocal and public exchange of ideas that was dependent upon the invention of the printing press and the creation of a French postal system, established in 1603. We might view the salon as a microcosm of what was happening at a national and international level. See *Republic* (15–23).

12. In *Utopiques: Jeux d'espaces* (1973), Louis Marin points to the interconnections between space and/as discourse in the fashioning of early modern utopias. He reminds us that utopia means no-place (*ou-topos*), and situates utopia in texts, the only places or no-places where utopias are realized. Thus utopias are textual places, as well as spaces of play. The production of utopic spaces

entails the exclusion of difference and the inclusion of the same, resulting in the creation of an isolate, homogenous, insular group and space. Marin characterizes difference not only in terms of different political ideals, socio-economic differences, or cultural differences, but also in terms of any kind of change, including temporal change or bodily change (sickness or death): in utopia time stands still and people live forever.

13. In the following lines, Théodamas likens Sapho to Midas: "tout ce que votre main touche / Devient joli, poli, galant" ["everything your hand touches / Becomes pretty, polished, and galant"] (88). Later Acante compares Sapho to Midas and Callicrate, a character in *Cyrus* who also turns things into gold and who is a key for Vincent Voiture: "Pensez-vous, Mademoiselle, que tout le monde soit comme vous qui faites tout ce qu'il vous plaît et qui changez en or comme Midas ou comme Callicrate tout ce que vous maniez" ["Do you think, Mademoiselle, that everyone is like you, who do everything that you find pleasing and turn into gold everything you touch like Midas or like Callierate"] (131).

14. In order to counter the effect of the unofficial, clandestine press which tended to be "biting, satirical, and willingly seditious," Louis XIII and Richelieu gave exclusive, official rights to Théophraste Renaudot to publish the *Gazette* in 1631. Essentially the *Gazette* provided official gossip about the monarchy, the *Gazette*'s news consisting of *petits faits* regarding the Court, the royal family, and the king's nominations. Its success resulted in Renaudot's nomination as *historiographe de Sa Majesté*. See Moureau (123–24).

15. Pellisson had finished his law studies in Paris in 1645 and permanently returned to the capital in November 1650. Isarn and his mother were in Paris as early as 1651. From 1653–1654 Donneville regularly made trips to Paris, but never established himself permanently. See Niderst (*Madeleine* 11, 93–94, 115–16).

16. Here Scudéry is referring to the Fête des Rois, a celebration of the Epiphany, where a token or charm is baked in a cake, and the person who finds the token is named king or queen.

17. The original manuscript reads "sainte Déesse" (ms. 76), but the editors of the critical edition use "puissante déesse" ["powerful goddess"] (103).

18. See for instance Montaigne (I: 237–3)8 and Charron (197, 489).

19. See Mary Skemp's discussion of friendship in *La Coche* in her forthcoming article, a version of which I had the pleasure of hearing at the 2000 M/MLA in Kansas City.

20. On books as gifts, see Davis (*Gifts*, 44–46); on Erasmus, see Davis, *Gifts*, 36.

21. In this section the *Chroniques* do not suggest that Georges de Scudéry is the unambiguous author of *Cyrus* or of Donneville's portrait. Because it is Sapho who is offended (or who pretends to be offended), the text intimates that she indeed is the portraitist.

22. This opposition between the universal and the particular, and the connection between universality, ontology, and the capital, cannot be better expressed than by Flaubert in *Madame Bovary*, where Emma contrasts Parisian high society with her provincial surroundings: "C'était une existence au-dessus des autres, entre ciel et terre, dans les orages, quelque chose de sublime. Quant au reste du monde, il était perdu, sans place précise et comme n'existant pas. . . . Tout ce qui l'entourait immédiatement . . . lui semblait une exception dans le monde, un hasard particulier" ["It was an existence above all others, between heaven and the earth, in the storms, something sublime. As far as the rest of

the world, it was lost, without a precise location and as if not existing at all. . . . Everything that immediately surrounded her . . . seemed an exception in the world, a strange coincidence"] (119). For Emma, in Paris a person "is someone," whereas in the provinces it is as if one does not exist.

23. Kettering discusses the importance of having *crédit* as a broker, who arranged the exchange of resources for patrons and secured connections for clients. An individual's *crédit* or trust derived from his or her reputation, rank, family name, wealth, clients, and patrons. In other words, an individual's *crédit* was an expression of both his or her trustworthiness and social value (42–43).

24. Just to cite a couple of examples, the lady plays the role of "lord" and the knight Yvain that of "vassal" who must go through many ordeals to earn her hand in Chrétien de Troye's *Yvain, le chevalier au lion*. Troubadour poetry often uses the language of vassalage to describe the poet's love for a lady, the poet asking to be his lady's "serviteur" and the lady playing the role of his "protectrice." See for instance Arnaud de Mareuil's "Domna, genser que no sai dir" (32–40) and Arnaud Daniel's "En cest sonet coind' e leri" (186–89) in *Anthologie*.

25. Kettering maintains that clients could secure the attention of a patron in several ways: as a family member; through the recommendation of kinsmen or clients of a patron; through his military exploits; or by writing (38). It is interesting to note that writing also attracted friends to each other. Montaigne notes that part of his attraction to La Boétie was a satire he had written (I: 236). Chapelain writes to Heinsius that his wit and way of writing "furent les premiers attraits qui m'engagerent a vous aymer" ["appealed to me and brought me to like you"] (*Heinsius*, 201).

26. In a letter to Acante, Sapho argues that a good portrait should not only flatter its model, but it should furthermore embellish it (61). In other words, the portrait is an embellishing, idealizing fiction based on certain traits of the person represented. Arguably all exchange within the salon has the function of embellishing its addressee. Jean Starobinski is quite justified in maintaining that in the social milieu of the salons reciprocal exchange is "a transaction in which fictitious perfections mutually authorize each other" (69).

27. Elsewhere in the *Chroniques*, Méliante also makes the analogy between the pen and the sword: "Rendre la plume en bonne foi / Est proprement rendre les armes / Pour un poète comme moi" ["Surrendering the pen in good faith / Is truly surrendering one's arms / For a poet like me"] (157).

28. In *Le Grand Cyrus*, Sapho is said to be the daughter of "un homme de qualité apellé Scamandrogine" ("a man of quality called Scamandrogine"). Her father's name, *Scamandrogine*, contains the word "androg[y]ne," suggesting that Sapho herself is somehow androgynous (10: 330).

4. BOILEAU AND PERRAULT

1. Because the position of the Ancients has come to be equated with misogyny and that of the moderns with feminism, critics have been, I would argue, too lenient in their assessment of Perrault's response to Boileau's Satire X. Critics who have given some credit to Perrault for taking a feminist position include Michael Moriarty (176), DeJean, (*Tender*, 164–67) and Timmermans (146, 166–67). Marina Warner calls his *Apologie des femmes* "a rather touching hymn of praise to conjugal love," and though she is somewhat critical of his

infantilizing of women, she refers to him as "the champion of womankind, defender of old wives' wisdom" (169). In a later discussion of the *Querelle*, DeJean goes so far as to argue that Perrault defended the modern position by suggesting that "it was necessary to think, to judge, and to reason as a Woman" (*Ancients*, 67). I would tend to agree with Lewis Seifert's assessment of Perrault's position: "Ultimately, however, women's 'innate' qualities were appropriated by men to enhance their own position in the Quarrel of the Ancients and the Moderns as well as the polite society of the salons. Indeed, concerned above all to answer Boileau's vendetta, Perrault, in *L'Apologie des femmes*, lauds above all the ideals of feminine domesticity and subservience" (94).

2. Unless otherwise noted, all references to *Les héros de roman* are from the 1961 edition of Boileau's *Oeuvres*.

3. In his Satire III, Boileau ridicules unsophisticated social climbers, and in Satire V, he condemns misalliances and the nobility's moral degradation in ways that anticipate the theories of Henri de Boulainvilliers.

4. Although Antoine Arnauld asserted that Boileau never attacked the author of *Cyrus* and *Clélie*, this would be difficult to argue in the case of *Les héros de roman*, given the fact that contemporaries immediately would have made the connection between Sapho and Scudéry.

5. The scene is taken from volume 3 of *Clélie*. The first sentence reads: "Qu'il seroit doux d'aimer, si l'on aimoit toujours! / Mais, hélas! il n'est point d'éternelles amours" ["How nice it would be to love, if one loved always! / But, alas! there is no eternal love"]. The response is: "Permettez-moi d'aimer, merveille de nos jours; / Vous verrez qu'on peut voir d'éternelles amours" ["Let me love, miracle of our times; / You will see that eternal love exists"] (297–98).

6. Scudéry was known to be rather unattractive, which is emphasized in the dialogue when Pluto first meets Sapho, exclaiming: "On me l'avoit dépeinte si belle. Je la trouve bien laide!" ["They painted her so beautiful for me. I find her quite ugly!"] (299). Scudéry also was known to have fairly dark skin, reproduced in the portrait with Tisiphone's "brun mâle et noble" ["male and noble brown"] (301).

7. The opposition between true/false, reality/illusion was an important topos in works by demonologists. They argued that the devil tricks people into believing in him through false knowledge, false stigmata, and false rituals that are illusionary and inauthentic copies of the true knowledge, stigmata, and rituals of the Catholic Church. See, for instance Jacques-Chaquin and Lancre.

8. It should be noted that Boileau wrote a similar satire, Satire IV (1664), in which he attacks human folly in the figure of the pedant, the gallant, the zealot, the libertine, the miser, the spendthrift, and the gambler. Despite the similarities between Satire IV and Satire X, including the use of madness to discredit each of the character types represented, Satire IV does not sexualize nor essentialize—nor demonize, for that matter—the vices of men.

9. Unless otherwise noted, all references to the satires are from the 1969 edition of Boileau's *Oeuvres I*.

10. Holly Tucker has determined that there were over thirty French reprints of the *Malleus Maleficarum* between 1487 and 1669 (64). In Lyon alone it was republished in 1595, 1604, 1620, and 1669. Interestingly, this corresponds somewhat to the two main periods in which antiwomen pamphlets were on the rise.

11. Fénelon obviously is thinking here of Plato, who excluded from his Republic Ionian and Lydian music, which he viewed as soft and indolent and to which he opposed the Dorian, perceived to be a military, virile mode of music.

12. See for instance the anonymous fifteenth-century *Miroir aux Dames*, in which the use of *cornes* is called a "diablerie" ["piece of devilry"] and women who wear them are compared to horned beasts (19–20).

13. La Brinvilliers was executed in 1676 for poisoning several people, including her father and two brothers. La Voisin, implicated in the Affair of the poisons and accused of witchcraft, was executed in 1680 (see Mossiker, 142–48 and 174–88). Canidie is a witch who appears in Horace's *Satires*. Gacon also portrays the debauched courtisan who has sex with a dwarf, a reference to La Fontaine's tale "Joconde," borrowed from Ariosto, itself probably influenced by written or oral versions of the *Arabian Nights*. Presenting the reader with women who threaten the order of the patriarchal family, Gacon also depicts the adulteress; the woman who conspires to destroy her father; the woman who abandons or murders her children; the woman who murders her husband; and the incestuous woman.

14. Moriarty is among those critics who argue that Boileau's attack on women must be read within the terms of the quarrel. Focusing on the idea of bad taste in the Satire X, Moriarty does not take into account the ways in which bad taste is gendered (171–72).

15. Chaussé argues that men have obligations to four main bodies which compel them to marry and reproduce, including: the human race; the political body; the domestic body; and the ecclesiastical body (130–58).

16. All references to Regnard's *Satire contre les Maris* are taken from his *Oeuvres complètes*.

17. In his edition of the *Contes*, Jean-Pierre Collinet notes that Perrault initially wanted to use the name "Griselde," based on Boccaccio's "Griselda," because "le nom de Griselidis m'a paru s'être un peu sali dans les mains du Peuple" ["it seemed to me that the name of Griselidis soiled itself a bit in the hands of the People"] (quoted in Perrault, *Contes*, 307n.). On the following references to the publishing history of "Griselidis," see Perrault, *Contes* 274–77.

18. In his *Les Triumphes de la noble et amoureuse dame et l'art de honnestement aymer* [Triumphs of the Noble and Loving Lady and the Art of Loving Virtuously[(1530), Jean Bouchet argues that women must nurse their children and must never be idle: "une fille ne doit estre oyseuse mais tousjours filler, tistre, broder, couldre ou faire autres ouvrages appartenans à leur estat" ["a girl must never be idle but must always spin, knit, embroider, sew or do other tasks appropriate to their state"] (*Miroir*, 47). Women must also be "solitaire" and "recluse en la maison" (*Miroir*, 48). On Chaussé's discussion on the imperative to reproduce, see note 15. Chaussé argues that men are responsible for women's behavior because they are more enlightened and noble, and must provide good examples for them to follow (185–86). Fénelon generally argues that women need to be educated in the area of household duties and religion, and must avoid reading novels and becoming educated in *mondain* ways.

19. At least one husband found the tale to be too oppressive to be held up as an example his wife should imitate. In the fifteenth century, a bourgeois of Paris produced an adaptation of "Griseldis" for his young wife. While he first explains that "les bonnes dames" ["good wives"] must obey their husbands and patiently endure their wishes, he later states that the lesson of the story is too harsh. Addressing his wife, he informs her that he does not think she should apply the story to herself, and that he is not worthy of such obedience: "l'ay mise cy, non pas pour l'appliquer à vous, ne pour ce que je vueille de vous telle obeissance, car je n'en suis mie digne et aussi je ne suis mie marquis, ne ne

vous ay prise bergiere, ne je ne suis si fol, si oultrecuidié, ne si jeune de sens, comme je ne doye bien savoir que ce n'appartient pas à moy de vous faire telz assaulz, ne essaiz ou semblens" ["I included it here, not so that it would apply to you, nor that I would want you to be so obedient, for I am hardly worthy of it and I am not a marquis, I did not take you as a shepherdess, and I am not so mad, arrogant, nor immature, as I know well that it is not my right to assault you and try you in such a way"] (quoted in Golenistcheff-Koutouzoff, 125).

20. In his letter to Boccaccio, Petrarch maintains: "My object in thus rewriting your tale was not to induce the women of our time to imitate the patience of this wife, which seems to me almost beyond imitation, but to lead my readers to emulate the example of feminine constancy, and to submit themselves to God with the same courage as did this woman to her husband" (Boccaccio, *Decameron*, 186). In her reading of the tale, Marga Cottino-Jones highlights the allegory of Griselda as patience and as a Christ figure and the marquis as the figure of wisdom and as the divine king or father (297–98). Perrault's Griselidis views her husband's torments as God's way of testing her faith (75).

21. In his preface to the *Contes* Collinet argues that Perrault was parodying La Bruyère's "Des femmes" in the prince's speech on women (13). Yvette Saupé suggests that "Griselidis" is an ironic or parodical tale and as such we must not take his depiction of Griselidis to represent his ideal for women (120–30). Again, I would emphasize that nowhere in his oeuvre does Perrault put into question negative stereotypes of women or the need to subjugate them. Perrault satirizes his Ancient rivals by having them tyrannize women, at the same time that he shares their fundamental beliefs about women.

22. The portrait of the gambler in "Griselidis" epitomizes the association Perrault makes between public women and women of ill repute: "Cette autre s'érige en Joueuse, / Perd tout, argent, bijoux, bagues, meubles de prix, / Et même jusqu'à ses habits" ["This other one sets herself up as a Gambler, / Loses everything, money, jewelry, rings, expensive furniture, / And even her clothes"] (*Contes*, 62).

23. When discussing dyes for clothes, Tertullian states: "those things cannot be the best by nature which do not come from God, who is the Author of nature. Hence, they must be understood to be from the Devil, who is the corrupter of nature" (126). Later he states: "those women sin against God who anoint their faces with creams, stain their cheeks with rouge, or lengthen their eyebrows with antimony. . . . Whatever is born, that is the work of God. Obviously, then, anything else that is added must be the work of the Devil" (135–36). Tertullian constantly reiterates his view that the "alluring display of beauty" through finery is "bodily prostitution" (146).

24. Although hospitals could be viewed as public spaces, women tend to play within them the domestic role of caretaker.

25. It is interesting to note that in Perrault's version, Griselidis and the prince only have one child, a daughter, whereas in most versions they have a daughter and a son. At the end of Perrault's tale, the prince has a definite successor in the worthy lord who marries his daughter. One could read this in terms of Perrault promoting a transfer of power between men based not on blood, but on merit.

26. For a nice summary of early modern notions of "male-dominated processes of reproduction," see Tucker (90–91).

27. In his *Mémoires*, Perrault recalls the conversation he had with Colbert regarding his marriage. Colbert suggested that he marry the daughter of a

businessman, who could bring him a bigger dowry than Marie Guichon, and asked Perrault if this was a marriage of inclination. Perrault responded: "Je n'ai vû la fille . . .[] qu'une fois depuis qu'elle est hors de religion, où elle a été mise dès l'âge de quatre ans" ["I only saw the girl . . . once since she has been out of the convent, where she was put at the age of four"] (120). He goes on to explain that he married her because he knew the parents well.

28. Of course, Perrault draws from medieval as well as humanist and Greco-Roman tradition to articulate his model of the ideal woman and his critique of "bad women." Nevertheless, he combines these earlier traditions in such a way as to set the groundwork for the more "bourgeois" misogyny of Enlightenment and post-Revolutionary France.

29. It is important to note that Perrault in fact did believe in witches. In his *Pensées chrétiennes*, he remarks: "Il y a beaucoup de choses très vraies dont on doute souvent, parce que les faits qu'on rapporte pour les prouver sont faux, et cela est injuste. Cela se voit particulièrement sur le fait des sorciers, des apparitions, des miracles et des possédés. Car il est certain qu'il y a des sorciers, les uns qui ne sont que des empoisonneurs, les autres qui font des choses surnaturelles à l'homme, comme de faire tourner le sas, d'empêcher le beurre de prendre, etc." ["There are many things that are true, which people often doubt, because the facts related to prove them are false, and this is unjust. This is seen particularly with respect to witches, apparitions, miracles, and the possessed. For it is certain that witches exist, the ones who are nothing but poisoners, the others who do supernatural things to people, like making the sieve turn, preventing butter from taking, etc."] (114–15).

30. In her discussion of "Cendrillon," Patricia Hannon maintains that the female body is an "object of pleasurable consumption" in Perrault's tales (68).

31. Marina Warner underscores the associations that were made between women's speech, sexuality, and the Fall: "The seduction of women's talk reflected the seduction of their bodies; it was considered as dangerous to Christian men, and condemned as improper *per se*. Female folly had brought about the Fall, so must be quelled. In the Vulgate, Jerome used *seducta* for Eve's transgression: the serpent led her astray, and she then 'seduces' Adam, too" (31).

32. In some ways, the situation recalls that in Jean Racine's *Phèdre*. When Thésée is believed dead, and paternal authority is momentarily lifted, Phèdre acts on her incestuous desires. In the absence of male authority, the law of the father is no longer respected.

33. Regular edicts were issued regarding parental consent from 1556 to 1638. Since 1556 clandestine pregnancy and childbirth were deemed illegal. See Hanley (9–11).

34. Marie-Catherine d'Aulnoy, on the other hand, uses a female cat in her rendition, "La Chatte blanche" ["The White Cat"].

35. The 1697 illustration tones down the luxuriousness of the 1695 illustration. Bluebeard appears much more austere, while his wife, plainly dressed, looks much more penitent. It is possible that in modifying the illustration, Perrault wished to portray Bluebeard as appearing to be a God-fearing man, only to highlight the degree to which the devil could appear to be *honnête*. It is much more subtle than the 1695 illustration, where Bluebeard exhibits far more recognizable signs for the early modern reader of his "barbarity" and ungodliness.

36. Jacques-Chaquin discusses the correlations that were made between secret knowledge and women's knowledge, all of which was associated with

witchcraft: "With the *Malleus Maleficarum*, one of the first texts to define witchcraft, the obsession about a female power over especially sexuality, birth, and death is evident, as a preoccupation with a specifically feminine transmission of a knowledge dangerous to men" (116).

37. For many demonologists, boundless curiosity and a thirst for novelty led to heresy and witchcraft, distracting one from thoughts of God (Jacques-Chaquin, 109).

38. Although the passage sounds like Fénelon is about to put into question this bit of "common knowledge," he in fact does not go on to refute the statement. Instead, he argues that a girl's education is necessary in order to make her a better wife and mother, and it must be restricted to religious and domestic concerns.

39. For Fénelon, the danger of the novel and such genres is that nothing corresponds to "real life." Women consequently do not accept household chores, for they want to live like these imaginary princesses: "Quel dégoût pour elle de descendre de l'Héroïsme jusqu'au plus bas détail du ménage" ["What disgust for her to descend from Heroism to the lowest detail of the household"] (15).

40. Perrault discusses what he calls "positive" and "negative" pleasures in his *Pensées chrétiennes*. Negative pleasures are those associated with the body and have to do with alleviating physical discomfort, such as stopping hunger or quenching thirst. Positive pleasures, however, have to do with the true satisfaction of the soul (57–59).

41. I am thinking in particular of Jean-Marie Apostolidès's article, "Des choses cachées dans le château de Barbe bleue," but other critics have touched on the theme of adultery as well.

42. Demonologists seem to agree that women's excessive curiosity leads them to make pacts with the devil, pacts believed to be consummated through sexual acts (Houdard, 122–23; Jacques-Chaquin, 109–14). They overwhelmingly use sexual imagery to characterize women's relation to the devil, even when this involves knowledge. For instance, Lancre maintains that the false sciences of sorcery "nous font entrer en des curiosités exécrables, et *nous prostituent* à tant d'abominations" ["introduces us to foul curiosities, and *prostitutes us* to so many abominations"], distracting us from the true knowledge of God that leads to salvation (245; my emphasis).

43. Kathryn Hoffmann discusses the mutual influences of these various discourses in her article "Flying through Classicism's Night: The Witch in Myth and Religion."

5. THE TYRANNY OF PATRIARCHS

1. According to Jean-Louis Flandrin, women who were heads of households, usually widows, had voting rights in many regions until the Revolution, and exercised varying degrees of authority. He notes that in the Basque country eldest daughters were heiresses of their houses and "traditionally exercised authority over husbands and younger brothers. Until 1794, they continued to vote on behalf of their families" (117).

2. On Louis XIV's attempts to consolidate the public sphere, see Apostolidès (*Roi*, 34).

3. Joan DeJean notes that the last fifteen years of the seventeenth century

"witnessed a veritable explosion" in the ranks of women writers, despite the fact that "the salons were displaced by the academies" (*Tender*, 128–29).

4. On censorship in this period, see Harth (*Ideology*, 184–86).

5. The English version I consulted contained the story of Anne Boleyn, but the French 1674 version did not. However, apparently the 1680 French editions do include the story, so at present it is unclear to me as to whether or not this story came in later editions, or if some 1674 editions do contain this story.

6. On Dunoyer's biography and political position, see Goldwyn "Journalisme" and "Mémoires", and Nabarra.

7. Curiously, the historic marquis of Northampton, though a supporter of Lady Jane, was never executed, and died nearly twenty years after Northumberland was killed for conspiracy.

8. In *Les Nouvelles d'Elisabeth*, Percy is depicted as a more perfect lover than Henry VIII and is unrivaled in Anne Boleyn's heart. In "La Belle aux cheveux d'or" ["Beauty with the Golden Hair"], the worthy Avenant earns the princess's hand for a rather unworthy king with the help of fairies, and in the end marries her. The legitimate heir to the throne in "Le Prince Lutin," Furibond, is a repulsive and cruel monster who is envious of the noble Léandre, and even tries to kill him. With the help of the fairy Gentille, Léandre defeats Furibond and wins the hand of the princess. In *Le Comte de Warwick*, king Edoüard is consistently portrayed as an inconstant lover who finds himself to be Warwick's rival for Madame de Dévonshire. The comtesse, however, prefers Warwick over the king.

9. Fearing his proximity to the throne, the historical Henry VII imprisoned Edward of Warwick in the Tower of London. The rumor that Edward had died gave rise to the rebellion of Lambert Simnel, a young man used as a political pawn to impersonate the Earl of Warwick to gain the crown. To avoid further such problems, the king had Warwick executed in 1499 (see Elton, 5–37).

10. Whereas Protestant women who refused to abjure were locked up in convents and hospitals that served as prisons, Protestant men were sent to the galleys. It is remarkable that Warwick survives some eight years on the galley of Dragut-Rais, for the average life expectancy for most galley slaves was two to three years (see Richard, 186–88).

11. It is important to note that parental consent was required for women until the age of twenty-five, and for men until age thirty. After 1639, "even children over age could be disinherited if they married for the first time against their parents' will" (Davis, "Ghosts," 107).

12. Anne's relationship with Percy was viewed to be an obstacle to Henry VIII's wishes to marry her. Anne's father, Thomas Boleyn, and the earl of Northumberland, Percy's father, conspire with Wolsey to write an "artificial letter" stating that Anne had agreed to marry the king. Northumberland shows Percy the letter, and Percy falls into the trap, believing Anne to be unfaithful. Percy consequently marries the daughter of the earl of Shrewsbury in accordance with his father's wishes. But later, when Percy sees Anne again, he laments: "unfortunately for me, my condition is only changed, my heart is altogether the same as it was" (*Novels*, 67). Like Percy, Julie falls into the trap, and marries Bedfort. And like Percy, upon seeing Hypolite again, she declares: "l'infortunée Julie, en changeant de condition, n'a point changé de sentimens" ["upon changing status, the unfortunate Julie did not change her feelings"] (101). The close wording of these two passages would suggest, again, that d'Aulnoy was familiar with the text.

13. At one point Hypolite refers to Bedfort as "le tyran de Julie" ["the tyrant of Julie"] (116).

14. When Julie finally escapes from the convent at Saint Menoux and flees to Italy to stay with Lucile and Léandre, the abbess tells Bedfort that Julie died. Bedfort consequently remarries, but when he discovers Julie is in fact alive, he arranges to have her kidnapped and sent to a convent so as not to lose the Becarelly fortune.

15. This will not be the case, however, in her tale "Riquet à la houppe" ["Riquet with the Tuft"], which nevertheless ends on a pessimistic tone, again suggesting that true love is not possible.

16. Julie's critique of the old pursuing the young is scathing: "une vieille qui s'éclate de rire pour en paroistre plus aimable, laisse voir des dents qui font peur, et quelquefois elle n'en a point à montrer; le Cavalier qui veut paroistre enjoüé, laisse par malheur tomber sa perruque, il découvre alors sa tête chenuë, et perd tout d'un coup le peu d'avantage qu'il tiroit de ses cheveux blonds" ["an old woman who bursts out laughing in order to appear more likeable, lets her teeth show, which scares people, and sometimes she does not have any to show; the Cavalier who wants to appear cheerful has his wig fall off, his bald head is discovered, and he suddenly loses the little advantage he had from his blond hair"] (151). This scene is another example of how certain characters fail—or perhaps in this case refuse—to assimilate the lessons they are taught within the story. Jean Mainil provides several examples of how d'Aulnoy uses inscribed readers who fail to integrate the message communicated by the tale or story. As such she problematizes the relation between storytelling and the communication of pedagogical lessons. See Mainil, 148, 152–53, 157.

17. I will be using the terms "bienséance," "virtue," and "honor" somewhat interchangeably. "Bienséance" basically refers to social and moral norms appropriate to one's age, sex, and condition, and can be translated by "decorum." "Virtue" and "honor" are acquired by adhering to the norms of *bienséance.*

18. I am drawing very generally here from Louis Althusser's notion of interpellation. For Althusser, interpellation designates individuals as subjects within a particular ideology by "hailing" them, which also means that the individual must recognize himself or herself within this ideology in order to respond to the call. See Althusser, 170–77.

19. Hypolite continually insists that he can never be separated from Julie. Before Julie and Hypolite are fully aware of their love for each other, Hypolite remarks: "je vous conjure ne me parlez jamais que nous devions quelque jour nous separer" ["I beg you, never talk to me about us having to separate one day"] (16). Later, when Julie is given the choice to marry Bedfort or enter a convent and fears for their future together, Hypolite responds: "si vous ne m'estes point contraire, qui pourra séparer nos coeurs?" ["if you are not contrary to me, who will be able to separate our hearts"] (34). Throughout the novel it is Hypolite who perseveres, who never gives up on their love.

20. Day argues, and rightly so, that Hypolite is often "in the grip of his emotions" (79). However, Julie is as emotional as Hypolite in the novel, and moreover, d'Aulnoy does not seem to propose that being emotional is necessarily a sign of weakness. I would argue that Julie and Hypolite are not constructed in oppositional terms of weakness and strength, but rather in terms of complementarity. Hypolite embraces his "feminine" side at the same time that he pushes Julie to be more "masculine" in the pursuit of her freedom. Their complementarity is exemplified by their transvestitism, which can also take the

form, in a tale like "L'Oranger et l'abeille" ["The Bee and the Orange Tree"], of interchangeable gender roles. See my "Nature and Culture," 154–57.

21. Perhaps a closer analogy with Julie and Lucile would be between Aline and Léonore of Sade's *Aline et Valcour* (1786, publ. 1795), although I would argue that Sade's Julie and Juliette also are similar characters whose stories should be read allegorically and not literally. It is interesting to note that Sade names one of his characters who engages in a clandestine marriage Léonore, recalling d'Aulnoy's Léonor who runs away with Don Fernand. Both d'Aulnoy's Léonor and Sade's Léonore also are abducted by the Turks.

22. I do not mean to suggest, however, that d'Aulnoy always deals with "true love" in a serious way. For instance, in "Don Gabriel," the treatment of love is quite comical. Don Gabriel falls in love with Isidore without having seen her, and is prepared to take extravagant measures to make her acquaintance. When Don Gabriel and his friend the comte d'Aguilar disguise themselves as pilgrims to gain entry into Isidore and Mélanie's home, the count immediately falls in love with Mélanie. But Isidore is attracted to the count, and Mélanie is taken with Don Gabriel. In a sort of "double inconstance," Isidore finally resolves herself to love Don Gabriel, and Mélanie similarly decides to love the count. Despite the fact that the young women renounce their original choice, they nevertheless are satisfied with the marriages. Arguably, d'Aulnoy plays on the relative interchangeability of positive characters in this *nouvelle*.

6. Fairy Tales and *Mondanité*

1. On the historical background of the writers of the 1690s fairy-tale vogue, see Zipes, "Rise of the French Fairy Tale," also reproduced in *When Dreams Came True*, as well as his introductions to tales by each of the individual authors in *Beauties, Beasts and Enchantment*, and his *Fairy Tale as Myth*, 17–29. See also his *Oxford Companion to Fairy Tales*. For background on d'Aulnoy in particular, see Mcleod.

2. On "Riquet," see Seifert, 205–18, and Hannon, 126–31. Both Jennifer Montagu and Betsy Rosasco discuss the extent to which enigmas and allegory remained essential forms of visual and linguistic expression in the latter part of the century to discuss current events as well as court intrigues.

3. It should be noted that court ballets, *divertissements*, and *théâtre à machines* also likely influenced the shape of d'Aulnoy's tales. However, I will limit the scope of my discussion to French opera.

4. Although questions remain as to the accessibility of Basile to seventeenth-century French audiences, it is very likely that French fairy-tale writers were familiar with his *Pentamerone*, suggested by specific references in the French tales. Originally written in Neapolitan (1634–1636), the *Pentamerone* was translated into Italian, the lingua franca of the salons, as early as 1674.

5. Zipes notes that the color "red was generally associated at the time with sin, sensuality, and the devil," and argues that "the helpless girl . . . subconsciously contributed to her own rape" (*Trials*, 9–10). "Red" could be understood as the sign of her sin (she is vain and spoiled) that leads to her victimization. As we saw in chapter 4, Perrault has his heroines bear the sign of their sin, clearly the case in this tale as well.

6. In *Discourse of Modernism*, Timothy Reiss connects ordered discourse to ordering the world: "The systematic discourse that names and enumerates

becomes, replaces, the order of the world that it is taken as representing" (35). Later Reiss states: "Well-ordered writing thus provides us with an automatic analysis of the world, a logical analysis" (*Discourse*, 211). Along these lines, we might view Perrault's unembroiled style as an expression of his desire to provide a clear literary and moral order to the world. We should keep in mind that Perrault was indeed a religious man and adherent to the Counter Reformation, which clearly impacts his tales, particularly in the associations he creates between women and disorder.

7. Although we generally associate iconoclasm with the Protestant Reformation, the Catholic Reformation also had iconoclastic strains.

8. On the rags-to-riches motif in Straparola, see Bottigheimer.

9. On perceptions of salon women promoting *mésalliances*, see Lougee, 41–55. On the demographics of the second half of the century pertaining to marriage, see Farr, "Pure," 413–14.

10. Bottigheimer argues that "Straparola's fairy tales of rags-to-riches through marriage were compensatory fictions that lent their readers (or listeners) hope for magically-mediated future wealth" (292). She notes that such narratives are absent from the medieval oral tradition, which could be explained by the changing social structures of western European societies.

11. Lewis Seifert discusses the solidification of aristocratic identity and the use of the pastoral to "reinstate a lost or obscured identity" in relation to "La Princesse Belle-Etoile" in particular, and the genre in general (82–83).

12. Another story by Basile, "The Three Fairies," similarly concerns the low-born and ugly Grannizia who tries to take the place of her beautiful stepsister Cicella as the nobleman Cuosemo's wife (see Zipes, *The Great Fairy Tale*, 544–50).

13. The idea that Maintenon was domineering is evident in popular songs of the period. A song transcribed in 1698 reads: "Au Dauphin, irrité de voir comme tout va, / Mon fils, disoit Louis, que rien ne vous étonne, / Nous maintiendrons notre couronne; / Le Dauphin répondit: Sire, Maintenon l'a" ["To the Dauphin, irritated by how everything was going / Louis said: My son, nothing should alarm you, / We will maintain our crown; / The Dauphin responded: Sire, Maintenon has it"] (*Nouveau Siècle*, 187). Another from 1699 depicts Maintenon as the actual possessor of the crown: "Une femme en pénitence, / Veuve d'un petit crotté, / Tient le timon de la France" ["A penitent woman, / Widow of a wretched little poet, / Controls the helm of France"] (*Nouveau Siècle*, 193).

D'Aulnoy dedicates *Les Contes des fées* to the Princesse Palatine, who despised Maintenon for several reasons. Most notably the princess blamed Maintenon for pushing the king to marry his and Madame de Montespan's bastard children, whom Maintenon loved as her own, to La Palatine's "pureblood" son and daughter (Orléans, 55). In many respects d'Aulnoy's "L'Oiseau bleu" could be read as an attack on Maintenon: the king marries a "fine veuve" ["shrewd widow"] who dominates him and who tries to marry her ugly daughter Truitonne to King Charming, to the detriment of the king's own noble daughter, Florine.

14. In an ARTFL database search, "souillon" appears in its masculine form in a satire by Régnier dated 1609, in a 1623 text by Auvray, and does not occur again until Perrault's 1695 publication of "Peau d'âne."

15. In the same vein, the heroine dressed in an animal skin takes on different meanings in d'Aulnoy and Perrault. Perrault has a princess wear a donkey skin, the skin of a domesticated animal, to escape her incestuous father, and she con-

sequently becomes "an object of ridicule, a social outcast." In d'Aulnoy's "L'Oranger et l'abeille," however, Aimée wears the skin of a tiger, which becomes on the contrary a sign of her strength. See Duggan, "Nature," 153–54.

16. In Marie-Jeanne Lhéritier de Villandon's "Ricdin-Ricdon," Rosanie, unaware that she is in fact a princess, despises spinning: "elle avoit pour le métier de filer, une aversion insurmontable, qui lui faisoit regarder comme un affreux supplice l'obligation de donner quelques heures à ce travail" ["she had an insurmountable aversion for the task of spinning, and she regarded the obligation to do such work for a few hours as a terrible torture"] (30–31). Like d'Aulnoy, Lhéritier characterizes domestic work for a princess in oppressive terms.

17. According to Mary Louise Ennis, Perrault, Catherine Bernard, and Lhéritier all composed a version of the tale "for a literary salon contest." See her entry on "Riquet" in Zipes, *Companion*, 423.

18. The 1694 *Dictionnaire de l'Académie Française* defines a universal man as one who "sçait de toutes choses" ["knows about everything"], a definition slightly modified in the 1798 edition, which reads "Il a une grande étendue de connoissances" ["He has a great breadth of knowledge"]. Of course, there are no examples in the dictionary of a woman being "universelle."

19. On the image of the castrated monarch in "Belle-Belle, ou le chevalier Fortuné," see Zuerner.

20. Tales with usurpers include: "La Bonne petite souris," "Le Serpentin vert" (the fairy Magotine and her marionettes temporarily take over Pagodie), "Belle-Belle," and "La Princesse Carpillon" (a usurper ousts Subtile). In "La Princesse Belle-Etoile et le Prince Chéri" d'Aulnoy does not provide background explaining the royal family's downfall, but we do know that the widowed queen lost her kingdom.

21. In relation to the grotesque adornment of Grognon, see Duggan, "Nature," 160–61.

22. For worldly paintings of Venus, see Titian's "Venus with a Mirror" (c.1555), Rubens's "Venus at a Mirror" (c.1615), and Velázquez's "Venus at her Mirror" (1649–51). For examples of "Allegory of Vanity," see the version of the unknown "Candlelight Master" (c.1630) and that of Jan Miense Molenaer (1633).

23. "Hermaphrodite" signified everything from an atheist to a dandy to a homosexual. See Dubois's introduction to *L'Isle des Hermaphrodites* and Stone.

24. For another perspective on the neutral construction of gender in d'Aulnoy's tales, see Duggan, "Nature," 154–58.

25. See for instance Apostolidès (141–43), Robert (366–79), and Seifert (110, 151). For a general discussion of the monarchy's use of the marvelous, see Mainil (46–52).

26. Without defining exactly what he considers the "corpus féerique," Mainil seems to be referring to the works of Ariosto, Tasso, and Ovid, authors who generally are not categorized as fairy-tale authors. Works by these three writers provided the principal source material for both opera and themes prevalent at Versailles. Mainil does not suggest, however, that Louis XIV was influenced in any way by the Italian fairy-tale writers, Straparola and Basile, whose works served as inspiration for the French 1690s fairy-tale writers and form an essential part of the "corpus féerique" of at least late seventeenth-century France.

27. Norman emphasizes this in speaking about quotes and references to opera in Sévigné's correspondence.

28. See for instance Norman, 105–6 and 263–64.

29. Norman notes that "a text destined for performance at court and subject to approval at several more or less official administrative levels was certainly not the place for making a strong statement about one's political or social views" (236).

30. On the importance of the marvelous in opera, see Thomas, 170–71.

31. On changing representations of Louis XIV, see Ferrier-Caverivière, 178–91.

32. In *Jerusalem Delivered*, the closest we come to a flying coach is Armida's chariot, which is drawn by four unicorns (Book 17, canto 34). Basile's "The Golden Root" contains a reference to a coach of diamonds drawn by four flying horses, but this is the only flying coach I have found in the *Pentamerone*. Other forms of marvelous displacement for the most part are not present in such works.

33. Other tales include characters capable of flying, such as Zephir in "L'Ile de la Félicité," and Léandre of "Le Prince Lutin," who magically travels all over the world in a flash.

34. Robert maintains that forms of supernatural transport like flying carpets were not used frequently in marvelous tales, meaning that writers must have been influenced by opera, court ballets, and royal fêtes, a speculation my research also leads me to conclude. See Robert, 372–73.

35. Due to the fact that the tale "Mira" is atypical of d'Aulnoy's oeuvre, I did not include it in the corpus of twenty-five tales.

36. It seems to me that d'Aulnoy indeed was familiar with Quinault's librettos which, as Norman has established, would have been true for most aristocrats of the period. It is also possible that she simply uses the same sources, notably Ariosto and Tasso, for different ideological purposes than Quinault. Nevertheless, my examination of Quinault's librettos and d'Aulnoy's tales has convinced me that d'Aulnoy was drawing on the overwhelmingly popular genre of opera to the same degree that she drew from novels, the Italian tradition, and folkloric material.

37. Thomas argues that at the end of *Armide*, for instance, the sorceress effectively is "dispossessed" of her power, while the hero "regains self-control through his liberation from (female) desire" (182).

38. In *Orlando furioso*, Medor is described as "a demon" and Angelica as a rather lascivious woman of ill repute. Quinault considerably tones down the degree to which the two lovers are immoral.

39. In act I, scene 2, Angélique's confidant Témire expresses surprise at Angélique's choice of Médor, reminding her of his obscure birth. Angélique herself recognizes that her glory demands she banish Médor from her heart. Later, Angélique explains to Médor how she feigned love for Roland, only to escape with him. She remarks: "Ne nous armons que d'artifice" ["Let us arm ourselves solely with artifice"] (3.3).

40. Norman notes that at the time *Isis* was produced, many considered it an allegory for Louis XIV's long-term relationship with Montespan, the model for Junon, and his new interest in Madame de Ludres, the model for Io/Isis (186).

41. Literary precedents exist in which the noble is favored over the king, *Clélie, Histoire Romaine* being a case in point. However, the fact that opera was such a prevalent genre and probably had the cultural impact of popular television shows, it is also possible that, wittingly or unwittingly, d'Aulnoy was responding to opera's privileging of the king.

42. Upon close examination of Quinault's librettos, tensions clearly exist be-

tween the glorification of the king in prologues and representations of kings in the play itself.

43. The aerial chariot fight takes place in "La Princesse Printanière." It is important to note that male and female characters both are objects of contemplation. In "Le Prince Lutin," for instance, the princess finds Léandre sleeping in her palace, and is mesmerized by the sight of him: "Elle eut tout le temps de le regarder sans être vue et de se convaincre que c'était la personne dont elle avait le portrait dans sa boîte de diamants" ["She had all the time in the world to look at him without being seen and to convince herself that this was the man whose portrait she had in her diamond case"] (*Contes I*, 154).

AFTERWORD

1. Although d'Aulnoy's feudal-like worlds could be read as her hope for the future, the feudal-type society d'Aulnoy envisions no longer was a feasible, realistic, or even possible ideal. By the end of the seventeenth century, there was no going back to a decentralized society governed by feudal lords. The state had become a historical reality, which makes d'Aulnoy's utopic feudal worlds more of a longing for an imagined past than a prospect for the future.

Works Cited

Primary Sources

Anthologie des troubadours. Edited and translated by Pierre Bec. Paris: Union Générale d'Editions, 1979.

Ariosto, Ludovico. *Orlando furioso.* Oxford: Oxford University Press, 1983.

Arnauld, Antoine. "Lettre de M. Antoine Arnauld à M. P. . . au sujet de la dixième satire." *Oeuvres.* By Nicolas Boileau-Despréaux. Introduction by Georges Mongrédien. Paris: Garnier, 1961, 326–44.

Aubailly, Jean-Claude, trad. *Fabliaux et contes moraux du Moyen Age.* Paris: Librairie Générale Française, 1987.

Aubert de la Chesnaye-Desbois. *Lettres sur les Romans.* Paris: Gissey, 1743.

Aulnoy, Marie-Catherine, baronne d'. *Le Comte de Warwick.* Amsterdam: Desbordes, 1704.

———. *Contes II.* Introduction by Jacques Barchilon. Edited by Philippe Hourcade. 1698. Paris: Société des Textes Français Modernes, 1998.

———. *Contes I.* Introduction by Jacques Barchilon. Edited by Philippe Hourcade. 1697. Paris: Société des Textes Français Modernes, 1997.

———. *Les Mémoires de la cour d'Angleterre.* Paris: Barbin, 1695.

———. *L'Histoire d'Hypolite, comte de Duglas.* Edited by Shirley Day Jones. 1690. Somerset: Castle Cary Press, 1994.

Balzac, Jean-Louis Guez de. *Premières Lettres.* 2 vols. Paris: Droz, 1934.

———. *Le Prince.* Paris: T. Du Bray, 1631.

Basile, Giambattista. *The Pentameron.* Translated by Sir Richard Burton. London: Spring Books, c1955.

Bellocq, Pierre. *Lettre de Madame de N . . . A Madame la Marquise de . . . Sur la Satyre de M. D*** contre les Femmes.* Paris: Nicolas Le Clerc, 1694.

Bernard, Catherine. "Riquet à la houppe." *Contes de Perrault.* By Charles Perrault. Edited by Gilbert Roger. 1696. Paris: Garnier, 1967, 271–78.

———. *Les Malheurs de l'amour. Première nouvelle: Eléonor d'Yvrée.* Introduction by René Godenne. 1687. Geneva: Slatkine, 1979.

Boccaccio, Giovanni. *The Decameron.* Translated and edited by Mark Musa and Peter E. Bondanella. New York: Norton, 1977.

Bodin, Jean. *Les Six livres de la République.* Paris: Librairie Générale Française, 1993.

———. *De la démonomanie des sorciers.* 1580. Hildesheim: G. Olms, 1988.

Boileau-Despréaux, Nicolas. *Oeuvres I: Satires—Le Lutrin.* Edited by Jérôme Vercruysse. Paris: Garnier-Flammarion, 1969.

———. *Oeuvres*. Introduction by Georges Mongrédien. Paris: Garnier, 1961.

———. *Les Héros de roman*. Edited and introduction by Thomas Frederick Crane. Boston: Ginn, 1902.

Bossuet, Jacques Bénigne. *Traité de la Concupiscence*. 1694. Paris: F. Roches, 1930.

Buffet, Marguerite. *Nouvelles observations sur la langue françoise avec Les Eloges des Illustres Sçavantes*. Paris: Jean Cusson, 1668.

Cent Nouvelles Nouvelles, Les. Paris: Garnier, 1926.

Chapelain, Jean. *La Pucelle, ou la France délivrée*. 2 vols. 1656. Paris: Marpon & Flammarion, 1891.

———. *Lettres de Chapelain*. Edited by Philippe Tamizey de Larroque. 2 vols. Paris: n.p., 1880–1883.

———. *Soixante-dix-sept lettres inédites à Nicolas Heinsius (1649–1658)*. Edited by Bernard Bray. The Hague: Nijhoff, 1966.

Charron, Pierre. *De la Sagesse*. 1601. Paris: Chaignieau Aine, 1797.

Chaussé, Jacques, sieur de La Terrière. *Traité de l'Excelence du mariage*. Paris: Jouvenel, 1686.

Corneille, Pierre. *Horace*. Edited by Jean-Pierre Chauveau. Paris: Gallimard, 1994.

Cousin, Victor. *La société française au XVIIe siècle d'après Le Grand Cyrus de Mlle de Scudéry*. Paris: Perrin, 1905.

Descartes, René. *Discours de la méthode*. 1637. Paris: Garnier-Flammarion, 1966.

Donneau de Visé, Jean. "Les Dames Vengées." *Trois comédies*. Edited and introduction by Pierre Mélèse. Paris: Droz, 1940, 152–285.

Dryden, John. *Secret-Love, or, The Maiden-Queen*. London: Henry Herringman, 1668.

Dupleix, Scipion. *Liberté de la langue françoise dans sa pureté*. 1651. Geneva: Slatkine, 1973.

Fauchet, Claude. *Fleur Maison de Charlemagne*. Paris, J. Perier, 1601.

Fénélon, Francois de Salignac de la Mothe. *Education des filles*. 2nd ed. Paris: Aubouin, Emery, and Glousier, 1687.

Ficino, Marsilio. *Commentary on Plato's Symposium on Love*. Translated by Sears Jayne. Dallas: Spring Publications, 1985.

Flaubert, Gustave. *Madame Bovary*. Paris: Flammarion, 1986.

Gacon, François. *Apologie pour Mr. Despreaux, ou Nouvêle Satire contre les Femmes*. Paris [?]: n.p., 1695.

Herodotus. *The Persian Wars*. New York: Modern Library, 1942.

Hugo, Victor. *Ruy Blas*. 1838. Paris: Gallimard, 1997.

Isle des Hermaphrodites, L'. Edited and introduction by Claude-Gilbert Dubois. 1605. Geneva: Droz, 1996.

Juvenal. *The Sixteen Satires*. Translated and introduction by Peter Green. Baltimore: Penguin, 1967.

Karr, Alphonse. *Sous les Tilleuls*. 1832. Paris: Calmann-Levy, 1888.

Kramer, Heinrich, and James Sprenger. *Malleus Maleficarum*. Translated by Rev. Montague Summers. London: John Rodker, 1928.

Lafayette, Madame de. *La Princesse de Clèves.* Edited by Jean Mesnard. 1678. Paris: Flammarion, 1996.

La Guette, Madame de. *Mémoires de Madame de La Guette.* Edited and introduction by M. Moreau. 1681. Paris: P. Jannet, 1856.

La Mothe Le Vayer, François de. *Oeuvres.* Geneva: Slatkine Reprints, 1970.

Lancre, Pierre de. *Tableau de l'inconstance des mauvais anges et démons.* 1607. Paris: Editions 00h00, 2000.

Lee, Nathaniel. *Lucius Junius Brutus.* Edited by John Loftis. 1681. Lincoln: University of Nebraska Press, 1967.

Lenclos, Ninon de. *Lettres de Ninon de Lenclos.* Edited by A. Bret. Paris: Garnier Frères, 1870.

Lenglet du Fresnoy. *De l'Usage des Romans.* Amsterdam: Veuve de Poilras, 1734.

Lhéritier de Villandon, Marie-Jeanne. "Ricdin-Ricdon." *Le Nouveau Cabinet des fées.* 18 vols. Geneva: Slatkine, 1987, 7: 25–131.

Livy. *The Early History of Rome.* New York: Penguin, 2002.

Maeterlinck, Maurice. *L'Intérieur, Pelléas et Mélisande, L'Oiseau bleu.* Paris: Club des Libraires, 1956.

Maintenon, Madame de. *Comment la sagesse vient aux filles.* Edited by Pierre-E. Leroy and Marcel Loyau. Paris: Bartillat, 1998.

Manifeste de la Noblesse de Normandie. Le. Paris: Simon Le Porteur, 1652.

Marmontel, Jean-François. "Essai sur les Romans." *Oeuvres complètes.* 19 vols. Paris: Verdière, 1818–1820, 10: 287–361.

Mayer, Charles-Joseph *Cabinet des fées.* 37 vols. Paris: 1785–1786.

Méré, Antoine de Gombaud, chevalier de. *Oeuvres complètes.* 3 vols. Paris: Fernand Roches, 1930.

Miroir aux Dames: poème inédit du XVe siècle, Le. Edited by Arthur Piaget. Neuchatel: Altinger frères, 1908.

Miroir des femmes I: Moralistes et polémistes au XVIe siècle, Le. Edited by Luce Guillerm et al. Lille: PU de Lille, 1983.

Molière. *Oeuvres complètes de Molière.* 2 vols. Paris: Gallimard, 1951.

Montaigne, Michel de. *Essais.* 3 vols. Paris: Garnier-Flammarion, 1969.

Musset, Alfred de. "Lettres de Dupuis et Cotonet." *Revue des Deux Mondes.* Paris: 1836, 3: 524–657.

Navarre, Marguerite de. *La Coche ou le Débat de l'Amour.* Geneva: Droz, 1971.

Nicole, Pierre. *An Essay on True and Apparent Beauty in Which from Settled Principles is Rendered the Grounds for Choosing and Rejecting Epigrams.* Translated by J. V. Cunningham. 1659. Los Angeles: William Andrews Clark Memorial Library, 1950.

Nouveau Siècle de Louis XIV ou choix de chansons historiques et satiriques, Le. Paris: Garnier, 1857.

Nouvelles d'Elisabeth, reine d'Angleterre, Les. Paris: Barbin, 1674. Amsterdam: Elzevir, 1680.

Novels of Elizabeth, Queen of England; Containing the History of Queen Ann of Bullen. London: Black Raven, 1680.

Orléans, Elisabeth Charlotte, Duchesse d'. *A Woman's Life in the Court of the*

Sun King: Letters of Liselotte von der Pfalz, 1652–1722. Translated and introduction by Elborg Forster. Baltimore: Johns Hopkins University Press, 1984.

Ovid. *Metamorphoses.* New York: Penguin, 1981.

Pasquier, Etienne. *Des recherches de la France.* 1560. Paris: Champion, 1996.

Pellisson, Paul. *Lettres historiques.* 1729. Geneva: Slatkine, 1971.

———. *Histoire de Louis XIV, depuis la mort du Cardinal Mazarin en 1661 jusqu'à la paix de Nimègue en 1678.* Paris: Rollin fils, 1749.

———. *Relation contenant l'histoire de l'Académie Française.* 1652. Paris: Didier, 1858.

Perrault, Charles. *Parallèle des Anciens et des Modernes en ce qui regarde les arts et les sciences.* 1688. Munich: Eidos Verlag, 1964.

———. "Apologie des femmes." 1694. *Oeuvres choisies de Ch. Perrault.* Edited by Collin de Plancy. Paris: Peytieux, 1826. 259–67.

———. *Mémoires de Ch. Perrault.* Edited by Paul Lacroix. Paris: Librairie des Bibliophiles, 1878.

———. *Contes.* Edited by Jean-Pierre Collinet. Paris: Gallimard, 1981.

———. *Pensées chrétiennes de Charles Perrault.* Introduction by and edited by Jacques Barchilon. Seattle: Biblio 17, 1987.

———. *Le Siècle de Louis le Grand.* Paris: Jean-Baptiste Coignard, 1687.

Pizan, Christine de. *La Cité des dames.* Paris: Stock, 1986.

Plutarch. *Lives.* New York: Modern Library, 1992.

Pradon, Jacques Nicolas. *Réponse à la Satire X du Sieur D***.* Paris: Robert J. B. de la Caille, 1694.

Pure, Michel abbé de. *La Prétieuse ou le mystère des ruelles.* Edited by Emile Magne. 2 vols. Paris: Droz, 1938.

Quinault, Philippe. *Livrets d'opéra.* Edited by Buford Norman. 2 vols. Toulouse: Société de littératures classiques, 1999.

Quinze Joies de Mariage, Les. Edited by Jean Rychner. Paris: Droz, 1967.

Radcliffe, Ann. *A Sicilian Romance.* 1790. New York: McGrath, 1972.

Regnard, Jean-François. *Oeuvres complètes.* Paris: L. Tenré, 1820.

Robert, Louise Keralio. *Collections des meilleurs ouvrages françois composés par des femmes.* 6 vols. Paris: 1786–1789.

Sade, Donatien Alphonse François, marquis de. *Oeuvres.* 3 vols. Paris: Gallimard, 1990.

Sainte-Beuve, Charles Augustin. *Causeries du lundi.* 15 vols. Paris: Garnier, 1850.

Sand, Georges. *Histoire de Ma Vie.* 1855. Saint-Cyr-sur-Loire: C. Pirot, 1993.

Scudéry, Madeleine de. *Choix de Conversations de Mlle de Scudéry.* Edited by Phillip J. Wolfe. Ravenna: Longo Editore, 1977.

———. *Clélie, Histoire Romaine.* 10 vols. 1660. Geneva: Slatkine, 1973.

———. *De la poësie françoise jusques à Henry Quatrième.* Paris: Chez Sansot, 1907.

———. *Conversations Nouvelles sur divers sujets.* Amsterdam: H. Wetstein and H. DesBordes, 1685.

———. *Artamene, ou le Grand Cyrus.* 10 vols. 1649–1653. Paris: Augustin Courbé, 1656.

————. *Les Femmes Illustres, ou les Harangues Heroiques*. 1644. Paris: Compagnie des Libraires du Palais, 1665; Paris: côté-femmes, 1991.

Scudéry, Madeleine de, Paul Pellisson, and Valentin Conrart. *Chroniques du Samedi suivies de pièces diverses (1653–1654)*. Edited by Alain Niderst, Delphine Denis, and Myriam Maître. Paris: Champion, 2002.

————. *La "Journée des Madrigaux" suivie de la "Gazette de Tendre" (avec la Carte de Tendre) et du "Carnaval des Prétieuses."* Edited by Emile Colombey. Paris: Aug. Aubry, 1856.

————. *Chroniques des Samedis de Mademoiselle de Scudéry*. Arsenal ms. 15156. Bibliothèque de l'Arsenal. Paris.

Sévigné, Marie de Rabutin-Chantal, marquise de. *Corréspondance*. 3 vols. Paris: Gallimard, 1973–1978.

Somaize, Antoine Baudeau de. *Le Dictionnaire des précieuses*. Edited by Ch.-L. Livet. 2 vols. Paris: P. Jannet, 1856.

Tallemant des Réaux, [Gédéon]. *Historiettes*. Edited by Antoine Adam. 2 vols. Paris: Gallimard, 1960.

Tasso, Torquato. *Jerusalem Delivered*. Translated by Edward Fairfax. Edited by Henry Morley. New York: Colonial Press, 1901.

Tertullian. *Disciplinary, Moral, and Ascetical Works*. The Fathers of the Church vol. 40. New York: Fathers of the Church, 1959, 111–49.

Troyes, Chrétien de. "Yvain, le chevalier au lion." *Romans de la table ronde: Le cycle courtois*. Paris: Gallimard, 1970, 227–322.

Urfé, Honoré d'. *L'Astrée*. Introduction by Louis Mercier. 5 vols. Lyon: Pierre Masson, 1925.

Vaugelas, Claude Favre de. *Remarques sur la langue françoise*. 1647. Paris: Droz, 1934.

Vertron, Claude Charles Guyonnet de. *La Nouvelle Pandore ou les Femmes illustres du siècle de Louis le Grand*. 2 vols. Paris: C. Mazuel, 1698.

Villedieu, Madame de (Marie-Catherine Desjardins). *Les Désordres de l'amour*. Geneva: Droz, 1970.

Watriquet de Couvin. "Li Mireoirs as Dames." *Dits de Watriquet de Couvin*. Edited by Auguste Scheler. Brussels: V. Devaux, 1868, 1–41.

SECONDARY SOURCES

Adam, Antoine. *L'époque de Pascal; L'apogée du siècle (Boileau, Molière)*. Vol. 2 of *Histoire de la littérature française au XVIIe siècle*. Paris: Albin Michel, 1997.

————. "La théorie mystique de l'amour dans *L'Astrée* et ses sources italiennes." *Revue d'Histoire de la Philosophie et d'Histoire Générale de la Civilisation* (1936): 193–206.

Althusser, Louis. *Lenin and Philosophy and Other Essays*. Translated by Ben Brewster. New York: Monthly Review Press, 1971.

Apostolidès, Jean-Marie. "Des choses cachées dans le château de Barbe bleue." *Merveilles et Contes* 5.2 (Dec. 1991): 179–99.

————. *Le roi-machine: Spectacle et politique au temps de Louis XIV*. Paris: Minuit, 1981.

Ariès, Philippe. *Histoire de la vie privée.* 5 vols. Paris: Seuil, 1985–1987.

Badinter, Elisabeth. *L'Amour en plus.* Paris: Flammarion, 1980.

Bamford, Paul W. *The Barbary Pirates: Victims and the Scourge of Christendom.* The James Ford Bell Lectures 10. Minneapolis: The Associates of the James Ford Bell Library, 1972.

Barbaza, Louis. *L'Académie de Castres et la société de Mlle de Scudéry 1648–1670.* Castres: Imprimerie Abeilhou, 1890.

Batany, J. "Le vocabulaire des catégories sociales chez quelques moralistes français vers 1200." *Ordres et classes: colloque d'histoire sociale.* Edited by Daniel Roche. Paris: Ecole Pratique des Hautes Etudes and Mouton, 1973, 59–72.

Baudrillard, Jean. *Le miroir de la production.* Paris: Galilée, 1985.

Bayley, Peter. *French Pulpit Oratory 1598–1650.* New York: Cambridge University Press, 1980.

Belmont, L. "Documents inédits sur la société et la littérature précieuses: extraits de la *Chronique du Samedi* publiés d'après le registre original de Pellisson (1652–1657)." *Revue d'histoire littéraire de la France* 9 (1902): 646–73.

Billacois, François. "La crise de la noblesse européenne, 1550–1650." *Revue d'histoire moderne et contemporaine* 23.2 (1976): 257–77.

Bitton, Davis. *The French Nobility in Crisis: 1560–1640.* Stanford, CA: Stanford University Press, 1969.

Bloch, R. Howard. *Medieval Misogyny and the Invention of Western Romantic Love.* Chicago: University of Chicago Press, 1991.

Bottigheimer, Ruth B. "Straparola's *Piacevoli Notti*: Rags-to-Riches Fairy Tales as Urban Creations." *Merveilles et Contes* 8.2 (1994): 281–96.

Braudel, Fernand. *Les Structures du quotidien.* Paris: A. Colin, 1979.

Brun, Pierre Antonin. "Jean Chapelain (1595–1674)." *Revue d'Histoire littéraire de la France* (1902): 608–32.

Brunelle, Gayle K. "Dangerous Liaisons: Mésalliance and Early Modern French Noblewomen." *French Historical Studies* 19.1 (Spring 1995): 75–103.

Butler, Judith. *Gender Trouble: Feminism and the Subversion of Identity.* New York: Routledge, 1990.

Caillois, Roger. *Les jeux et les hommes (Le masque et le vertige).* Paris: Gallimard, 1958.

Church, William F. *Richelieu and Reason of State.* Princeton: Princeton University Press, 1972.

Clarac, Pierre. *Boileau.* Paris: Hatier, 1964.

Clark, Henry C. "Commerce, the Virtues, and the Public Sphere in Early-Seventeenth-Century France." *French Historical Studies* 21.3 (Summer 1998): 415–40.

Clarke, David. *Pierre Corneille: Poetics and Political Drama under Louis XIII.* Cambridge: Cambridge University Press, 1992.

Collins, James B. "The Economic Role of Women in Seventeenth-Century France." *French Historical Studies* 16.2 (Fall 1989): 436–70.

Cottino-Jones, Marga. "Fabula vs. Figura: Another Interpretation of the Griselda Story." *The Decameron.* By Giovanni Boccaccio. Translated by and edited by Mark Musa and Peter E. Bondanella. New York: Norton, 1977, 295–305.

Cousin, Victor. *La Société française au XVIIe siècle d'après Le Grand Cyrus de Mlle de Scudéry*. Paris: Didier, 1858.

Crane, Thomas Frederick. "Introduction." *Les Héros de roman*. By Nicolas Boileau-Despréaux. Boston: Ginn, 1902, 1–161.

Damon, Pierre. *Mythologie de la femme dans l'ancienne France, XVI–XIX siècle*. Paris: Seuil, 1983.

Davis, Natalie Zemon. *The Gift in Sixteenth-Century France*. Madison: University of Wisconsin Press, 2000.

———. "Women in the Crafts in Sixteenth-Century Lyon." *Women and Work in Preindustrial Europe*. Edited by Barbara A. Hanawalt. Bloomington: Indiana University Press, 1986. 167–97.

———. "Ghosts, Kin, and Progeny: Some Features of Family Life in Early Modern France." *Daedalus* 106.2 (Spring 1977): 87–114.

———. *Society and Culture in Early Modern France*. Stanford, CA: Stanford University Press, 1975.

Day, Shirley Jones. "Madame d'Aulnoy's Julie: a Heroine of the 1690s." *Writers and Heroines: Essays on Women in French literature*. Edited by Shirley Jones Day. New York: Peter Lang, 1999. 71–88.

DeJean, Joan. *Ancients Against Moderns: Culture Wars and the Making of a Fin de Siècle*. Chicago: University of Chicago Press, 1997.

———. *Tender Geographies: The Politics of Female Authorship under the Late Ancien Régime*. New York: Columbia University Press, 1991.

———. "Classical Reeducation: Decanonizing the Feminine." *Displacements: Women, Tradition, Literatures in French*. Edited by Joan DeJean and Nancy K. Miller. Baltimore: Johns Hopkins University Press, 1991, 22–36.

Deleuze, Gilles. *Proust et les signes*. 1964. Paris: Presse Universitaire de France, 1998.

Delumeau, J. "Mobilité sociale: riches et pauvres à l'époque de la Renaissance." *Ordres et classes: colloque d'histoire sociale. Saint-Cloud 24–25 mai 1967*. Edited by Daniel Roche. Paris: Ecole Pratique des Hautes Etudes and Mouton, 1973, 125–34.

Dewald, Jonathan. *The Formation of a Provincial Nobility: The Magistrates of the Parlement of Rouen, 1499–1610*. Princeton: Princeton University Press, 1980.

Dictionnaire de l'Histoire de France. Edited by Jean-François Sirinelli and Daniel Couty. 2 vols. Paris: Larousse-Bordas, 1999.

Dubois, Claude-Gilbert. *La Conception de l'histoire en France au XVIe siècle (1560–1610)*. Paris: Nizet, 1977.

Duggan, Anne E. "Nature and Culture in the Fairy Tale of Marie-Catherine d'Aulnoy." *Marvels & Tales* 5.2 (2001): 149–67.

———. "Feminine Genealogy, Matriarchy, and Utopia in the Fairy Tale of Marie-Catherine d'Aulnoy." *Neophilologus* LXXXII.2 (April 1998): 199–208.

Elias, Norbert. *The Court Society*. Translated by Edmund Jephcott. New York: Pantheon, 1983.

Elton, G. R. *England Under the Tudors*. 1955. London: Routledge, 1991.

Engel, Claire-Eliane. *L'Ordre de Malte en Méditéranée (1530–1789)*. Monaco: Rocher, 1957.

Farr, James R. *Authority and Sexuality in Early Modern Burgundy (1550–1730)*. Oxford: Oxford University Press, 1995.

———. "The Pure and Disciplined Body: Hierarchy, Morality, and Symbolism in France During the Catholic Reformation." *Journal of Interdisciplinary History* XXI.3 (Winter 1991): 391–414.

Farrell, Michèle. "Griselidis: Issues of Gender, Genre and Authority." *La contestation et ses limites au XVIIe siècle: l'instance du burlesque et du grotesque*. Paris: Biblio 17, 1987, 97–120.

Ferrier-Caverivière, Nicole. *L'Image de Louis XIV dans la littérature française de 1660–1715*. Paris: Presse Universitaire de France, 1981.

Festugière, Paul. "Vie de Jean-François Sarasin." *Oeuvres de J.-Fr. Sarasin*. 2 vols. Paris: Champion, 1926, I: 1–71.

Fineman, Joel. "The History of the Anecdote: Fiction and Fiction." *The New Historicism*. Edited by H. Aram Veeser. New York: Routledge, 1989, 49–76.

Flandrin, Jean-Louis. *Families in Former Times: Kinship, Household, and Sexuality*. Cambridge: Cambridge University Press, 1979.

Foucault, Michel. *Histoire de la folie à l'âge classique*. Paris: Plon, 1961.

Fumaroli, Marc. "Rhetoric, Politics, and Society: From Italian Ciceronianism to French Classicism." *Renaissance Eloquence: Studies in the Theory and Practice of Renaissance Rhetoric*. Edited by James J. Murphy. Berkeley: University of California Press, 1983. 253–73.

———. *L'Age de l'éloquence: rhétorique et 'res literaria' de la Renaissance au seuil de l'époque classique*. Geneva: Droz, 1980.

Génetiot, Alain. *Les genres lyriques mondains (1630–1660): Etudes des poésies de Voiture, Vion d'Alibray, Sarasin et Scarron*. Geneva: Droz, 1990.

Genette, Gérard. *Figures II*. Paris: Seuil, 1969.

Gibson, Wendy. *Women in Seventeenth-Century France*. New York: St. Martin's Press, 1989.

Godenne, René. "Préface." *Les Malheurs de l'amour. Première nouvelle: Eléonor d'Yvrée*. Geneva: Slatkine, 1979, vii–xvi.

Goldsmith, Elizabeth. *Exclusive Conversations: The Art of Interaction in Seventeenth-Century France*. Philadelphia: University of Pennsylvania Press, 1988.

Goldwyn, Henriette. "Journalisme polémique à la fin du XVIIe siècle: le cas de Mme du Noyer." *Femmes savantes, savoirs des femmes: du crépuscule de la Renaissance à l'aube des Lumières*. Geneva: Droz, 1999, 247–56.

———. "Les Mémoires d'une 'affranchie': Mme du Noyer." *Oeuvres et Critiques* XX.3 (1995): 273–79.

Golenistcheff-Koutouzoff, Elie. *L'histoire de Griseldis en France au XIV et au XV siècle*. Paris: Droz, 1933.

Goodman, Dena. *The Republic of Letters: A Cultural History of the French Enlightenment*. Ithaca: Cornell University Press, 1994.

———. "Public Sphere and Private Life: Toward a Synthesis of Current Historiographical Approaches to the Old Regime." *History and Theory* 31.1 (1992): 1–20.

Gordon, Daniel. *Citizens without Sovereignty: Equality and Sociability in French Thought, 1670–1789.* Princeton: Princeton University Press, 1994.

Gumbrecht, Hans Ulrich. "'Phoenix from the Ashes' or: From Canon to Classic." *New Literary History* 20.1 (1988): 144–49.

Haase-Dubosc, Danielle. *Ravie et enlevée: De l'enlèvement des femmes comme stratégie matrimoniale au XVIIe siècle.* Paris: Albin Michel, 1999.

Habermas, Jürgen. *The Structural Transformation of the Public Sphere: an Inquiry into a Category of Bourgeois Society.* Translated by Thomas Burger. Cambridge: MIT Press, 1989.

Hamscher, Albert N. *The Parlement of Paris After the Fronde 1653–1673.* Pittsburgh: University of Pittsburgh Press, 1976.

Hanley, Sarah. "Engendering the State: Family Formation and State Building in Early Modern France." *French Historical Studies* 16.1 (Spring 1989): 4–27.

Hannon, Patricia. *Fabulous Identities: Women's Fairy Tales in Seventeenth-Century France.* Atlanta: Rodopi, 1998.

Harth, Erica. "The Salon Woman Goes Public . . . or Does She?" *Going Public: Women and Publishing in Early Modern France.* Edited by Elizabeth C. Goldsmith and Dena Goodman. Ithaca: Cornell University Press, 1995.

———. *Cartesian Women: Versions and Subversions of Rational Discourse in the Old Regime.* Ithaca: Cornell University Press, 1992.

———. *Ideology and Culture in Seventeenth-Century France.* Ithaca: Cornell University Press, 1983.

Heinsohn, Gunnar and Otto Steiger. "Birth Control: The Political-Economic Rationale behind Jean Bodin's *Démonomanie*." *History of Political Economy* 31.3 (1999): 423–48.

Heyden-Rynsch, Verena von der. *Salons européens: les beaux moments d'une culture féminine disparue.* Paris: Gallimard, 1992.

Hoffmann, Kathryn. "Flying through Classicism's Night: The Witch in Myth and Religion." *Racine et/ou le classicisme.* Edited by Ronald W. Tobin. Tubingen: Narr, 2001, 459–70.

———. "Monstrous Women, Monstrous Theorizing: Mothers, Physicians and *les esprits animaux*." *PFSCL* XXIV.47 (1997): 537–52.

Houdard, Sophie. "Possession et spiritualité: deux modèles de savoir féminin." *Femmes Savantes, Savoirs des femmes: Du crépuscule de la Renaissance à l'aube des Lumières.* Geneva: Droz, 1999, 119–29.

Huizinga, Johan. *Homo Ludens: a Study of the Play Element in Culture.* 1944. Boston: Beacon Press, 1955.

Huppert, George. *Les Bourgeois Gentilshommes: An Essay on the Definition of Elites in Renaissance France.* Chicago: University of Chicago Press, 1977.

Jacques-Chaquin, Nicole. "La curiosité sorcière: représentations du désir féminin du savoir chez les démonologues (XVIe-XVIIe siecles)." *Femmes savantes, savoirs des femmes: du crépuscule de la Renaissance à l'aube des Lumières.* Geneva: Droz, 1999, 107–18.

Jalby, Robert. *Le folklore du Languedoc.* Paris: Maisonneuve & Larose, 1971.

Jauss, Hans Robert. *Aesthetic Experience and Literary Hermeneutics.* Minneapolis: University of Minnesota Press, 1982.

Jonsson, Einar Már. "Le sens du titre *Speculum* aux XIIe et XIIIe siècle et son utilisation par Vincent de Beauvais." *Vincent de Beauvais: Intentions et réceptions d'une oeuvre encyclopédique au Moyen Age.* Edited by Monique Paulmier-Foucart, Serge Lusignan, and Alain Nadeau. Paris: Vrin, 1990, 11–32.

Kelly, Joan. "Early Feminist Theory and the *Querelle des Femmes*, 1400–1789." *Signs* 8.11 (1982): 4–28.

Kettering, Sharon. *Patrons, Brokers, and Clients in Seventeenth-Century France.* Oxford: Oxford University Press, 1986.

Köhler, Erich. *L'Aventure chevalresque: Idéal et Réalité dans le roman courtois.* 1956. Paris: Gallimard, 1974.

Kristeva, Julia. *Pouvoirs de l'horreur.* Paris: Seuil, 1980.

Lanfant, Marie-Françoise. *Les Théories du loisir: sociologie du loisir et idéologies.* Paris: Presse Universitaire de France, 1972.

Le Roy Ladurie, Emmanuel. *Saint-Simon ou le système de la cour.* Paris: Fayard, 1997.

Lewis, Philip E. *Seeing Through the Mother Goose Tales: Visual Turns in the Writings of Charles Perrault.* Stanford: Stanford University Press, 1996.

———. "Bluebeard's Magic Key." *Les contes de Perrault: La contestation et ses limites. Furetière.* Paris: PFSCL, 1987, 41–51.

Lougee, Carolyn C. *Le Paradis des Femmes: Women, Salons, and Social Stratification in Seventeenth-Century France.* Princeton: Princeton University Press, 1976.

———. "*Noblesse,* Domesticity, and Social Reform: *The Education of Girls* by Fénelon and Saint-Cyr." *History of Education Quarterly* 14.1 (Spring 1974): 87–113.

Mabille de Poncheville, A. *Valentin Conrart: Le père de l'Académie Française.* Paris: Mercure de France, 1935.

Maclean, Ian. *Woman Triumphant: Feminism in French Literature 1610–1652.* Oxford: Clarendon Press, 1977.

Mainil, Jean. *Madame d'Aulnoy et le rire des fées: essai sur la subversion féerique et le merveilleux comique sous l'Ancien Régime.* Paris: Kimé, 2001.

Marie, Alfred. *Naissance de Versailles.* 2 vols. Paris: Vincent, Fréal & Cie, 1968.

Marin, Louis. *La parole mangée et autres essais théologico-politiques.* Paris: Meridiens Klincksieck, 1986.

———. *Utopiques: Jeux d'espaces.* Paris: Minuit, 1973.

Mcleod, Glenda K. "Writer of Fantasy: Madame d'Aulnoy." *Women Writers of the Seventeenth Century.* Athens: University of Georgia Press, 1989, 91–99.

Michaud-Quantin, P. "Le vocabulaire des catégories sociales chez les canonistes et les moralistes du XIIIe siècle." *Ordres et classes: colloque d'histoire sociale.* Edited by Daniel Roche. Paris: Ecole Pratique des Hautes Etudes and Mouton, 1973, 73–86.

Miller, Nancy K. *Subject to Change: Reading Feminist Writing.* New York: Columbia University Press, 1988.

Montagu, Jennifer. "The Painted Enigma and French Seventeenth-Century Art." *Art Journal* 48.2 (Summer 1989): 307–35.

Moriarty, Michael. *Taste and Ideology in Seventeenth-Century France.* Cambridge: Cambridge University Press, 1988.

Mossiker, Frances. *The Affair of the Poisons.* New York: Knopf, 1969.

Moureau, François. "Les débuts de la presse en langue française (1631–1715)." *Australian Journal of French Studies* XVIII.2 (May–August 1981): 122–33.

Muchembled, Robert. *Popular Culture and Elite Culture in France: 1400–1750.* Translated by Lydia Cochrane. Baton Rouge: Louisiana State University Press, 1985.

Mueller, Marlies. "The Taming of the Amazon: the Changing Image of the Woman Warrior in Ancien Régime Fiction." *PFSCL* 22.42 (1995): 199–232.

——. *Les Idées politiques dans le roman héroïque de 1630 à 1670.* Harvard Studies in Romance Languages. Cambridge: Department of Romance Languages. and Literatures of Harvard University, 1984.

Munro, James S. "Richardson, Marivaux, and the French Romance Tradition." *Modern Language Review* 70 (1975): 752–53.

Nabarra, Alain. "Madame Dunoyer et *La Quintessence*: La Rencontre d'une journaliste et d'un journal." *Femmes savantes et femmes d'esprit: Women Intellectuals of the French Eighteenth Century.* New York: Peter Lang, 1994, 45–75.

Niderst, Alain. *Madeleine de Scudéry, Paul Pellisson, et leur monde.* Paris: Presse Universitaire de France, 1976.

——. "Sur les clefs de *Clélie*." *PFSCL* 21.41 (1994): 471–83.

Norman, Buford. *Touched by the Graces: The Libretti of Philippe Quinault in the Context of French Classicism.* Birmingham, AL: Summa, 2001.

Palmer, Melvin D. "Madame d'Aulnoy in England." *Comparative Literature* 27 (1975): 237–53.

——. "*The History of Adolphus* (1691): the First French *Conte de fée* in English." *Philological Quarterly* 49 (1970): 565–67.

——. "Madame d'Aulnoy and Cervantes." *Romance Notes* 11 (1970): 595–98.

Palmer, Melvin D., and Nancy Palmer. "English Editions of French *Contes de fées* attributed to Mme d'Aulnoy." *Studies in Bibliography* 27 (1974): 227–32.

——. "The French *Conte de fée* in England." *Studies in Short Fiction* 11 (1974): 35–44.

Pessel, André. "De la conversation chez les précieuses." *Communications* 30 (1979): 14–30.

Portemer, Jean. "Le statut de la femme en France: depuis la réformation des coutumes jusqu'à la rédaction du code civil." *Recueils de la société Jean Bodin pour l'histoire comparative des institutions 12.* Bruxelles: Edition de la librairie encyclopédique, 1962, 447–97.

Pugh, T. B. "Henry VII and the English Nobility." *The Tudor Nobility.* Edited by G. W. Bernard. New York: Manchester University Press, 1992.

Ranum, Orest. *The Fronde: A French Revolution.* New York: Norton, 1993.

——. *Artisans of Glory: Writers and Historical Thought in Seventeenth-Century France.* Chapel Hill: University of North Carolina Press, 1980.

——. "Courtesy, Absolutism, and the Rise of the French State, 1630–1660." *Journal of Modern History* 52.3 (September 1980): 426–51.

Reiss, Timothy. "Denying the Body? Memory and the Dilemmas of History in Descartes." *Journal of the History of Ideas* 57.4 (1996): 587–607.

——. *The Discourse of Modernism.* Ithaca: Cornell University Press, 1982.

Richard, Michel. *La vie quotidienne des Protestants sous l'Ancien Régime.* Paris: Hachette, 1966.

Riggs, Larry W. "Moralism in a Constructed World: La Rochefoucauld's Semiotics of the Empty Center." *Cahiers du dix-septième* 4.2 (Fall 1990): 119–31.

Robert, Raymonde. *Le Conte de fées littéraire en France de la fin du XVIIe à la fin du XVIIIe siècle.* Nancy: Presse Universitaire de Nancy, 1982.

Roche, Daniel. *Le siècle des lumières en province: Académies et académiciens provinciaux, 1680–1789.* 2 vols. Paris: Editions de l'Ecole des Hautes Etudes en Sciences Sociales, 1978.

Rosasco, Betsy. "Masquerade and Enigma at the Court of Louis XIV." *Art Journal* 48.2 (Summer 1989): 144–49.

Rousset, Jean. *La littérature de l'âge baroque en France: Circé et le paon.* Paris: José Corti, 1985.

Sankovitch, Tilde. "Inventing Authority of Origin: The Difficult Enterprise." *Women in the Middle Ages and the Renaissance: Literary and Historical Perspectives.* Edited by Mary Beth Rose. Syracuse: Syracuse University Press, 1986, 227–43.

Saupé, Yvette. *Les* Contes *de Perrault et la mythologie: Rapprochements et influences.* Seattle: PFSCL, 1997.

Schiebinger, Londa. *The Mind Has No Sex? Women in the Origins of Modern Science.* Cambridge: Harvard University Press, 1989.

Seifert, Lewis. *Fairy Tales, Sexuality, and Gender in France, 1690–1715: Nostalgic Utopias.* Cambridge: Cambridge University Press, 1996.

Shannon, Laurie J. "Emilia's Argument: Friendship and 'Human Title' in *The Two Noble Kinsmen.*" *ELH* 64.3 (1997): 657–82.

Skemp, Mary. "Reading a Woman's Story in Marguerite de Navarre's *La Coche.*" *Explorations in Renaissance Culture* 31.2 (Winter 2005): forthcoming.

Stanesco, Michel. *Jeux d'errance du chevalier médiéval: aspects ludiques de la fonction guerrière dans la littérature du Moyen Age flamboyant.* New York: E. J. Brill, 1988.

Stanton, Domna C. *The Aristocrat as Art: A Study of the* Honnête Homme *and the* Dandy *in Seventeenth- and Nineteenth-Century French Literature.* New York: Columbia University Press, 1980.

Starobinski, Jean. *Le remède dans le mal: Critique et légitimation de l'artifice à l'âge des Lumières.* Paris: Gallimard, 1989.

Stierle, Karlheinz. "L'Histoire comme Exemple, l'Exemple comme Histoire." *Poétique* 10 (1972): 176–98.

Stone, Donald. "The Sexual Outlaw in France, 1605." *Journal of the History of Sexuality* 2.4 (1992): 597–608.

Thomas, Downing A. "Opera, Dispossession, and the Sublime: The Case of *Armide.*" *Theatre Journal* 49.2 (1997): 169–88.

Timmermans, Linda. *L'Accès des femmes à la culture (1598–1715).* Paris: Champion, 1993.

Tucker, Holly. *Pregnant Fictions: Childbirth and the Fairy Tale in Early-Modern France.* Detroit: Wayne State University Press, 2003.

Velay-Vallantin, Catherine. *L'Histoire des contes.* Paris: Fayard, 1992.

Viala, Alain. *Racine. La stratégie du caméléon.* 1990.

———. *Naissance de l'écrivain.* Paris: Minuit, 1985.

Warner, Marina. *From the Beast to the Bonde: On Fairy Tales and Their Tellers.* New York: Noonday Press, 1996.

Weinbrot, Howard D. "Enlightenment Canon Wars: Anglo-French Views of Literary Greatness." *ELH* 60 (1993): 82–88.

Wiesner, Merry E. "Women's Defense of Their Public Role." *Women in the Middle Ages and the Renaissance: Literary and Historical Perspectives.* Edited by Mary Beth Rose. Syracuse: Syracuse University Press, 1986. 1–27.

Williamson, James A. *The Tudor Age.* New York: Longman, 1979.

Yates, Frances A. *The French Academies of the Sixteenth Century.* London: Warbug Institute, 1947.

Zipes, Jack, edited and translated by *The Great Fairy Tale Tradition: From Straparola and Basile to the Brothers Grimm.* New York: Norton, 2001.

———, ed. *The Oxford Companion to Fairy Tales: The Western Fairy-Tale Tradition from Medieval to Modern.* Oxford: Oxford University Press, 2000.

———. *When Dreams Came True: Classical Fairy Tales and Their Tradition.* New York: Routledge, 1999.

———. "The Rise of the French Fairy Tale and the Decline of France." *Beauties, Beasts and Enchantment: Classic French Fairy Tales.* Edited and translated by Jack Zipes. New York: NAL, 1989. 1–15.

———. "Marie-Catherine d'Aulnoy." *Beauties, Beasts and Enchantment: Classic French Fairy Tales.* New York: NAL, 1989, 295–97.

———. *The Trials and Tribulations of Little Red Riding Hood: Versions of the Tale in Sociocultural Context.* South Hadley, MA: Bergin & Garvey, 1983.

Zuerner, Adrienne E. "Reflections of the Monarchy in d'Aulnoy's Belle-Belle ou le chevalier Fortuné." *Out of the Woods: the Origins of the Literary Fairy Tale in Italy and France.* Edited by Nancy L. Canepa. Detroit: Wayne State University Press, 1997, 194–217.

Index

abject, 143–44, 146, 148, 149–50, 151, 152, 163

absolutism: in d'Aulnoy, 166–69, 202, 241, 242; historical circumstances, 29–30; ideology, 82–83, 227, 238, 248; and public sphere, 35–36, 48, 242; in Scudéry, 85–87. *See also* Louis XIV

Académie française, 46–47, 113, 139, 147, 164

academies, 41, 46–48, 131, 165–66, 242, 248; and women, 47–48, 147, 151, 165, 224

Aligre, Madame, d', 102

allegory, 86, 103, 140–41, 167, 201, 204, 210, 218, 227, 237, 262

Althusser, Louis, 261

Amazons, 118, 120, 128, 129, 213, 229

amitié. See friendship

Ancients, 135, 163, 254

Apostolidès, Jean-Marie, 36, 48, 161, 223, 248, 259, 264

appearance (vs. reality), 38–39, 157, 162–63, 255; *Carte de Tendre* and discernment of, 75–77, 102; and madness, 126, 128, 129; and nobility, 206–9, 218, 221; unmasking, 128, 130 132, 161–62

Aragonnais, Madame, 92, 96, 102

Ariosto, 225, 232, 256, 264; *Orlando furioso*, 174, 225, 233

aristocracy. *See* nobility

Aristotle, 104

Arnauld, Antoine, 123, 134, 221, 255

Arpajon, Mademoiselle de, 92

Astrée. See Urfé

Auchy, Charlotte des Ursins, vicomtesse d', 42, 46

Aulnoy, Marie-Catherine d', 35, 121, 201–39, 240–43, 244–45; "Babiole," 213, 231–32, 235–36, 237; "La Belle aux cheveux d'or," 213, 218, 229, 232–33, 260; "Belle-Belle, ou le chevalier Fortuné," 264; "La Bonne petite souris," 210, 213, 214, 223, 226, 228, 264; "La Chatte blanche," 213, 214, 218, 223, 229, 258; *Le Comte de Warwick*, 167, 169; *Contes des fées*, 226, 229; *Contes nouveaux ou les fées à la mode*, 202; "Le Dauphin," 205; "Don Fernand de Tolède," 183, 192, 196, 262; "Don Gabriel Ponce de Leon," 183, 192, 195–96, 262; "Finette-Cendron," 214; "Fortunée," 205; "Gracieuse et Percinet, 197–98, 208, 222–23, 226, 228, 229; *Histoire d'Hypolite*, 14, 165–200, 201, 244, 260–62; "L'Ile de la félicité," 171, 197, 214, 225, 226, 227, 228, 235, 236, 265; *Mémoires de la cour d'Angleterre*, 169; "Le Mouton," 198, 204, 227; "Le Nain jaune," 203, 218; *Nouvelles d'Elisabeth, reine d'Angleterre*, 167, 185; "L'Oiseau bleu," 203–4, 208, 210, 263; "L'Oranger et l'abeille," 206, 262, 264; "Le Pigeon et la colombe," 206, 213; "Le Prince Lutin," 198, 203, 214–15, 223, 226, 228, 229, 232, 233, 235, 236–37, 260, 265, 266; "Le Prince Marcassin," 205; "La Princesse Belle-Etoile et le Prince Chéri," 205, 236, 263, 264; "La Princesse Carpillon," 227, 229, 236; "La Princesse Printanière," 198, 226, 266; "La Princesse Rosette," 208, 209; "Le Rameau d'or," 203, 207, 211, 212–13, 226, 229; "Le Serpentin vert," 210–11, 212–13, 226, 264

authority: in family/marriage, 146, 152–54, 156, 160, 183; female, 150–51, 224; patriarchal, 127. 151, 163–64, 165, 209; political, 154, 192, 231

Autriche, Marie-Thérèse d', 115

280